the
lost whole moose
catalogue

DON'T LET YOUR CHILDREN READ THIS BOOK. AS A MATTER OF FACT, **YOU** SHOULDN'T READ THIS BOOK. JUST PUT IT DOWN AND RUN OUT OF THE STORE, SCREAMING.

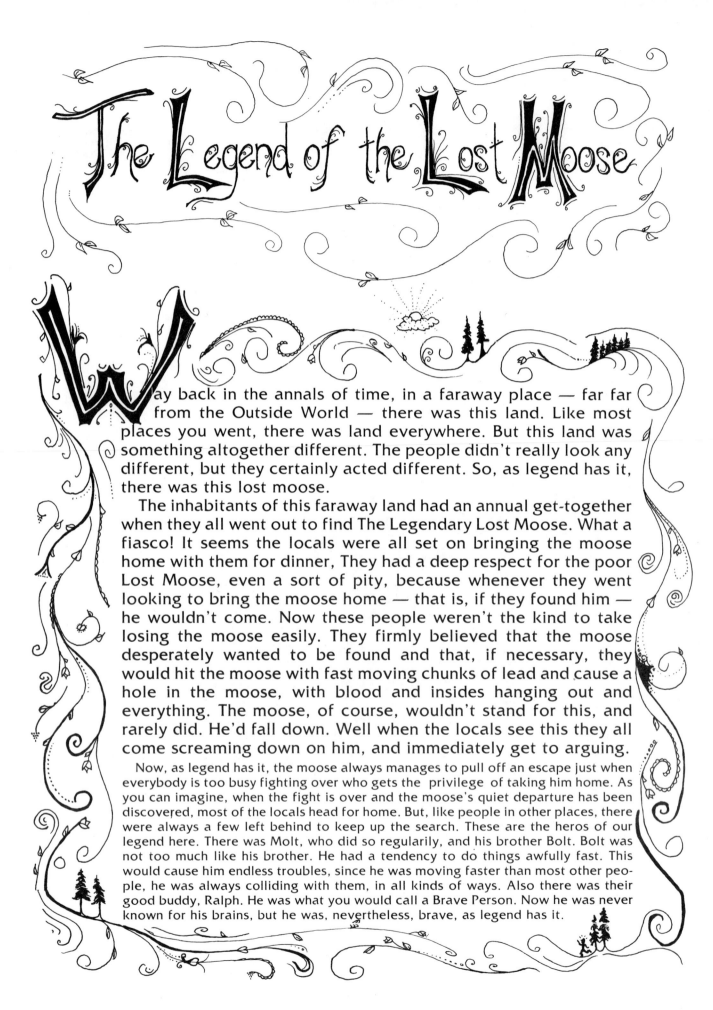

The Legend of the Lost Moose

Way back in the annals of time, in a faraway place — far far from the Outside World — there was this land. Like most places you went, there was land everywhere. But this land was something altogether different. The people didn't really look any different, but they certainly acted different. So, as legend has it, there was this lost moose.

The inhabitants of this faraway land had an annual get-together when they all went out to find The Legendary Lost Moose. What a fiasco! It seems the locals were all set on bringing the moose home with them for dinner, They had a deep respect for the poor Lost Moose, even a sort of pity, because whenever they went looking to bring the moose home — that is, if they found him — he wouldn't come. Now these people weren't the kind to take losing the moose easily. They firmly believed that the moose desperately wanted to be found and that, if necessary, they would hit the moose with fast moving chunks of lead and cause a hole in the moose, with blood and insides hanging out and everything. The moose, of course, wouldn't stand for this, and rarely did. He'd fall down. Well when the locals see this they all come screaming down on him, and immediately get to arguing.

Now, as legend has it, the moose always manages to pull off an escape just when everybody is too busy fighting over who gets the privilege of taking him home. As you can imagine, when the fight is over and the moose's quiet departure has been discovered, most of the locals head for home. But, like people in other places, there were always a few left behind to keep up the search. These are the heros of our legend here. There was Molt, who did so regularily, and his brother Bolt. Bolt was not too much like his brother. He had a tendency to do things awfully fast. This would cause him endless troubles, since he was moving faster than most other people, he was always colliding with them, in all kinds of ways. Also there was their good buddy, Ralph. He was what you would call a Brave Person. Now he was never known for his brains, but he was, nevertheless, brave, as legend has it.

So the heroes of our legend left in pursuit, still arguing over who should have the privilege of taking the now-gone moose home. Throughout the search Bolt would take off running at what he thought was the moose. But the others never knew if Bolt saw the moose or not, because he invariably hit a tree from running too fast in the woods. Ralph would come over to where Bolt was spinning around the tree that had blocked his path and give him a lecture on coordination. Throughout these numerous breaks in the search, Molt would stand by and watch.

If Bolt wasn't finding trees where he thought they shouldn't be, Ralph would be bravely climbing rotten trees and leaning over cliff faces, looking for The Lost Moose. Because of the sheer determination of our heroes — and the fact that they weren't quite sure of the way home — they managed to keep up the search for well over a reasonable period of time. Our heroes were extraordinary people. (Aren't all people in legends extraordinary?) They wanted to bring that Lost Moose home.

As the story goes, our trio of heroes finally happened upon The Lost Moose. Fortunately for them, but unfortunately for the poor lost moose, they somehow see him before he sees them. And you know what's going to happen. Yes, they're going to again hit the moose with fast moving chunks of lead, so they can go home with the moose and nobody will laugh at them ... once they find their home.

So you know what happens? The moose collided with the heroes' lead, then they run down screaming on him, but before they start quarrelling about whose moose it is, they tie him to a tree, A classic example of forethought. (Extraordinary people, right?) Our trio of heroes now have The Legendary Lost Moose tied to a tree, and now that they have him there, they are quite sure that they can go home without being laughed at. As soon as they decide whose moose it is. And as soon as they can decide which way is the way home (double argument, and the moose is tied to a tree).

How are our heroes going to overcome this problem? This is the kind of situation that makes men out of men.

Now don't worry about wounds, legends have a way of overlooking these things, and so shall we. While Molt, Bolt and Ralph were busy with their dispute as to whose moose it was, and which way it was to home, the moose was busy untying the knots in the rope.

"I saw him first and I hit him first," said Bolt. "Not really. I saw him first, and I hit him, so he's mine," Ralph replied. "He's mine cause I want him!" Molt stated, then added, "Isn't that the way home, down through that gulley? See where the moose is going down there? Do you think he knows the way home?"

Bolt took off in a dead run, and hit the first tree in his way. Ralph gave him a short lecture on optics and how to prevent physical damage by using your eyes. Molt stood by, and watched the moose take off over a distant hill.

So our trio of heroes took off again in dogged dispute (or is it moosed pursuit?) still bickering over whose moose it was, and whether or not the moose knew the way home (which he did, as he was fed up with getting hit by fast-moving chunks of lead; and he wanted to get rid of these heroes). He took them on a very short trip through the woods to the top of a hill, where the homes of Molt, Bolt and Ralph could be seen quite clearly, nestled in the valley below.

"How can we go home without the moose? They're going to laugh at us," said Bolt.

"Yah, you're right," Ralph agreed.

Molt stood and looked at his cabin down in the valley, and listened to his stomach rumble. "I'm hungry", he said. "Well, I'm hungry too....but I want to keep going. That moose is mine and I want him," persisted Ralph. "No, he's mine," said Bolt. "Mine, mine MINE!!" screamed Ralph. "He's lost again," mumbled Molt. "How's he expect us to bring him home if he won't come?" "Stupid Dumb Moose," reflected Ralph.

So our heroes sat on the side of the hill and argued late into the night, and the moose went deep, deep into the woods, hoping that next year the extraordinary people with their extraordinary ideas about him would not find him, and if they did, he hoped that at least they would quit hitting him with their fast moving chunks of lead that caused him holes with his insides hanging out and everything and maybe, with a bit of luck, they would change their religion or philosophy or whatever it was that caused them to chase him about and never leave him a moments peace during their annual idiocy that made them act so foolishly, so different from "normal" people. He hoped.

—Mars Bonfire II

contents

The story of Seamus

PART I

The beginnings of a dog's life in the Yukon are simple and straight-forward. No one asked me to come here. No one conceived me in love in the middle of winter. No one welcomed me to the Indian village of Whitehorse on a cold December night. Things were made very clear from the beginning; my mother wanted to forget the whole thing, the Indians couldn't care less (they didn't hardly feed the grown-up dogs they already had) and to cap it all off, people shot dogs on sight found running around looking for food.

True, nobody wanted me then and there, so survival became paramount and education cheap and constant.

My name is Seamus, I'm a fuzzy brown husky-type of dog. I'm not too big, not too pretty (having had my share of lost causes) but I can make a man respect me in his guts, a child love me from the heart and I can take you for everything you've got. Some call me a "mutt" or a "cheesehound." Well, let them. It's all true and I've been called both with affection and love. People come from somewhere too, but they don't think about it much, it seems. I'm going on five years old now — that's old for the Yukon; most don't see three years, due to guns, trucks, starvation and disease — not to mention other dogs.

Actually it's not so bad what people call you, but how they call you — I have been lucky — if you like that word; it also means "worked hard at." I have been lucky to have been loved as a cheesehound because those that labelled me loved me for what I am. I've always been hated for it but I'm still around.

I'm just another traveller on spaceship earth with some stories to tell. Some are short and to the point, others babble right on into the night. I don't care, I just tell stories, I don't have to sit and read 'em. Sometimes I talk like I'm addressing an idiot, but you know I don't know if you're reading this in Ross River or Rome, so bear with me, whoever you are. Sometimes if I use terms and jokes you don't understand, please don't waste your time on your pride. It may be none of your business because it ain't your life.

As this is an introduction, I have to say all this to appease the varieties of skeptics who will read these lines. There are bound to be questions like: "What's this farce, a dog writing a story? Ridiculous!" Well, I'm not writing it, I just told the stories to Toby, and he's recording it — how I told him, etc. is none of your business. Well then: let's begin to bullshit in earnest.

PART II

Stories usually begin at a beginning, and even though I would like to tell you a story in chronological order, it's just not possible due to length and other complications so I'll only do it to my early history (and try to make it brief. It's about the same as most pups born in winter in the Yukon anyway. I had two distinct advantages, though. I was wild from the start; no one cared so no one tied me up. Two, I never forgot a lesson learned from events that happened around me. I'm a dog to be sure, but, I'm not a servant of anyone but myself, no matter how much Toby would like to believe that I'm his dog; or the other people that he knows nothing about.

My first waking decision came one night (it may have been day, can't tell in December) when I got cold and woke up to find my mother gone and my two brothers and one sister huddled together with me, shivering and beginning to cry. I guess I was different from the start because I began to wonder if something was wrong. I felt something inside.

We were in a den she had hollowed out of a snowbank under some willows. The den mouth looked out onto the Yukon River. It was fine when food and warmth, in the form of mother, was near. But now all was strange and I felt very scared when I heard men's voices close-by. I'd heard and seen the men before. They came out when it was warmer and sat and drank and shot the shit about each other. Today was a little different and the conversation went as such:

"Hey partner, where'd you get that gun?"

"Oh hell, I found her in Stanley Joe's and borrowed it for a minute."

"Here, lemme . . ."

"No way, he said to return it right after I use it, and I don't want to get caught by the man."

"There's that bitch-dog returning from Adam's place across the river. He's always complaining about the noise his team make when she's around."

"That's what this is for, partner."

Two shots rank out in the semi-darkness. I crawled up and saw my mother lying about two hundred feet away on the ice, her body still twitching, but one shot was in her face and the other in her gut. I went into shock at the very back of the den and stayed there for a long time. I was nearly four weeks old.

. . . Seamus continued on bottom left-hand corner throughout the catalogue.

YUKON — GEOGRAPHICAL LOCATION

The Yukon Territory is the North West corner of Canada. Its boundaries are roughly the 141st meridian to the west, the Arctic Ocean to the north, the Mackenzie Mountains to the east and the Coast Range Mountains and British Columbia border to the south.

It is a land totalling 207,076 square miles; 1,700 sq. miles are fresh water, and all of it — except downstream from Whitehorse and a few other communities — is clear and good.

It is a land of mountains and valleys with streams and rivers cruising through them. There are high plateaus in the north that seem to stretch forever and valleys in the south that're big enough to stop your mind from comprehending it all.

To the south west are the spectacular heights of the St. Elias Mountains. Mount Logan, Canada's highest peak, measures 19,500 feet and many others are in the 12,000 to 17,000 ft. range. The glaciers and ice fields form what some suspect to be the largest non-polar ice cap in the world.

The Mackenzie Mountains, to the east, are smaller in elevation but more scenic, their sharpness rising out of the interior plateaus of the territory. Most of the interior of the Yukon averages about 2,400 feet above sea level, with hills and mountains rising to 9,000 feet high.

About 40 per cent of the territory is forested, albeit mostly by black spruce.

The water drainage is handled by four major river systems. The Yukon River, 2,000 miles long, runs north and west from the southern part of the territory to the Bering Sea. The Liard River flows south into the Mackenzie River as does the Peel in the northeast. The Alsek, one of the wildest rivers in the world, drains the south-west corner into the Pacific and boasts glaciers for riverbanks.

As for the lakes of the Territory, there are the 153-sq.-mile Kluane Lake, the 143-sq.-mile Teslin and enough others — complete with connecting navigable rivers and streams — to stagger an explorer's imagination.

There are lots of places up here that are truly unique — hot springs, sandy deserts and valleys missed by the last ice age — that will reveal secrets to those who choose to look.

In Old Crow, there's a guy named Grafton Njootli. He's about 30 years old and is the Council for Yukon Indians representative for the area. **National Geographic** magazine did an article on the territory in its April, 1978 edition, and they quoted him thusly about the future of his people and the land claims:

"We want progress, yes. But not at the expense of our culture. People may go to the Old Crow flats, to trap by bush plane, but they will still go. And some day I'd like to see running water and bathtubs. You know, luxuries."

HUMAN HISTORY

The Indians were here first.

What now is called the Yukon Territory was on the Mongolian peoples' migration trail between Asia and the Americas. There is every evidence that they went back and forth across what is now the Bering Sea, which was possibly a land bridge long ago.

The Yukon River Basin was never glaciated during the last ice age, and was probably navigable during that time. Even the animals and fish are similar to eastern Siberia's. The tools of the people have been dated back to 30,000 years in Old Crow Flats, 20,000 years on the Firth River to the North and 10,000 years in the Kluane-Dezadeash area.

The Indians have been trying to tell this to the white man since he got here, but because they don't have a written history he has trouble finding the time to think about how new he is to the scene. Throughout the history of the Indian people in this part of the world, things have changed very little. They settled in a large area and adapted to the local environments, another kind of being on the land, with a place reserved for them in the eco-system. When that system was no longer sufficient they moved to another. Their population was never great in terms of the White-man, but evidence points out that before the first whites penetrated the Interior, their diseases made it in from the coast and practically halved the Interior people's population. This had led some to wonder if the whiteman ever really saw the Indian culture, or only the final decline and separation from the land.

There were three distinct cultural groups established in the Yukon; the Inuit, who were just passing through the arctic and north coastal areas east and west; the Tlingit, who are an off-shoot of the Coast Indians of the Alaskan Panhandle and the Northern British Columbian coast; and the Athapaskans, whose language group extends across Canada to Hudson's Bay and south to the Apache and Navajo lands.

The Indians here had no classifications for each other, only cultural groups containing the inter-marrying groups called "moieties" of Crow and Wolf. These two groups had compulsory intermarriage and property ownership was also expressed in these terms.

The modern ethnographers, searching for a way to categorize groups for study, designated by language divisions.

This method of course, is a very inaccurate way to talk about Indians, but enabled them to look at the geographical effects on tribal movements in the present territory (at the time of contact with the Whiteman).

All languages in the territory are Athapaskan except Tlingit in the Teslin area and Tagish (a blend of Tlingit and southern Tuchone) around the Carcross area. Roughly the language divisions in the Yukon Territory break down as such:

Kutchin — north of the Yukon and Stewart Rivers.

Han — on the Yukon and westward from White River to Eagle, Alaska.

Tuchone — on the Yukon, Pelly, Ross, Stewart and Macmillan Rivers from Carmacks to Stewart, including west to the White River.

Southern Tuchone — in the Kluane Lake area to Lake Lebarge and Quiet Lake and from the Carmacks area south to the Coast Mountains.

Tagish — at Marsh and Tagish Lakes.

Tlingit — in the Teslin and Atlin areas.

Kaska — in the southeast corner of the present (White-man-bounded) territory.

Basically, beyond this, nothing is written except ethno-

graphic accounts and stories told by the Indian people.

Two sources for more information are a book called **"MY OLD PEOPLE SAY"** by **Catherine McClennan**, published by the National Museum of Man, Publications in Ethnology No. 6 (1) c/o Marketing Services, Ottawa K1A 0M8; and a book by **Julie Cruikshank** called **"THROUGH THE EYES OF STRANGERS,"** a report to the Yukon Territorial Government and the Yukon Archives, available from them if you're nice to them.

Before the white man penetrated the interior lands the coast Tlingit, who were trading for years with the Russians, middled furs for the interior Indians. Because of the wiping out of the sea otters, the trade was lucrative for the coast Indians and drew people from as far north as Old Crow to trading areas around the junction of the Yukon and Stewart Rivers. The Russians on the coast never came inland (except a few up the Yukon River in present-day Alaska) and traded furs with the Tlingit middlemen. Apparently the Kutchin in the north middled for the Russians and northern tribes as well. The people came together for the trade and also for pot-latches, fish camps and caribou migrations, to hunt together.

What has been referred to as "tribes" were groupings of families, and a chief was chosen as a representative and a final authority to guide the groups' movements. Most of the time, people travelled in small family groups spread out over the land.

Meanwhile, back in whiteman history, Alexander Mackenzie had heard about a great river to the west in 1789 and Franklin hit the north coast by boat in 1821. In 1839, the Hudsons Bay Company sent John Bell across the Richardson Mountains from Fort MacPherson. Robert Campbell came up the Liard River to found Fort Frances in 1842. Fort Yukon was established in 1847. The British still had no idea where the Russians were and made a fort stockade in case of attack. The Russians weren't anywhere near them and couldn't have cared less.

Campbell was the first whiteman to lead a party into the interior. He always seemed to do things the hard way, losing men to the Liard Rapids and nearly dying of starvation in what is now northern B.C. Things began to go good, though, in 1848 when he established Fort Selkirk at the confluence of the Yukon and Pelly Rivers. The Chilkat Indians weren't too enthusiastic about someone breaking their monopoly and siphoning furs off to the east so one night in 1852 they canoed into Fort Selkirk and burnt it to the ground. They took everything of value that they wanted and sailed off, leaving Campbell & Co. to look after themselves. They didn't kill anyone, but they effectively stopped and reversed the Hudson Bay Company's role in the southern Yukon.

Robert then set the all-time record for voluntary suffering endured by a human being by snowshoeing all the way to Minnesota in an effort to get to England, tell the HBC directors what happened and get back at the Indians when he got there. The HBC told Campbell to forget it.

The Porcupine River route across the mountains to Fort MacPherson and up the Mackenzie River became the supply-line for the entire territory for a while and things settled down for the Bay. The churches were also in the race, and in the Mackenzie River area the Catholics were winning. One Reverend Kirby from Ft. Simpson was determined that the Anglicans be first, and became the first to travel over the Richardson Mountains. On his second trip he was accompanied by a Catholic priest but the Indians stayed Protestant and to this day the Anglican church is still winning over here.

Another enterprise that was happening was the building of an overland telegraph, in 1866, from the USA across The North, over the Bering Sea and across Asia to Europe. [This was significant because it became the first modern economic failure (besides the Bay in Fort Selkirk) in the northwest, setting the stage for mines, highways, pipelines and a host of others to present times.] Everything was going well and a fantastic amount of data about the north was being collected when the news came that a cable had been laid across the Atlantic Ocean. End of the overland telegraph project.

In 1867 the Russian territory of Alaska was sold to the USA for a song, and the Bay got kicked out of Fort Yukon, it being illegally in the U.S. So they moved everything up the Porcupine River to Rampart House, and got kicked out of there when the news came that they were still in Alaska. So they packed it all up again and moved further upriver

. . . continued . . .

Nice Day if it Don't Rain

The weather up here is similar to the prairies, with those wide open skies and the most incredible cloud formations. It is basically a dry climate, about an inch of rain a month in most areas. The average annual rainfall is 10.6 inches; snowfall 48 inches. The last spring frost is usually somewhere between May 28 and June 10, and the frost free period lasts between 80 and 100 days.

The greatest extremes of temperature are registered in the central interior. High temperatures have reached into the 90's and lows have dipped to minus 80. For the most part, though, temperatures tend to hover around 25 below (F) in the winter and 70°(F) in the summer.

The most noticeable thing about the climate up here is the long long winter followed by a gradual spring, a quick intensive summer and an early fall with colours that can catch the eye of everyone. The other big difference up here is the daylight, which averages over 20 hours in July and five hours or less in mid December, depending on how far north you are.

One of the nicest things a person can do in the summer is sit up on a hillside and watch the sun rise and set, all in a couple of hours. There is no other experience like it.

POPULATION OF THE YUKON

MOOSE.	30,000
BLACK BEAR	lots
GRIZZLY BEAR . . .	5,800
DALL SHEEP	17,000
STONE SHEEP	3,500
MOUNTAIN GOATS . .	1,400
YAKS	two (domestic)
LLAMAS	none, but we'd like to see them
CARIBOU	105,000 barrenground 10,000 to 20,000 mountain (1975 estimate)
ELK	60 (seldom seen)
DEER	a few, but increasing
HEFALUMPS.	none, but we'd like to see them, too
FUR BEARERS	lots (beaver, muskrat, otter, fisher, mink, marten, lynx, coyote, wolverine, wolf.)
BIRDS	lots; many stay just for the sumnmer, though. (ravens, eagles, whiskey jacks, owls, ducks, geese, loons, grouse, ptarmigan, falcons, hawks)
FISH	lots (Arctic Grayling, Salmon, Trout, Pike and others)
PEOPLE	23,306 (Medicare enrolment at July, 1978)

Although the wildlife population estimates are far from precise because of lack of funds for thorough surveys, it's clear that people are outnumbered. Wise up, folks!

. . . continued . . .

built another fort and settled in. This fort barely paid for itself before closing in 1894. The men working there didn't think they had it so bad though, despite all the work. The land was beautiful, the game abundant and the people friendly. After all, that's what they came here for.

Private traders began moving into the interior around 1870. McQuesten established Fort Reliance, six miles below the Klondike River (1874), and McQuesten, Harper and Mayo built a post at the mouth of the Stewart in 1886. The Indians began to trade at these posts and their migrations changed to accommodate the seasonal trade movements. Those men who built and ruled the posts became a little short of legends in their own time. They held power, were trusted and respected for their character, which was exceptional. They knew better than to blow it — life was good in those days.

The small miners came into the country and flocked to the places where gold was to be found. There was always another strike around the corner, and part of your duty as a man in the Yukon was to spread the news of every colour and rumour in every pan from B.C. to Alaska. Everyone moved through the country on this note — miners, traders, Indians and missionaries. The coast Tlingits, meanwhile, still wouldn't let anyone across the mountains all this time and a man named George Holt got his name into history by somehow sneaking through the blockade sometime between 1875 and 1878. That wasn't very long ago.

Deals were struck a little after this time by whites and Indians to allow passage across the mountains. This was done by convincing the Chilkats that there were so many white men coming anyway that it was useless to resist them all, and the gunship anchored in Lynn Canal was thrown in as an added bonus. The Indians saw the logic behind this and said it was alright with them, and they'd even help the whiteman with his bags, for a fee. This they did, and made a lot of money at it too. So the Chilkats may have been responsible for the beginning of the tourist business in the Yukon. Holt eventually got murdered by the Copper River Indians and that is all we know about him.

The territory was still a "little man's land," where a man's freedom was earned by his mastery of life in the frontier. (The big entities like governments and the big mining concerns still have to fight the little guys to this day. Yukoners have always had a deep distrust of all large enterprises, because, as this history points out, virtually none of them have ever done as much good as they have other things.)

The town of Fortymile sprang up gradually as gold began coming out of that river around 1883, and continued to do so at first as a summer digging with the miners wintering at Ft. Reliance. The settlement became more of one in 1892 when Bishop Bompas arrived and further in 1894 when NWMP Inspector Constantine arrived to collect export taxes and keep law and order among the miners. You can imagine just about how well that one went over with the men on the creeks.

There is some disagreement as to whether there was all that much lawlessness in the Yukon. The independent traders and men didn't seem to mind, but one John Healy of the newly-established American Transportation & Trading Co. got into shit at a miners' meeting (partially because nobody liked him, and partially because they had a reason) and wrote a letter to a friend in Ottawa about it. He wasn't much liked because, unlike Harper, Mayo and McQuesten, he was there to make a buck. He didn't extend charity, called for his bills on time and lived a mental attitude that a lot of people still come up here to get away from.

Where was McQuesten during all this? He saw it all coming and moved far downstream, built Circle City, and continued much as before. Another man who wrote to Ottawa was William Ogilvie, who was afraid that the pro-American attitude on the creeks would lead to trouble if a major strike happened. He wasn't without just cause in doing this, seeing as most of the men on the creeks were Americans anyway. These letters landed on the desk of the NWMP in Ottawa, and they sent Charles Constantine back the following summer with 19 men. The miners tried him out soon after and were met on the diggings by eleven mounties who pointed out that **they** were now the law.

There still is an undercurrent of dislike for the force in the territory. It seems to stem from the fact that they derive powers from beyond the peoples' control; and these powers are stronger than almost any other police force in the free world. However, when the gold rush hit in 1896 there weren't any shoot-em-ups in Dawson City or Wyatt Earps and Soapy Smiths roaming around the country, and it was the police who were responsible for the peace with which it was all carried out.

Life continued to be more settled in the Yukon. The Chilkoot Pass was letting in one-way traffic mostly, and those who did not stay for lack of work, etc. had a nice float down the river to St. Michael, and then a ship home. Ladies had gardens, men had dogs as pets and wives; beef cattle, carpets and lace curtains made appearances. Old hand miners began to drift off to obscurity to get away. Then in August of 1896 a whiteman named Carmack, and two Indians, Skookum Jim and Tagish Charlie, brought gold out of

a creek with an Indian name no one could pronounce. As soon as the miners could figure out that George wasn't lying (an apparent habit of his), Fortymile became a ghost town as did Circle City. Everyone went to Bonanza and the Klondike River. Dawson City became a reality and the whole country freaked out and had a party that lasted four years.

The gold rush is the largest chapter of every history of this land, but here it's pretty short. Much has been written, and anyone can be bombarded with as much bullshit as reality wherever they go here in summertime.

Hardship and pain were present to be sure, but no one seems to have noticed that these were young men, many just into their twenties and hell-bent for some action. There was a depression on. Men were leaving their wives and kids and going on the equivalent of a big fishing trip with the boys. Most of them had a gas, got to breath good air and ate a lot of Spam. The ones from the south had lots of company and the ones who tried to come overland from the east were fools. Dawson City had a population of 30,000 and telephones, sawmills, a railway, a bridge across the Klondike, and all the trappings of a miniature San Francisco. Some people went into hiding and the government decided something had actually happened up here and made the Yukon, despite cries for provincial status, a separate colony of Canada in 1898.

It all disintegrated fairly swiftly but some good stuff got left behind. Lots of settlements everywhere were serviced by a railway from Skagway to Whitehorse and at one time 200 riverboats were working the rivers. Meanwhile, back in Indian history, the people had a hard time comprehending all this. Their fish camp on the Klondike was now called Lousetown, and what happened to the swampland across the river was just science-fiction, and it didn't include Indians. They were moved downstream to a place someone called Moosehide, and some still live there. Jim Lotz pointed out in his book "Northern Realities" that while some folks are running around up here playing frontiersman, the real frontiersmen are living in those shacks up in Dawson to this day, but are frowned on.

The almost instantaneous uprooting of the country, the overwhelming numbers of strange people who never even saw the people they were running over, just about finished the Indians as a culture. Only the ones who stayed out of the way, trapping and living close to the land, kept their sanity and made it through to the quiet years and peace. Everyone settled down after 1900, the population of the territory dwindled to about 8,500 by 1911 and life continued a little as it had before, only a lot more civilized. There were now people who never got dirty. There was government. There were police; as a matter of fact there were more after the rush than during it all. There were silver rushes to Keno Hill and Mayo in 1910 and copper mining near Whitehorse until 1921.

The land basically decided who could adapt and who couldn't. People worked on the dredges and in the mines for a steady wage. No one went hungry and the Yukon was once more a safe place from wars and famine — things were pretty comfy. Everything ran down to 1941 and the population of the whole territory dipped below 5,000 souls when all hell broke loose again. The Japanese attacked Pearl Harbour and tried to take everything and split it with Hitler. All this prompted someone in Washington, D.C. to build a series of airports across the north to Alaska. True to modern technology applied in the Yukon, they tried to build the airports then a road to service them. Thirteen planes set out from the south for Alaska; five crashed on the way. The Alaska Highway came in with the same impact as the gold rush, and has had the same amount of bullshit attributed to it. We're not going to get into it, either. Whitehorse's population rose to 40,000 and the city was born into the present southern lifestyle, complete with subdivisions. Again all kinds of people (mostly the American army) trampled in and, in 1946 trampled out, leaving more litter and more stuff that needed maintenance.

The Canol Project happened around the same time. Like the highway it was all American money (a habit of the country that persists to this day, with the Haines Road and Alaska Highway paving projects and the natural gas pipeline). It consisted of building a pipeline from Norman Wells, N.W.T. to Whitehorse, with the construction of a refinery in the latter. The thing was built at a cost of 134 million dollars, run for less than a year and closed in 1945. Then they came back and took it all out again except the tanks in Whitehorse, the road, and some of the vehicles which they drained the oil out of and left them running. What the hell, it's only money, and the people down south were a long way from even caring what happened up here. They still are.

Now we had two nice country roads, one going from nowhere to nowhere and one going from nowhere to somewhere; but not many people went there and everyone settled down again. The Canol Road is still there in spots and is a beautiful hike. The Alcan, meanwhile, set the stage for modern times in the territory. It opened up the Kluane region and led to a game sanctuary there. It established Whitehorse, which already had the railroad from Skagway, as the main transportation center and the capital was switched to there from Dawson City and the river closed to traffic in 1956. New settlements like Beaver Creek, Haines Junction and Watson Lake opened up and the native people were told to move there. The established Indian villages of Burwash, Teslin and Upper Liard grew as the people left

1942 Alcan Highway Construction Camp

i live here now

I am a Yankee, born and raised in sunny California. By now I'm getting used to the horrified "What in the —— are you doing up here?" Sometimes I wonder; boy do I wonder.

We arrived in the north in August, 1968. It was 107 degrees F. when we left California, and now it was a cool, cool 60 degrees. I sat in the campground, wrapped in a blanket, teeth chattering, lips blue, watching with amazement people scurrying around in shorts. As one rather stout, shirtless chap wiped his brow and expostulated "Man, oh man, it's hot," I suddenly got real homesick. These people were crazy, pure crazy!

We finally, after much searching, found a house. (We were pleasantly surprised to find that the dire warnings of our parents and friends that all Yukoners lived in igloos to be erroneous.) We **were** surprised to know that water had to be delivered, and we had never heard of a chemical toilet, much less seen one. A bucket with a toilet seat perched on top was not my idea of luxury (until it got 20°, 30°, then 40° below outside, then I blessed it). Of course it was a trifle disconcerting and a wee might embarrassing to know everyone in the house could hear even the faintest tinkle in the contraption. The hardest part, of course, was retraining the whole family to flush after we got the real McCoy.

We were surprised, and heartened to learn that Texas can't claim all of the biggest things in North America. The Yukon can claim the biggest mosquitoes (and the most), the biggest, healthiest crops of dandelions, and the dubious distinction of having a biting bug that isn't there. No one who's lived in the Yukon, or even passed through, can doubt the existence of the no-see-um.

Nothing I had ever seen or heard about prepared me for a Yukon winter. Believe me, you only "dash" outside once in -40° weather barefooted.

You learn very quickly what that "funny little electric cord" hanging on the front of the cars are for. I admit that I still can't convince my poor, sleep-ridden body that it's time to get up in the morning when it's cold and dark outside, but I'm working on it.

Sometimes when winter seems ten years long and I yearn for green grass, paved roads and the aroma of chicken coops, I ask myself that question, just what **are** you doing here?

Well, where else is the air so clean and the people so friendly? After ten years of gazing at the enchantment of a "winter wonderland," snow so dry it crunches when you walk on it, so clean and sparkly, that when hit by the sun it explodes into a million glittering diamonds, I know. Can anyone describe the ice fog that insidiously creeps like a living, ghostly apparition over an open door sill?

How do you describe the ice fog? Cold, glittering shards of glassy ice, beautiful beyond description, or the Northern Lights, fantastic, dancing across the heavens, never still, surely painted by the hand of God.

The North grows on you, from the croaks of the ravens in the winter to the twenty-four hours of daylight in the summer. I remember once, getting up in a panic because the sun was already high in the sky, cooking a hurried breakfast, urging a harried husband he'd be late for work, and discovering it was 3:30 a.m. (He wasn't amused.)

Well, here I am ten years later, groaning how hot it is at 60° — saying "eh," like an old pro, and never considering living in old sunny California again.

Guess I'm just an old dyed-in-the-wool Canadian-Yankee.

— Kay Chappell

the land. This trend continued until 80 per cent of the entire population was centered on the highway.

For the Indians, it was just another kick in the head. The highway construction came hand in hand with a drop in fur prices that helped families decide to winter in the posts during 1942. Many went to Whitehorse to find work on the highway, and people have continued to come in from the bush ever since. For the first time there was a permanent non-Indian majority in the territory. Government welfare money flowed into the Yukon in greater amounts because of everyone's assessability.

These words were spoken a week before this history was written.

"I remember when I was little and the Indian Agent was talking to my father, saying that the government wanted to give him lots of money but only if I was sent away to the Mission School, and if they left Champagne and the trap lines and moved to Haines Junction or Whitehorse. The mission schools were in Whitehorse, Lower Post and Carcross and run by the priests. The government left the running of these places to the churches. They cut off my hair and punished me if I ever spoke my own language, ever.

"The law said that the parents had to send their children to school, so they did. We were educated to grade 8 or 16 years old, whichever came first. Then the education was to be paid for by the parents. Not many of us ever got past that because there was work to do. Then we were divided into status and non-status Indians. Status Indians were people on a Band list and recognized by the Indian Act. Non-status Indians were Metis or half-breeds and got nothing from anyone. They were non-people."

People began to talk about the Alaska Highway "corridor" and the areas around the highway began to lose their fish and game. There was a short time when everyone went back to sleep. Mayo was linked to the south by a road in 1950 and in 1958, Dief the Chief announced his "Roads to Resources" program. The government would pay the full cost of building the highways and 85 per cent of the maintenance costs. The Dempster Highway got started that year and is due for completion in 1979. That's how much they really wanted it.

Development began to pick up in the mid and late '50s. It started to resemble a boom in its own right. Anyone could get a job. There were roads to build, bridges to erect, suburbs for Whitehorse, sewers, hospitals. . . . The squatters in Whiskey Flats got the boot so that the residents of Riverdale didn't have to see them anymore on their way over the bridge. Strange new things began to happen. People began to putt golf balls on real lawns in front of their houses, and stare at dogs pulling toboggans for downtown shoppers. The "developers" became the new gold rush and everyone was going to work with them and make lots of money. Well, the developers came alright and brought their own men with them. They did the jobs and got out. Fat lot of good that did everyone here.

Things did not happen magically. By 1967 the Clinton Creek mine (now closed) was opened with $4 million in government assistance. New Imperial near Whitehorse opened and did well, thanks to the high price of copper and a hell of a lot of Japanese money. Anvil-Dynasty opened with Faro, and the government paid a third of that. As an example, the government poured $23.4 million into the Yukon in 1962-63 to maintain the southern lifestyle it had founded. Revenues only totalled $6.69 million in 1964 and the population actually dropped between 1961 and 1966. This is a very expensive place to run, much more than most people realize.

There always is the prospect of another mine, another pipeline, another big charge to the economy; but it takes a lot more than big talk and fancy brochures. Now, in the 1970s, we have another population increase. There is another pipeline coming billed as "The largest construction project in the history of man." New mines are being talked about in Macmillan Pass and oil is supposedly hiding somewhere up the Dempster Highway. If the Alaska Highway pipeline goes through there will be another one coming down the Dempster and Klondike Highways. The folks in Pelly Crossing are going to love that. Urban land prices have gone crazy, and most of the rural property is frozen until the Indians are "dealt with." The U.S. Congress has delayed the pipeline a year already, and before it's started two of the remaining three mines are planning on closure. History teaches us to believe half of what we see, and that hasn't been much.

We can count only on the fact that things are changing fast. The commissioner quit recently because of a "small minority" of people. This is hogwash because he wasn't elected. He didn't have to pay any attention to anyone. The so-called minority, made up of the same type of little people who hung out in Fortymile, just succeeded in getting rid of someone they supposedly had no power to influence at all.

The most stable part of our economy now is tourism. They come up here and spend over $30,000,000 or more a summer. Some learn some of what is in this catalogue, others get told a song and dance about the "Trail of '98" and that's all. It doesn't really matter. What does matter is that people up here trying to do things learn from the lessons of the past. That's where the Indians come into the picture. That's why they are so important. We can't just run over them, no matter what Trudeau's style is.

All these people — companies, plans, schemes, etc. — mentioned in this history make up the "lesson of the land" which is: Take it nice and easy and listen to the land; and the land will take it easy on you. It's only fair. Judge Tom Berger put it this way:

". . . what happens in the north will be of great importance to the future of our country. It will tell us what kind of people we are."

— *Dirigible Pundy Gumby*

YUKON COMMUNITIES

STEWART CROSSING ...Mile 213 Klondike Highway... population 7, according to Medicare...river crossing and junction to Mayo...hotel...restaurant...gas station...campground...

WATSON LAKE
...Miles 635 Alaska Highway...junction with Robert Campbell Highway...population area 1,100...almost all white...born 1939 with airport...school to grade 12...7 cops...hospital...2 doctors...seven nurses...CBC radio and TV...large creation complex...downtown...airport...bus station...ski slope...440 phones...lots of bars...golf course.. saw mills...

CARMACKS
...110 miles north of Whitehorse on Klondike Highway and Yukon River...population 400...25% white...unorganized community...old caribou crossing and hunting camp...Carmack built traiding post 1895...Faro and Watson Lake road turn off...school to Grade 9...2 police...full time nurse...CBC radio and TV...bank...community hall...library service...hotels...store...gas station.. post office...air strip...bus service...55 telephones...coal mine...highway camp...stock car racing track under construction.

CLINTON CREEK
...25 miles north on Top-of-the-World Highway...population 500...mining town to 1978...ghost town 1979...

DAWSON CITY
...Mile 334 Klondike Highway...340 miles north of Whitehorse...population 950...70% white...old Indian fish camp...centre of gold rush 1898...gambling hall...tourism business, old ghost town...school to Grade 12...4 police...hospital 10 units...1 doctor...3 nurses...old folks home...CBC radio and TV...bank...stores...hotels...library...several community halls...3 museums...post office...airport...bus and air service...275 telephones.. vehicles with slugs prohibitted...

DESTRUCTION BAY
...Mile 1083 Alaska Highway...population 80...mostly white...born 1942 during highway construction...road camp...school to Grade 8...no police...1 nurse...CBC radio and TV...post office...no airstrip...bus service...hotel...gas station...library...curling rink...32 telephones.

FARO
...30 miles west of Ross River...population 1500...25% single...founded 1968...mining town...situtated in Yukon's newest large burn area...school to Grade 12...3 police...hospital...one doctor...six nurses...dentist...CBC radio and TV...bank...department store...jewelry store...2 gas stations...library...recreation centre...airport...Alcoholics Anonymous...theatre...

MAYO
...200 miles north-west of Whitehorse...35 miles east of Stewart Crossing...population 470...75% Indian...local improvement district...Al Mayo trading post 1880's...tied to fortunes of mines...river landing...school to grade 12...4 police...hospital...2 doctors...5 nurses...CBC radio-TV...community hall...revival hall...library...Tony the game warden...hotel...store...bus service...post office...165 telephones...

OLD CROW
...on Porcupine River, at 68th parallel...population 200... 90% Indian...settlement...30,000 year history...trading post since 1912...not accessible by road...school to Grade 9...2 police...1 nurse...community hall...library...air service...CBC TV...post office...12 telephones...

PELLY CROSSING
...175 miles north of Whitehorse on Klondike Highway... population 180...mostly Indians...born 1952 with the Highway...school to Grade 7...1 nurse...bus service...short airstrip...post office...store...community hall...

ROSS RIVER
...225 miles northeast of Whitehorse by road...population 371...majority Indian...old Indian camp...born 1942 with Canol...highway junction and strategic drop-off point for the boonies...highway camp...school to Grade 10...3 police...1 nurse...2 community halls...CBC radio...post office...air strip...library...store...a famous bar...Matthew Sills in summer...70 telephones...bus service...air service.

TESLIN
...Mile 804 Alaska Highway...Hudson Bay Post 1903... born 1942 with Highway...population 350...50% Indian... canoe factory...school to Grade 10...3 police...1 nurse...2 community halls...museum...post office...CBC radio and TV...air strip...bus service...70 telephones...1 banana...

SWIFT RIVER
...Mile 733 Alaska Highway...786 miles from Fairbanks... population 33...highway camp...hotel restaurant sells beer at $15.00 per dozen in summer...CBC radio...library service...gas station...bus service...

HAINES JUNCTION
...Mile 1016 Alaska Highway...100 miles west of Whitehorse...population 500...25% Indian...local improvement district does not include Indian village...born with the Alaska Highway...two pipelines have been built through it...school to Grade 10...3 police...1 nurse...highway camp...CBC radio and TV...110 telephones...bank... 2 community halls...post office...air strip...bus service... hotels...stores...good pie at Mom's...

UPPER LIARD
...Mile 643 Alaska Highway...8 miles west of Watson Lake ...population 250...mostly Indians...born with madness in 1946 or so...lodge...church...nursing station...Indian band hall...CBC radio and TV...6 telephones...

WHITEHORSE
Mile 918 Alaska Highway...population 15,000...white man's dream...metropolis...born in gold rush 1898...died and went to hell with Alaska Highway, 1941...everything you would expect...a lot of bars...a lot of people looking for someone to be...close access to the Yukon Territory...

ELSA
...62 miles by road east of Stewart Crossing...mine town...health centre...doctor...school to Grade 8...cafe... store...post office...bank...CBC radio and TV...curling rink...

TAGISH
...21 miles from Carcross...closer to Jakes Crystal Palace...Indian camp, later Mounties Post...cottage area...one-year old post office...famous for fishing...and the late Tagish Annie's home-made bread and pies...store ...gas...campground...noisy on week-ends and holidays... hello Archie... *continued on next page...*

CANADA
DEPARTMENT OF
ENERGY, MINES AND RESOURCES
SURVEYS AND MAPPING BRANCH

YUKON
TERRITORY

SCALE 1:2,000,000
1 inch equals approximately 32 miles

Road
Railway
Territorial capital

POPULATED PLACES

500 to 2,000
Under 500

Lambert Conformal Conic Projection with Standard Parallels at 49°N and 77°N

Reproduced from the 1:2,000,000 map of Canada by the
Surveys and Mapping Branch, Ottawa, 1976

MCR 47 THIRD EDITION

Copies may be obtained from the Canada Map Office, Department of
Energy, Mines and Resources, Ottawa, or your nearest map dealer.
Canada Copyrights Reserved 1976

communities continued...

CARCROSS

north end Lake Bennett . . . . 45 miles south of
Whitehorse on Klondike Highway . . . pop. 250 . . . .
80% white . . . unorganized community . . . white
contact 1898 . . . Indian hunting and fishing gathering
spot . . . school to grade 6 . . . two police . . . doctor and
nurse visit once a month . . . hotel . . . store . . . radio
and TV from Whitehorse . . . community club hall . . .
Indian band hall . . . railway north and south daily . . .
flying club on gravel air strip . . . bus service . . . 53
telephones . . . post office . . . community school . . .

BURWASH LANDING

. . . mile 1093, 177 miles northwest of Whitehorse on
the Alcan . . . pop. 65 . . . mostly Indians under 25
years old . . . designated an unorganized community
. . . 1904 trading post built . . . Indian Band Office
center of community . . . Indians run own primary
grades school . . . no police . . . nursing clinic . . . 10
miles north of Destruction Bay . . . no radio or TV . . .
no post office . . . gravel air strip . . . bus service . . .
five telephones . . . water from wells and lake . . .
communal washroom . . . Roman Catholic mission . . .
27 unit tourist lodge . . . museum . . . gas station . . .
outfitter . . .

BEAVER CREEK

Designated as an unorganized community . . . pop.
126 . . . 80% Whiteman . . . first prospected 1900 &
1914 . . . tourist and transport oriented . . . located at
mile 1202 of the Alaska Highway . . . 21 miles east of
Alaska border . . . customs station . . . school to Grade
Eight . . . nursing station visit once a week from
Destruction Bay . . . doctor visit once a month . . .
dentist visit twice a year . . . three police . . . CBC
radio . . . town pays $1,000 a year for CBC-TV . . . no
bank . . . swimming pool in summer . . . gravel air
strip . . . curling rink . . library service . . . post office
. . . stores . . . 50 telephones . . . hotels . . .

CANOEING

HOW TO GO ABOUT IT ALL:

Maps. It is handy to know where you are going, especially if you want to get to a specific place or come back to where you started. Maps are also useful for knowing what is over the next rise and from where the creek flowing in on the right-hand side is coming. However, some veteran bushpeople have lived decades in this country without maps, using their wits and — above all — their memories. There is little security to be gained from an arsenal of maps and charts if you couldn't find your way to safety should you become separated from your two-dimensional, paper-world images. We advise you to try to appreciate the country in your mind as well as in terms of topographic maps.

If you're looking for a river, go to a map of the Yukon, the whole thing, find the area in which you're interested and buy the specific large-scale maps you need. The index and map lists are free at Canada Map offices. The local one is at 200 Range Road in Whitehorse, phone 668 5151. Scales vary from the continent size 1:4,000,000 (which means one inch on the map is 61 miles or 100 kilometers) to territory size 1:1,000,000, on up through 1:500,000 (one inch is eight miles or 12 km.) and 1:250,000 (an inch for every four miles or almost seven km.) and 1:50,000 (one inch equals 1¼ miles). Quickly now, what is one centimeter at 1:50,000?

The 1:250,000 are best for river tripping with 1:50,000 used for specific areas of interest, such as whitewater. If you are really interested in an area, inquire about land use maps as they have lots to tell you.

Map prices vary from $1 to $3. The Mapping Branch of the Department of Energy Mines & Resources Canada has a pamphlet and map guide called "Maps and Wilderness Canoeing." Besides a complete list of 1:250,000 maps of Canada it carries information on map reading (rivers), compass reading, aerial photographs, Hydrographic Charts and Symbols. It is available free from the Map Offices.

Maps are also available in downtown Whitehorse now, which saves you the hassle of going "up the hill" to government offices at Takhini. You can buy them at Yukon Gallery, which is downstairs from Mac's Newsstand (Mac's Fireweed). The door is on the left hand side past the counter but before the magazines.

The Yukon Voyageurs Canoe Club can be contacted through Yukon Tourism Dept., Box 2703, Whse. The membership fee is $2 and they are there to serve you and go on trips with you. They are into buying better equipment cheaper, receiving and giving instructions, and most of all meeting others who are into it all. It's not a ho-hum club and the people we've met are pretty knowledgeable and friendly . . .

Rob Lewis, President, Kayak Instructor.
Bob Sharp, Vice President, White Water and Wilderness Canoeing.
Vicky McCandless, Vice President, Recreational Canoeing.
Al Omitani, Vice President, Flatwater Canoeing.

Some Things Need Mentioning

1. The RCMP has a registering service for river travellers. The only trouble is that a lot of people don't tell them that they're still alive at the journey's end. They may scrap it because of the cost of hunting people down who aren't lost . . .
2. The weather office can tell you what the week-long picture looks like for your trip. Actually they can't, but it's fun to think you might know something for about three days. Call 668-2293 in Whitehorse.

3. The easiest way to pack a canoe on top of a car is pieces of foam pad under the gunwales and ropes fore and aft. Then throw a rope over the canoe and while pulling tight from the inside, slam the door on it. Don't make five loops of rope and 15 half-hitches, it's a waste of time if the rope's gonna break anyway.
4. One time when I was on a trip to Dawson on the Yukon River, I stopped at Yukon Crossing for the night. Two guys were shooting beer bottles from the log butts of the old round house. I threatened to tell the RCMP and they left. Don't be stupid — there's a lot of people on the Teslin and Yukon Rivers. Don't spoil their time with your popguns.
5. We're not going to list rivers and where, how, etc., because you can get that information somewhere else. (See books on canoeing.)
6. It's worth fiberglassing the tips of your paddles, no matter what their make. It's worth it, believe me. I've had the same paddle now for 5,000 miles of both haywire and smooth river, but I used four unfiberglassed paddles up on one run to Dawson City from Quiet Lake.

There are three types of fiberglass: mat, cloth and roving. Coat some mat (cloth tends to wear off the bottom and peel back) and lay on the end ¾ inches of the paddle with ¼" overlap. Do this on both sides and fill the groove between the two layers at the end with some strands of roving, also soaked in resin. Sand off excess when dry and you will have a virtually indestructible paddle tip. There is a paddle in existence up here with more than 10,000 miles on it, preserved by this method.

7. Try the Mylar tape instead of Duct Fiber tape. It's stronger. Also try Ambroid glue instead of Epoxy, because of low temperature hassles with the latter.
8. For long extended lining and wading in freezing temperatures, try wet suit booties inside running shoes. The old ankle-high Hong-Kong getaways work best. However, there are wet-boots made in England that seem to be alright.
9. About lifejackets: air cell are good, closed cell are better and anyone who goes boating with Kapock and virtually anything else needs their head read. Buy one as an article of clothing and when it gets cold, put it on. Some people never use one, that's

their prerogative. Some people aren't around to argue about it anymore. All we say is that if you start thinking about how many people drown every year who know how to swim and all, maybe you'll get one.

10. A word about the medical kit. There is a book by Bradford Angier called "Be Your Own Wilderness Doctor," but there is a better one by Peter Steele, a local, entitled "Medicine For Mountaineers." We recommend it. Published by William Heinemann Medical Books Ltd., London, England. Also, the best medicine on the market for the shits (Aztec two-step, Montezuma's Revenge) is Lomotil. We have mentioned morphine, and we feel it will do the job except for the fact that you may be unable to take proper care of yourself after using it, and it does have some after-effects, like tiredness and general veginess the next day.

Chuck's ultra-comfort one-man Canoeing List

From his drafty, snow-covered cabin on Lake Lindeman, the old fart himself imparts this wisdom. We reproduce his summer river tripping list verbatim for your prerusal.

canoe, two paddles

yoke, spray cover (if needed)

sponge for bailing. If it has that much water in it, tip it over.

25' ropes bow and stern, 50' roll of cord, two elastic straps

tent

stuff bag containing clothes and sleeping bag; foamy

1 pocket warmer with enough fuel (for those cold nights; throw one in your sleeping bag 15 minutes before retiring)

1 Deluth pack or other packsack (there is no place in a canoe for a packframe)

1 waterproof bag (Phoenix or Voyageur) for camera, books, money and other valuables tied to thwart

small grill, cloth, pot cleaner, forks, spoon, cup, flipper, pots and frypan

matches (wooden), bug dope (It's worth noting that many bugs up here like the taste of Cutters. Repex is stronger but it burns holes.)

axe (with sheath), file, knife (one that is cheap but good, so that you can replace it and not be mad if it's lost)

gun, 20 rounds

pen, log book, reading matter, rolling papers, camera and film, pipe

repair kit (roll of duct tape, epoxy glue, snare wire, needle and thread, fiberglass and resin if canoe is fiberglass)

CLOTHING: raingear, down vest, sweat shirt, 2 t-shirts, wool sweater, running shoes or moccasins, shorts or cut-offs, two pants, two socks, bandana, toque.

sunglasses, belt, water-proof match safe, soap, brush, toothbrush, towel, roll of bumwad, package of fire starter.

FIRST AID KIT (with help from a doctor who
continued on next page...

understands) should include all this: sharp Swiss Army knife, tweezers, 3" by 5 yds. adhesive tape, 30" rubber tubing for a tourniquet, elastoplast assortment, triangular bandage and safety pins, hypodermic syringe, long needles, ¼ grain morphine, ammonia salts, peroxide, antibiotics (penicillin), 292's, cotton, ointment, (antibiotic/anesthetic), shit pills for diarrhea, needle nose pliers for pulling porcupine quills out of mutt, scissors, 2 field dressings, needle and suture, twine, piece of candle, emergency bug dope and matches.

This kit fits into a surprisingly small bag and is quite light.

FOOD [sampling of goodies] all veggies and fruits dried, all items packaged and labelled in plastic bottles, squeeze tubes and plastic bags. (Heavy plastic geology sample bags work best, fold over the tops several times, and put a large elastic band around it. Using garbage bags and baggies etc. causes brain damage.)

If you're just going down the Teslin or Yukon or other smooth-flowing rivers without portage, you can treat yourself to fresh veggies etc. - you can take a half a ton of food if you want.

Dry meat, onions, peas, carrots, beans, mix veg., spaghetti, macaroni, soups (Swiss and Knorr), oatmeal, granola, cream of wheat, cornmeal, flour, vitamin C pills, coffee (French/Columbian blend), rice, egg (powdered real egg, not Highland), milk powder, baking powder, lard, butter, tomato paste, cocoa, tea, tang orange (blows heads in the morning), cheese, raisins, cognac, whiskey, dry fruit, nuts, sunflower seeds, jam, honey, peanut butter, marijuana, brown sugar, salt, pepper, cinnamon, thyme, basil, oregano, curry, cloves, garlic, soya sauce, sambal, lemon powder (concentrated lemon) and fruit cake.

What's this, no ice cream?

✱ Where-to-get-it-in-Whitehorse suggestions:

Teslin wood/canvas freighters - Go-fer Sales
Grummans - Horwoods
Frontiersman Fiberglass - Igloo Sporting Goods

Lund Aluminum - Whitehorse Motors
Faber wood/canvas - " "
Cadorette fiberglass - Woolworths
Coleman plastic - Hector Mackenzie
paddles - Igloo has solid wood paddles, very sturdy
Duluth pack - Horwoods
waterproof bags for food and to line inside of stuff bags with - try geological surveying companys
cooking gear - Horwoods has the best selection
knife - try Normarks sheath knife, $13 at Horwoods
fishing tackle - Hougen's (and tell them who sent you)
repair materials - Whitehorse Motors and Northern Metallic
snare wire - Horwoods
clothing - is cheapest at Woolworths, but you get what you pay for
first aid - from any drug store, plus a doctor's note. If you can't get the drugs from one doctor, try another.
food - best bought down south, can be ordered from: Galloway's Speciality Foods, 1084 Robson St. Van., phone 685-7927.

A decent freeze-dried food list is available from Kamp-pak Foods, 120 Sunrise Ave. Toronto, Ontario.

Chuck's How to Pack a Canoe Method: –

Lay a 9' by 12' tarp in a canoe under the thwarts, one side overlapping one to two feet and other side at least three to four feet. Place food and equipment (being heaviest) where you want to balance your canoe (keep the bow down).

Place clothing, stuff bags and foamies, tent in the other compartment (presuming the centre thwart forms two compartments). Fold the 2-foot overlap down and the end pieces up like a butcher's wrap.

Pull the large overlap over the load, pulling it tight and tucking it down the other side. Tie rope or stretch elastic cord across the top or around the load to secure it. Load paddles, tie camera bag or thwart and it's done.

When this tarp technique is done tightly and neatly, you can roll your canoe right over and not only lose nothing, but everything will stay dry too! Involuntarily tested and proven effective.

"Come a Long Journey", Alan Fry, published by Doubleday, 1971.

Without qualification, this is my vote for the best book written on the Yukon River. The author, who was an Indian Agent in the territory for many years, has created a gourmet's stew of adventure, history and travel, and seasoned the blend with a few lessons in human understanding. This is the book that best captures the spirit of the river as I feel it. Unfortunately the book appears to be out-of-print at the moment, which is a shame because it is ten times better than Berton's drivel, "Drifting Home".

Dear Folks,

For what it's worth, here's a song (or perhaps dirge?) composed during a mad paddling battle against the rain, hail and **cold** wind enroute to Minto. The tune is borrowed from "O Lord, won't you buy me a Mercedes Benz" and should be sung dolefully, loudly and in beat with the paddle strokes. (It works! After two damp days of fervent singing, we were rewarded by a week of sun.)

THE CANOEIST'S LAMENT

O Lord, won't you send us a bright sunny day
Take all of these storm clouds and blow them all away
I'm wet and I'm soggy as I kneel here to pray
So Lord, won't you send us a bright sunny day.

O Lord send us sunshine and ninety degrees
My body is so cold that my toes won't unfreeze
I'm wet and I'm shaking from my neck to my knees
O Lord send us sunshine and ninety degrees.

O Lord I'm so weary of this mold and this damp
My bedding's green and rotten, I just can't dry out this camp
My nose won't stop running and I feel like a tramp
O Lord, please deliver us from this mold and this damp.

O Lord, won't you remember what summer really means
Those long sultry days and those wild nude beach scenes
Straw hats and lemonade and cut off blue jeans
O Lord, please remember what summer really means.

Repeat first verse.

—*Helen D.*

YA DON'T SAY!

Chilcoot Chuck says:
"Always have a good story ready to tell the tourist when you mooch a tow!"

CAMPING EQUIPMENT

The first reality is, of course, that everything is too expensive in the Yukon. An example: a spray cover for a Grumman canoe was bought at REI Co-op (figuring we'd save money there) for $295 plus customs and freight. While on the river of our choice, we met some guys who'd paid $160 for the same thing from the factory in New York. And as far as I know, you can't buy one in the Yukon anywhere, at any price. The moral is: go to the manufacturer if you have time.

The following listings are just to give an idea on sources of camping and canoeing equipment and maybe to say a word on their effectiveness as a supplier.

LARGE MAIL-ORDER OUTFITS

Recreational Equipment Inc., better known as REI or simply "the Co-op," Box 21685, Seattle, Wash., USA 98140. Probably the biggest (with ¾ million members) and best of the American suppliers. Excellent catalogue. Cheaper by far than most other mail-order houses plus you get a yearly dividend as a co-op member of between seven and 10 per cent of your expenditures. Customs will charge 25 per cent or more for the Queen. Sew-it-yourself kits available for some of the clothing.

ABC Equipment, 555 Richards Street, Vancouver, V6B 2Z5, B.C. Expensive, mostly climbing and hiking gear, for those who like to spend lots, be modern and look good in the bush.

Happy Outdoorsman, Box 190, St. Vital, Manitoba X 2M 4A5. Canadian, trying hard and presenting a good selection. However, a silva ranger type 15 compass is $31.75 from here and only $21 from Mountain Equipment Co-op and a Phoebus 625 stove costs $42.50 here and $28.00 again from

Mountain Equipment. Nice catalogue, though.

Mountain Equipment Co-op, 2068 West 4th Ave., Vancouver, B.C. V6J 1M9. Probably the best. Specializing in mountaineering and backpacking with lots of information on other places if you ask them. They don't sell crap, they won't rip you off and they'll get it to you quickly. What more could you ask?

Eddie Bauer, 22 Bloor Street West, Toronto, Ont. M4W 1A1. For the complete suburban camper. Virtually everything in their catalogue looks like it can be bought somewhere else. Their sleeping bags are $200 to $300 but very warm indeed. National Lampoon did a spoof on them but didn't do half as good a job as Eddie Bauer does on itself.

Thomas Black & Sons, Canada, 225 Strathcona Avenue, Ottawa, Ont. K1S 1X7. Famous for their sleeping bags. Much of their equipment is made of cottons and natural products and is a welcome relief from the rush towards high-tech plastics and synthetics. Expect to pay more for the quality.

Gerry Division of Outdoor Sports Industries, 5450 North Valley Hwy, Denver, Colo. 80216. Gerry Cunningham designs superb packs and interesting mountaineering tents, as well as supplying those re-usable squeeze tubes for your honey and peanut butter. He also co-authored a book called "Lightweight Camping Equipment and How to Make it" which is an excellent resource book.

Woods Bag & Canvas Co., 401 Logan Ave., Toronto. Franchised locally at Horwood's in Whitehorse. Sturdy, rugged-use tents, sleeping robes and parkas. Their Arctic 5-Star sleeping robe is big enough for two and doubles as a sauna in warm weather.

L. L. Bean, Freeport, Me., 04032, USA. Three or four

catalogues per year with the most comprehensive selection of canoeing-oriented clothes and equipment known. Their store is like Disneyland for a camper and open 24 hours a day and only a 4,000-mile drive from Ross River.

Outdoor Stores Ltd., 615 Bowes Road, Concord, Ont. A modern sporting goods mail order house, also with a chain of stores. A modern sportings good selection, which means you can't get super specialized equipment here but they have a large selection of fishing gear and family camping stuff.

Herters Inc., Route #2 1-90, Mitchell, South Dakota. What they say about themselves is true: "the authentic world source for fishermen, hunters, guides, gunsmiths, tackle makers, trappers and expeditions since 1893."

King Sol Outdoor Stores, 639-647 Queen Street West, Toronto, Ont. Phone 363-9944. Save a lot of money on camping, fishing, hunting, boating, cottage needs. Lots of government surplus stuff. Cheap stuff — but goodies can be found tucked away in their catalogue. Big store in Toronto.

Holubar Mountaineering Ltd., P.O. Box 7, Boulder, Colorado, 80306. Phone 303-442-8413. Good quality gear and you get what you pay for. Impressive catalogue. As a matter of fact, the canoe equipment dealt from here is the best on the market. Prices aren't too far out of reach. Gets our recommendation.

Fairydown Polar Equipment, c/o Arthur Ellis and Company, Private Bag, Dunedin, New Zealand. Listed here because it's the best you can buy in the world. Amaze yourself and drool on a catalogue from them. Surface mail transit time 10-12 weeks. Air mail one week. Seven per cent duty at least, but there it is — sleeping bags, jackets, hoods, gloves, boots, pants for Arctic use.

TEA ALARM CLOCK

Before going to sleep, drink lots and lots of tea and you won't need an alarm clock in the morning to wake you up.

65-MILE CANOE TRIP

Go to kilometer 53 on the Robert Campbell Highway where the Frances River crosses the road. The Frances River flows into the Liard and you come out at Upper Liard, Kilometer 1032 on the Alaska Highway. There are 11 rapids within the first eight miles. At the 4-5 mark the rapids are at their worst (best) and you may have to make one or two short portages.

— *W. Lanz*

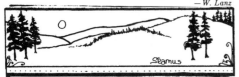

PART III

Hunger forced me out of the den. The Ravens had done a number on my mother's corpse and I turned and ran. Direction didn't matter; I just had to get away, brothers and sisters forgotten. I didn't get very far when I saw a huge orange thing coming at me. The next thing I saw was a dark hole under a small porch and ran for it. From my hole, I watched the thing go by, smoke and steam coming out from under it. I also got a chance to watch my fellow inhabitants of this world of white as they went about their business. I'll tell you about some of them.

First I noticed that I was the only dog not tied up that I could see. I saw no advantage to a five foot chain on a ring pole so I made up my mind not to indulge in it if I could help it. Across the street was a huge malamute tied to a steel pole. The pole was about six feet high and he revolved on a chain of about twice the length around it. The pole itself was about two inches wide but the bottom two feet or so was about a one foot thick column of yellow ice. He revolved about this is an ever deepening hole and recycled his food over and over again. The people who owned him were like most in the village in that they hardly fed their dogs, unless they were about to use them for hauling. So, thin and crazy, the big idiot went round in circles and made hoarse sounds at any thing that moved. A lot of dogs up here, pure breed dogs mostly, cannot bark and make some really pathetic sounds.

The other big thing that added to his brain damage was that scourge of the north, the almighty Raven. You may think that a raven is just a dumb frozen idiot that eats garbage, but then let me tell you something. The oldest one people **know** of was 69 years old when it croaked, and ravens have an entire vocabulary. I've known a few people who talked to them (that's another story) and also they eat better than any other animal in the north. So, with all this information do you know what they do for fun? They complete the damage of the poor dog's brain in a multitude of ways.

I lay there and watched the ravens and dogs, and as I watched them, I noticed that they all fought; the ravens fought each other for food just like the dogs did, but the ravens also stole food from the dogs. The most common way was to swoop down in a relaxed manner and rip off their fancy and fly off. This was okay for dumb dogs who were fed a lot. Most were tied up all their lives and ate their own droppings half the time. Another way the ravens would feed was to bother a dog who had something and kept an eye on it — one would jump around just inches from the chain radius (I call them "life-lines" and the area inside the circle the "snap-zone") and another would perch behind him on his post or a wire nearby. One partner would peck away and cause him to snap at it in total frustration (a raven's beak and claws hurt!) and the other would nab the morsel. Then there were the odd "bad-guy" ravens that could humble a dog by flying at his eyes enough and take their fill. I couldn't fly, and I couldn't run very fast, being about the size of a rugby ball — but hunger makes the world go round, and on the third day of hiding I made my way out to try my luck in the "main game."

KAYAKING:

1/SLALOM

Highly manoeuverable boats suitable for whitewater found on many Yukon rivers, constructed out of fiberglass or A.B.S. plastic.

2/TOURING

Longer and less manoeuverable but has more space for packing and will track better. Constructed out of a variety of materials including the above plus wood and canvas. Suitable for quiet rivers but can navigate grade II rapids.

Additional equipment used for whitewater

—Helmet—plastic with holes (hockey helmets have actually proven better than most).
—Lifejacket—vest type with closed cell buoyancy have proven best.
—Spray skirt—cover for cockpit fastened with shock cord around waist of paddler.
—Paddle—double paddle either left or right handed.
—Buoyancy—essential in fiberglass boat.

WHERE TO BUY OR MAKE

Kayaks—Yukon Canoe Club has molds that you can do-it-yourself. Yukon Fiberglass makes a slalom kayak for $175, but the quality may not be too good. Check carefully.

Helmets—generally about $25. Once again Igloo Sporting Goods gets undersold; they want $17 for a helmet that Scotties Sports (a new place on 4th Ave.) only wants $7 for.

Lifejackets and spray covers—are available from catalogues, probably less than you'd pay in Whitehorse.

Paddle—If you buy one, be prepared to pay $50-$100. Varnish should be stripped off and the paddle well oiled otherwise it will probably splinter. Make your own either by laminating strips of wood or by using a fiberglass mould.

Bob Sharp has a mould for paddles. Contact him through the canoe club. Laminate the blade you make to a wooden shaft. (See the book listing in the Misc. section for a good book on homemade paddles.) Beware of the quality of locally bought paddles.

Buoyancy—anything that can be fixed into the boat, foam blocks, plastic bags.

Phoenix Products, US Route 421, Tyner, Kentucky 40486, USA — Kayak company with an impressive list of equipment, some of which is outstanding. Try the floatation and water-proof bags.

Needle Rock on the Pelly

INEXPENSIVE BUYS

A cheap way to buy sporting equipment that is U.S.-made is to go to Haines, Alaska, and buy there. If you stay the weekend and take a crowd along you can bring lots back legally through customs duty-free. Check out: Alaska Sports Shop, Box 577, Haines, Alaska 99827.

They carry Buck and Gerber knives, Winchester, Remington, Ruger, Colt guns, as well as nets, traps, clothing and boots.

— *a. d.*

OUTFITTING AIRCRAFT — CHARTER

B.C. Yukon Air Service
Box 68
Watson Lake, Yukon   **Phone:** 536-7485

Frontier Helicopters
Box 10
Watson Lake, Yukon   **Phone:** 536-7766

Watson Lake Flying Services
Box 7
Watson Lake, Yukon   **Phone:** 536-2231

Mayo Helicopters
Box 130
Mayo, Yukon   **Phone:** 996-2375

Terr-Air
Ross River, Yukon   **Phone:** 969-2240

Globe Air Service
Hangar "A", WHSE International Airport
Whitehorse, Yukon   **Phone:** 668-2228
* Britton — Norman — Islander 9 passenger.
  Cessna 206   Wheels, Floats, Skis
  Cessna 185   Wheels, Floats, Skis
  Cessna 172   Wheels, Floats, Skis
  Piper Seneca

Northward Airlines
Hangar "A", WHSE International Airport
Whitehorse, Yukon   **Phone:** 668-2101
* F-27   40 passenger
  Whitehorse, Mayo, Dawson City, Old Crow, Ft. Macpherson, Inuvik, Tuktoyaktuk, Sachs Harbour.
  Flys once a week at least. Phone for full schedules.

Trans North Turbo Air Limited
Box 4338,
Whitehorse, Yukon   **Phone:** 668-2177
* Twin Engine Otter and DeHavilland
  Cessna 404
  Cessna 402   WHEELS ONLY
  Piper Seneca   2 Beachcraft
* Single Engine Otter
  2 Turbo Beavers   FLOATS, WHEELS, SKIS
  1 Standard Beaver
  1 Cessna 185
* Helicopters:
  Alouette 3   2 Hughes 500
  9 Bell Jet Rangers   5 Bell 47
Hangar "A"
Whitehorse, Yukon   **Phone:** 668-2354
* Beech 18 — 18 passenger
  Cessna 337 — 5 passenger
  Piper Seneca 1 — 5 passenger
  Cessna 206 — 5 passenger
  Cessna 2X185
* Helicopters: Miller 12E4T
  Hughes 500 D   Miller 12E — 2 passenger
Bases in Whitehorse, Haines Junction, Carmacks, Ross River, Mayo and Dawson City.

Transwest Helicopters
Hangar "A"   Open May - September
WHSE International Airport   Based in Vancouver, B.C.
Whitehorse, Yukon   **Phone:** 668-5504
* 6 Hughes 500
* STOL
  Helio Courier — 5 passenger with ski wheels
  Based Kluane Park at the Arctic Institute

We would like to add that you can do better, farther for less sometimes by flying Moose Air Chisel Charters and other people who have their commercial licence and need more hours in their books. They will be happy to rent a plane and fly you all over the place. Ask around, as usual up here, the grapevine is waiting to help you.

BOOKS ON CANOEING

There is a virtual stampede of books and publications on how-to-canoe and where-to-canoe, etc. Most of these books are just copies of other good books. Some are actually written by people who have canoed real rivers and are worth mentioning. For this reason the following list is small but good; you shouldn't need more this. By the way — you can buy all these and maps, too, at Mac's News Stand on Main Street, Whitehorse.

WHERE TO CANOE

"Canoe Routes: Yukon Territory"

By Richard Wright and Rochelle Wright/112 pages/ w/photos. Antonson Publishing Ltd., 12165-97th Ave., Surrey, B.C. One edition, published in 1977. Price: $5.95 in Whitehorse.

Outlines 23 of the most travelled Yukon rivers in the best detail yet available. However, don't believe it all. Upon examination it is obvious they were never near some of these rivers.

"Boaters Guide to Upper Yukon River"

Paperback, price $4.75. From the Editors of Alaska Magazine.

Includes sectional maps covering the 800-mile journey from Lake Bennett to Circle, Alaska. Lots of information on how to run the Yukon, supplies, etc. Not the best, but sufficient.

"Yukon Channel Charts"

By Bruce T. Batchelor/55 pages/w/photos. Published by the author.

Now out of print but scheduled for second printing in Spring 1979. May be ordered through Mac's News Stand, Whitehorse. The best maps available covering Whitehorse and Dawson City on the Yukon River.

Other information on the following rivers is available from the Yukon Territorial Government, Box 2703, Whitehorse. These rivers (16) were surveyed and written up in 1971-72 by the Dept. of Indian and Northern Affairs, National and Historic Sites Branch, Planning Division.

Too many comments on them have already been made — it's just a case of go and find out for yourself. Take a write-up along though, they'll tell you where the rough spots are.

Ross River, Nisultin River, Yukon River, Teslin River, Pelly River, Bell River, Porcupine River, Peel River, Lake Bennett, Tagish Lake, Atlin Lake, Atlin River, Marsh Lake, Macmillan River, White River, Sixty Mile River, Klondike River, Big Salmon River, Stewart River, Ogilvie River.

Yukon Archives has these reports plus the Lapic River and other smaller wild rivers.

HOW TO CANOE

"The Complete Wilderness Paddler"

By J. W. Davidson and John Rugge/260 pages with illustrations. Alfred A. Knopf Publishing, New York. Price: $12 in Whitehorse.

The very best modern canoeing manual on the market. Lots of illustrations — sections on flatwater navigation, whitewater, map-reading, canoe packing, and equipment tricks. A must for anyone who's really interested in making a canoe trip more efficient and safe.

"Pole Paddle Portage"

By Bill Riviere/259 pages/w/photos. Van Nostrand Rienhold Company, Toronto. Price: Approx. $6.

This book is excellent too. The difference between "Wilderness Paddler" and this one is that Bill Riviere is a traditional paddler and poler — a wood and canvas man. This information is so nice to know because it is lessons learned through hundreds of years. A wealth of experience and he never ever takes his pipe out of his mouth!

BOAT BUILDING

"Boat Builder's Manual"

(Building Fiberglass Canoes & Kayaks for Whitewater, 1977) Charles Walbridge-Steve Rock. Published by Wildwater Designs Kits, 230 Penllyn Pike, Penllyn, Pennsylvania, USA.

These guys are hotshots. THE best book on the subject available. Section on spray skirts and decks, too.

Excerpts from a Yukon River diary

What a godawful day. Down to the core of what this trip is really about. Felt like a paddling machine all day today. Numbed my brain out of existence and concentrated on being an automaton. Regular as clockwork. But tired. I am a human. Muscles at back of arms and lower back were protesting. Couldn't do perfect mechanised strokes at all. Got discouraged, snappy. Performed only out of mindlessness. Didn't care about anything, didn't look at the scenery. Half the time I paddled in my sleep. And the rain . . . what can be said about the rain? It was awful. Soaked right through my rain-jacket, pants, all. Once in a while the rain would break a little, and I had looking breaks. The scenery has never been so beautiful. Shades of blues in amorphous layers, silhouettes of mountains down to infinity, clouds fluffing around ethereal peaks, spiky treetops lacing the slopes of mountains . . .

Had a floating soaked lunch during a drier spell and finished just in time for the downpours to begin again.

—Joy Proulx

Spring break-up and flood on the Yukon

RIVER SERVICES, GUIDING, OUTFITTING IN THE YUKON

JET BOAT MINOT
Bill Harris, Minto, Yukon
Afternoon and evening, four hour charter trips to Fort Selkirk.

YUKON EXPEDITIONS
Monty Alford, 2 Kluhini Cresc., Whitehorse.
Mountain climbing, river running in kayaks.

GOLDRUSH RIVER TOURS
P.O. Box 4835, Whitehorse
Down by the White Pass Freight Yards on the river. Rentals of canoes and most camping equipment. Guided riverboat trips.

ADVENTURE YUKON LTD.
Dave Griffiths, Gordon Miller
510 Steele Street, Whitehorse (667-6934)
Five 14-day guided canoe trips, outfit and canoe rentals.

YUKON CANOE RENTAL
6159 - 6th Ave., Whitehorse (667-7773)
One of the first rental companies — also guided river trips.

YUKON MOUNTAIN & RIVER EXPEDITIONS
Hector Mackenzie
52 Sunset Drive, Whitehorse, Yukon Y1A 3G4   668-5918
Guided river trips (canoe and kayak), from one to ten days on fast and white water rivers; transportation and meals provided. Canoeing instruction and equipment.
Guided mountaineering and mountaineering instruction. Rock climbing, snow and ice climbing and glacier travel to all mountain areas in Yukon including Kluane National Park. Cross country ski instruction and touring from one to ten days. Special trips organized with dog team support. Equipment, transportation and meals provided.

YUKON RAFTING
Allan Dennis and Greg Capol. P.O. Box 23, Dawson City (993-5391)
Klondike River 2½ hour tour $6. Two days on the Yukon River and Forty Mile River $90. Five days on the Stewart and Yukon Rivers $215. Fourteen-day tour Lake Bennett to Dawson City $560 per person. Customers interviewed were very happy.

RUDY BURIAN
Stewart River, c/o Dawson City Post Office, Y.T.
River freighting.

YUKON WHITE WATER RECREATION (Canoe Yukon Ltd.)
Al Omitani, P.O. Box 4478, Whitehorse (667-6071)
Private or group canoeing lessons. Introduction to kayaking. Guided white water trips. Equipment available (see equipment, under this company).

YUKON WILDERNESS UNLIMITED
John Lammers
P.O. Box 4126, Whitehorse Yukon (Radio: 2M-3908)
Guide and outfitted for river float trips and base camp wilderness vacations. Small groups. No hunting.

AIRCRAFT
For canoe trips and general messing about we have tried two and examples of rates are:
Ross River to Moose Ponds (Nahanni River) $380 (2 people, 1 canoe).
Via Territorial Airways, Ross River, Yukon.
Watson Lake to Moose Ponds $564.
Via B.C.-Yukon Air, Box 68, Watson Lake, Yukon.
Trans North Turbo Air
Box 4338, Whitehorse, Yukon (668-5504)
The largest outfit in the Yukon.

We didn't want to print things twice, so if you're looking for a specific type of plane or a number of an outfit somewhere in the boonies, please refer to the Aircraft List opposite.

MISCELLANEOUS SUPPLIERS

Grey Owl Paddle Company, 101 Sheldon Dr., Cambridge, Ont. N1R 6T6. Hardwood paddles. Orders of 10 or more only. Very impressive brochure.

Phoenix Products, US Route 421, Tyner, Kentucky 40486, USA. The best waterproof camera and equipment bags available. Also makers of kayaks.

Voyageur Enterprises, Box 512, Shawnee Mission, Kansas 66201. Huge plastic waterproof bags at good prices. Very strong, made to hold 30 pounds of clothes. A good camera bag available, too.

Al Beletz, Bog 9301, Richmond Heights Station, Richmond Hts., Montana 63117, USA. Are you going into poling canoes? It's the fastest way to go up or down the river; with the new light aluminum poles, a person who learns how can do wonders where a paddle completely fails.

Teslin Tlingit Wood Products, Teslin, Yukon Territory. Freighter canoes to drool over. Beautifully hand-crafted cedar strip and canvas. As good as any others on the market, probably better. The native people there also make snowshoes and toboggans.

Western Canvas & Cotton Ltd., 3594 W. 4th, Vancouver, B.C. Write for a brochure.

Calgary Tent & Awning Ltd., 3624 Manchester Rd., Calgary 24, Alta. Phone (403) 243-4666. Dealing in all kinds of things, including TIPIS.

Sample prices: 18' Sioux 12 oz. unbleached canvas	$350
18' liner (10 oz.)	$200
18' Sioux (Boat Duck)	$490

Archer's Bible, c/o Kitteridge Bow Hut, Mammoth Lakes, California. Send 50 cents for a catalogue. Complete archery gear, plus camping accessories. Interesting stuff, worth looking at.

Kluane Mountaineering Ltd., 8223-104th St., Edmonton, Alta. Phone (403) 433-9986. John Faulkner has been busy designing some worthwhile stuff like Duluth-style packs that can hold two large plastic waterproof stuff bags. Never seen a catalogue, but we were made aware of this source by some people who seem to know that they're about . . .

SCOOP . . . You can now order the canoe that you really want. Forget Grummans and Chestnuts, Hougens, Igloo and Woolworths. Here is a local supplier who can order a canoe like a Langford or an Old Town, and can beat the costs of any supplier up here (save Hector Mackenzie, who's right after this piece). Offering a month and a half delivery (air is shorter but costs a lot but if you've got the money . . .) and with a markup of only 20 per cent it looks like we can now own some class equipment. Here's the Info:
Yukon Whitewater Recreation Ltd., P.O. Box 4478, Whitehorse (403) 667-6071. Al Omitani. Sale and service of:
(Canadian) — Langford Canoes — cedar & canvas
　　　— Pleasure canoes,　　— Royalex (ABS), Blue Hole
　　　　Freighter canoes　　　Canoe (US)
(USA) — Old Town Canoes — cedar & canvas
　　　　　　　— Oltonar (ABS)
　　　　　　　— 17' chipewyan — recommended as the best whitewater tripping canoe available.
(Canadian) — Woodstream canoes
(USA) — Sawyer
　　　— Also dealing Clemente (Canadian) paddles, recommended as the top wood laminated canoe paddle in North America

Yukon Mountain & River Expeditions, 52 Sunset Dr., Whitehorse. Phone 668-5918. For about $400 Hector Mackenzie is selling the Colman plastic canoes, which most people who have tried them recommend highly over aluminum for the rough spots. Our particular quote comes from Boris, who says, "On our trip down the Nahanni we came across Grummans wrapped around rocks, and we actually hit a rock dead on, bending the bow. We stopped, did some fishing and when we returned, our canoe was back in its original shape, ready to go."

Try the mighty Yukon

The perennial travellers' favourite, the Yukon River, is probably the best river for newcomers to canoeing. It is a tremendous two-week trip from Whitehorse to Dawson but it is a gruelling maniac-paddle in anything less than ten. "Don't push on the river, it flows by itself". Take your time, keep to yourselves, and take your garbage with you, or burn it and sink it. Leave the river people alone; summer is a busy enough time for them without 800 tourists visiting.

Last summer, 1978, Parks Canada and YTG Playgrounds tried to extend their empire onto the river but made such an embarrassing mess of it all that I doubt they will want to show their faces for at least another few years. No one needed patrolmen motoring all over asking silly questions and bureaucrat-planners making fools of themselves.

Have a good trip!

b.b.

RODNEY RIVERDALE'S RIVER LIST

For four people (never travel alone)

Buy everything at Hougen's and charge it.

- two zodiac rubber rafts (one for people, one for gear)
- eight small plastic paddles
- foot pumps for inflating said rafts, 20 lb. rubber patch kit
- 1000 square ft. two mil. plastic sheeting
- four u-vic floater coats (tested on the oil rigs)
- 200 ft. 1/8" plastic rope (yellow)
- three boat sponges
- one package green garbage bags w/ties for everything
- Coleman stove, gas, 40 piece PALCO alum. mess kit
- 15 lb. newspaper
- cameras, film, more film
- fishing rods, tackle boxes, four packages worms and herring
- Y.T.G. Parks Yukon River Guide, R.C.M.P. checklist
- tool box, spare parts, four food coolers
- First aid kit: tweezers, bandaids, aspirin, speedsew
- clothes (too numerous to mention), dirty laundry basket
- Bushnell's shock resistant sunglasses
- soap, shampoo, Tide, Ivory liquid soap, towels, paper towels
- sleeping bags, foam pillows, blankets, deck chairs
- chain-saw, gas and oil, carrying case, spare chain, tools
- Matches, butane lighter and fluid, white gas , fire starter
- *FOOD* - Kool aid
- In cans: fruit, veggies, spaghetti sauces, soups, milk, butter
- beer, cigarettes, scotch
- four rolls toilet paper
- 10 lb. hamburger (florescent green)
- 10 lb. steak
- vitamin pills
- corn flakes, six loaves white bread
- mayonnaise, three rolls summer sausage
- eggs, 5 lb. bacon, marshmellows
- potatoes, onions, mushrooms, ketchup
- Rolaids
- wieners, hot dog buns, relish, mustard

Rodney got scared at this point and left hurriedly. However, we expect to learn more from him after he returns from a hunting expedition at Jake's Corner.

Blue vs. White foamies

Backpackers, canoeists, skiers, virtually everyone who does any camping will tell you not to buy the thick soft foam underpads because they are too bulky and soak up moisture "like a sponge." There is little agreement beyond that about which to use between the closed cell blue polyethylene pad and the white, more expensive ensolite pads.

For the winter, a caribou hide is best of all, but bulky. If your bag isn't very warm it is a good idea to sleep on two foamies (and your parka, and any other spare clothing handy). Be careful about unrolling foamies if they have been wet and frozen, as they will pull apart in chunks if not thawed by the fire first. A length of wax paper rolled up with the foamie will keep it from freezing too badly but you still have to be careful. Some people sew a nylon cover for their pad to minimize wear and tear. Blue foamies cost about $5 mail-ordered and are less durable; white foamies are $10 but you can expect to pay double that in Whitehorse.

—A.D.

A Midsummer's Raft Dream

Excerpts from a River Journal

DAY THREE: Thunder storms, marauding cloud warriors, black in a sky of billowy white others, hurl their light then ROAR at me snug in a dry tent, a dry warm bag; within minutes of my being ready for rain.

Look at that. I try to start descriptive, then ZOOM! directly at me, me, me. I've a story to tell, of how I came to camp in a tall old cottonwood stand, the duff soft below me, a full moon mattress.

Oh, yeah? Well, where's your ensolite sleeping pad?

What does the ensolite have in common with a Guatemalan sarong? With Roastaroma Mocha spice tea in a small sour cream container? Or with a wildflower bouquet of onions and sage, fireweed, goldenrod and yarrow?

Gone to the sea, M'dear, to the Bering Sea.

Using the well-known tool of levers, how would one get a six-log, five metre raft to return to the right-side-up from the up-side-down? What does a lack of attention at the end of a conserve-energy day, then a huge log-jam in a Pelly River side channel, have to do with a full moon?

Male Salesman Voice: Wah, try our new special all-improved type river raft, Ma'am. You alone of all your friends, Ma'am, would have a river raft with the forward sunbathing platform, the rear storage area, the bouquet and the driftwood section. Wah, they're all under water, Ma'am.

This somewhat slick rendition is made possible because it's all under control again; I am safe and my losses are few, and Huey even sent a new vase as I started the dry-out job by a cool evening's warm fire. An old sherry bottle floated right up to the raft and I nabbed it, much as when my newly-inverted vehicle caught up at last to the little teapot, given up as lost as it bobbed ahead in the cold, muddy Pelly.

Funny, but it didn't seem at all cold through those minutes — no, seconds — in the water, though my teeth chattered after I stood elemental on the raft, my steering sweep lost, waiting to strike shore. Like a dream I recall standing ready, sweep poised to push off after the inevitable crash. Instead of bouncing off, though, the raft crept higher and higher on the jam. In slow motion I see my warmly-clothed body, the gear, the raft sliding up and over and still the river takes us. I am clinging to the outer log, legs stuck instinctively up and pressing on the scantily-tied gear on the raft's underside. The ensolite pad makes the first exit. Goodbye. Then the little teapot and the Roastarama mocha spice tea in the small sour cream container. By now the river has pushed us past the jam into a deep, open run and I realize that everything is carrying on regardless. Well-timed revelation it was, for the food sack, escaping off to one side, was calling out for rescue. *Kersplat,* the water-heavy bag is on deck and I'm off again for my bobbing packsack, for my North Face mountain tent, summer home . . . shelter me, shelter me . . .

A brief back-to-the-now to report that it's nicely dry in here and the second rain shower splatters my fly.

DAY 4: "Stay tuned for the second half of this here river drama folks." The old male salesman again. Imagine his rasping drawl from Tucson, Arizona . . . imagine his suit from Sears . . . imagine him chairman of the lawn-bowling club meeting. . . . But I digress.

I am going to trick you.

I'm going to miss out a whole block of time and start at now.

Gone swimmin'.

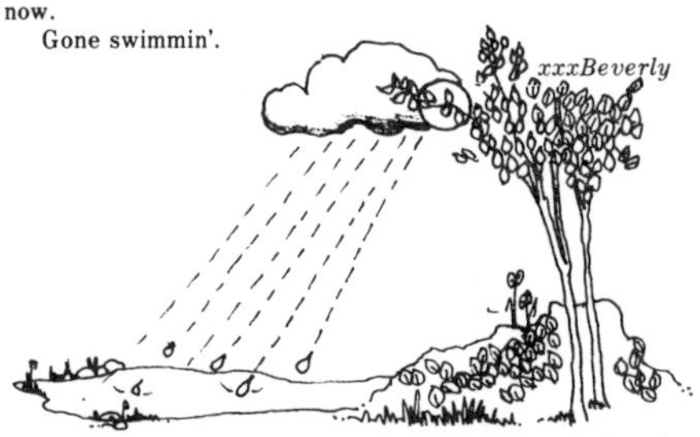

DAY 5: Tired from the flurry of activity necessary to get floating again. Scared of the river now, although my earlier fear of ranging too far from the raft has been overcome. I will trade you one fear for another.

My exploratory ventures are increasing. Only yesterday I ran up dry clay cliffs, said hello to hoodoos, found strawberries and sunshine and a layer of volcanic ash in the soil. As the day ended my feet took me looking for fireweed tea and new poles for sweeps — a barefoot evening walk through the soft green woods, wandering further from my camp each time. I suppose I'll mellow into this trip again — all I need is to go a while with no mishaps. Log jams and treacherous side-channels, newest bogeymen. A family of kestrels dwelt high high above my tent in an old dead cottonwood tree. They all stared at me from their woodpecker peephole when pa (or was it ma?) shrilled some hidden sunset message. I didn't see the babies fly.

The buzzing of insects is like the noise of motor monsters, incredibly irritating if it gets through your shell. Along the complaint line — I don't want to tie and untie and tie and untie anymore plastic bags!

EL DIA NUMERO 6: A rainy low-cloud day, fog like the coast. Last night I wanted to write that no matter how that day begins and regardless of the middle-time, evening brings peace and inner calm. I wanted to write that, but hot milk and driftwood fire glow put me in dreamland real quick.

Feelin' good! Maybe a rainy tent morning will be good practice for my Glacier Bay trip . . .

I fought with myself all day yesterday, tricked and trapped by future-time, wanting to get to people again, planning and coordinating my river-folk visiting, fish camping, Glacier Bay tripping . . . round and round I went. Turmoil.

# # #

Mental debate: one little voice — get yer shit together, make a sweatlodge, do some stretching
other little voice — oh so nice to listen to the rain and the river, to drink tea in the sleeping bag

# # #

Some *Islandia* quotes (from the only realistic Utopia novel I've read, about complex and independent people):

"I was being floated almost most happily in the stream of their lives." Now there's good hosts.

"It appeared that one hated to destroy or even change an aspect of things found pleasing, and never did so without creating another in its place."

"It seemed to me that she evaded the grim side of life in her constant concentration on its visual beauty."

DAY 7: Have you ever, for example, been stuck with your raft on a rock in the mid-Pelly, and considered the possibilities?

# # #

What a phenomenal place to be. I hear the background roar of jet planes, high above the clouds, almost constantly. They seem to fade in and out, and it's hard to tell their direction. Probably old man river playing ventriloquist.

Very noisy — I sit perched on a rock as tall as me, its downstream edge just a few inches under water, its upstream edge a few feet under raft. The river seems spurty and the raft is rocking slightly side-to-side. The optimist in me thinks the river might rise, after yesterday's rain. Regardless, I've decided to stay and watch. Weren't Siddhartha's talents (when thusly questioned) to watch, to listen and to wait? Incredible to be quite stationary in among cresting white waves, and looking upstream the whole river flows at me, steady and wide. . . . Big swirls around both ends of the raft, angled slightly downstream but exactly centered on the rock.

And I laughed at the Eddie Bauer survival kit, with the eight foot yellow plastic tube tent I'm keeping dry and windproof in.

A few more hours till sunset, then the dark of night and another change. It's been Huey ☼ and warm air for most of my afternoon stay, with a thundercloud that threatened and chilled for an hour, sprinkled for a minute.

How warm and dry and comfy and not-uptight will I pass my night? Will I be ta da ta da (with a bravado I'd scarcely feel) rescued by a concerned John or the folks at Pelly Crossing who know of my trip and intended visit? John predicted a five-day trip, the old Indian a week. Today is number seven.

This is the north. I will learn more of its character through this drama, and just a little of my own too, eh? I'm stoned now so objectivity comes easier; this could be a *(SHUDDER)* torture-chamber place.

I feel a little like the guy who sat on a telephone pole for some absurd length of time.

Nearest swimmin' shore is half a mile away, with the current.

A big silver plane passed over a while ago and I thought I saw it start to circle as I madly waved a red poncho, but it was hope pulling tricks again.

Now an inner tube to ferry the goods ashore would be handy indeed.

My first impulse today, right after "oh fuck it's happening again" was to pack my bags and get out of here. Swim for it. Actually that came when I realized that the raft wasn't going to budge despite vain, chest-deep water levering attempts, and equally vain jumping up and down efforts on both ends of the raft. I even tried to rig a water sail, throwing the red poncho and lengths of rope into the current in hopes of being pulled off the rock, but to no avail.

Is this thing steady enough for me to crash out for the night? Two logs are dry, and the magic yellow Eddie Bauer tube will keep off the splashes. It will be cold on the water. It would be even colder in the water, sure folly to be in the water in my sleeping bag. If the raft moves, will it be quick? It shouldn't fall apart, with three two by fours and very long spikes holding the logs together. From the last mishap they're on the raft's underside now, sandwiched between the logs and the rock, pushed into the raft by the current.

DAY 8: Lobster for dinner, fresh sprouts and salmon for lunch — at least the cuisine is fair on my two-log river perch. Passed a much better night than I anticipated, and through the grey-clouds gradually-clearing day I sit all bagged up, finally warm again after an early-morning plunge for one final levering attempt. This raft ain't goin' nowhere — all six logs and flush with the rock, wider than I imagined it. I got chilled pretty quick from such a short immersion and that, combined with frustration and apathy, keep me raft-bound still, the swim-for-it plan abandoned for now.

What to do? I am safe and warm and well-fed right here, and two sloping logs are almost as comfy as my usual bedspots (spikes and nails next for this girl — sky's the limit).

Option A — wait some more. The long arm of concerned rescuers and the little "help-me" vibes I'm projecting are bound to have me safely plucked from my prison, with time. Is this being too irresponsible? too dependent?

Option B — Alternately I could chance swift rapids, with my will-it-float gear (about $700 worth, I can't see leaving it behind), then stash everything but clothes, food, magic yellow bag and first-aid kit, and strike off. I'd have to swim the MacMillan River (on the map it looks Pelly-sized but very meandery — dare I guess it slow-moving?) after a

seven kilometer walk. A little black square on the map says there was, or is, a cabin across the confluence; most likely was, as the new cabin I saw upriver was unmarked, the caving-in remains of another duly indicated. From there it's a 28 kilometer hoof to a cabin just above Granite Canyon, where there may or may not be people. And from there a 40 kilometer saunter, trail-less of course, to town.

Ought I take the risks? Is my desire to be not dependent that strong? Am I exaggerating the risks? Am a good swimmer, and even my truckin' Nike runners along.

To take Option B eliminates the possibility of taking Option A in the future — the converse is not true. The worst that could come of staying put is the shame of having to be saved, and maybe the cost. Havoc in the bank account. The worst that could come of a get-there-yourself attempt is drowning or otherwise bidding a permanent adieu. Now how scared am I really of that? Other baddies — lose all my gear, get hypothermia (can I be sure enough, in these mid-summer days with all my woolies and waterproof matches along, that I won't?).

The helicopter noises I've been hearing all along are the sounds the boulders make rolling along the river-bed. The water is slightly higher and only one log remains dry. Thanks again yellow plastic bag — a bit wet inside but the fiberfill sleeping bag is still warm. If the water comes higher or the raft breaks apart, I may be forced to leave. Until then, or my patience breaks, I stay.

\# \# \#

Smoked a joint and went for it. Nice refreshing dip, now Huey dries a few things and heats my oiled body (Ooh Ooh feel gooood); I play on skree slopes with a raven-feather crown I found the minute I touched shore.

—beverly

p.s. — sure is quiet here, no wonder I was freaked on the noisy raft.

\# \# \#

Such a gentle and peaceful confluence . . .

Easy truckin' in these woods — I think I'll keep me and my gear together, including tomorrow's MacMillan swim. My trip continues, how happy I am. Stuck on a rock with a raft was no fun.

Warm summer evening (or am I biased by three light cashmere sweaters and my favorite men's dress pants, wooly and grey and just a dollar at the Sally Ann?) Half the sky is clearly blue and sunset clouds flame yellow and pink on their bases. A grey rainstorm looms up the mountainous MacMillan drainage — my vista is wide.

Tired now; not exactly deep sleeping last night on the raft. So glad not to be there. Feels great being with just me. I wonder if I'll see people tomorrow?

Unafraid at last, and two more days until my birthday.

DAY 9: Garden campsite. Purple aster and show-off white yarrow twinkle at me from between smooth grey boulders.

And old buddy onion, right now complementing my chicken broth soup (thanks again Eddie Bauer). Food is getting low and I have just twelve kilometers left to the cabin at the canyon. I hate like hell to plan the future but methinks I'll be there tomorrow. Birthday treat. Maybe there'll be people but I'll settle for food alone. Can probably slide by if the cupboard is bare too — lots of berries today, the rosehips so firm and sweet and appley, and fat juicy strawberries as well. The currants taste awful although purple-ripe, and the cranberries are still too new.

About sixteen kilometers of heavy-duty truckin' today, lots of up and down and thrash crash bang. Bear shit and tracks absolutely everywhere but I don't feel afraid. I wonder why?

Started my day with maybe three in-the-bag hours reading *Islandia* and procrastinating the MacMillan River swim; procrastinating even getting up. Finally did, and packed my gear watertight, oiled up, then . . . procrastinated some more. Had to wait till I felt the sun right through me, until I stretched and stanced enough to feel powerful, then in . . .

The first half was scary as I saw little progress and felt very cold water. At last I was in the meeting-of-the-rivers current, which whisked me towards my desired shore, then I was safe in a still back-eddy for my hoped-for sandbar landing. Towards the end my legs numbed out a little but an hour on black sand with $\cdot Q \cdot$ and I was off again.

Almost no shore travel; little benches just above the present water level, or ridge-walking atop new or old cut-bank cliffs, were the order of the day. Some really shitty areas, deadfall in mature spruce or else tangles of willow trees, but at last half was decent going. The animal paths are always in the easiest places.

Heard two beavers talking today, a nasal whispery sound with lots of tone range. Another first. Saw several old fire-rings and rusty tin cans — past use of the Pelly.

Tomorrow's birthday present for yours truly will be a hair wash and condition in the clean cold stream I'm camped by, a mid-day destination choice that I actually made it to.

DAY 10:   Happy Birthday to you
           Scratched-up sad missy-poo
           This hot mid-day truckin'
           Just ain't made for you
           Have a rest and a toke
           Maybe swim the odd stroke
           Don't be trapped by the future-time
           As this song is by rhyme.
Happy 24th, strong lady.

\# \# \#

Shaggy mane mushroom feed after seeing only dangerous red-rimmed boletus for two days. Thanks Huey, I was just feelin' hungry.

\# \# \#

So I lay back in the soft green horsetails, not even minding the blackflies, drinking in the sun. Hot to the point of hallucinations, I sat up to debate a swim — and — I — S A W — (you won't believe it) my raft with my foodbag floating down the opposite shore. And this after two days of nuts and raisins, honey and berries, and a morning of nagging doubt as to the food content of the Canyon Cabin.

I lost nearly a kilometer's ground on the swim across, but beat the raft so had time to grab a pole from the bush, in anticipation of manoeuvering the bugger back across the Pelly. A stroke of luck — as I swam out to my refound logmobile — logmobile? I hereby christen the LOGMOBILE, brother of BUSHMOBILE (this will probably call for a sign to be carved) . . .

Anyhoo, one of the boards from the previous floor was floating alongside, held on by a few nails. A makeshift sweep, and I managed to cross back in about three kilometers and not the unknown greater distance had I used the pole. Everything still there! Oh canned butter, oh blue swede-saw, given up as lost. . . . A hasty meal of milk and wheatgerm (protein please, after all the sugar I've had) and the speedway continued. I'll not deny the old heart was racing. Abandoned boots to keep thorns out and the red tarp sarong-style against the rosebushes; I was off. Against the gathering grey clouds and oppressive heat I marched on, and back at my gear now, I am . . . a . . . very . . . tired . . . girl.

\# \# \#

Islandia in the tube, not sure whether I'll pack up and head for the raft and cabin tonite or not. For many days I've thought I'd be at the Canyon Cabin **tomorrow**. Feel a little impatient but also feel tired, want to mellow out.

\# \# \#

"There had been too much thinking all these last days, not the good first-hand thinking of actual things, but thoughts removed from reality by various stages of generalization and theorizing."

DAY 11: Lazy but hungry, a dilemma with the food a few kilometers downstream and my gear strewn all over the tent. Slept long and deep these last few nights; I think I'm tiring, ready for this trip to end.

Oh christ, timing . . .

It's a bird, it's a superman, no it's a plane, and sweet kind John steps out to my hug. He worried so he and a pilot friend, out for a Friday spin, just happened down the Pelly.

Sheets and sweet dreams at Pelly Farm. Maybe tomorrow the logmobile will float by, having been set free as I climbed into the plane.

—Beverly

KEEP CLEAN EVEN WHILE CAMPING IN WINTER

While we are packing up to move camp in the morning, we put a last pot of snow on the fire to melt for wash water. By the time most everything is packed, there is hot water ready so everyone can at least wipe his or her face and hands with a soapy cloth. We do this even at forty below and it feels good to start out warm and clean.

—a d

tents

Remember that whether you make your own tent or buy one, the roof colour is probably going to be the first thing that your waking mind will notice. If it is blue, you will be convinced that it is a cloudless day and wake up happy. If it is a colour like white or brown or gray, you might not want to get up at all. Don't ask what psychoses will develop to campers with a bright orange tent, but if they get diarrhea and pimples you'll know why.

FLOORS

In places where there are dangerous snakes a floor might be handy, but there aren't any snakes in the Yukon except in certain Dawson bars. Plastic floors on tents were probably invented by the same joker who swears by green garbage bags. Some tourists' tents have a rubberized floor which continues up the sidewalls a few inches and is proudly proclaimed by the manufacturer as an added feature, a bath-tub type floor! Apparently this is supposed to keep your freeze-dried foods dry if you are dumb enough to camp in a puddle.

A small piece of canvas ground-cloth under your bedding will keep it dry and be lighter to pack than a whole floor. And without a floor, you can bring your boots inside on a wet or snowy day and not have the drops off them meandering all over your tent in search of the lowest point. If there is a small leak in the roof of a floorless tent, it isn't a grand calamity; you just put a can under it, instead of looking for your rubber ducky.

Semi-permanent wall-tent camps often utilize plywood and two-by-four framing inside the canvas and a plywood floor is a logical extension of such luxury but make sure it is raised off the ground a few inches for proper drainage.

DESIGNS

A distinction must be made at the outset as to where the tent is intended to be used. Persons planning to go climbing mountains and glaciers have to consider the wind as the dominant factor. Expeditions have perished in recent times from exposure when their tents disintegrated under the force of high-altitude gales. Best buy an expedition-quality tent from a well-known source and you can expect to pay an arm and a leg for it.

Camping below timberline is quite a different matter. Here you can experiment with inexpensive original designs in a much more forgiving environment. We'll map out a few design points to help you start creating the exact tent for your personal needs.

BUGS

The north is famous for them so insist on netting that is marked "no-see-em cloth." Nylon netting is very lightweight and doesn't soak up any water but don't set your tent close to the campfire as it is quite flammable.

PEGS

Look around. Just about everything in the forest is a potential peg or peg-substitute. Tie the guy-lines to a tree, a branch, a rock, a stick piled over with rocks, bushes, a log, pound a stick

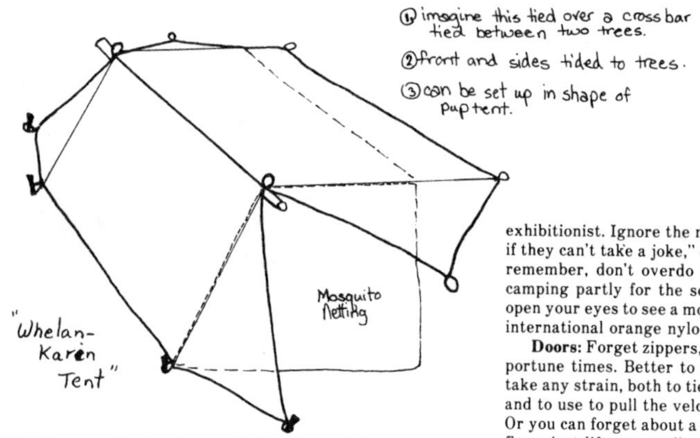

(1) imagine this tied over a cross bar tied between two trees.
(2) front and sides tided to trees.
(3) can be set up in shape of pup tent.
Mosquito Netting
"Whelan-Karin Tent"

into the ground even. Long spiral nails work fine or you can appropriate the pegs from an old discarded tent.

I've found lots in campgrounds after the tourists leave. If you aren't up to scrounging or making do, it is possible to buy just the pegs from any camping goods supplier. They stock them because so many people lose them.

Waterproofing: If you don't stay dry, you might as well not pack that tent around with you. Coated rip-stop nylon taffeta is a good material to work with, as long as the seams aren't in critical places. If they are, seam-sealer is available but must be bought locally as postal regulations prohibit mailing flammable products.

The steeper the roof pitch, the less critical the water proofing as the rain will mostly all run off. Make sure though that when it runs off that it has somewhere to go, not like some of the new tents that have a rainfly smaller than the tent itself. It is fine to have only a single water-proof roof, rather than a breathable roof with a rainfly over it, providing there is lots of wall ventilation. Waterproof light duck canvas works well with a little once-a-season maintenance. Prospectors lived under linseed-oiled canvas for a long time before nylon hit the scene. Forget nylon in the winter, use canvas.

Netting—Windows vs. Walls: If you are scared of bears, you'd better put a window in every wall so you can see at a glance whether it is a noisy whiskey jack or a quiet bear outside. Walls are handy in crowded campsites if you aren't an

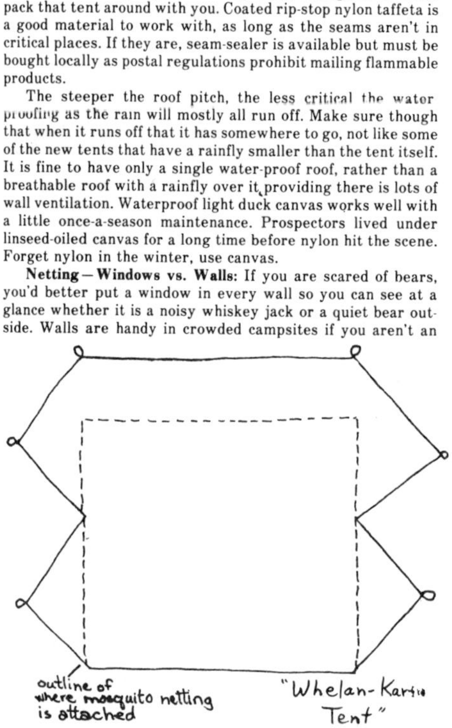

outline of where mosquito netting is attached
"Whelan-Karin Tent"

exhibitionist. Ignore the neighbours: like John says, "Fuck 'em if they can't take a joke," or go where there are no people. And remember, don't overdo the walls because you are probably camping partly for the scenery. It is much more inspiring to open your eyes to see a mountain or a river or a tree than to see international orange nylon wall from two inches away.

Doors: Forget zippers, they jam and break at the most inopportune times. Better to use a velcro strip with a few ties to take any strain, both to tie it securely shut in a windy situation and to use to pull the velcro apart when opening the doorway. Or you can forget about a door altogether if you don't have any floor, just lift up a wall and crawl in.

Poles: Here again you can improvise. Tie your tent between two trees and you don't need any poles. Wooden poles are lying all over the Yukon, free for the taking. I've used paddles and also ski poles, though not on the same trip. If you want to pound a post into the ground as a support, pound in a short stick first to make a hole, wiggling it as you pound so you can remove it. Then the post will not be so awkward to hammer in. Again, you can often scrounge poles from an old tent. If you plan to tent during the winter months, be leary of plastic or fiberglass poles as they get brittle in extreme cold.

Size: The idea of sleeping in a coffin sounds claustrophibic to most people but a coffin is larger than the so-called "two-man pup-tents" on the market today. A tent has to be tall enough to sit up in without brushing your head against the roof, long enough to lie down without touching either end, and wide enough for you and your gear and someone else and their gear unless you plan to travel alone.

SUGGESTIONS

The Bug Tent. This is four walls of mosquito-netting with a lightweight roof of either more netting or thin cotton. The roof can be either formed in a peak or be flat. This tent would only weigh about two pounds (one kilogram), without pegs or poles, yet be large enough for three or four people. When rain threatens, a tarp would have to be thrown over the tent and secured, probably to the same guy-lines as the bug tent.

The Fly Tent. The same idea as the bug tent but with the tarp, which could be oiled canvas or coated nylon, forming the roof and with netting sewn all around the edges to drape down to the ground. Any way that you can set up a tarp-shelter will work for this model. The tarp should have loops and ropes attached all around the circumference to enable you to set it up as a lean-to or peaked tent.

A refined version of this is the Whelan tent, also called the the Karin tent, after the people who invented it fifty years apart . . .

The Whelan-Karin tent is best explained with a diagram. It uses the same amount of material as a floorless pup-tent but it gives you much more flexibility of use. With bug netting sewn around the central area, and the walls made from coated canvas or nylon, the sleeper is protected from the nasties at night and has the option of raising one side wall for a sheltered porch for cooking or whatever.

If you still can't picture this tent, make a model out of paper to get a better idea. To hold the netting down on each of these examples, you can pile stones or earth or wood or your boots, whatever is handy, on the excess netting just as you do on a sod-cloth of a wall-tent.

—*Bruce*

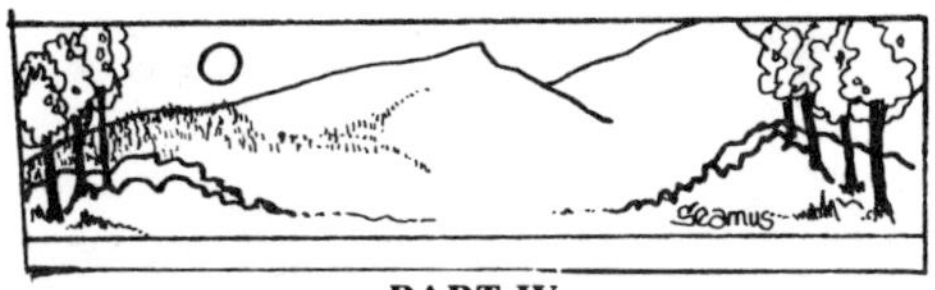

PART IV

I guess I was the youngest urban guerrilla in Whitehorse. My chances were as thin as I was getting, and relief was not in sight. But I had something going for me: I'm a hustler and when it all comes down, I go into a state of mental suspended animation and cease to think at all. I just do things. It's part of being a cheesehound. We are survivors and the world is a hustle. Don't ever kid yourself.

The one big break in the big malamute's routine of eat, shit and whine was a little girl who lived nearby. Every day she came home in the afternoon and, from a pocket in the folds of her parka, produced a piece of food and a pat on the head for the poor beast. I made up my mind to get that food — to hell with the pat on the head. She came down the road, scarf around her head, white frost layered on it and on her hair, humming and kicking ice balls. The ravens clustered on the old derelict cars and garbage, the dogs stood silent in the twilight, the whole world held its breath with me.

I ventured forth, staying calm and cool, walking slowly and deliberately towards her. As I got closer, though, I got nervous. I had never communicated with a human before and, being four or five weeks old, I couldn't control myself and my hunger got the best of me. I began to wag my whole body and then freaked right out all over legs! She didn't seem to like that . . .

"Hey cut it out stupid."

"Arf, yip, yap, bark, bark, bark."

"G'way, leave me alone silly little pup, git!"

I got a kick in the stomach for my troubles. I got up and ran to my hole and watched her give the oaf his food. That was a long night, one spent in thought and hunger. How was I to do it? Obviously I had to remain calm, even in the face of hunger. I had to be her friend, I had to get through to her somehow. I had to follow the source of that food.

Next morning in the darkness, a little girl found a new friend following her to school. We walked along together. I couldn't go away and she didn't give me any food, but I got a pat on the head, and that was a good start. The big thing of course was that I ended up alone bang smack in the middle of Whitehorse, at Whitehorse Elementary School, next to a huge shopping mall with more people, smoke belching machines, dogs, ravens, pussy cats, children and noise than I ever thought possible. I found a hole in a concrete block, watched the door she went in and waited for her to come back.

Two-in-a-Bag

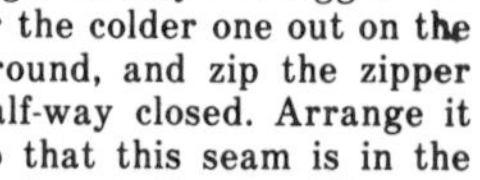

For years I slept alone in my sleeping bag dreaming of the day when I could find a lady with a left-hand zippered sleeping bag to attach to mine. Finally, I saved enough money to buy a matching bag and coerced a nubile young waif to come with me and explore the misty (musty?) forests. I've decided that camping with a lady is definitely more fun but I was surprised that the shared body heat wasn't keeping me as warm through the night as I'd been in my single mummy bag before.

The difference seems to be that a double bag is far too big for two people, especially if they cuddle. I tried all sorts of different ways to attach the bags and overlap them and wrap blankets and flannel sheets. Here are my suggestions for bags that will zip together first, then for bags that won't zip together.

Zip only one side together. That seam will be the centre of the top of your bedding. Now tuck the foot of one bag into the foot of the other. If there will be a draft coming in at the end of the zipper, stuff a sock in the way. Next, lay the bottom of one bag on the ground lay the bottom of the other right on top of it. This way, the weight of your bodies will keep the bags from sliding apart and the toe-inside-toe arrangement keeps your feet crowded but toasty-warm. You will be sleeping on two thicknesses of bag and will not have extra space to have to heat.

For bags that don't zip together, lay the bigger one or the colder one out on the ground, and zip the zipper half-way closed. Arrange it so that this seam is in the centre on the top. Then zip the other bag about a third closed and stuff its foot into the foot of the bag already on the ground. The top bag's seam will be down and you will sleep with your feet inside the top bag which is inside the bottom bag. Each of you will have to grab at the top and lie on the edge so that your partner doesn't steal all the cover during the night. If you have ten minutes spare, stitch (baste) the top bag to the bottom bag with long looping stitches so you don't bunch up the down too much. Farting in the bag also helps warm things up.

—B. B.

hiking –
"you experience more"

We all know that the way to travel the vast northland and see as much as possible of it is to gas up our Chevy and hit the highway. Right? Wrong! Not only is hiking cheaper, but it is much better for your mind and your body, not to mention the environment. Best of all, you actually see more of the Yukon. Or, rather, you experience more. The hiker gets the close-up view of plant and animal life the motorist misses.

He finds beauty in the changes of weather which are a nuisance to road travel and gains strength of mind and body from overcoming obstacles on his own. Rather than limiting you to one type of scenery, hiking can provide an amazingly varied panorama. If you are up to hikes such as the Chilkoot Trail (33 mi.) you can enjoy hiking through rain forest, then bare rock, then tundra, then sand dunes and boreal forest — all in a three and-a-half day hike. Of course the same thing is possible to a lesser degree by climbing any large hill.

Hiking can be a part of other activities. Canoe trips provide many opportunities to hike back from the river and explore. There is no better way to get the most exciting photographs — whether they be close-ups of plant life or of a grizzly met on the trail. Others may choose to preserve the beauty in paint, poetry or memory.

The best hiking experiences are the ones where the hiker follows an undeveloped trail — the only markings being those left by animals or the trappers or miners who went there before. For these hikes you should obtain topographical maps of the area from Room 103, Federal Building, Whitehorse or from downstairs at Mac's Bookstore, Whitehorse. To be of use, these must be on a scale of at least 1:150,000.

Of course everyone is not advised to head into the wilderness on an unmarked trail. If you are inexperienced in survival skills such as compass use, firebuilding, first aid, etc. or lack proper equipment you can still experience solitude and a close awareness of nature by taking a day-hike down a lakeshore or mining exploration trail. Even experienced hikers are wise to respect the potential dangers of the wilderness and to travel with a companion and register with RCMP or park officials before leaving on an overnight hike.

If you are an experienced hiker packing for your first trip here is a general rule on what to take: Pack only what you need for existence, not comfort — then unpack half of it. The reason for the second half of the procedure will be evident if you put your pack on as you first packed it. The staggering weight will persuade you that you don't really need that change of clothes or that tin of raspberry jam. What you will need is good boots, extra socks, a hat, rain gear, polyster or down sleeping bag, tent, lightweight cooking utensils, bug repellent, a good knife, a first aid kit and lightweight food. Only experience will tell you what and how much you will eat on the trail, but it is best not to learn the preferences of bears from experience. It is a good practice to hang your food in a tree well away from your tent and burn all tins before packing them out.

Though there are set trails such as the Chilkoot or some of those in Kluane Park, the entire Yukon is a potential site for hiking. Here are a few reviews by Walter Lanz who has hiked the following areas.:

HIKES
The Ogilvie Mountain Range
Go to mile 31 on the Dempster Highway. Here a creek crosses the highway. Follow it upstream (there are game trails but it is quite heavy bush). A ridge will rise to your right. The destination is the end of the ridge about 1½ days walk. There is no wood or water on the ridge, although patches of snow remain into August.

From the top you have a spectacular view of the two deep blue lakes which feed the creek you followed. Surrounding the larger of the two lakes are 1,500-foot cliffs which are in the forefront of "The Monolith," an Ogilvie landmark. You are able to see down three valleys from this vantage point.

There are good day hikes from Mile 31 to Mile 50 on the Dempster, also around the Ogilvie River at Mile 123.

At Solsticetime go to Mile 260 on the Dempster to the Richardson Mountain Range. (This is just north of the Arctic Circle.) Climb any peak of the range. They are really just hills, void of trees, and take 1-2 hours to reach the top. A well chosen peak will allow you to watch the sun all night as well as afford you a spectacular view.

Hike the Chilkoot without taking the train
Go south on the new Skagway highway from Carcross

to Log Cabin, which is the junction of the railway tracks. Walk northwest on the tracks for a couple of miles until you find a trail on your left leading to the Chilkoot Trail. Or head through the bush at the first large right curve with the beaver pond. This will allow you to gain an impressive view of Lindeman and Bennett Lakes from the ridge which divides the White Pass and Chilkoot valleys, although a day of bushcrashing is involved. You will meet the Chilkoot between Mile 25-30 depending on the route you choose. Continue to Skagway.

Atlin
Rent a boat for a day and go down to Llewellyn Glacier. There is a 1½ mile trail to go and view the glacier, and another two miles to go up onto it. If you have extra time you can hike up along the right hand side of the glacier for an overview without walking on the ice.

Find someone to take you straight across the lake from Atlin townsite and climb Atlin mountain. It's not easy, but you get the best view of B.C.'s longest natural lake and a lot more!

Watson Lake Area
From the Frances River bridge you are able to see some peaks to the northeast. A good day hike is to climb the treeless peak which is the leftmost of the three you are able to see. A few hundred yards south on the highway there is a four-wheel drive road which leads to the mountain in 3-4 miles. A short cut through the bush and you are on the slope. Stay to the left of the rifts for easiest hiking. The mountain is 4,910 feet high, while the bridge is at 2,300 feet. There is a beaver pond along

the road and lots of berries in August!

At Mile 514 (823 km) on the Alaska Highway in B.C. you cross the Smith River. Follow this upstream for 1½ miles to a waterfall. (There is a dirt road.)

North Canol Highway
This is a beautiful road, but don't turn back before you reach the N.W.T. border as the climb to the Macmillan Pass is incredible. Lots of good hiking there. For old car nuts there are hundreds of old army vehicles lined up alongside the road. Last gas at Ross River.

—Hike Reviews by Walter Lanz

Kluane National Park

Kluane Park is a naturalist's dream. Located in the southwest corner of the territory, it spreads over 8,500 square miles or approximately four percent of the territory. This area has been dedicated as a national park because Canada's highest mountain, Mt. Logan, towers over its companions here; Kaskawulsh Glacier and many other rivers of ice carve the landscape; alpine tundra and a unique montane forest of white spruce, trembling aspen and balsam poplar grow in the valleys and because there are internationally significant populations of Dall sheep, grizzly bear, and peregrine falcons.

First contact with the park occurs when you (going northwest) get to Haines Junction and continue down the Alaska Highway or Haines Road. Most people never get beyond these borders, which means that it represents one of the best examples of an environment unaltered by man and exists as an unsettled and virtually untouched region of the world.

Plans are still being made, though, to open up the park so visitors can experience its interior. Right now hiking and mountain climbing are the best ways to participate and enjoy this unique wonderland of nature.

PARK HIKING
Here are a couple of tips about trails from people that have been there:

The infamous Kaskawulsh Glacier is not as difficult to go and see as its ruggedness suggests. Go to the Sheep Mountain registration/information hut on the south end of Kluane Lake. Register and start walking upstream on the Slims River. One and a half to two days will bring you to Canada Creek. One long day hike will be enough to cross the very wide Canada Creek, climb Observation Mountain for a view of the glacier and return to your camp. Observation Mountain can be both easy or difficult to climb, depending on your approach. Imagine yourself as approaching at six o'clock. You must walk clockwise around the mountain to approximately two o'clock before attempting to climb.

SHEEP MOUNTAIN PLATEAU is an excellent place for a day hike. For a longer walk (52 miles - about six days) try the route from Beloud Post to Kathleen Lake. The trail follows the old road to Mush Lake. It turns up Dalton Creek (part of the Dalton Trail) and then down Cottonwood Creek to Sockeye Lake. Two final days are needed to walk out on the south side of the two Kathleen Lakes. The Dalton/Cottonwood plateau, although only 2,000 feet higher than the starting point of the hike, is a spectacular, isolated mountain valley.

There a lot more trails, and exploring this park depends on you. Additional information can be readily obtained by writing to the Superintendent, Kluane National Park, Haines Junction, Yukon Territory, Y0B 1L0, or phone 634-2251.

The Lost Whole Dog Pack

Some dogs who are useless in harness still make excellent summer pack dogs. Since most dogs can't pack more than fifteen or twenty pounds and keep up all day, the load should be light and bulky. We get Casey to carry his food plus dog chain plus our tent and maybe a blanket if it is cold. He acts very solemn throughout the day's work and seems to feel useful and happy.

Besides the obvious advice such as: don't put sharp edges where they will rub the dog and don't let him pack anything delicate like a camera, there is little else to it. Be firm and consistant from the start and he will understand this is business. Don't let him go to a side stream to drink or chase squirrels unless you take off the pack first so he knows the work has stopped and play can start.

To tie the pack on, use one length of rope.

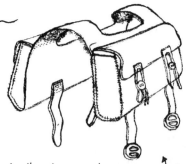

Another home-made pack ➜
Another way to tie one on...➜

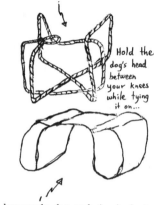

Hold the dog's head between your knees while tying it on...

A home-made dog pack is simply two pouches attached together with a strip of canvas.

Bruce

JEAN LE PHILOSOPHER

It had to be. We talked it over, weighing all sides, examining every possibility. One by one we quickly, easily dismissed every other factor.

Mind you we weren't rushed at all—there was lots of time to decide as we were being pulled up the old road. The dogs were not breaking any speed records but neither of us felt like yelling at them and smacking the lazy ones. Sunny, hot; it was a nice day to be lying on the toboggan watching the world pass by and discussing our situation. The March sun was streaming through the sparce spruces and jewelling the snow around us. We were mushing through a carpet of diamonds and eiderdown.

When the trail became steep, I got off and skied, running up the hills to keep ahead of the dog team, and arrived breathless and sweating at the little log building.

It is, indeed a perfect place for a cabin, in its chapel-like setting, halfway over the pass and an easy day's journey on to the village. We would stop here tonight. Jean guided the team past the front door, then proceeded to unharness them, and chain them in the woods for the night. I split some wood and had supper started by the time Steve had arrived and tied up his dog team.

On the hand-hewn log bench inside, with a short pencil tied on with a string, was the 'Guest Book'. The first entry, by the builders, invited all travellers to use their little chalet overnight, and subsequent notes indicated that many had, like us, taken up their offer. Comments, like "I'm sure glad this place is here" and "Far out place, man" and "new snow today" made interesting reading as we waited for the rice water to boil. Surely this was the place, we decided, this book would be where we would first record our findings. Thus, other outdoors people would benefit from our revelation---perhaps it would help them get over any great guilt or embarassment they felt—after all, it wasn't their fault at all. So we each solemnly signed our name and Jean wrote it out . . . **"Fresh Air** makes you fart!"

The author of this story gave only the following bibliographic material: "I don't want to be bothered. I live with the Trolls in a cave under Mount Haldane."

From the Dawson Daily News files at the Yukon Archives, we learned that during the winter of 1921, an energetic young man walked behind a dog sled all the way from Whitehorse to Dawson along the stage road in a time of seven days and 13 hours.

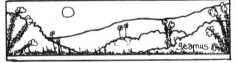

PART V

Lots of things went by that day. I sat and watched the world roar, beep, and smoulder before me. Everything human and animal moved so fast I went unnoticed and I came to realize that if they didn't notice me, then my power to live was so much stronger. I had to move, go somewhere, but I didn't know where or how. I was becoming aware.

A big noise went off in the morning and everything became very quiet except for the machines. More noises went off that meant nothing to me, then one that did, and all the children came running out, and doggie heaven was revealed to me for the first time — they all had bags of food! Every last little grommett had some food and as I rubbed against them they all gave me some of what they had plus a hug or a pat.

I ate and ate and ate and never noticed the noise going again until the children leaving and the ravens coming to clean up until a sharp pain in my back startled me. I looked back and a raven as big as me flapped and went to tear at me again. I looked around for my hole and didn't know where I was. I ran, directionless, while they circled and pecked at me. I knew I was cut but I didn't know what to do and hugged the side of the building as I ran and cried at the same time. They wouldn't stop the attack. I was going to die if I didn't find my hole. I turned a corner and crashed into a pair of boots belonging to a man taking a smoke by a back door. The pecking stopped and quiet descended — except for the cries that came from me — as I writhed in agony from my wounds. I don't remember much more after that but I owe those legs my life. Whoever was attached to them may have been sending me to my room because I came to inside a cage in the Whitehorse city dog pound. I had eaten, which was my first priority; I had learned about ravens; I had learned that where there were children clustered inside fences, there was food, and I was alive. I had my shit together pretty good and I wasn't going to be caught unaware again. I'd get out somehow . . .

A Love Story For Lucy

Three years ago, my partner, Greg, placed a "lost" advertisement in the paper when his puppie, Maggie, ran away. The next day, an Anglican minister tourist found a young dog wandering around Miles Canyon and promptly delivered her to Greg. She didn't come close to matching Maggie's description, but Greg thanked the reverend gentleman for his trouble and said that he would take her to the dog pound himself. However, Maggie failed to materialize and little Lucy crawled into his heart, and he began to change his mind.

The first time I saw Lucy — she didn't have that name yet, of course — she was a furry-fat black puppy with floppy ears and thick sloppy feet, sitting beside a puddle of her own piss on Greg's warehouse floor. "What'll we do?" Greg asked me. "Shall we keep her?"

"It looks to me as if she's already decided," I laughed as she started chewing on his pant leg. The two partners had acquired a new sidekick.

Somehow she became mostly "my" dog. Greg went off to Alaska for a week and I was left to housetrain Lucy and teach her "come," "sit," and "shake a paw" and all the other important dog words. She learned very quickly, and I began to wonder if this piglet-shaped bundle was perhaps from german shepherd stock. The colouring matched — she was mostly black with brown eyebrows and paws and already there were signs of the shepherd's fierce loyalty. Whatever she was, judging by the size of those feet, she was going to be BIG. We guessed her to be just weaned, perhaps six weeks old, when we got her. That was mid-July . . .

In August, Ralph Nordling and I set off from Johnson's Crossing to go moose hunting on the Teslin River. We each had a small fiberglass canoe,

and planned to drift with the current and hoped to add a half-ton of moose meat to our cargo as we floated to Dawson City. Each of us had our dog along, Lucy with me and Ralph's puppy, Babe, with him. Babe looked like a spaniel mixed with a black lab, with a silky black coat and happy, bouncy disposition. After a dusty two-hour drive with Jon in his ¾-ton truck, we were at the water.

"Have a good trip!" Jon yelled, and waved good-bye as the current caught our boats and swung us round and off downstream. Lucy climbed up into the gunwhale for a look round. She walked to the bow and peered long and hard over the port side, her hind-quarters high in the air and her head thrust downwards, nose sniffing and forehead wrinkled in concentration. After a moment's deep thought she decided not to venture onwards; she retreated, backing right over the other side and into the icy water. "Kersploosh!"

Up came a sopping furry struggle and then she sank again. Up she bobbed a second time, but only for a quick flurry of splashing. The third time, I was able to scoop her out of the water with my paddle and flip her into the canoe — a cold, matted huddle of scared and sorry dog. There she stayed a long time, licking her fur and slowly regaining composure before she ventured forth again. But she had learned something too and she never fell in again. Back on the shore, though, Jon almost fell in, he was laughing so hard . . .

Babe and Lucy were early risers, something neither Ralph nor I could honestly claim. We would sleep late in our little tent until the sun was well up and baked us out of our lodgings. The dogs, however, learned how to speed up the waking process: they pulled out all the tent pegs and collapsed it on us. By the time we struggled out of our claustrophobic canvas cocoon, they would be half-a-mile down the beach chasing butterflies.

For fourteen days we floated the rivers, and never tired of the antics of our two entertainers. The puppies were our court jesters and we their proud audience.

Weeks passed and soon September was half-over. Nightly frosts had killed the mosquitoes and the crisp air was just right for hauling in winter cordwood. Then a job opened working out-of-town and I grabbed the chance. As there were no job

Going to the dogs

My first sled came from an old cabin way up on Slim's Creek. I called it a sled because it's the closest thing it resembled. It was a "hang-on and watch out." By this time I had developed an image of what this dog-sledding was all about. Hitch them up, point them in the right direction, yell mush once or twice and look out. Well, it didn't exactly happen like it was supposed to.

Putting them in home-made harnesses wasn't too bad, and even getting them in the right direction was alright. It was really everything that was supposed to happen next that went awry.

Looking back now, the whole thing of having a good team seems to be largely dependent on discipline, self-control and genuine care for the dogs. I learned, and not always the easy way either, that dogs will not freely run in the presence of anger. They may move because you're bigger and can scare them, but they'll be uptight and uneasy and, beyond all, they won't like or respect you for it. Without an openness to learn from the dogs, you are doomed to frustration.

Only after I truly "learned to learn" did I feel the experience of being part of a team. I still vividly remember one bright sunny day being out on the trail to a lake to pick up some water, feeling very calm and peaceful when I yelled, "okay, let's run" and they actually did. Well, my smile was pretty large that day. Everything seemed to be in unison. The energy flow was smooth, free and beautiful. I felt a responsibility to do my part and not be just a lump on the back of the sled.

I'm writing this now (in the fall) but really thinking of the fast-approaching winter, of winding forest trails and frozen lakes. The closest thing I can compare to sledding is an experience I had as a child in a sailboat: the gliding sensation, the sense of being attuned with your surroundings, no mechanical interference.

One of the nicest things is to wake in the morning, roll over in the loft to look out the window and see the trees shining in the sun, and then go out and welcome the new day with the dogs. I feel very lucky.

Oh yeah. Last night I pulled a few porky quills from Hooker and am trying to get ahold of Chico to pull more from her today.

Frank Turner

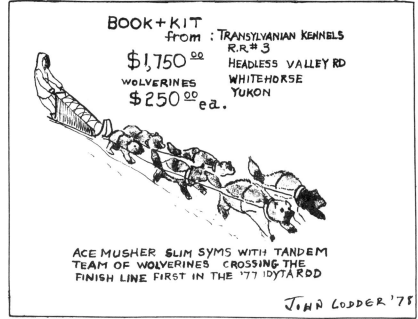

Wolverine Mushing For Fun and Profit
Issued by: Transylvanian Kennels Inc.

BOOK + KIT
from: TRANSYLVANIAN KENNELS
R.R # 3
HEADLESS VALLEY RD
WHITEHORSE
YUKON
$1,750⁰⁰
WOLVERINES
$250⁰⁰ ea.

ACE MUSHER SLIM SYMS WITH TANDEM TEAM OF WOLVERINES CROSSING THE FINISH LINE FIRST IN THE '77 IDYTAROD

JOHN LODDER '78

"One of those great ideas somebody should've come up with a long time ago. It's fun and adventure all rolled into a unique learning experience. Transylvanian sells a complete kit to the novice Wolverine musher, including reinforced steel sled, chain harnesses, heavy-duty wire muzzles, tranquillizers, shot-loaded whip and .357 Magnum pistol. Also 600 lbs of dried rancid fish. Ought to be just the thing for that heavy north-of-sixty mushing."

---

vacancies for rod-dog or chain-puppy on the survey crew, Lucy stayed behind with friends in town. Greg had taken her for rabies and distemper shots at the RCMP station two days before and with Spring long past, distemper seemed hardly a possibility. I was far more worried about the dog-catcher finding her running loose. "You be good, Lucy. And stick around," I hugged her as I left. "See you later, little buddy!" She looked at me intently with her big brown eyes, not wagging her tail, somehow knowing she wasn't coming along this time.

The next ten days seemed to whiz by. We were working near Stewart Island just as the geese migration hit its peak, and even over the whine of the chainsaws, we could hear the incredible honking of 300 Canada Geese, flying overhead at 500 feet in a great vee formation. At times we would count up to thirty of those patterns winging their way south, covering the sky from horizon to horizon.   But while the colours of leaves were changing around us, events were happening faster back in town.

Young Lucy had lost her spunk. Her appetite was waning and she began watering at the eyes and nose. A switch in brands of dogfood interested her for one meal only, and she was losing weight and strength noticeably. After a few more days she began to howl at night: erratic, sudden bursts of high-pitched puppy cries which woke friends and neighbours alike. Then, as suddenly, she'd stop and drift back to sleep as if she'd only been scared in a dream.

When I returned there was another problem. My friends were being evicted, and partly because of Lucy's noise. I felt terrible, because of Lucy's sickness and also because of the problems she'd caused. They shared my anguish, feeling somehow responsible for Lucy's condition in my absence. Luckily, they were able to find a better place to live immediately, and I returned to my cabin outside town and turned my attention to my little companion.

I cooked her dogfood in milk and added vitamins, and saved her large scraps of cooked meat from my supper. She only ate a bit but offered me a paw to shake — I hoped she was improving. While she slept that night, covered with a blanket in her

little doghouse, she was shaking, almost like a shiver in her jaws. Watching by moonlight, I heard her yelping in her dreams and saw her churning and twisting body; the sounds and motions of fright and confusion. I stroked her neck, trying to comfort her as she writhed until her eyes opened and the panic stopped. Those soft dark eyes, shiny under the moon's light, looked tired and frightened. She looked at me vacantly, showing no signs of recognition, then closed her eyes and was asleep almost instantly.

Three times more that night I awoke to hear her delirious yelping and I knew what I would have to do come morning. In those days there was no real veterinary doctor in the Yukon, but I carried Lucy into Whitehorse to a lady who ran a small clinic. She agreed that Lucy must have distemper but was abhorred by the idea of putting her to sleep. "You don't murder a person who gets pneumonia, do you?" she said and recommended some medicines. "Wait a week," she added.

By evening, Lucy could hardly walk. Her balance was so bad that she stumbled into trees and her strength hardly up to supporting her weary body. Her jaws were shaking more frequently and her mad yelping was no longer confined to night-time. It was tearing me apart to listen to her. Her suffering was wrenching my heart. I got my .22 rifle out of the cache and looked for ammunition. One solitary bullet was all I found; I looked everywhere but there were no more. One shot was all I would have — it would have to be from point-blank range, face-to-face.

I put the single charged shell into the magazine and went to where Lucy lay shivering beside her doghouse. Her food was untouched and she had fouled herself, but hadn't the strength or will to move away from the stench. With my one free arm I tried to lift her but she seemed heavy and too awkward to manage gently. She tried to raise herself but couldn't, her wild wet eyes huge in delirium. "It will be okay, little Lucy," I whispered softly, "not long now."

Twenty yards I walked down the path, laid down the rifle and turned to bring Lucy. Then I saw her.

She was staggering, falling and then pulling herself up and forward again, struggling down the path to follow me. She was so pathetic, yet so

valiant, this loving faithful shepherd puppy, her matted fur crusted with pine needles and excretia, her eyes and nose gleaming wet in the sun. My eyes went cloudy with tears and I felt my mouth and face distort with emotion. I knelt to hug Lucy and stroked her tired face as the tears rolled down my own. How could I shoot this dog I loved so much? I couldn't and carried her into the cabin to lay beside the stove on a blanket. More pills I fed her, pushing each one into her throat and then holding her mouth shut with one hand while massaging her neck until she swallowed it. I made beef broth soup and she managed to drink a little. She soiled the rug but I couldn't scold her, knowing her pain. "Perhaps she is passed the worst," I prayed, but didn't believe my hopes.

That night I hardly slept at all, and when I did there were dreams of Lucy painfully struggling, stumbling and falling down the path to follow her master. I'd awaken covered in sweat. For many hours I lay there, listening to Lucy's laboured breathing, always expecting the insane yelping to begin again, wondering how much longer we could both go on. I was scared and felt my insides knotting with each whimper she made.

At dawn, she was a dismal sight. Her jaws were clenching and unclenching spasmotically and her eyes looked sunken and sore. She couldn't lift her head to drink. Those dark brown eyes seemed to have seen only horror; they weren't the same soft Lucy eyes that had danced and sparkled on the Teslin River or had laughed and played learning to "shake a paw." I think Lucy as I knew her was already gone.

Quietly I picked up her limp body and cradled it in my arms. At the door I tucked the .22 under my arm and walked quickly down the path. Fifty feet away I laid my bundle softly under a tree. Slowly I worked the rifle's action, then slid the safety off and placed the barrel's end behind her ear. "With only one bullet," I reminded myself and forced myself to not look away as I squeezed the trigger. Then I dropped the rifle and turned away, closing my eyes until the only thing I could see was the memory of Lucy walking towards me and I cried like I'd lost my only friend in the world. I cried and felt so very lonely.

—bruce batchelor

ZEN AND THE ART OF SKIDOO DESTRUCTION
BY RIMPOCHE SHI-GY

Just about the best book I've seen on how to deal with balky machinery

B.S.

from:
Hotchka Imports
32 Gung-ho Ave.
Pearl Arbor
Hawaii

5.95 PREPAID

D'ICHI A'ANG
(LUNG-BLOW)

TS'HAING-KO
(FACE-CRUSHER)

BUTO-SAN
(ASS-KICKER)

NGO-D'GLO'-SÏ
(FINISHING BLOW)

GI-CHAI
(BROW-BUSTER)

John Lodder '78

ZEN-MASTER HATO NAGOUCHI GIVING PERFECT DEMONSTRATION OF SKIDOO DESTRUCTION AT SH'I'IN TEMPLE, KYOTO. NOTE PURITY OF MOVEMENT AND ECONOMY OF FORM WHICH PERMITTED HIM TO TOTAL THIS MACHINE IN FIVE CLASSIC BLOWS.

"Having divested myself of all inner storms and turmoils I approached the irrepairable machine in a state of perfect Sotu Gopu, or "Soul-tranquility". Remembering the admonitions of the Old Sage Ao-Kai, I prepared for the actual act with great care and deliberation, focusing particular attention upon the weight and form of my hammer-head the slender but supple t'chai of the rosewood handle, remembering too that my implement was above all an extention of my dispassionately pure need to destroy this symbol of all worldly attachments keeping me from true Enlightenment.

After sprinkling water thricely around the machine to ward off demons, I clearly delivered the first blow in one abrupt off-handed motion, the classi **Tshong-Cha'i'**, cleaving perfectly the plastic motor cowling and thoroughly shattering the head, block and pistons. Circling the machine with continued tranquility, I next dealt a lightening side-long blow to the rear of the machine, destroying the suspension, the seat and the bogeywheels. This was my own personal variation of the classic **Buto-San** blow. Almost with the same motion, and no interruption in speed from the just-completed destruction, I smashed the dash, steering handles, carburetor and what remained of the seat and chassis, in the **Ts-Haing-Ko** blow. Spinning about from the momentum of this stroke, I executed a flawless **Dzu-Kodo**, or Nose-Flattener. And finally, I drew back, gathered myself and with all my Force and Concentration delivered a consumate **Ngo-D'glo-Si**, or Finishing Blow upon the remnants of the motor.

After this I was still calm and full of breath. My triumph meant nothing to me - mere vaingloriousness. Quickly, I struck a match and tossed it into the gasoline-soaked wreckage and placidly boiled myself a pot of sweet **gonang** (fireweed tea). It was only after this, as I turned to face the twenty mile walk in a wind-chill of seventy below back to town, that I permitted myself one small display of emotion:
"Fucking junk!"

PORKIES

If you are planning to be out of reach of veterinary services (available only in Whitehorse) and your dog or team has an appetite for porcupine, it is best to be prepared. Always take along a small pair of pliers and if possible, obtain some "doggie knock-out medicine" at the pharmacy. Peoples Drug Mart in Whitehorse will sell you a $6 supply which would do several dogs.

Dog Mushing — How To

"Novice Sled Dog Training," by Mel and Lee Fishback, pub. by Raymond Thompson, 15815 - 2nd Place West, Lynwood, Washington, USA 98036. $3.30. A clearly-written, sensible philosophy for training a dog to work, with lots of concrete advice. Illustrated.

• • •

"How to Drive a Dog Sled," by Peter Gzowski, pub. by the CBC, Toronto and Whitehorse, February 1978. Free.

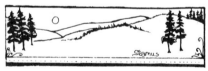

Seamus

PART VI

The cages were small, green plastic things piled one on top of another in tiers five or six high. The big dogs were at the bottom and there were pussy cats, too. The cats made the most noise — they never seemed to get tired of squeaking. I learned to hate them fast. The other dogs went crazy too, but only when someone came in the room.

I lay and watched and waited. There was blood on the cage I was in and it belonged to me. I wasn't cut bad but I wasn't in prime condition either. I was hurt, thin, hungry, scared and awaiting future developments. There was one man who was the dog catcher and he had had the job for a while. He never communicated with any of us at all. We got fed twice a day, hosed down with water sometimes, our cages cleaned out once a day and that was about it. The one big happening was when someone would come to buy a dog or cat, which was about five a day, being close to New Year's. Everybody would make as much noise as possible and scream, howl, kick, scratch, beg and freak right out; that is, everyone except one large husky in a cage against the opposite wall and me. We sat, stared ahead, watched and waited. I guess we saw no need to make a lot of noise, even though about 50 per cent of the people went away with animals.

About three days went by. We stayed in our cages and people came and prodded me, patted me but no one wanted me. I was a mess and not up to begging at all. Then came the end of the week, the cages now held about thirty dogs, and the man came in with a gun and began to take us out of the cages, one at a time, and shoot us.

DOG FOOD

Dog Food can be purchased from **Paul Sheridan** at Klondike Kennels, in Porter Creek. Paul also carries a supply of doggie equipment, webbing, snabs, rope and such.

Northwest Feed and Tuck (Box 4122, Whitehorse), is located at Mile 5.2 on the Mayo Road. Mostly they are dealing with farm animals but mushers who cook their dog food will appreciate a source for herring meal, soya meal and bone meal.

A trapper has suggested the following combination when cooking for a dog team: mix rice, soya meal, herring meal, quick oatmeal and fat scraps. "Count on it costing at least 50 cents per dog per day to feed a team. Mushers generally don't feed dogs as much as pet owners. A skinny dog is healthier, especially in summer."

Wooden Toggles

Here's one way to save money if you are just starting out with a dog team: homemade hardwood toggles. Instead of paying two dollars each for big harness snaps that may break on you anyways, why not take that old hockey stick handle or that broken axe handle or any other piece of scrap hardwood and wittle some toggles. They should be about four inches (ten centimeters) long and up to an inch (two centimeters) in diameter at the centre, tapered to both ends and rounded, with a deep groove around the middle so that the cord will stay in place. You have to make loops to receive the toggles, and you should learn how to splice the ends together. The advantage of toggles besides price (free) is that you can manipulate a toggle with your mitts on in cold weather and a toggle won't freeze shut.

—Agnes

Once again, in mid-December, the Whitehorse Sled Dog Club began to prepare for the 2nd Annual Mail Run between Carcross, Yukon and Atlin, B.C. a distance of 80 miles. It was decided to produce special envelopes with an insert describing the route taken; 3,000 were printed and sold at 50 cents each. The envelopes were well received in Whitehorse and in many parts of Canada and the United States, and have become collectors items. These envelopes were all carried by dog team as well as the regular mail.

It was all set. We were to leave Nares Lake in Carcross at 9:30 a.m. on March 19, 1976 — 18 teams and four cross country skiers. The mail carriers, John Bryant, Bill Thomson and myself, were to leave first. A non-existent trail greeted the dogs as the wind had blown over the trail during the night. Bill left first, followed by John, then me with Neepek in single lead. He was excited but confused ... all there was in front of him was a big white plateau. Chris Camping finally got Neepek straightened out and we took off with the other teams following. Neepek kept looking back at me and at Spottie, the female who often runs lead with him. His expression seemed to say, "Someone come up here and keep me company in this wilderness." I put Spottie up and in the meantime, Fred Stretch, Ralph Lee and Bob Erlam passed me.

For our journey, I had borrowed a big heavy freight sled and had it loaded with two of the cross country skiers' gear, some of our own, and the mail. How I wished for our small training sled many times during the run! The dogs ran well; in fact they thought they were racing as that was all they knew. I looked back for Ken (my husband) but couldn't see him. He had waited (I found out later) until the last team had left.

The day was perfect — slight wind, clear sky and high rugged mountains on all sides of the lake. It made me forget all the work that was done to make this trip possible; it helped erase the picture of my livingroom filled with bags of mail for the last three weeks. Yes, I decided it was worth putting up with the mess. After 10 miles we turned on to Windy Arm.

By now I was running by myself. There were dog teams in the distance, in front and back, but, I was essentially alone. Windy Arm lived up to its name. It was windy and cold with ground drifting. Consequently the trail left by the teams in front was blown over. We passed Terry McBride and Peter Steele, the cross country skiers who left earlier than the dogs. I was beginning to get cold and was thinking of stopping and donning another sweater when I caught sight of what I hoped was Strikers Pass. The scenery along Windy Arm was spectacular with high rugged cathedral peaks rising out of the snow-covered lake — green and white for a while, then, just masses of white. (By now, Bill Yankee, the musher from Juneau, Alaska, was well past me, as was Bob English.)

When I arrived at the cutoff to Strikers Pass, I wondered if I should go along alone or wait for Ken, as he had suggested. Mike Stackhouse arrived shortly so we started up together. It was steep, rugged and unbelievably beautiful. Soon we were up to the others; their eight teams winding with the terrain, along, up, over and around. The trail was well packed as long as you stayed on the straight and narrow. Once off, you would easily sink to your waist or higher. After a few dives the dogs soon learned to stay on the trail. On the first few hills the dogs would almost reach the top then stop and all turn around. As a dutiful musher I would get off and push to the top. Well, this happened once too often for my liking and besides, I was getting tired. We soon came to an understanding — unless very steep they pulled me and soon we were all working together. This was a totally new experience for my dogs and they needed reassurance and encouragement.

My team consisted of Neepek and Spottie (both 13 months) in lead. In single swing was their littermate, Sedna. Behind her was Brother and Chimp and, in wheel were Mitas and Kesik, also littermates. All were working well, in fact too well as far as I was concerned for whenever possible they broke into a run and with that large freight sled loaded to the hilt it was difficult to manoeuver. I prayed for slowness and no trees close to the trail. To move the sled I had to jump in the air in order to get enough weight and power. Doug LaMond of Alberta was close now so I had lots of help if I needed it. By now we had passed the other two skiers.

"ONE BAD HILL"

There was one bad "hill." It looked bad but I wasn't to know how bad until it was too late to do anything about it. The trail went along a narrow scenic ridge when suddenly! it went **down** in front of me. At the start of the descent a big hole had been dug by previous mushers breaking to slow their teams. My sled was too heavy for me to manoeuver around the hole so, over we went! There we hung over the edge with only the leaders on the trail — the rest of the team, and me, buried in the snow. While buried to my chest in snow I dumbly watched the contents of my sled bag tumble all the way down — SPLASH, that's right, water! There sat my lunch, my bottle of water, my lipstick, comb and last but not least, my toothbrush, in this ice cold creek which stubbornly refused to freeze. I shivered but refused to contemplate further. Calmly and rationally I announced to the dogs, the creek, the trees and anything that wanted to listen, that I wasn't going down for them although the lipstick and comb were only a week old. I decided to eat some of Ken's lunch. Still amazingly calm, in voice only, I gave some commands to the dogs; Spottie and Neepek picked up my tone of voice and were very responsive. They pulled the other dogs, the sled and finally me, up onto the trail.

The best approach, I decided, still cool and collected (too afraid to be anything else), was to let them pull the sled down on its side, thus ensuring a slow, controlled descent. As I regained my strength at the bottom my knees refused to stop shaking, a reaction from our episode as well as for what was in store for me up ahead. Fortunately, the rest of the "hills" were a piece of cake after that one.

By now we were over the roughest part of Strikers Pass and were on a plateau with scenic lakes connected by rolling hills. On one of these lakes Ken caught up to Doug and I. Mike had gone on by himself. On another lake we watched with great amusement as Bob Erlam's team pulled out the snowmobile which was accompanying the teams in case help was required. As it turned out the only one requiring help was the snowmobile.

After 20 miles we came to what became a nightmare, especially for the big or fast teams. (How I cursed that big loaded sled and my racing dogs.) Ken had a long

toboggan loaded with the rest of our stuff and the other two packs of the skiers, pulled by 10 eager Siberian Huskies. The trail had more twists, turns, was very overgrown and trees in the worst places ... just ideally placed for fast removal of brushbows. Believe me, if one went over the trail after the mushers had used it one could have built several sleds with the many pieces. Every time we rounded a turn my dogs broke into a trot ... goodness, I wanted them walking at this point as I was getting very tired heaving around this damnable sled and going around turns on one runner. Finally, the trail began to open up and life became more pleasant. At the entrance to Taku Arm was a trapper's cabin where, it was reported, they served the "best coffee," with probably additional flavour added. Twelve miles further brought us to Moose Arm and the cabins. Happy shouts and faces met us as well as a nice old beer. Delicious! It's amazing how thirsty one can get driving dogs.

Before musher socialization and eating the dogs had to be fed and bedded down for the night. This took some time as we had to wade to our waists in snow in order to stake them out; however we soon had our own trails made. Most of the mushers followed this pattern — caring for the dogs first, themselves later.

COMICAL SCENE

It was comical to see the state of the sleds arriving — brushbows missing, runners gone, etc. I felt good with only a brushbow missing. Now it was time for socializing, another beer and some Moose Stew which had been provided by the Atlin Fun Committee. It was great fun sitting in the one heated cabin listening to the guys relate their experiences of the day. By now the cross country skiers and the mushers had arrived. It was a clear, cold night (-30°F), stars out in full regalia, and, with the dogs providing the background music, we experienced pleasant feelings and sounds. By 9:30 we were in our own little tent anticipating a restful, dreamless night. Well, every time I closed my eyes I saw trees coming towards me, and, with 200 dogs (18 teams) including 10 loose ones, you can imagine the amount of sleep any one of us got.

Up at 7:00 a.m. and golly it was cold! Treats for the dogs (what was left after the loose dogs had their fill). Breakfast for us, and, we were off once again. An easy pleasant day with 12 miles of rolling bush and then 22 miles on Atlin Lake — warm and sunny, a great day to get a tan.

A rather humorous incident occurred on the second day. We caught up with Dave Hodgson in the bush and as I attempted to pass him the handle bars slipped out of my hands, and off went the dogs. Shouts were only added to their speed of departure. Quickly Ken gave me his team and sprinted off to catch mine.

I couldn't believe he could run so fast. Dave and I watched in awe as those size 13's flew over the ground. In retrospect I should have entered him in the Olympics. Two hundred yards brought us up to Ken and the dogs. Ken had a strange haggard look and held happy tail-wagging dogs. Needless to say he had a few choice words for his laughing wife.

Atlin Lake travel was uneventful, warm, sunny and boring for both dogs and musher. We let the dogs set their own pace and we stopped only once as we found that stopping broke up that rhythmical pace. We passed and were passed by several teams and finally we rounded a bend in the lake and caught sight of Atlin. The dogs sensed the closeness of the end of the trail and picked up their own pace. The teams were to congregate at a certain point so that a group could enter Atlin together, therefore, when enough teams were together for a presentable entrance into Atlin we all drove our teams into town, going directly to the Post Office where we lined up on the muddy streets (it was 30°F).

Bill and I officially passed over the mail to the Post Mistress who was dressed in the style of '98. Pictures were taken and a lot of laughter and comments were exchanged between the mushers and the public.

—*Jan Weagle*
Carcross Road

. a hand-crafted
freight-sleigh
for packed trails.

. an oak
toboggan
for deep
snow.

LAND OWNERSHIP

"I hope one day to see a plan here like PEI's whereby only residents can own land. That would eliminate most of the land speculation which drives the prices up. If you aren't going to hang around the territory to use the land, I don't figure you have any real moral claim to that land.

"In Ontario, the government has introduced a Speculation Tax which limits the increase possible in land prices. We could use that here but the civil servants and the businessmen and the politicians all want to be able to make a killing off the pipeline themselves so they encourage land profits. Probably just bringing in a few Revenue Canada auditors would reveal that some of these people are making a lot of dubious dealings and crooked business."

—an oldtimer

"Tell 'em that if they're too old to go back to the land or to give up some of those awful, wasteful things they've worked all their lives to get, the least they can do is encourage their kids to start conserving and doing with less."

acquiring land

The Yukon Territory covers just over five percent of Canada. The total area is 207,076 square miles or 132,529 x 1000 acres. That's a fair chunk of land. In 1976 there were 21,836 of us here in the Yukon, according to the "mini-census". That means there was a population density of approximately 0.1 person per square mile or 1 person for every 10 square miles. Not too bad an average, eh?, especially when you remember that 13,311 of those people were living in Whitehorse.

That leaves a lot of land available, and you'd think a young couple would be able to get themselves a piece of land in the country. Forget it! This isn't happening. We're young and this is the place we call home. Our future is here in the Yukon. All we want now is a small piece of land so we can build our homes, but we can't get it. Unless you have just robbed Diamond Tooth Gerties, it's almost impossible to get some acreage legally so some of us squat. Why? What's going on? Who are the people that are stopping us from settling? What is being done with the land?

The federal government has 99.8 percent of all of the land under their control, management and administration. We are like a colony. The territorial government or YTG is responsible for an estimated 0.2 percent of the land, and its located mainly around established communities. Very little land is held privately - individuals have less than 0.0003 percent, yet the feds have issued all kinds of leases to corporations interested in "developing" or establishing industries in the Yukon.

Land Use Permits granted in 1977-78:

Type	Number
Oil and Gas Drilling	2
Seismic	3
Mining (Drilling)	7
Mining (Geophysical)	3
Roads	39
Airstrips	2
Government	83
Power Lines	3
Campsites	46
Hydro Projects	3
Research Projects	2
Quarrying	21
Gas Gathering Systems	1
Woods Operation	22
Miscellaneous	5
Applications but no permit issued or permit not required	13

For the individual determined to get his piece of land, there are two choices. Squat, and take your chances - a few people do and have gotten away with it so far because there is no definite policy on dealing with squatting. The other alternative is to follow the procedure for applying for Crown land. It's rather hopeless! There is a freeze on the land, even if they deny it.

If you have found the setting of your dreams and don't want to move, the procedure for applying for land is outlined in the Territorial Lands Regulations. You can file an application for primary residential lots, seasonal residential lots, commercial acreage, or land for agriculture. People also stake placer claims and live on them.

Federal crown land is supposed to be made available under lease, lease with option to buy, or sale agreement. It isn't. The present policy of the government is to make land available on a lease-only basis. If you're lucky enough to get land, the terms range from 3-30 years depending on your location and intended use. Once it expires, they may not grant another one.

Applications for land are considered only where your intended use for the land conforms with all the rules and regulations and plans for the area in which you are situated. This means you can't farm in areas where the government has concluded agriculture is impossible or unnecessary. Maybe this is why there are only 17 farms in the Yukon in 1976.

If you have been rejected, welcome to the club; if successful, congratulations. Now come the bills. A legal survey is a must somewhere in the future. You have to pay federal rental charges and YTG taxes annually. In addition, you must live on the land for a major portion of the year or use the land for the purpose indicated in the application. You must also complete specified improvements such as building a home and clearing some land and/or sowing a crop within an agreed time period. They are usually considerate at this stage of the game.

The main steps followed in processing most applications are briefly summarized in the following diagram...

1. Application for land recieved by "Supervisor of Lands", Diand Whitehorse.

2. Preliminary Review, including Lands Inspection (if required). Here is where most applications stop. → Application rejected and returned with reasons - usually failure to confirm to their plans.

3. If it meets requirements it is forwarded to Federal - Territorial Lands Advisory Committee for review and clearance.

4. To Regional Director Yukon Region, Northern Affairs Program, Diand with recommendations.
→ Rejected - you should expect the worst.
→ Decision reversed pending additional information - welcome to limbo
→ Approved - subject to modification.
→ Approved - you are one of the rare ones and I'd like to meet you.

-j. maxwell

If justice Ruled on earth, it would be sufficient to have built one's cabin; it would require no further protection than this manifest Right of possession. But because injustice is the order of the day, whoever built the house must also be in a position to protect it.
— Schopenhauer "Essays & aphorisms"

Mail Order Tools

Woodcraft Supply Corp., 313 Montvale Avenue, Woburn, Mass. 01801, U.S.A., (617) 935-5860.

Send 50 cents for a catalogue. They've got all kinds of specialized quality tools for lutheirs, furniture-makers, log builders, and even some strange looking Japanese cabinet-makers tools.

Ringing Anvil Tools, R.R. 1, Black Creek, B.C. V0R 1C0.

Send a stamped self-addressed envelope for a price sheet. This is a one man shop specializing in hand-forged tools for wood carvers and log builders. . . . so if you'd rather use your money to support other craftsmen, check this out.

The Blairhampton Alternative, Norplast Limited, Box 748, Haliburton, Ontario K0M 1S0.

Send 50 cents for a catalogue. They already have a good selection of log-building tools and they have plans to expand their catalogue in the future. Among other things, they carry a hand-powered washing machine. *(Ladies and Gentlemen, rid yourself of the back-ache earned by beating your clothes with rocks along the North's frozen creekbeds!)*

100 and 1 uses . . .

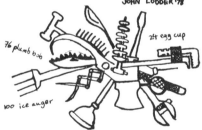

MULTI-TOOL
3168 CHIANG KI-SHEK BOUL
TAIPEI,
TAIWAN **5.95**

Well, we found we could go on all day figuring out the infinite uses of this handy little machine. Suffice it to say that it is indespensible for anyone living or travelling in the bush. Wonder how anyone ever got along without it before?

RESEARCH PUBLICATIONS

The National Research Council's Division of Building Research has a list of publications on permafrost and building in the North. Also available are translations of some Russian reports. Copies can be obtained from the Publications Section, National Research Council, Division of Building Research, Ottawa, Ontario.

For more information on housing, consult these government publications:

Glossary of House Building Term.	$1
Canadian Wood Frame House Const.	$1
Housing the Handicapped	$2
Use and Design of Space in the Home	$2
The Conservation of Energy in Housing	$3
A Study of Medium Density Housing	$2.50
Modest House Designs-Metric	$1

The books and pamphlets can be acquired by sending a money order or cash to: Cashier, Financial Services Division, Central Mortgage and Housing Corporation, National Office, Ottawa, Ontario K1A 0P7.

Building Your Home With Logs

by Swede Saw Sam

My advice, as a person who's somewhat of a fanatic log home builder, is that people should build their own; simplify and improvise and use hand tools instead of power tools. We put up our home for $200, and it's the warmest and nicest place I've ever lived in. In one and a half months we put it up, eliminating a 30 or 40 year mortgage and a nine-to-five lifestyle to pay it off.

You can do without chainsaws, a vehicle and sophisticated tools, and build a better quality home than most you'll find in the Yukon. You'll spend more time at it, but you'll save money and have that peace of mind that comes with doing something and doing it well — for yourself.

A 24 or 30-inch swede saw is the best asset any log home builder can have for every kind of cutting from felling trees to cutting window stops. (You'll also need an axe and hatchet for notching and shaping.) With one 24-inch swede saw, a person can fell enough trees in one day for a good-sized log home. And for cutting firewood, it shouldn't take more than half an hour per day to cut and split enough for the heater and wood cookstove during the winter. A swede saw is a remarkable tool that is quiet, doesn't smell, is safe and doesn't cause the dreaded "white hand" disease. With heavy use you may go through five or six blades a year, or sharpen them if you like. Maintenance is nill. (Chainsaws can give you headaches in more ways than one.)

I have numerous friends who have built their own log houses, some who are experienced in carpentry but most have never built before, each house reflects something about that person. A friend of mine who knew nothing about building and who violated every structural rule in the book, including building in January and peeling after completion with a paintscraper, has created the most imaginative and beautiful house — that I'm sure will outlive all of us.

So let your home be a creation and an extension of yourself and don't be confined by rectangles, building codes, or "how to" books.

Maybe use them as a guide but not as a Bible. The Yukon is full of log builders — from perfectionists to those who slap them together in a day on the trap line. So put your efforts into building your own house instead of working in town for a mortgage.

"Just Go Do It!": Rick

Build your own place - out of logs and don't take any bullshit from government inspectors or anyone else, unless they've lived in the area longer than you. Just do it, if you want it. And you can scrounge a lot of material you'll need. Just look around. It's worth it. No sense in paying for something you could get for free.

There are good books about building a log cabin or a log palace, log shithouse, log dog house, cache or darn near anything else that strikes your fancy. Here is some information about trees that grow here. When someone wants to construct a log building, this is what they have to start with. What you do yourself is up to you.

TREES

Black Spruce - has club shaped crown/ found in boggy areas/ cones less elongated/ less tapered trunk/ light, strong, resilient.

White Spruce - light, strong/ more tapered/ lots of limbs/ fairly straight grained. White spruce is best for building logs.

Jackpine - heavier/ slightly harder/ not as strong as spruce/ harder to limb (less limbs - but big ones)/ less, small taper-sometimes straight/ small 4" pine is great for poles

Alpine Fir - found in higher elevations/ two sided needles, grayish bark/ soft, rather weak wood/ extreme taper/ stunted at higher elevations

Birch - interior rots quickly/ beautiful wood grain/ good for furniture

Poplar - soft wood, weak/ beautiful, light sapwood and heartwood/ great for tables, doors, shelves, finishing work/ splits easily/ rots quickly/ hard to find standing dead wood that is sound.

Summary: Spruce best for logs and shakes (if clear)/ pine for ridge, purlins, and pool roof/ poplar for siding and table tops/ birch for furniture.

BOOKS

"Shelter" (a catalogue), 1973, Random House
"Shelter Shacks and Shanties ," D.C. Beard, illustrated, New York, 1932
"Building a Log House in Alaska," Alex R. Carlson, Co-operative Extension Service, University of Alaska
"How to Build Your Home in the Woods," Bradford Angier, Hart Publishing, New York
"How to Build and Furnish a Log Cabin," W. Ben Hunt, MacMillan Publishing, New York, 1974
"Building with Logs," Alan Mackie, Published by the author, P.O. Box 1205, Prince George, B.C.

The Whole Stackwall

If you are tired of squares, rectangles and horizontal lines, and if you plan to build within reach of dry, standing deadwood, clean sand and water, and a supplier of portland cement, then the Whole Stackwall Cabin may be for you.

It will take a bit longer to build and, depending on the thickness of the wall, more wood but it is: stronger, heavier, fireproofer, soundproofer, lighter (on the inside), and definitely warmer.

The wood, although it has to be **very** dry, does not have to be straight, long or thick since it is all cut to 1 foot lengths anyway. Another obvious advantage to this type of construction is that the heavy labour involved is minimal and it can therefore be built independently by the feebliest of people

The mortar suggested by the Department of Engineering, University of Manitoba is type"S": 4 parts sand, 1 part of portland cement and 1 part lime. The sand should be coarse and the water very clean (We hauled our water in empty kerosene drums and the trace of kerosene was enough to prevent the mortar from getting any harder than corn bread.)

CONSTRUCTION

A solid foundation is essential because the walls are gonna be pretty heavy. We used the largest logs (14" diameter) and cut them in half lengthwise and supported them frequently with 3 to 4 foot posts creosoted, sitting on drainage stones and cemented in.

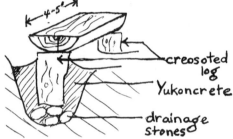

creosoted log

Yukoncrete

drainage stones

Lay your floor joists across these, and begin the long peaceful job of laying your stack wall.

If you have spent winter in the Edgewater designing and redesigning the location of bedroom, kitchen, den and bay window—if you have cut up your 4 cords into 1 foot lengths (we found that if the logs vary a few inches, which they invariably will, it gives the outside a charming, careless, cottage effect which casts shadows like a dappled fawn) and have them in 3 or 4 piles of dissimilar thickness,—and if your partner enjoys mixing the mor-

seamus

PART VII

The blood from the first dog's head ran into the gutter in the center of the floor and everything in the place became very quiet. We just stared at the dog while the man never stopped moving. He opened cage after cage on the far side of the room and one by one hauled whatever it was out, and set it on the floor. Holding the animal between his feet and legs, he dispatched it with one shot from a .22 rifle. Most animals went quietly. They didn't or couldn't fathom what was taking place. I stayed quiet and when I got tired of watching the blood and twitching bodies on the floor I focused on the big husky who focused on me.

I felt he was going to do something. He just stared at me sadly and waited. He was going to do a number on that man and I began to feel excited. The next dog beside him got his and then the man quickly unlatched the husky's cage and without any warning reversed his rifle and with one smack of the butt, knocked my friend unconscious, then without a break put a bullet in the back of his skull where he lay and started on my side of the room.

I began to get worried and started to stand up and fret. Then the cold icy feeling came over me and I lay down and watched, or rather, I just stared ahead with my head on my paws. The phone rang and the man put down the gun and left the noise of the execution room to the outer office and spoke for awhile. When he returned he began hauling the corpses outside to the back and piled them in two big bins. He began to hose down the floor.

The back door opened and two young men walked in. One was taller and thin with long blond hair and patches all over his jeans. He had blue searching eyes that darted quickly around the room and covered a lot of ground. The other fellow was shorter and chubby with glasses and neater clothes, but with long brown hair and beard. He was steadier and more cautious than his friend and looked more at the place than the dogs. I was still waiting for the bullet.

tar, —and if you are far enough away from the threat of gov't officials with clipboards and polaroid cameras, then the task ahead will be truly long, lazy and peaceful.

Window and door frames, especially door frames, should have a whole bunch of nails knocked partially in for strength.

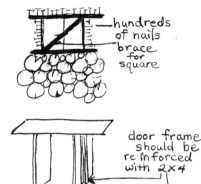

hundreds of nails brace for square

door frame should be reinforced with 2x4

2x10

When you get to the top of the walls you must finish with a round of two sided interlocking logs laid length ways for a top plate before any roof beams are layed on.

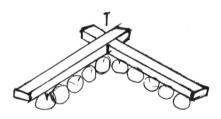

If you don't you will get a big crack running down your wall like the one we got.

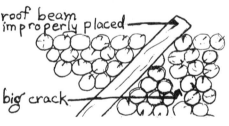

roof beam improperly placed

big crack

We followed the advice given in some magazines that the mortar should be applied in two globs, one at each end of the log with the space in between filled with sawdust. Add some lime to the sawdust to keep out bugs.

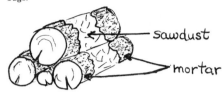

sawdust

mortar

The sawdust will insulate the two globs of mortar from each other and help to fill cracks. Use rubber gloves as protection from the lime and the cold.

If you want straight flat walls on the inside simply erect a form of oiled plywood, level it, brace it, and place the butt ends flush against it and throw in the mortar. Take down the form before the cement is completely set and brush away the excess and fill gaps for a better looking wall than our first one.

The corners are no big problem. Ours look like this:

Our cabin is 16 by 20 with a flat roof using one main roof beam and it held the snow no problem. Flat rooves are sooo easy. Who wants to sleep in a hot sweaty loft anyway?

Stick an airtight in the middle and you've got yourself a nice warm home.

-dave c.

"Try Using Fire-Killed Logs"

Use fire killed logs for building. They're good and strong, dry and ready to build with.

They're better than hacking down growing, living green trees, and then having to wait a year so they can dry out. If you do build with them soon after you've cut them down, you're going to have to wait a year before putting in doors and window frames because otherwise everything will twist and turn and get whacked out of shape as they dry.

-rick & avril

TIPI LAND!

Within the last year the popularity of tipis has mushroomed. And no wonder — the atmosphere is peaceful, the fresh air life promotes basic health and nature's spirits come alive. As for aesthetic value, anyone who has seen a tipi will tell you how beautiful it is.

Now on to practicality: the shape seems to confuse bugs, bears and people. Bugs because of the swirling draft upwards — they rise up to the tipi's apex and ascend into the blue. Bears are confused with the circular shape of this structure. They walk around the tipi feeling for the door; sometimes they discover the opening by falling through. This event scares the critter back into the forest. As for people, the right angle support system is just not there. But then the human being is noted for his/her adaptability! Right?

Now for the creatures that don't get confused. There has been many a sleepless night when mice have danced upon my head, in the pots, on the liner, up my pant leg, and into the food. "The mindless dancers!" I have found the tipi bandits to be the CUTE squirrels. They rob pet food, mocassins (must be signs of a cold winter), peanuts, etc., daily.

If ever the chance may come, do not turn down a night in a tipi.

— Morothy & Dady

The 45-gallon Drum as alternative Housing

Govt of Canada Pamphlet No. 326

Free From:

Housing Canada
Suite 36
Shanghri-la Bldg
Chimera St
Toronto, Ont.

JOHN LODDER '78

A FAMILY OF TYPICAL DRUM-DWELLERS AT ABANDONED EXPLORATION CAMP, BONNET PLUME LAKE.

"WHEN LINED WITH MOSS OR DISCARDED FIBREGLASS INSULATION AND COVERED WITH SNOW, A FAMILY OF FIVE CAN EASILY KEEP WARM IN THE MOST RIGOROUS ARTIC WINTER IN ONE OF THESE DRUMS. SNUG, EASILY PORTABLE AND SCATTERED EVERYWHERE, THESE DRUMS BECOME AT ONCE THE MOST LOGICAL SOLUTION TO THE NORTHERN HOUSING PROBLEM."

"I think this very definitely is a breakthrough in housing in Canada, the biggest since Habitat, or even the igloo."
— Warren Almond
Minister of Northern Affairs

Hot tips from the Tipi

Out on the river, ladies, and no more tampons? A diaphragm holds it in as well as it holds the other out. Now why didn't our mothers share this knowledge from their pre-pill contraception days?

When mother nature calls and it's 20 below and you're having massages and tokes around the airtight, would you be tempted to have a poop on newspaper and send it to the fire-god for painless combustion? The subject of many a mid-winter debate.....

Are your coconut oil massages getting redundant? Try cottonwood buds, or juniper berries, or alpine fur sap (bubbly bark blisters identifies this tree), added to any vegie oil or a combination of vegie and mineral oils. There must be tons more too - I'm trying sage leaves now, and as the typewriter clicks I'm realizing mint leaves might be dandy.

.....Just got toid that clove oil (a little numby) and wintergreen oil (but watch those mucous membranes!) also dilute to good massage material. And the lady that told me volunteered to trade massages too! Welcome to right now...

— beav.

The Heritage Tipi
Box 910
Calgary, Alberta T2G 0P3
You can get a 20' tipi from them for under $500. Heritage figures that about ⅓ of the people who buy tipis from them live year-round in tipis....there are even year-round tipi-dwellers in the Yukon and they claim that they're not too uncomfortable, (although they spend a lot of time warming up in the 'Boo Tavern).

We make tipis All sizes

Karin Shell
Leigh Cole
Box 65
Carcross
Y.T.

DOMES

A few observations after living in a log-cabin-geodesic dome-shack for years:

—domes are beautiful spiritual places to be in.

—they have an incredible number of wall-edges so that makes them finicky to build, difficult to weatherproof, a pain in the ass to finish the inside.

—they are incredibly strong. (Our sixteen-foot half-sphere frame weighs about 300 pounds but will support a dozen fools dancing on the roof.)

—normal square furniture looks lost, wastes space. You'll have to build your own. Wire spools make excellent tables.

—insulation is expensive, because it is hard to figure a way to use moss as filling or to use thick logs other than as framing.

—the shape almost necessitates using plastics and plywood — expensive imported materials for remote bush cabins.

One closing remark though; I'll never live in a four-sided place again if I can help it.

—bruce

Bury your house — and your heating bills...

Dutch Van Tassil offers the suggestion for northerners that they bury their homes to reduce heating costs. Information can be gathered from Popular Science, April 1977 issue, an article on "earth cover housing", or by writing the American Underground Space Association at the University of Minnesota.

For insulation, pour eight inch cement walls, paint them with tar for waterproofing, then spray on foam insulation one or two inches thick inside and out and on top of ceiling. Foam insulation under the cement floors is also a good idea. A minimum of two feet of soil should cover the roof.

To light your bunker, Dutch suggests taking advantage of natural lighting, by using skylights over the central hallways. Then the inside partitions of the bedrooms would have three foot high solid walls with non-see-through glass and curtains to the ceiling.

One problem seems to be getting women to like the thought of living underground, but Dutch mentined that it wasn't too much of a problem getting housewives to stay all day long in underground shopping centres in the .south.

a. r.

———— Sharpening ————
———— Stone ————

If you are working in a mine or close to a diamond drilling operation, excellent sharpening stones are available for free. Drill core, when the rock tested is hard, like quartz or granite, makes a perfect sharpener. The core is perfectly smooth and round and is available in different thicknesses from AQ (small) to HQ (large diameter). I've used a piece of quartz-type HQ core on my Puma for years and am quite happy with the results. And it sure beats paying $18 for a silver-dollar-size slice of Arkansas rock.

-b.b.

PART VIII

They looked so out of place with their soapy smell and colorful clothes. They were gazing wide-eyed at the dogs who were left. They didn't know what they wanted but I thought they really did want a puppy. I watched, in a trance, knowing that if they left without me, my number was up completely. I was scared shitless.

"Well boys, this is what's left. I just snuffed twenty and these ones aren't much to look at."

"They've all gone nuts, mister, that's what's happened."

"Yeah, probably for sure, but listen, kid. You don't want any of these mutts. Come back Wednesday."

"Hey Alex, what do you think?"

"Well let's take a good look at them for ourselves. I mean we're here aren't we?"

"Yeah. Hey, haul that one out on the floor."

"Hey get offa me little muttso."

"He's spun right out — cute, though."

"Hey Toby, you notice this one?"

"Hey now there's a cute dog."

"He's so still. He's watching us."

"Yeah, like a hawk. Let's put him down here."

"Well okay you guys but this one is a real cheesehound, all scratched up, obviously an Indian village dog. He'll be nothing but trouble — just a garbage hound."

"That's it fella, stretch and take it easy . . ."

"See what I mean? Right over to the garbage pail."

"Jesus! He knows how to get into it fast enough."

"Alex, that's our puppy right there."

"You're right. That cheesehound doesn't give a shit."

"You guys are crazy, you know. I'll just end up with him again and shoot him then."

"Yeah sure mister, but if we like him we'll come and bail him out again."

"It'll cost ya."

"Maybe, but a good cheesehound is hard to find, so here's your money."

"Sign right here for receipt of the mutt."

"We'll both sign."

"You guys are crazy."

"No man, but we're trying."

"Fucking hippies."

There was a rush of night air, a dark shape engulfed me. A machine started and the voices continued.

"Well, we've got another one. Hopefully he'll be happy."

"You never know with a little guy like this, but I like his style. He was staring his death in the face with a lot of cool. I think he kinda knew that we'd take him."

"Toby, he doesn't know shit, but somehow his personality makes him mellow and he pays attention. There is something different about him."

"Well, cheesehound, welcome to the club — you're going home."

I didn't know what was going on, but I kinda felt that they wouldn't shoot me. I was out and awaiting further developments.

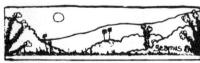

Part IX

The truck pulled up beside an old house surrounded by garbage. I was carried inside and put on the floor. A bowl of greasy food was put in front of me. I ate and went to sleep. As I awoke later and dozed, I heard those two talking softly in another part of the house.

". . . How about Bob?"

"I don't want a dog called Bob, man."

"A dog called Bog?"

"Bog the dog?"

"Bogdog, dogbag."

"Ratbag."

"Jabber-jabber, let's smoke some hash."

"O.K. . . . how about Storm?"

"You're an idiot, you know that?"

They were rather strange — but they fed me and left me alone. I'd stay awhile.

Chain Saw Advice

A friend has worked long hours the past few years repairing all brands of chainsaws. He felt compelled to give us some advice so he wouldn't have to spend the rest of his life just catching up to the workload. He also wanted it made clear that Husqvarna makes the best saws.

He advises:

1. Buy a good saw, not a throw-away item.

2. If you've got a good saw, run good oil in it: good 2-cycle oil in the gas mixture, good chain oil in summertime and motor oil in winter or cut the summer oil with kerosene.

3. Add a couple tablespoonsful of methyl hydrate in each tankful of gas (or more in gas can container) if really cold, say twenty below (F.) or more.

4. Important to use good oil in oiler if automatic pump (summerweight could seize that little pump).

5. If you don't know much about sharpening, buy a cheap chain sharpening guide and you can't go too far wrong. Unless you go through a lot of chains or live completely in the bush, forget an expensive clamp-on sharpener. Go to a sharpener service.

6. If you have a felt-type gas filter (in gas tank), throw it away every year and get a new one, regardless if it appears to work well. It only costs a couple bucks at most. Worth it.

Husqvarna saws, accessories, and service are available from Jon Rudolph at Box 4689, Whitehorse.

-a.d.

A sensible alternate to the "Alaska Mill", this device is simpler, faster and cheaper. Essentially it is a clamp-on, hinged 'boat' which slides along a 2x6 or 2x4 nailed to the log. It weighs less than four pounds and costs forty dollars (american).

Write to: Haddon Tools, 47719 West Route 120, McHenry, Illinios, U.S.A. 60050.

i.m.

Agnes' ~Woodpile~ Etiquette ~

A sturdy sawhorse without cross braces can be constructed if the ground isn't frozen. All you need are four long green poles, two spikes and the means to dig four post holes. When you've decided where to put the sawhorse, dig the pairs of holes, the deeper the better, at a slant so that when you insert the poles they lean out, away from each other. Then you have to bend the poles so they will cross. Spike them there. And if you only have two pairs of poles, you don't have to be exact on your measurements. With no cross poles or braces, your wood-cutting goes a lot faster -- you don't have to worry about sawing through anything but the log you want cut!

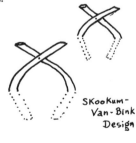

Skookum-
Van-Bink
Design

To cut a short piece of wood that is too short for your sawhorse, hold the swede saw with your foot and lean it against your stomach. Hold the wood with both hands, bend over the saw and move the wood up and down over the blade to make the cut.

You'll be surprised how accurately you can make cuts this way if you are doing a little pole carpentry.

When you are trying to split wood, give the axe just a little twist as it hits the wood, so that some of the force is directed sideways to force the wood apart. This way the axe never gets buried into the wood, but bounces off. It sounds odd, but it works better than just hacking away. Also, if you can wait until it is forty below or more, the wood, even if green, will be easy to split.

To cut a length of cordwood into stove lengths, it is easiest if you put it on a sawhorse and cut through almost all the way in several spots. Then turn the log over and break each length off with the axe.

The Verdict: Airtight or Barrel

At the turn of the century, about 40,000 people passed a winter in our territory as part of the Gold Rush. They came from all over the world. A few didn't return home because they liked it here; a few others didn't go anywhere because they froze to death.

Heating is a serious business in this territory. We get temperatures forty degrees colder than anywhere in continental USA. If you want to know about wood stoves, just about every crazy type of heater in the world has been imported and tried by someone here. However, throughout this time, the best buy on the market has remained (by unanimous decision), the oval sheet metal "airtight". Cost is only twenty-five bucks plus six-inch stove pipe, a damper, and a chimney "jack" or "safety". What you get is the only heater that can heat a cabin fast. Apparently something special about the oval shape makes it effective, and it can be shut right down to idle all night. I've had one burn for twenty hours—and a friend on Labarge managed a record 36 hours using only softwood. These heaters come in different sizes: a 24 inch is a nice size for a small cabin and are light enough to be backpacked into remote places.

There are a few simple things to know that don't get explained by salesmen and I've never seen an instruction booklet with an airtight.

There must be ashes or sand in the bottom, at least two inches deep or the bottom will burn out.

To start it: open the damper, close the draft, take off the lid and build a fire just like it was a campfire. When you light it, replace the lid, but leave it slightly ajar so air can slip in, and then open the draft. When it is a roaring inferno, slide the lid closed and shut the draft. Wait a minute, then close the damper.

To adjust it: you have to open the damper a bit if you want to open the draft at all, or else expect the airtight to puff smoke around the lid.

To feed more wood: open the damper and wait a minute for the smoke inside to rise out the pipe. Then remove the lid—leaving the draft closed.

If it "takes off" during the night and gets red and hops around the room, open the damper only. Then open the cabin door and look at the stars while the cabin cools down.

Once a day, open 'er up and let 'er roar. Creosote buildup causes chimney fires and sometimes a chimney fire can get out-of-control and burn the whole cabin down. So burn it out once a day, or take a dog chain, climb onto the roof and rattle it around inside the pipe. Then chain up your white samoyed-huskey again with the chain.

Airtights have a problem. They burn out eventually because they are only made out of sheet metal. If someone ever markets a completely cast iron oval, buy one. Ashley sells an oval airtight with cast-iron top and bottom and a bi-metal thermostat for automatically controlling the temperature, but it costs about two hundred dollars.

I'd love one with some kind of heat-proof glass window in the side so you could watch all the smoke swirling around and the wood compressing but the inside would just creosote up. Still, if you see one....

Before buying a heater, you should know the few possibilities. The best way to explain them all is to outline a heater that you can get a welder to assemble from, mostly, scrap parts. The design is adapted from one that a space cowboy has near Dawson. I thank him for finally putting together in one heater every feature possible except a roach clip.

This model will heat a warehouse but illustrates what possible features are missing from small heaters. But if you still want to buy a silly southern heater, dealer's addresses are lised in Harrowsmith magazine's "Wood Heat Compendium" on pg 32 of issue fourteen, volume 3: 2. It's at the library.

—a.d.

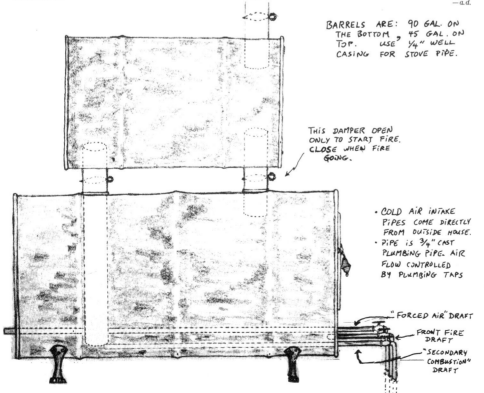

BARRELS ARE: 90 GAL. ON THE BOTTOM, 45 GAL. ON TOP. USE 1/4" WELL CASING FOR STOVE PIPE.

THIS DAMPER OPEN ONLY TO START FIRE. CLOSE WHEN FIRE GOING.

- COLD AIR INTAKE PIPES COME DIRECTLY FROM OUTSIDE HOUSE.
- PIPE IS 3/4" CAST PLUMBING PIPE. AIR FLOW CONTROLLED BY PLUMBING TAPS

"FORCED AIR" DRAFT
FRONT FIRE DRAFT
"SECONDARY COMBUSTION" DRAFT

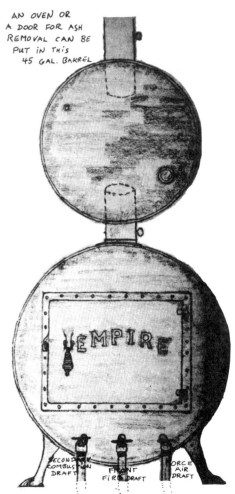

AN OVEN OR A DOOR FOR ASH REMOVAL CAN BE PUT IN THIS 45 GAL. BARREL

EMPIRE

SECONDARY COMBUSTION DRAFT
FRONT FIRE DRAFT
FORCED AIR DRAFT

—Smoke Chimneys in old cabins—

In many of the old trappers' cabins along the Yukon, you will see a smoke chimney. This is usually a long wooden tube-like box constructed of milled lumber which hung down from the roof to just above head level, with a flap door on it. Sometimes a smoke chimney was built to vent out the end wall, but always high up. This device would allow the occupant to let out smoke from the inside of the cabin but only as far as the level where it would offend the eyes. This kept heated, albeit smokey, air near the roof in and saved on fuel.

—agnes

Part X

My hearly history ends about here. It's really rather par for the average dog in the Yukon but I've had my moments.

Over the weeks I learned about my new place of residence. I was to live with Toby, who talked a lot and ran around searching for an identity, and Alex, who worked hard in a bookstore, read a lot at night and didn't worry about Toby. We were in an old house in a nice area by the river under the cliffs in Whitehorse. It was a cul-de-sac and no one came up the winding road unless they lived there or were lost. We didn't have many visitors. It was nice..

Also in the cul-de-sac were eight other houses — some nice, some not so nice, none bad. And in those houses lived about six children, ten adults, six freaky people counting Toby and Alex and about nine dogs. The biggest dog was about 160 pounds and the smallest just a tad smaller than me.

So I settled in and I liked it. I had my freedom after I made it clear I wouldn't take off. I didn't make friends with the other dogs and I still don't have any good friends that are dogs. They don't have anything to give me.

So I got mellow, played by myself a lot, got beat up a lot by the others, learned the routine around the area and polished up my act.

Toby spent a lot of time with me, Alex worked all the time and wasn't speedy like his partner. We ran around a lot and played games together. Toby understood me a lot, and I'd never felt a feeling like that before. They both took me places and let me do what I wanted, fed me lots and gave me shit. So I cared for them too, as far as that went. We got along really well.

Oh yeah — there was another dog that lived there too, name of Jock. He was an asshole and I don't want to talk about him. We played sometimes but he was a jam-tart, brought up on butter and never took any chances. In short, a house pet.

So that's the first story in a sense, and I'm glad it's done because it's all old history and better left alone. I suppose it does explain why I am like I am, but life becomes less crazy in some ways and more mellow in others. Once I had a home and some friends, things became less of a fight, and I began to have fun, gradually.

I was now Seamus the cheesehound, I had a lot of friends, and I made good use of my time with them.

keep your pipes clean

If the kitchen is the heart of every home, then your heater or stove pipes are the main arteries, and equal care is due. Anyone who has known the feeling of watching their home go up in flames, the loss of loved ones, or just all your worldly possessions turned to crispy black ashes, knows what a bit of forethought can do in avoiding such calamities.

Keeping your pipes clean is easy, and the advantages go beyond safety. When they are clean, they give off more heat because the build-up of creosote and ash acts as an insulator. After you've installed them, give them a light tap with a small hammer or kitchen knife. Listen to this sound and get to know it.

ALADDIN LAMPS

There is a brand of kerosene lamp that is called "Aladdin." These lanterns have a thick tubular wick and a flame spreader and are supposed to throw off 100 watts of light. An advantage over propane lights is that these ones don't roar or hiss. They do burn a lot of fuel though, up to a pint for a long winter evening.

Aladdins are really touchy about draughts and changes in temperature. They will respond by pouring black smoke all over the room. One way to make them burn better is to extend the glass chimney's height. You can do this by bending a piece of tinfoil into a cylinder and placing that over the top of the glass to make it taller. Or, you can just place a second glass chimney over the first.

I tried burning diesel in one but found it plugged up pretty fast. Maybe mixing in JP-4 would help. Sounds dangerous.

—a. d.

If, after some time, they begin to get a dull or thick sound, you're overdue for a cleaning. These are a few simple ways of keeping your pipes clean.

1. A small green leafy branch with ropes tied at either end, then drag it up and down the pipes.

2. Using a length of tire or tow chain, lower it down the pipe then rattle it about so that it scrapes the sides of the pipe.

3. Hire a chimney sweep.

4. Take your pipes outside (careful not to drop ashes on the floor) and beat them senseless (careful not to dent).

If you're burning greenwood, about every week to ten days should be good, and regular use of soot remover helps. One thing you should avoid is burning plastics. These produce deposits on your pipes that act as a kind of glue to the ashes, and produce rapid build-ups of soot, and are also far more dangerous as far as the potential for fire is concerned. Clean pipes give you more heat, and if you're the fire-phobiac type, easier sleepful nights.

—*Mars Bonfire II*

Woodstove Hints

To get a pan hot faster, you can remove one of the lids and place the pan over the hole. This will soot up the bottom of the pan, so watch where you put it when you take it off the stove.

To clean the surface of a cast-iron stove, rub it with a pumus stone. This is a porous rock, shaped like a brick, that is used in commercial restaurants to clean their grills at the end of the day.

—g.s.

Franklin Barrel Fireplace/Heater/Stove

Everyone enjoys the aesthetics of a fireplace, but its efficiency as a primary heat source in a cold climate is far inferior to an air tight type heater. So normally, if one wants the luxury of an open fire, it's in conjunction with another wood heater and possibly a cook stove. This situation complicates the whole process of acquiring, cutting, and storing wood, in addition to increasing the number of stove pipes, maintenance, fire hazards, heat loss, and most important, wood consumption. In a small cabin two or three wood burners occupy too much space and can create sauna-like conditions.

This dilemma can be overcome by simply combining the three heaters into one all purpose stove. There are many forms the finished product may take on, but the basic principle is to create a Franklin-type heater which will close airtight for use as a heat source and lend itself to cooking both on tip and inside.

Here is a suggested design that is well tested: Start with a forty-five gallon barrel, preferably the roundish beer barrel-shaped galvanized drums that were used on the old river boats as water containers. They're heavy duty barrels and their shape is more aesthetically pleasing than the more contemporary drums. (Two possible drawbacks are the health dangers of welding galvanized metal and the difficulty of cooking on the rounded top surface.)

With the barrel resting horizontally, cut out a

door opening eleven inch by twenty-one inch. Weld angle iron around the opening to create a flat door frame. Hinge at the bottom a ¼ inch thick steel door with a draft at the bottom. Latch the door at the top and line the perimeter of the inside of the door with asbestos strips fastened with small stove bolts and/or stove cement. Weld a stove collar towards the back of the drum with a minimum eight inch flue. (Mine is ten inch to guarantee a good draw when the door is open.) I also have a seven inch long handle welded on the door so when the door is opened it rests on the floor creating a level hearth.

The greatest care should be taken in fitting the door so it is airtight. If tight enough, the finished heater will keep a fire going twelve hours or more and will take two foot long logs. The top surface can be used for cooking and keeping steaming hot water. A flat cooking plate could be welded to the top for greater ease in cooking.

When the door is open it acts as a fireplace. A makeshift screen keeps ashes off the rug. With the screen removed you can cook with or without a grill, as if camping outdoors, or you can use a dutch oven for stews or baking; or simply lay back and roast dinner on a willow stick while you roast your feet on the hearth at the same time.

peter frankbink

Airtight Gourmets:

Do you make your toast on the top of your airtight heater? And are your eggs getting cold while you wait? If you hold the bread slices against the side of the heater, they will stick there. Turn them with a flipper, but chose a new spot because they mightn't stick in the same place again. If you still insist on making the toast on the top, sprinkle salt in the surface of the heater first and the toast won't stick.

j.v. & b.b.

Airtight Summer Cooking

For cooking on an airtight during the summer there are two methods that work well.

You can lower a lidded pot inside the airtight, using some heavy wire, to get it closer to the fire.

Or cut the ends out of a big juice can and split it down the side. Then put this curved tin inside the airtight around the in-vent and heap up the ashes to keep it in place. Fill up the airtight with sand or ashes to the level of the top of the can. The can should keep air circulating from the vent and you can build the fire higher now so the flames heat the top better.

—a.d.

TOP SHOULD BE 3/8" to ½" CAST IRON PLATE. DOOR IS ANGLED FOR MORE EFFICIENT LOADING.

BARREL STEP STOVE.

Airtight Servicing

"If people have trouble with their airtight, I'll service them", says Alyx. He has an airtight servicing company and will make housecalls. Find him in the Kopper King Tavern, listed under "angry young men".

— b.b.

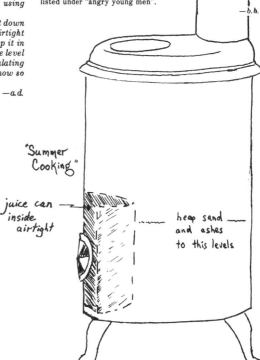

"Summer Cooking"

juice can inside airtight

heap sand and ashes to this levels

GRAVITY-FEED WATER SYSTEM FOR CABINS

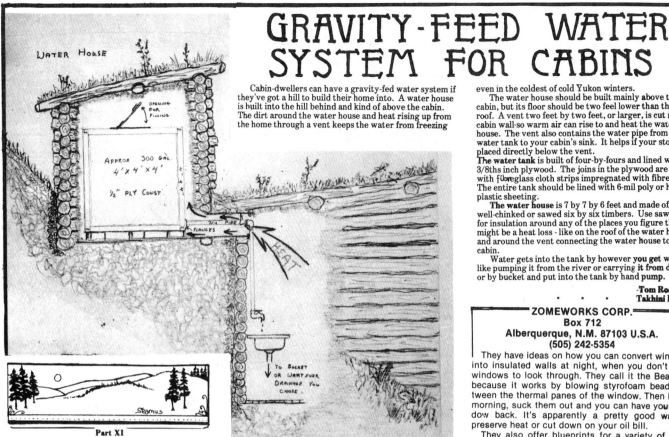

Cabin-dwellers can have a gravity-fed water system if they've got a hill to build their home into. A water house is built into the hill behind and kind of above the cabin. The dirt around the water house and heat rising up from the home through a vent keeps the water from freezing even in the coldest of cold Yukon winters.

The water house should be built mainly above the cabin, but its floor should be two feet lower than the cabin roof. A vent two feet by two feet, or larger, is cut into the cabin wall so warm air can rise to and heat the water house. The vent also contains the water pipe from the water tank to your cabin's sink. It helps if your stove is placed directly below the vent.

The water tank is built of four-by-fours and lined with 3/8ths inch plywood. The joins in the plywood are sealed with fibreglass cloth strips impregnated with fibregum. The entire tank should be lined with 6-mil poly or heavy plastic sheeting.

The water house is 7 by 7 by 6 feet and made of well-chinked or sawed six by six timbers. Use sawdust for insulation around any of the places you figure there might be a heat loss - like on the roof of the water house and around the vent connecting the water house to the cabin.

Water gets into the tank by however you get water, like pumping it from the river or carrying it from drums or by bucket and put into the tank by hand pump.

—Tom Roscoe
Takhini River

* * *

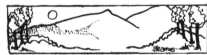

Part XI

One of the basic rules of dogdom is never to raid your own place's garbage; always go somewhere else. So I did.

The good people of Whitehorse built racks to keep the dogs from tipping their garbage cans over. These were a godsend to a little puppy who could climb. Being suitably upwardly mobile in my own right I quickly learned to climb and nose open the can and dive in.

The main drawback, of course, was getting out. Twice I was stuck for a solution to the problem. Garbage cans are hideous prisons. They stink, albeit nicely, and my first rescue didn't come for a whole day and a night until an early morning Larry Lunchbag dropped a green bag of crud on me. I damn near died trying to get around the cans and had to tear the bag apart and burrow through some really strange garbage to get out on top.

Garbage is great if it's food, but if it isn't, it's awful. When I got home Toby and Alex tied me up and didn't talk to me for two days. That's the price you pay, I guess. The second and last time came when I got stuck inside a nearly empty one and no one came for two days so I started to yell and raise hell. I got rescued by an old lady with three cats. She decided to keep me for another week in her house and made me shit in a box filled with perfumed weirdness. I made a break one afternoon and never stopped running until I got home.

I got locked up for two days again but I had a good time thinking about the fact that the old dear only had two cats after I'd left. If I'd stayed one more day, she would have had none. I never got caught in the can again. That box of kitty crap still makes me shiver when it slips into my memory.

Part XII

Travel was no problem in Whitehorse up until 1976. That's the year they got into meters in taxicabs and more companies moved in. Until then I rode in them just like anyone else; except the drivers always used to try and keep me out of sight. Black Top Cabs was a choice favorite. A lot of Toby's friends worked there and I used to go down to their office on Main St. and lie around inside. I'd listen to the man yell at the talking box and answer phones, or go sit on the hood of a cab and wait for a ride.

This was the way to do it, you see, because the driver would come out, shoo me off the hood and jump in his car. Then I'd pounce back on the hood or the roof. The trip behind this is that he can't take off down the street with a dog on his hood — the cops would have his number in minutes and he can't just zoom off down the road and take a turn at forty because the second he speeded up I'd get my claws into the wiper wells and block off his vision full force on the windshield. So he'd have to let me in.

I got to see a lot of ground that way because I could get out whenever I wanted — or if someone got in.

something that came to me one day when I was sitting in my outhouse:-

Oh I hate As It Happens
I hate Barbara Frumm;
I hate Allan Maitland
and I'll tell you how come.

Each night I listen,
faithful I'll get the call,
Each night As It Happens,
I do nothing else at all.

Oh there's kindling to cut,
there's wood to chop,
must dump my bucket,
my bucket of slop.

Many chores to do,
including water haul,
When As It Happens,
Nothing's done at all.

—Max Fraser
June, 1978,
near Whitehorse, Y.T.

TOILET SEATS

A mid-winter's night trip to the old "shitter" can be much less traumatic if the toilet seat is made out of styrofoam. No matter how cold it is, the seat feels toasty warm within a few seconds.

—s. s.

Styrofoam works fine but it looks pretty gross after a few months' use. What we use is an old thick wooden toilet seat, like the ones off the sternwheelers, and we hang it right behind the airtight. When you go out you take it with you, and bring it back afterwards. With your parkie on and pants pulled up to your thighs and the hot seat almost burning your ass, you could even read a book out there.

Better remember to bring it back inside though, or the next person will be right put out about it.

—b. s.

Editor's note: at sixty below, be very careful about metal zippers. One trapper we know on the Dempster got frostbitten last winter but was too embarrassed to go to the clinic. He did get better, though.

SIMPLE SOLAR WATER WARMER

Hot water can be a problem for cabin and cottage dwellers in the summertime. You don't want to light your wood stove because you don't need the heat; you don't have the cook stove on long enough every day to heat up the water in your reservoir, so what do you do? Go to the Sun.

A 30-gallon barrel of water on your roof can be heated from cold lake temperatures in the morning to 90-100-degree (Fahrenheit) water by evening. All you need is a car radiator, painted black, on top of it, a piece of glass over that, and some insulation underneath. Hook the radiator to the barrel, point the radiator at the sun and let the light and heat warm the water. Convection will circulate the water in the barrel for you through the radiator.

The water ought to be 90 to 100 degrees, which is just the right temperature for a shower. And since most people use an average five gallons per shower, that's six showers! Or a bath, and some left over for washing the dishes!

This idea was contributed by Vern Toews, an electrical inspector with the YTG, who's been doing solar research for years. He adds that the warm water, if left overnight, ought to lose 10 to 15 degrees Fahrenheit on a "normal night." But by noon or afternoon the next day, depending on how much heat was lost and what the weather's like the next day, it'll be warm again for another shower, or more dishes. An old Chevrolet car radiator would be good for this system, he says. And don't worry that much about the direction at which you point the radiator. Angles aren't that critical. If you're into angles, though, any solar panel (whether a radiator or something a little more sophisticated) ought to be set so it'll be 90 degrees to the sunlight at high noon on July 1, or 10 degrees more than your latitude. The angles don't matter that much with a car radiator because it's got a lot of surface the sun's rays can hit.

Toews is trying now to do what everyone says should be tried: building a solar home in the north to see how practical that kind of thing is for North of 60. He's applied for some help, but as of publication time we hadn't heard if he'd gotten it.

One thing he has proven successful already is that a single solar panel three feet square can heat a swimming pool. Vern talked to Doc Branigan in Riverdale and they agreed to give the idea a whirl. Vern was a "bit disappointed" with his results at first because the water wasn't hot enough, so he decided to take a swim and check things out. He discovered Branigan's pool held 10,000 gallons of water, not the 5,000 he'd designed it for, but the design (one small solar panel) almost heated twice as much water to pool temperature!

HEATING GREENHOUSE SOIL

Solar energy can also keep the soil warm in a greenhouse. Set up the 30-gallon/radiator system and run plastic hose or pipes through the soil. The warmth will keep the frost out, so you can start growing earlier and get more "mileage" out of your greenhouse each year. Vern says people in the Yukon can start using the sun in March if they want to, because the strength of its rays and the hours it's available at that time of year are sufficient.

Another thing of interest about solar energy, and you'll find handy if you want to get more sophisticated, is that the sun at Whitehorse is the equivalent of 260-270 British Thermal Units (BTUs) of heat for every hour of sunlight. The hours of light are equivalent to those in Edmonton, says Vern, but the temperature is slightly cooler so a little more storage of heat is required here than there.

He recommends people stick with plastic pipes when building solar units, rather than

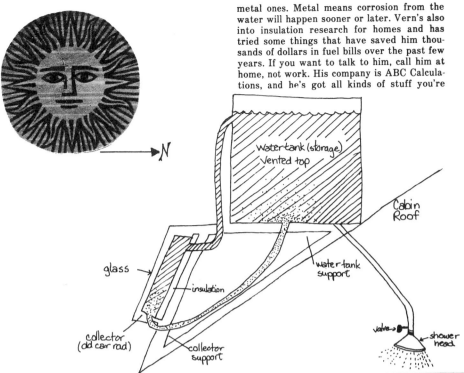

Keep conections between collector and tank as short as possible. Top of collector and top of tank (approx 12" from top) to be interconnected. Top of collector must be below bottom of tank. Water must be above top of the pipe connection.

metal ones. Metal means corrosion from the water will happen sooner or later. Vern's also into insulation research for homes and has tried some things that have saved him thousands of dollars in fuel bills over the past few years. If you want to talk to him, call him at home, not work. His company is ABC Calculations, and he's got all kinds of stuff you're bound to find useful.

Solar energy is a simple way of getting heat, and its potential is great. And it sure beats using fossil fuels and paying money to White Pass, NCPC and Yukon Electrical. With people like Vern around, we ought to get by just fine, and be able one day to say "so long" to the energy systems of the present and past.

YUKON'S ALTERNATIVE TO THE EXPENSIVE DRILLED WELL

Dear Catalogue People:

Many of us who are living in rural Yukon are often faced with the problem of finding a safe and adequate water supply for our homes. In a lot of cases we've constructed our homes in areas where there is no surface water available to us or what is available may be unsuitable for human consumption either through pollution or high sediment loads during the spring runoff.

When faced with these problems most people think of putting in a well but are soon turned off of the idea when they find out the price, which, incidentally, on the average is several thousands of dollars in the Yukon. But, there are alternatives to the expensive drilled well which in most cases produces water far above the daily requirements of an average household, so in most cases you are throwing money away on water you will never need.

Most of the alternatives are not new scientific breakthroughs in the art of water supply, but means that have been around for a long time.

The alternatives are the following: 1. Driven wells, 2. Jetted wells, 3. Dug wells, 4. Bored wells, 5. Springs, 6. Cisterns, and 7. Manmade ponds.

Many of these most people already know about or have even attempted; some with success, others with failure. Here is where I must say that though these methods are simple, there are proper techniques for installing all these water supplies if you don't want to meet with failure.

These methods of installation have become very well studied over the years and, if followed and installed with proper equipment, should meet all your water supply needs at a very inexpensive price.

If you're interested in learning more about these alternative water supplies or how to go about putting one in we would be glad to help you. We also are capable of putting in these water supplies for you if the conditions at your property are conducive to these alternatives. However, please remember in some areas a deep drilled well may be your only answer to an adequate water supply.

For further information, write—

Water Supply
c/o Box 4971
Whitehorse, Yukon
Y1A 4N6

or, if you see any of us on the street stop and talk to us, we will be glad to bend your ear. "Us" happens to be the following people.

Al Foster
Stu Withers
Ken Nordin

Twelve Volts

Bush dwellers who rely on twelve volt batteries for power can exchange information about twelve volt technology through Dave Clark at General Delivery, Whitehorse. Dave has a twelve volt television, twelve volt vacuum cleaner, twelve volt toothbrush, twelve volt franklin fireplace, twelve volt guitar and twelve volt pencil. If you have information to add to the pool, write to Dave who is eventually going to write a book on the subject. If you want information you can also write him, but better be specific and throw in a couple of bucks if you want a reply.

—a. d.

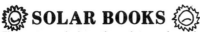

SOLAR BOOKS

There are many books on the market now about solar energy that your library probably has if you want to look at them before buying. Best titles we've heard are:

THE SUN BUILDERS

By Robert Argue, Barbara Emanuel and Stephen Graham. $7.50.

"A people's guide to Solar, Wind and Energy in Canada" is what it says it is, and what it really is. True-life stories of real people getting by with real new-energy methods, which tells you that solar can happen and is happening for people who devote a little time to it. Recommended, because it reviews solar, wind and other new energy sources *in Canada*, not Arizona. Includes consumers guide, list of manufacturers, access to books and other educational material. 256 pages.

THE SOLAR HOME BOOK

By Bruce Anderson and Michael Riordan. $8.50.

Called "an excellent book" that's clearly written to tell you how to heat, cool and design homes with the sun's energy. It includes do-it-yourself projects.

HARVEST THE SUN

By Nick Nicholson. $10.

Is about work done at Ayer's Cliff, Quebec, on new developments in solar energy in Canada. Includes new concepts for greenhouses, turbines, heat exchangers, and looks like you have to be able to understand a lot of technical stuff to really do something with it, as with most solar potentials. However, it's described as "a book you can build from" and definitely is worth checking out. Nice to know what's happening with new developments in Canadian solar research.

THE NICHOLSON SOLAR ENERGY CATALOGUE AND BUILDING MANUAL

By Nick Nicholson. $9.50.

The only solar energy building manual of its kind. Detailed sequential photographs of two solar houses being built in the heart of Canada's snowbelt. Includes lots of plans, specifications and details. This book is based on the practical use of solar energy. Nick Nicholson has built more solar homes in Canada than anyone else. Anyone about to build his own solar home can easily incorporate solar heating into their plans from the information contained in this book. Two volumes including updates.

THE FOOD AND HEAT PRODUCING SOLAR GREENHOUSE

By Rick Fisher and Bill Yenda.

A fine book detailing methods of both design and construction of solar greenhouses. Well illustrated and clearly written, with many photographs. Loaded with practical information on the design, construction and operation of solar greenhouses. Includes a state of the art review of many operating solar greenhouses. 168 pages.

SOLPLAN ONE

By The Drawing-Room Graphic Services. $2.

Originally billed as a booklet for solar houses for Canada, the information and solar house plans included here are excellent for any climate. Contains outlines for 17 different solar houses (building plans are available). Also contains vital information on design considerations, solar energy principles and selecting a solar house site. A book highly recommended. 32 pages, paperback.

SOLAR HEATED BUILDINGS, A Brief Survey

By William Shurcliff. $12.

This is the 13th and final edition of a book that has become a standard for the industry. Contains photographs and descriptions of 319 solar heated homes, schools and commercial buildings. An excellent book showing the variety of work that has been done in solar construction. Provides an excellent base for anyone attempting to design a solar installation. 306 pages, paperback.

PROTOTYPE CANADA

By the Ayer's Cliff Centre for Solar Research. $8.

Prototype Canada includes all the working drawings to build an efficient and maintenance free air-rock-water solar system. Designed for the Canadian context, on eight (18" x 24") sheets, the design takes into account: • Availability of materials • Simple erection procedures • Optimal efficiency on an energy-dollar basis • Flexibility for custom application • Oil, gas or electric back-up • Understandability • Solar heating of living space and domestic hot water, and ... all necessary details for fabricating the air handler, solar store, collector, including wiring diagrams, pressure drop calculations, etc.

Some books available at the Whitehorse library on solar energy are:

Harnessing the Sun to Heat Your House
By John Keyes, 1974.

Direct Use of the Sun's Energy
By Farrington Daniels, 1964.

How to Build a Solar Heater
By Ted Lucas, 1975.

Harnessing the Sun, the Story of Solar Energy
By David C. Knight, 1976.

ENVIRONMENTALLY APPROPRIATE TECHNOLOGY (Renewable energy, and other developing technologies for a conserver society in Canada).
By Bruce McCallum, Fisheries and Environment Canada, first published March, 1975 by the government Catalogue number En102-1/15 ISBN 0-660-01003-8 $3.75 in Canada.

ISLAND UNIVERSE BOOKS

At 415 Parkside Drive, Toronto, Ontario, M6R 2Z7 has a good selection of alternative-energy books, including "do-it-yourself" types. Write them for their catalogue.

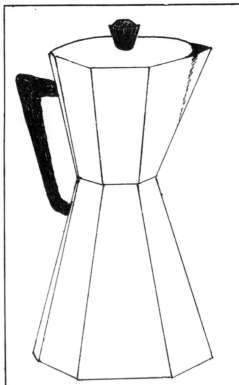

EXPRESSO COFFEE MAKER

For those expresso lovers who love the bush too much to live adjacent to a Vancouver coffeehouse but still crave that certain something...Alyx recommends a "near-expresso maker". It costs thirty dollars from the spice shop in the mall but is worth it. There is a bottom part (where the water heats) with a pressure outlet which jets into the upper half. He claims it works well for expresso-type coffee as well as regular blends and he uses a wood stove. Now if everyone buys one, maybe I'll get a decent cup of coffee when I visit...

— a.d.

LET BABY WASH HIS OWN DIAPERS!

At Fort Selkirk, there is the remains of an old hand-powered washing machine which had a lever on the side to rock the tub of laundry. It is this agitation that is the washing principal even on the electrical models. It might take something to rig up, but why couldn't junior's bouncing on his jolly jumper or rocking horse be used to agitate the laundry? Might as well make the blighter earn his keep.

-c.c.

CURIOUS ABOUT INSULATION?

If you've got any questions about insulating your home or energy conservation, call the government. One of the ways they're using our tax money is the ENER$SAVE HEATLINE. Call collect to 613-995-1801, extension 2618.

Radio telephones are an interesting alternative to regular service. A mobile phone in your vehicle means you are never out of touch with the world of princess phones, Ma Bell and As It Happens, if they want to talk to you. Small business owner/operators rely heavily on mobile phones and recording devices to keep in touch with their clientele. But in areas without regular telephones, radio is more than just added convenience; it is an emergency link to friends, hospitals, fire control and police.

Another sometimes-viable choice for bush dwellers is the C.B. citizen's band radio. C.B. s are usually cheaper but are less dependable in emergencies because circumstances such as road closures during a storm will knock out highway traffic which would relay your vital message. Both C.B. s and radio phones have the advantage of operating off D.C. power and so are not affected by power black-outs. The antenna for a citizen's band radio is about ten feet long compared to about two feet for the same effective distance on a radio phone.

CNT Radio Phones — Rates and Prices

A mobile phone is only registerable if it is installed in a "mobile," such as an automobile, trailer, truck, plane, boat, etc. A radio phone at a cabin would have to be registered as a "base station." This means, by CNT law, that the set must be connected to an expensive special directional gain antenna worth about $150. The same phone installed in a vehicle parked in the garage is called a "mobile" and can get by with a mobile unity gain antenna costing about $40. Either mobile or base phones usually are run off a D.C. battery such as a skidoo or automotive 12 volt.

CNT, which does all its billing from Edmonton, will want $7 per month for a mobile phone. Calls cost 70 cents for the first three minutes and 15 cents each additional minute. All calls are considered "Person-to-Person" so it is to your advantage to ask the mobile operator for a specific person. Long distance charges are calculated at the standard person-to-person rate between the closest tower and your destination. For example, a call from near Minto tower to Whitehorse would cost $2.25 for three minutes plus forty cents per minute after that.

Your actual cost is much higher than just those rates, however, because a mobile phone is an expensive piece of electronics. To lease a set from CNT will cost you $55 per month for a year contract or $68.75 per month on a six-month deal. Installation is a $50 charge.

Private enterprise has a scam for you here. Bob Reynolds of Northern Systems, 508 Wood Street, Whitehorse, 667-4987, will lease a "Spilsbury and Tindall" set for $50 per month on a six-month lease. The set is equipped with "selective call" which tells you when a call for you is coming in so you don't have to listen to everyone else's garbage and static. You can hook it up so that the car horn will beep ten times to call you if you are parked on a job site or even at home out in the garden. This set with three channels costs $525 to buy outright, installation is $35 and with the selective call $40. Bob says the selective call mechanism actually saves power because you don't have to have your set turned up as loud when monitoring for incoming calls. This is an important consideration for people without electricity, relying on recharged car batteries.

Bob sells a 5/8 wave mobile unity gain antenna for $40 which gives effective radiated power of 50 watts. There are 1/4 wave models on the market but they are "not recommended out of town."

Mobile phones and service are also available at Total North Communications at the Whitehorse Airport but their rates are higher.

Extending Your Range And Improving the Reception Of Your AM Radio Receiver

—an idea article courtesy of Dan and Lee Carruthers; the other by Peter Carr with the assistance of a Popular Mechanics article on radio.

This antenna design is to extend and improve the AM radio reception on radios using internal "ferrite" bar antenna systems.

MATERIALS NEEDED

Radio with internal or Ferrite antenna.
20 feet plus of yellow blasting wire or magnet wire. Extra won't hurt. (If you're working in a mine, the yellow blasting or signal wire is all around, and excellent. If you're not, know any miners?)
One grounding rod, preferably copper, four to six feet long.
Ten feet or more of 12 to 18-gauge wire.
Solder and torch.

PROCEDURE

Remove back plate of radio, making sure it is disconnected from power source and ignoring death threats of professional associations who wish your business and don't like people "improving their own."

Locate the internal ferrite bar antenna, usually at the top rear of the radio, wrapped in a fine wire (see first illustration).

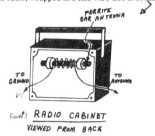

Figure 1: RADIO CABINET VIEWED FROM BACK

Take 12 to 18 inches of blasting or magnet wire and wrap it tightly around the ferrite rod, being careful not to break the wire already wrapped around the rod. Make sure the wire is secure to the antenna, pass both ends to the outside of your radio cabinet — one to be used as the antenna lead, the other for 'ground'.

The antenna wire length is not critical, but generally the longer you make it, the better the results will be. It should be mounted as high as possible and at right angles to the radio station broadcast antenna. (If you're trying to improve reception of a distant station, then obviously you won't know this, so guess away.) See figure two:

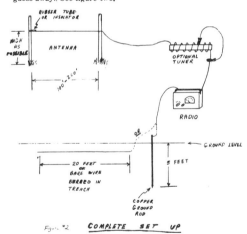

Fig. #2 COMPLETE SET UP

The ground rod should be four to six feet long and preferably driven into moist soil. An alternative, however, is that any long, heavy-uninsulated wire can be buried, say in a trench, in a horizontal position as deep as possible. With this method, you should use 15 to 20 feet of wire. This alone will improve the reception of existing or fringe AM stations but go one step further, and you will end up with a system that allows you to select the optimum antenna length (within limits) for various station frequencies. See figure three:

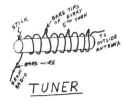

TUNER

Take a stick one and a half to three inches in diameter, or a cardboard tube (the designers of this idea use an old paint brush roller) and wrap with blasting wire for a length of 12 to 18 inches. At about every fifth turn of wire, strip the insulation for about an inch and twist at gap.

The selector wire seen in Figure Three with alligator clips at each end of its ends can be moved from tap to tap on the roll until station reception is at its peak. This tuner should be placed near the radio, attached on one end to the antenna outside and on the other to the antenna lead from the radio.

A home fitted with this system on the Carcross Road greatly improved its reception. Two local radio stations, poorly received, now join a number of Alaskan AM stations and the quality is very high. The system has another advantage: power requirements will be less since improved reception produces greater volume; better reception means you use less power for your radio. If your radio has other bands and is capable of receiving more of the radio spectrum than the AM broadcast area, or the medium wave band, then the above antenna system also may improve reception in other areas as well.

In the radio spectrum, the standard AM broadcast can be found at 535 to 1605 kilohertz (see diagram, figure four):

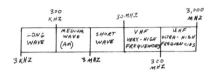

SPECTRUM ILLUSTRATED AS RADIO DIAL

Frequency is measured in cycles per second, referred to as *Hertz*, with the spectrum extending, in theory, from zero Hertz to infinity. One thousand *hertz* equal one kilohertz. One million Hertz is called a Megahertz and equals 1,000 khz.

For antenna purposes, at the lower end of the spectrum—the "long wave" area—length is important with "longer the better" being the rule. But shorter antennas will work well for casual listening. A normal AM radio will not tune these frequencies but begins in the 500 kHz range, called the Medium Wave band. Simple-home-built receivers are available, however, from a wide variety of sources for persons who wish to listen to the long wave frequencies in the three to 150 kHz area which features, among other things, the Omega Radio Navigation Beacons (near k2Hz), worldwide naval ship-to-shore signals (between 16 and 150 kHz) time, weather, iceberg patrol and other useful reports (between 16 and 150 kHz) and other weather and marine radio beacons.

In the middle wave band, beside the standard AM signals, one can hear the International Emergency Frequency for alarms from ships at sea on the 500 kHz and near 2100 kHz; the Amateur Radio 160-meter band at 1800-2000 kHz, the shortwave listener (SWL) 120-meter band at 2300-2500 kHz, and finally the airliners' two-way radio worldwide band on 2868-2987 kHz.

A type of receiver popular in the Yukon these days features middle band and portions of the short wave frequencies and the FM radio broadcastig band, coupled with cassette player/recorder, It picks up some of the above signals with just its built-in telescopic antenna, and can be easily and cheaply powered by a car battery if electricity from the utilities is not readily available.

Shortwave frequencies extend from 3 to 30 Mhz. The lower frequencies travel farther at night, while higher shortwave signals go farther during the day. A wide variety of gear can be used to receive short wave, from the very cheap to the sublimely expensive, and open up to your hearing 11 international broadcasting bands with hundreds of stations in all languages.

Citizens Band (that dreaded CB) as well as five amateur radio bands and their around-the-world conversations are also found on the short wave range. Continuing along, we find the Very High Frequency area, from 30 to 300 Mhz, containing three ham radio bands, the FM radio broadcasting band and the television channels 2 to 13. Also included are VHF-low and VHF-high (public service), police bands as well as the main frequencies for two way air-to-ground communications.

Short antennas, between 10, (25.4cm.) and 100 (254 cm.),inches long, work well; and so do the normal FM radio telescopic antenna so common today. Ultrahigh frequencies ranging from 300 Mhz to at least 3,000 Mhz include three amateur radio bands, a police public service band and in some areas more TV broadcast channels. Antennas become very small at UHF with lengths of less than 10 inches suitable, and most TV sets can be adjusted to bring in the channels; but listeners wanting to hear other UHF frequencies usually build small converters to move UHF signals down to frequencies that can be heard by shortwave sets.

Here are the frequencies where international radio shortwave broadcasts can be heard (all Mhz).
120-metre band—2.3 to 2.5 Mhz.
90-metre band—3.2 to 3.4 Mhz.
75-metre band—3.9 to 4.0
60-metre band—4.75 to 5.060
49-metre band—5.950 to 6.2
41-metre band—7.1 to 7.3
31-metre band—9.5 to 9.725
25-metre band—11.7 to 11.975
19-metre band—15.1 to 15.45
16-metre band—17.7 to 17.9
13-metre band—21.45 to 21.75
11-metre band—25.6 to 26.1

For more information, hobby organizations exist most places that deal with everything to be found in the radio spectrum, and a number of magazines deal with Ham Radio, international short wave broadcasts and the more than 5,000 standard broadcast AM radio stations around the planet.
Good hunting.

HAM CLUB

People wishing to know more about radios for broadcasting as well as receiving, are encouraged to write to the Yukon Amateur Radio Association, Box 4597, Whitehorse, Y.T. Tell them that a loose moose sent you.

Toys

"This is one of the best love songs I've written — it may be male chauvinistic, I don't know for sure — but I do know I feel this way about some of the most beautiful women I've ever met . . .''

I'd like to take you on a trip
And spend some time with you
Because you make me feel so good
The little things you do.

Chorus:

But we know we're not each other's type
We'd never get along
So let's love the day away, my friend
And make like all nite long.
I'd like to do a thing with you
Rational fun and fine
I'd like to play with all your toys
And you can play with mine.

I've had it to here with those
Intense relationships
Where you tingle to the toenails
With the touch of lips to lips
(But we know . . .)
　　　　　　　　　　　　—banjo jim

yukon natural edibles

I used to walk around through the woods without noticing anything but funny noises in the bushes. My paranoia created bears and wolves and cougars and snakes. After a while, I realized there weren't any snakes in the Yukon, that wolves were unlikely to attack me, that I wasn't far back enough in the bush for lynxes to be around and that I'd be able to hear a bear long before it'd arrived. (I still worry about bears but one of these days I'm going to save up enough money to buy a rifle.)

My release from the fears of the rustlings has freed my eyes to all the lovely plants that grow around; so the first thing you've got to do is open your eyes and look at all these things that are growing as presents for your mental photography files and try to find out a little more about them. I've tried most of the plants and mushrooms that I'm going to talk about, and hopefully your stomach won't react too differently from the way mine did. If you're in doubt about the identification of a plant, check out "Wild, Edible and Poisonous Plants of Alaska" published by the Cooperative Extension Service of the University of Alaska (Publication No. 28) available for only $1.00. It's small and handy to carry in a pack, and identifies the poisonous stuff as well as the edible. Me, I never bother. I eat everything and if it's horrible or makes me sick, I don't try it again.

Shall we start with *dandelions*? My father used to send out to the back yard to practice my golf swing on these poor innocents nesting in the grass; It was only years later that I learned that they could be used and didn't need to be despised.....dandelion wine recipes can be found in any wine-making book.

Most people will have no difficulty identifying this plant when it's in full bloom, but next time you see a dandelion with its yellow moppish crown, check out the structure of the leaves because in spring, the leaves - before the flowers appear - are tender enough to use in salads (and are full of vitamins A,B,C & G). Any later in the year and they're quite bitter. Even in spring, it's best to soak them in salted water for about ½ an hour before cooking or using in salads. The soaking removes some of the bitterness. In the fall, the roots can be dried on your handi-dandi (lion) drying rack set up above the stove and then ground fairly fine and used as a coffee substitute.

The root is the medicinal part of the plant, effective for obstructions of the liver, gall bladder and spleen. It's also good for skin conditions like scurvy and eczema. Drinking the herbal coffee helps get rid of excess mucous in your system...so do yourself a favour, even though the price of coffee has gone down a bit, it's still bloody expensive and the effects of large amounts of caffeine can be nerve wracking.

Fireweed shoots are also pretty good in salads if they're caught before they get big and tough. Look for them in burned over areas or in places where you saw all the purple and scarlet last summer.

While you're in burned places, someone told me that these are good places to seek out the morel, the succulent spring mushroom. *Morels* have sort of scrunched up caps. They look old and wizened even when young, and mycologists assure us that, when cooked in butter, tenderly, gently, and with love and care (mushroom enthusiasts sometimes get out of control), their subtle flavour is unequalled.

Lodgepole pine has an edible cambium layer (inner bark) that can be taken, stripped or scraped off the outer bark and then dried and crushed to make a sort of flour. The little seeds in the pine cones are also edible, and squirrels seem to find them delicious. I've never had the patience to extract very many of these tiny nuts, but just a few added to sweet bannocks contribute texture.

sage

Dandelion.

Well, that pretty well exhausts the spring edibles . . . there are probably more. Oh yeah . . . wild onions . . . I met up with a lovely patch just after three mile riffle on the Thirty Mile. They were growing in flood flats and looked just like garden chives - tubular green stalks with hollow purple heads. If you happen to be passing by there, by all means, pick a few; but don't be too greedy . . . . leave enough so that a few others can pick some and there'll still be enough for the patch not to die. Herb books caution against getting onions confused with Death Camus which also has an onion-like root, but their flowers (when they flower, which is mid-summer) are yellow. Death Camus is extremely poisonous so make sure you know what you're picking and eating.

BERRIES

RASPBERRIES...leaves are good in tea. You should be able to identify these by their taste

MOSS BERRIES...grow in clumps, the leaves are a little like pine needles and are evergreen

DEW BERRIES...like little raspberries, red-purple flower blooms in July, berries in late August

BEARBERRY...edible but not too impressive

WILD STRAWBERRIES...yum, eat as many as you can find

ALPINE or MOUNTAIN or LOW BUSH CRANBERRIES... close to the store-bought cranberries in taste and texture but much tinier

HIGH BUSH CRANBERRIES...sometimes get to six feet high. They taste tart and are red and translucent.

BLACK CURRANT...short bushes, leaves like high bush cranberries taste terrible until processed into jelly or jam

BLUEBERRIES or HUCKLEBERRIES...taste them and if you're immediately inspired to make blueberry pancakes or blueberry and corn-meal muffins, you've found them

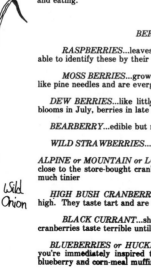

Wild Onion

Moss Berries!

MID-SUMMER STUFF TO EAT

The roots of *clover* are sweet and the leaves may be used for salads. You can partially dry the roots and then smoke them; dipped in warm oil, they make a pleasant addition to dinner.

Yukon sage, while not really something to eat, should be picked in the summer before it flowers. It can be found on clay banks near water and you should be able to identify it by smell; its fragrant odor sort of takes you off to the high deserts. Put it in stews and soups and fish and rabbit dishes, but use it sparingly as it has a much stronger flavour than the stuff you buy at Safeway.

Boletus are good mushrooms for pickling (boil in vinegar and spices); contribute themselves as a delicacy for feasts and sauteed mushroom pig-outs. Instead of having gills, they store their spores in a dense sponge. DON'T eat any boletus that are red-rimmed around the little openings in the spores 'cause they're poison/dangerous/not edible or doubtful. (Ref. Edible and Poisonous Mushrooms of Canada..Agriculture Canada) The older ones, when you press on their orange caps, turn a sort of inky blue-green.

Mushrooms come up after a rain (this'll give you something to look forward to while you're bitching about the weather) and there's nothing like going for a walk on a mushroom hunt, ambling through the damp wood's scent, keeping your eyes trained to the ground, and revealing in the fresh smell of moss and greenery and life.

While I'm muddling around with boletas, I'd like to make a few sort of general comments on mushrooms. First of all, a lot of people have a myopic fear of mycophagy (mean's mushroom eating...I was going to make you look it up in the dictionary, but it felt too pompous throwing around works that I didn't know what they meant until I looked them up this afternoon;. Anyway, to assuage your mycophobia, I'd just like to say that I haven't gotten sick from eating any mushrooms that I've found.

Secondly, mushrooms attract worms when they get older so it's best to cut open every one before cooking. If there are holes in the meat where the stalk joins the cap, throw the whole thing out (unless you don't mind surprises like a bite of worm.....mushrooms have almost no nutritional value....maybe the worms provide some).

orange delicious   shaggy mane   boletus

Some that you can be sure of are puffballs and orange delicious. I've heard stories about the Giant Puffball - mostly from people from Ontario - that grows to a foot across.......but if you're pursuing mushrooms in the Yukon, set your sights a little smaller. *Puff-balls* are small and round and white....they hang around in clusters and sometimes alone. When cooked, they have a slimy texture and a delicate flavour. I like them best when they're tiny, under an inch in diameter.

Never eat puff-balls after they've puffed. Only eat them when they're firm and white and plump. At any other stage of their lives they can make you sick.

Orange delicious' are the same sort of shape as super-market mushrooms when young. As they get older, they start to resemble umbrellas turned inside out by the wind...when they get older, greenish patches appear on the caps. I usually throw the stalks away (except on very small ones) because they're sort of woody or pulpy . . . . orange delicious' can be pale orange to a deeper, almost burnt orange.

Shaggy manes are also good to eat...they have grey caps that look like weathered shake roofs. The stalks are white and the caps have quite a steep slope to their overhang. The overhang extends down over the stalk about two thirds of the length of the stalk. I found some last year right in Whitehorse. They were perched, with a bunch of puff-balls right next to Qwanlin Mall (scratch one item off the grocery list).

Boletus, puff-balls, orange delicious, and shaggy manes are the best eating, there are also some thin-stalked, dark brown capped ones that I've tried but their taste is rather bitter. I don't know what effect they'd have on your stomach if you ate a whole meal of them, but I figure that they can safely be put in a wild mushroom melange. Another one that's okay to use for filler in a whole bunch of varied kinds of mushrooms is the one with the purplish cap, white stalk and a yellow patch at the base of the stalk. They shouldn't be eaten in large quantities, though, because they give some people stomach aches.

DON'T EAT mushrooms that have bright red caps and white stalks or white-capped mushrooms with white stalks and white collars just about one third of the way down from where the stalks join the caps (both of these belong to the amanita family). The red capped ones aren't usually fatal but if prepared properly they'll produce hallucinations. If prepared improperly, you can get *VERY* sick....so if you find some and want to get high, make sure you talk to somebody that's done them before and find out how to prepare them.

YARROW

When viewed from the top it looks like Japanese parasols with their wooden support spokes. These branchy things are topped with hundreds of little white flowers clustered together. They have tough, fibrous stalks that branch quite suddenly to form the network of even smaller branches that bear the flowers. Their leaves are a bit brighter than the brown-green stalk. They wear their feather boa leaves just like the ladies at Rendezvous do, sort of off the shoulder.

The plant sometimes gets more than a couple of feet high and the breadth of their umbrellas is a foot or so. Yarrow can be picked, tied in bunches and dried above the stove....crush some and put it in jars to preserve its freshness. This herb is a handy little item to have around.

My young man once had a tooth-ache. We were out of cloves, which will numb the ache, and in desperation I hit on yarrow. It eases the pain off quite nicely (at least, he wasn't hollering anymore). Drinking yarrow tea - though I don't consider it the best tea I've ever tasted - seems to gently draw fever down...also good for colds and gas. Leftover tea can be used for eye wash (make sure there's no floating stuff in it). The leaves can be used fresh on rashes and cuts, scrapes, and burns...if yer hemorroids are acting up, just pile some yarrow ointment on your piles. Well, I guess we've gone all the way from mouth to ass-hole......proper time to stop. (NOTE: Poison water hemlock could be confused with yarrow, from the description..even though they don't really look the same) to avoid eating this fatally poisonous plant , check the leaves. Yarrow's leaves are like feathers - water hemlocks are also narrow and up to 4 inches long, but they are veined and the edges are toothed. If you still can't tell the difference, split the root and lower stem length wise and check for chambers...water hemlock has them, and they exude a resin-like sticky substance called cicutoxin. The water hemlock has a bulb, and yarrow has roots.)

PLANTAIN

The leaves live close to the ground. They're like flat versions of the onion spires that you see in pictures of Russian churches. The veins are close-set at the white little connector to the root. They sort of swell out, following the curve of the leaf, and then meet back at the tip of the leaf (the same way lengthwise stripes on a stretchy nightie will form fit a fat lady).

The seeds are on a couple of stalks that come up from the centre of the leaf groupings. Culpepper uses the seeds for treatment of epilepsy and yellow jaundice. The Indian herbology book advises that the seeds and stem boiled in milk will check diarrhea in children (if they shit everything out, give them bananas cause it sort of firms up the bowel movement.) I think that the seeds are only there at certain times of year, but in the fall they are for sure.

The leaves can be used externally for burns, boils, scalds, bleeding of wounds and chronic sores. They've got lots of vitamin C and K in them so they're good things to put on the scourge.

You can make an ointment for piles and all the other external uses by boiling the leaves down for a couple of hours in just a little bit of water. You can also use the leaves for salad greens.

HORSETAILS

These plants grow along creeks and roads. You can use them for scouring pots and polishing stuff; sort of acts like fine steel wool.

It's good for your kidneys, so if a few days of hard drinking has made pissing a problem, boil up a tea and drink it. If your feet stink, horsetail has been found to make them a little less offensive.

They look a little like bottle brushes, a single centre stalk with the brush parts coming off at intervals. It's easy to pull the centre stalk apart where the brushy parts join in.

LABRADOR TEA

The dark green leaves of this bush have little rusty hairs on their undersides. The flowers are white or a little pinkish and grow in umbrella-like clusters at the tops of the branches - if you've found one bush, you've prob'ly found hundreds, they like to be near others of their kind and take over a whole area (Riverdalians aren't the only ones to find comfort in numbers).

If you come across a patch while out on a walk, stuff a few leaves in your pockets. (Labrador tea nor Riverdalians). It makes a good bedtime tea because it acts like a sedative......but don't make the tea too strong or you may end up sleeping at the kitchen table. It's also good for coughs, colds and lung infections.

The Indian herbology book says it'll cure bronchitis in two weeks . (1 ounce leaves to 2 pints boiling water...drink as required, a mouthful at a time).

Somebody told me that if you have crabs, you can boil it up into a thick gooey tea and apply it to the affected area (sounds better than kerosene.....although if you have money, Qualada at the drug store is the best sure-fire method to get rid of your unwanted "friends.")

The Russians boil the flowers in fresh butter to make an ointment for skin diseases, bruises, wounds, bleeding and rheumatism. Wash your hair in the tea if you want to clear up severe dandruff.

STRAWBERRY BLIGHT

The leaves of this plant make an acceptable spinach when you've got your wok out and nothing to cook in it. Go for a walk around the neighbourhood and look in open areas - one's that're maybe even a little rocky and look for the deep red fruits that grow along the stalk and up over the top. The red part is edible too, and tastes sort of sweet and juicy. Their leaves are a lot like Lamb's Quarters except they're much broader and the whole plant is much closer to the ground than the Lamb's Quarters.

LAMB'S QUARTERS

They have fruits also but these taste sort of mealy. Their leaves are much smaller than the Strawberry Blight's and are shaped a little like flint arrowheads. This plant is also called Pigweed. It grows fairly tall, up to maybe a couple of feet high, with branches rising off a fairly central stalk. The leaves, when they first come out in the early summer, are sweet and succulent. You can freeze the leaves for later use in salads and soups if you happen to have a freezer. Or dry them and use

labrador tea.

Yarrow

Common Plantain

red

Horsetail

strawberry blight

throughout the winter in soup and stews. Actually, they taste better than store bought spinach.....and are probably better for you too, unless the Territorial Government has taken to spraying the wilderness with whatever southern agribusiness puts all over their crops to protect them from bugs; what's not good enough for bugs isn't usually good enough for you either.

ROSEHIPS

During the summer, you may notice bushes a couple of feet high that bear simple pink flowers (the kind that went with peace symbols a few years back). Keep an eye on these bushes because when fall comes and the wild roses fall off, the fat red berries that remain are the Yukon's answer to high-priced imported fruit as a source of vitamin C (it takes about three rosehips to equal the amount of vitamin C found in one orange and don't let Anita Bryant tell you any different).

They grow along roadways and in the woods.....actually, they're everywhere..Dawson, Mayo, downtown Whitehorse, and all along the Alcan. I like to wait til after a couple of frosts when they're sweeter, riper, redder, and softer, then go out with a five gallon pail and pick (and pick) . . . it usually takes a couple of days. The thorns are fairly non-threatening but do be careful of your hands. Anyhoo, now that you've got five gallons of the little beggars, here are some ways to use them.

Some of them can be strung up (they provide a bit of colour in your house in the winter and you can string them around the tree at Christmas) to be used slowly for tea. To make tea, slip a few off their string and bang them with a hammer a few times, put the squashed berries in a tea-pot, pour in boiling water and let steep.

Others of your five gallons worth can be dried very thoroughly on a drying rack over an air-tight or cookstove (an ex-screen window suspended by string will work) and then ground into a fine powder. Put the powder in sealed containers and use with cereal in the morning to give your oatmeal or Red River a little bit of added flavour. Leave the seeds in for this as they contain vitamin E.

Cut another bunch in half and pull out the seeds and fluff....some of these can be pureed with cranberries and honey, after soaking in hot water for a fair bit of time......some can be pureed by themselves (with honey) and some, after soaking in warm honey, can be dried to just munch during the winter or for use as dried fruit in baking. Grind the seeds up until you can find a use for them.

And the last bunch of rosehips can be put in a big pot with some water, put the pot over a low flame and make sure you keep stirring it because cleaning burnt rosehips off the bottom of your pot will discourage you from doing all this next year.

Cook it for a while, boiling for a long time will remove the vitamin C so keep it just below...allow to boil for just a bit, then put the whole thing in a jelly bag and hang it over another pot for a day or two, giving the bag an occasional affectionate squeeze. Stir in honey and some applesauce and boil quickly and fleetingly. (this boiling is just for sterilization)

Pour into jars and you'll have a jelly or syrup depending (I guess) on luck or your conception of jelly or syrup.

Make sure that ALL the jars you're putting jelly or syrup or puree into are boiled thoroughly because mold likes vitamins just as much as we do. Seal all the preserves with parrafin wax. Put the purees down in the root cellar or out in the cold house or in the refridgerator (don't let them freeze and thaw, though).

One last thing about rosehips is that they freeze-dry on their bushes. If you're sitting inside during the winter and you've got enough firewood cut and you're looking for motivation or an excuse to get off your ass and go for a walk.......well, then go get yourself a visual as well as an edible treat. The red of the berries is so bright and startling beside the stark blue and white of most January days that the sight might add a little warmth to your day.

Rosehips

Free! Extra Information from Beverly

-wild rose petals make a colourful addition to salads and also produce a delicately flavoured tea

-one set of rosehips will make three pots of tea, the second of which is best. Leave the tea-pot brewing on the air-tight to get full flavour from the hips.

-if you throw a handful of rose-hips in the fire (even let them get good and black), it mellows them out, sort of takes the obnoxious green taste away.

-for making puree, mosquito netting is the ideal strainer because it lets the pulp pass (if you squish it) but keeps the seeds behind. If you add butter to the puree, it'll richen and thicken the spread.

-if you add more water to the mush that doesn't make it to the puree, and squish it through the netting for a second pass, it makes excellent pancake syrup. Add honey to sweeten.

-press rosehips together (with honey, if you wish) and let them dry to form nutritious "candy bars" packed with all that lovely vitamin C.

-lou-

uh.... this was going to be the Moose Section & it was here a minute ago.... but, um, I don't quite know how to put this.

I...uh.... LOST THE WHOLE MOOSE SECTION

so you can have 2 parts of Seamus.... and a list of reference books to help you deal with the next few pages.... and a few things that you can eat if you can't find your moose... like birds & rabbits & fish.... and for vegetarians and carnivores in trouble, we have...

Bradford Idiot's
"HOW to SURVIVE in the BUSH on $5 a DAY."

Part XIII

Toby had a cohort by the name of Woody. That wasn't his real name, but it was what Toby called him and everyone else did too. Woody was my next favorite human beside Alex and Toby, who shared the number one spot together. He had cool, and very seldom got really excited about anything. The only thing he liked better than hanging out with me and Toby was hanging out with loose ladies, of which there was always a prospect, though he never mentioned it to "the boys."

It was 1974 and we used to go up on the cliffs and run around. Woody just called me "cheesehound" and knew what I liked. We just hung out together and ran around Whitehorse. From the cliffs you can see all of downtown and all the animals, people and things going on and about. I used to spend a lot of time up there watching dogs do their rounds and people being sneaky. It helped me get around a lot quicker sometimes when the heat was on my tail.

One day we were up playing in the old airport foundations when Woody noticed smoke coming out of the smokestacks of the old river boats down by the rail yards. We had all spent lots of time there messing about and lovers used to go there a lot until the boats become popular, painted and fenced in.

Toby said he thought it was a joke but as we watched, a shaft of flame came soaring out of a smokestack and sirens began in the city. We ran down to the house, they got on ten-speeds, and we raced to the scene. The superstructures of both ships were aflame, pieces crashing down in showers of sparks. It was a sight all right; one I'll never forget. It only lasted about an hour and there was nothing but twisted metal left. Nobody ever seemed to care about those boats until they burned down, then some idiot made a poster of them burning and printed "end of an era" on it.

Part XIV

One of the more sinful parts of Whitehorse was the YWCA. Toby and Alex and most of their friends who came from the south stayed in the apartment there when they first hit town. For them it was easy living in decent surroundings, lots of ladies, lots of ladies and lots of ladies. When they no longer lived there it was still a good place to go to get laid and they used to use it quite frequently.

Toby used to use me frequently too. I didn't really mind but sometimes I'd split. What he did was clean up his act, the house, the yard and me and together we'd go to the Y. Under cover of a newspaper, he would spot a lady going out and it wasn't hard to tell what she was about before she hit the bar. Well that creep would "meet" them downtown by having me suck up to them, engage them in conversation, entice them for a walk on the cliffs and home to bed.

I must admit he did it well but he used me, so I'm ratting out on him because he's a creep.

"HOME BOOK OF SMOKE COOKING", Jack Sleight and Raymond Hull, 1975

Pyramid Books of New York, 161 pp. This very usable pocketbook is an excellent introduction to the arts of saving meat by not only smoking but also by salting, canning, making sausages, head cheese and dry curing. The sausage recipes sound particularly good. $1.50

"No man who is lost in the bush need starve if he has the Niggerhead at hand. More needless tragedies than can be told might have been averted if those in peril had known of the endless nutritional benefits of this much-denigrated plant. Yet a cross-section of it reveals a veritable corni-copia of good things to eat. The Northern Indians have always known of this course, and must have shaken their heads in pity or amusement at the distain whitemen who would sooner starve than partake at Nature's table. No more common and complete offering could she give, not even in the lushest tropical grove.

It can be eaten in a variety of ways, none requiring much preparation. For those too hungry, or without proper utensils, the plant may simply be loped off, the dirt beaten out of it against a convenient tree, and then eaten raw. My own favorite method is to skin the plant (this being a necessity in the larger, older plants whose exteriors are rather leathery) and cut it into thin strips lengthwise, laying these on a hot sizzling pan after rolling them in a mixture of milk and breadcrumbs. These same sort of strips, when dried in the sun, make an incomparable hiking food when passing through non-Niggerhead country. A whole Niggerhead, when thoroughly dried and then tenderized with a club provides, when its powdery interior is drained, a superlative flour, especially for gravies and pastries."

—Bradford Idiot

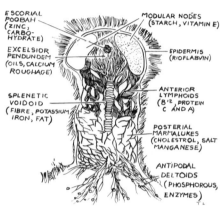

ESCORIAL POOBAH (ZINC, CARBO-HYDRATE)

MODULAR NODES (STARCH, VITAMIN E)

EXCELSIOR PENDUNDEM (OILS, CALCIUM ROUGHAGE)

EPIDERMIS (RIOFLABVIN)

SPLENETIC VOIDOID (FIBRE, POTASSIUM, IRON, FAT)

ANTERIOR LYMPHOIDS (B12, PROTEIN C AND A)

POSTERIAL MARMALUKES (CHOLESTROL, SALT MANGANESE)

ANTIPODAL DELTOIDS (PHOSPHOROUS, ENZYMES)

"IF I'M TRAVELLIN' IN NIGGERHEAD COUNTRY I NEVER BOTHER TAKIN' FOOD. JUST AN AXE TO CUT FIREWOOD AND A KNIFE TO CUT UP 'HEADS. WE BEEN EATIN' 'EM FOR GENERATIONS IN OUR FAMILY. PRACTICALLY LIVED ON THE BUGGERS IN HARD TIMES. SAVED MY LIFE A COUPLE TIMES TOO. ONCE, IN THE KOREAN DISPUTE I INADVERTENTLY PARACHUTED BEHIND ENEMY LINES, WALKED ALL THE 200 MILES BACK TO OUR SIDE OVER THEM THINGS, BUT THEY KEPT ME GOIN'."

—REMINISCENCES OF YUKON SLIM

A Solution to the world food problem?
— BS

John Lodder '78

"THE ALASKAN CAMP COOK", Alaska Magazine, 1962, Alaska Northwest Pub., 84 pp.

Here's a sample from this interesting cookbook, telling how to cook the part of the moose that whitemen usually throw away but Indians never do.

"Cut upper jawbone of moose just below the eyes. Put in large kettle of scalding water and parboil 45 minutes. Remove and cool in cold water. Pick off the hairs as you would feathers from a duck (the boiling loosens them), and wash thoroughly.

"Put moose nose in fresh water with onion, a little garlic and pickling spices. Boil gently until tender. Cool overnight in same juice.

"In the morning, remove bone and cartilage. The bulb of the nose is white meat, the thin strips along the bone and jowls dark. Slice the meat thin, pack in jars or cans, and cover with the juice. This jells, and when chilled it can be sliced. Serve cold. The meat of the nose may be pickled in vinegar if desired." *by Bertha Meier, Anchorage*

This collection of recipes used to cost $2 but probably is three times that now.

"PUTTING FOOD BY", By Ruth Hertzberg, Beatrice Vaughan and Janet Greene. 368 pages. The Stephen Greene Press, Brattleboro, Vermont, U.S.A. 05301, 1973.

Tells all about canning, freezing, the preserving kettle, drying, root-cellaring, curing, "the roundup" (a section of procedures not in other sections) and recipes.

The person who has it is still using it. Finds it very useful because it gives four or five alternatives for preserving food, other than freezing. "You probably couldn't find a more complete reference on the subject of storage," says Organic Gardening and Farming.

"EDIBLE AND POISONOUS MUSHROOMS OF CANADA", by J. Walter Groves of Agriculture Canada, Queen's Publication number A43-1112 Price $9.75

This is a good back-up manual for double-checking your field results. The are hundreds of colour photographs in the three hundred plus pages of technically-written information. Much of the data for identifying the individual species is in very scientific language but if you dig far enough each term is explained somewhere in the book. And the frontispiece painting of Aminita caesarea is beautiful and lends one to think that there might be hope for Agriculture Canada after all.

"NORTHERN COOKBOOK", Eleanor Ellis, 1967, Queen's Printer, 350 pp.

Certainly the most complete cookbook and nutrition guide yet published for northerners. The instructions are simple and easy to follow, designed to be used by people for whom English might be their second language and who may be more familiar with cooking over campfire coals than electric ranges. Recipes range from fried muskrat and boiled lynx to sourdough bread and cranberry muffins. The book abounds with good advice on caring for meat, furs, fish, fowl and even gives hints on saving fuel bills and what clothing to wear when hunting. A must for any northerner's kitchen. About $4.00

"THE TASSAJARA BREAD BOOK", By Edward Espe Brown, 1970. 14 printings 146 pages. $4.05 in Whse.

Published by Shambhala Publications Inc., 2045 Frisco St., Berkeley, Calif., U.S.A. 94709

A very compassionate approach to bread-making. Details health-wise information on all types of ingredients, stressing nutritional, taste and texture values.

"TEN TALENTS", Frank Hurd, and Rosalie Hurd., 354 pages. Published by themselves, Box 86A, Route 1, Chisholm, Minnesota. 55719, in 1968. Was $7.95 then.

Not everyday stuff for most people but useful. A lot of basic things. Really stresses nutrition. Philosophy of eating taken from the Bible. All natural foods. Good for vegetarians. No meat recipies, few with milk, cheese and eggs. Even has natural ice cream recipes, including "Eskimo ice cream". Also shows different ways of cooking.

"THE YUKON COOKBOOK" has all kinds of recipes using wild food with an illustrated section about plants and berries and mushrooms.

There is also an excellant book called *"ALASKA WILD MUSHROOMS"* or something similar. You will recognize it by its lovely pen-&-ink and water colour drawings....very helpful for identification.

BENT BRENT'S WILD BIRD STEW

Take a bottle of cheep red wine...you're allowed to drink half of it. Use the other half to marinate 2-4 grouse overnight. Put in whatever vegetables you have on hand and let simmer until everything's cooked....don't bring it to a boil or you'll lose all the alcohol.

TOILETTE BONNET McDOUFF'S OLD CROW MOOSE RECIPE:

Put large pieces of moose meat in a pot with water and a few spruce needles. Add salt if you like. Boil over a campfire until meat starts to fall apart. Eat.

food

BRAISING GAME BIRDS

One of the best ways to cook ducks, grouse, or any other bird is braising, or cooking with moist heat. First brown the bird in fat over fairly high heat. You can dip the meat in flour or spices before you brown it if you prefer. Then cut up some carrots and onions in very fine strips and cook in a little fat until wilted. Again if you have a preference for an extra flavour you can add in another vegetable, such as parsnips, leeks, celery or turnip to the wilted cooked vegetables. Sit the bird on top of a little nest of these vegetables and add a little water if you have some, add a little white wine or sherry. Put on a lid and simmer until the bird is done, which might take an hour or more.

CREAM SOUP

Put some butter in a pot. Let it melt slowly then take from the heat and mix in flour until the mixture is like mealy heavy cream. Add powdered milk and water and/or canned milk.

Put it back on a low heat and stir pretty steadily, thin with water, or milk. Add mushrooms that you've found in the woods or wild onions or strawberry spinach or canned asparagus or something fresh from the garden. Bacon's a nice additive, potatoes for extra thickness, whatever spices seem appropriate....good soup!

froski the snow-woman

PERHOGIES

Boil up a pot of potatoes...while they're boiling, find a bowl and put some white flour and a bit of oil in it....mix the two as much as they'll mix then add water until you have a flexible dough, one that will stretch quite a bit before tearing.

Put another pot of water on to boil and take the potatoes off the heat (provided they're cooked). Drain them (if you like, save the potato water for soup stock).

Put a bunch of torn-up, cut-up or just plain squished cheese in with the potatoes. I usually use cheddar or something else with an inoffensive flavour...but if you like being offended, by all means use gorgonzola or limburger. Put a couple of dollops of butter or margarine in, too, and mash it all together. Other addible edibles include pickled beets, sauerkraut, green onions, parsley or any cooked meats.

Go back to the dough and pinch a small ball off the main blob...press the ball flat...you may need to put a little flour on it so it doesn't stick to your hands. Working it with your fingers, gradually stretch the one inch ball into a disc about three inches in diameter. If you get holes in your disc, pinch them, being careful not to create new holes. Try not to tear the dough.

Put a plop of the potatoe mixture in the centre of the disc, then fold the dough around it (be careful not to tear the dough or its guts will leak out and you'll be left with a cooked, empty skin of dough.) Anyway , fold the dough in half around the potato blob and pinch the semi-circle closed so that its contents are sealed into it. Drop the little guy into the pot of now boiling water. Start on the next one and the one after and the one after that.

They're done when the perhogies float to the top. Serve them basking in sour cream (fresh or dehydrated kind) or smothered in a sauce of melted butter, onions, parsley and mushrooms.

kiz

How many times have you sat by a campfire and eaten canned beans and variations thereof...

How many times have you been forced out of the comfortable warmth of a winter's cabin by the smell of your own methane?

Beans

1 lb. dried navy beans
¼-½ lb. dried salt pork
½ tablespoon salt
2 tablespoons brown sugar

Wash beans, cover with water and leave overnight. Add salt and simmer until tender. Drain and save the liquid. Layer the beans with saltpork and put the sugar on top.
Add:
-1 onion
-2 to 4 tablespoons molasses
-1 teaspoon dry mustard, some pepper, and ¼ cup vinegar
-¼ cup maple syrup and a dash of worstershire sauce.
Line a shallow pit with coals....put the dutch oven in the pit for 6-8 hours. Add saved liquid whenever the beans get too dry.

excerpt from eric's bush book

RABBIT

The finest feed I've ever had on same-day rabbit was in northern Quebec where two young Quebecois showed me the secret. Prepare a big pot of baked beans from scratch, soaking the beans, and adding the onions and molasses and tomatoes and spices and baking until about two hours before ready. Then lay out the rabbit, right in the middle of all the beans, then finish cooking. The rabbit meat will fall off the bones when done and you'll have to be careful about the little sharp bones, but the rabbit gives a lovely flavour to the beans and vice versa.

sylvain and jacques

CURRIED GRAYLING

A nice change from traditional ways of serving grayling, and easy to prepare with a minimum of ingredients in the bush.

Ingredients

Lots of curry powder (to your taste)
Whole milk powder (or skim, if you prefer the taste)
Peanut butter, canned regular butter, a few onions or wild leeks
Salt, pepper, and whatever else you have

Fry up a bunch . . . more fish, more sauce. Fry the curry with butter in a hot pan. Add the onions to the pan and brown them, being careful not to scorch the curry. Have a pot of rice cooking in advance so that it will be ready when the sauce is done. Make up a quantity of milk powder balancing it so that it does not kill any of the curry-onion flavor. Just add more curry after warming the milk if it is too weak.

When this mixture is at the boil, add filletted grayling or halfed grayling, cover and simmer for a short period . . . you are actually poaching the fish in the sauce, so it will not take too long, especially in the case of fillets.

Peanut butter in a small quantity, can be forked into the sauce before the fish goes in adding its own special flavour. When the flesh of the fish separates easily, remove bones and serve the fish with the rice, utilizing the sauce as gravy for the fish or rice, or both.

—Peter Carr

Courtesy of University of Alaska.	Moisture %	Food Energy (Calories)	Protein Gms	Fat Gms	Calcium Mg[1]	Phosphate Mg	Iron Mg	A Values II[2]	Thiamin Mg	Riboflavin Mg	Niacin
Beef, Good Grade-66% Lean, 34% fat	54.7	323	16.5	28	10	152	2.5	60	.07	.150	4.0
Caribou, raw flesh	70.0	120	27.2	1.2	18	280	2.9	187	.182	.520	4.7
Moose, raw flesh	72.4	123	25.1	2.5	10	219	2.7	650	.074	.027	5.0
Moose, liver	73.5			4.3				96,000			
Reindeer, raw flesh	70.1	117	26.6	1.2	16	280	2.9	187	.186	.770	4.7
Bear, black, raw flesh	71.2	148	18.6	8.2	3	139	6.1	261	.160	.680	3.2
Bear, polar, raw flesh	70.3	130	25.6	3.1	17	40	6.1	1,400	.023	.573	4.0
Beaver, raw flesh	46.2	408	14.3	39	15	262	5.9	176	.061	.310	1.9
Beluga, raw flesh	72.5	107	24.5	0.5	7	270	26.6	335	.070	.400	6.8
Muskrat (Marsh Hare), raw flesh	73.4	101	22.4	1.3	25	220	7.6	2,820	.095	.372	6.2
Oil, salad or cooking	0	884	0	100.0	0	0	0	0	0	0	0
Oogruk, raw flesh	69.6	110	26.7	0.4	10	199	11.6	1,400	.168	.267	5.9
Rabbit, raw flesh (wild)	73.0	129	21.0	5.0	12	226	3.2		.030	.060	6.5
Seal, raw flesh	67.8	143	28.3	33.0	17	245	19.8	1,050	.135	.452	7.0
Seal, liver, raw flesh	74.2	115	18.0	3.2	13	285	13.7	36,600	.180	3.020	8.4
Seal, oil	0	900						4,860			
Squirrel, ground, raw flesh	75.4	115	10.1	3.8	2	168	4.5	220	.095	.372	6.2
Walrus	65.1	200	19.2	13.6	18	122	9.4	550	.180	.346	3.2
Whale, Baleen	73.0	110	23.9	1.6	17	212	14.0	330	.138	.550	7.4

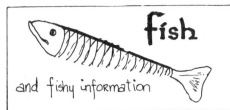

fish

and fishy information

To set a gillnet in a backeddy, stretch the net out on the shore and tie down the shore end securely. Then, use your boat to pull the net out straight and drop the anchoring weight. If properly set, the float-line should stay right on the border between the eddy and the current or reach across the eddy out to the current. You can use the plastic motor oil containers for floats and, if you can't get leaded line for holding the net down, you can use chain tied every foot or so.

If the fish are for Peoplefood as opposed to Dogfood, you should check the net twice a day. To check a net in an eddy, bring your boat from downstream up to the last float and, standing in the bow, check the net over the awayfrom-shore gunwale, moving along the net towards the shore. Try not to pull on the weighted end of the net or you will move the weight in.

Another method of setting a gillnet in a back-eddy involves using a long pole, long enough to reach out to the edge of the current. Stretch the net out on the shore and tie the shore end securely. Then tie the end of the float-line to the small end of the pole and push the pole straight out to the edge of the current. The anchor weight won't be as far out as if you use a boat to pull it out, and it shouldn't be too heavy, just enough to keep the net hanging down. Then you have to pile rocks on the shore-end of the pole to keep it straight out from shore. To check this type of set you pull in the pole.

AN INDIAN METHOD FOR CUTTING FISH TO HANG

To cut up a fish so you can hang it over a pole to dry, don't cut off the head and gut it right away. Instead, make your first cut along the fish's back, and cut down until you get to the spine. Then keep cutting down the outside of the rib-bones on each side, but don't cut through the belly skin. Do this all the way to the tail but don't cut it off either. If you are good, you can skim out all the flesh on the head, too. Finally, make a cut on the throat and you should be able to lift the entire head and back-bone up and you can push all the guts away into a pail for the dogfeed.

Now you can wash it all off and hang it over a pole with the head and backbone on one side and all the meat on the other so it sort of balances with the tail like a hinge. If the fish meat is thick, you have to make lots of cuts in it so the air gets to all the meat.

So that the meat doesn't all curl up together, cut a little stick and take the bark off it, and sharpen one end. Make maybe four holes in the meat and weave that stick in and out through these holes to keep it flat. To keep the blow-flies away, make a smokey fire under the poles, but not so big a fire so that the fish cook, only enough for keeping those flies and bugs away. If you find some little eggs get laid on the fish, just flick them off with your knife.

— f. m.

FISHING NETS

The Fisheries people in Whitehorse have been buying their nets form John Redden Net Co., 1645 West Third Ave., Vancouver, V6J 1K1. A five inch mesh gillnet hung to 8 feet deep by fifty feet long is $49.20. Another fishing supplies house is John Leckie Ltd., 14519 - 121 A Avenue, Edmonton, Alta., T5L 2T2.

Ice Fishing in the Yukon

Other Suggestions

Don't give that Ling Cod away if it is all you caught while ice fishing the other day. For its liver alone, the cod is to be cherished; that flavour rarely exists in a fresh water fish.

And due to a tremendous amount of public demand, I'm not going to include my recipe for Garlic Pizza in this catalogue.

peter truckk

SMOKED GRAYLING

1 part coarse salt
2 parts brown sugar

Moisten with grapefruit juice. Rub the fish down thoroughly with the mixture. Drain overnight on a slanted rack. Smoke until done, approx. 12 hours. Use leafy tree wood chips (poplar, willow).

karen kostiuck

Canning Salmon

"Canning" your salmon usually means storing the fish in glass mason jars rather than in tin cans. An advantage to canning fish is the availability of the calcium from the bones of these canned fish. The long processing time makes the bones easily eaten and digestible.

It is possible to store in cans but you need special equipment. For home canning in jars, you will need the following things:
1. a pressure cooker with a gauge or a gauge weight on it
2. glass jars with rings
3. new lids
4. salt
5. hot soapy water
6. a pot or pan of boiling hot water
7. a scrub brush

First thing to do is wash all the jars and rings and the cooker in hot soapy water and rinse them off. Don't get the gauge wet. If a jar is chipped, you can't use it. If a ring is bent or rusty, don't use it either. Boil the lids and the jars in a pot or pan of water while you are cutting the fish.

Cutting boards and utensils should be kept clean to prevent bacteria build-up. This is done with plenty of clean water, a scrub brush and elbow grease. When your cutting board becomes too slippery for safe working, throw on a handful of salt and scrub it down.

Take the jars out and put them upside-down on a clean cloth to cool a bit so you can handle them, but leave the lids in the water until you are going to use them.

Put a little salt in each jar and then fill up the jar with salmon to within one inch from the top. Some people like to put the fish in the jars so that the skin is towards the outside, but it doesn't really matter how you cut up or arrange the fish.

Don't put any water in the jars because the fish make lots of their own juice. Wipe the rim of the jar, then put a lid on it with the rubber-side down, then a ring over that and tighten it. Put the full jars onto the rack in the cooker and pour 1½ quarts of hot water into the cooker.

When the cooker is full or there is no more fish, close the cooker and lock the lid. Put it on the heat. Turn up the heat until steam shoots straight up for seven minutes or more. Then put the gauge-weight on the hole, set at "10." Keep the stove hot enough so that some steam hisses or bubbles out around the gauge-weight all the time. If you have a gauge, you want it to read "10" or more all the time. Cook for two hours. If the steam stops completely, you have to start again to cook it for two hours.

RED'S PICKLED TROUT

2 cups vinegar, ½ cup oil, 1 cup water, handful pickling spice, 1 tablespoon sugar, 1 tablespoon salt, some lemons.

Bring the above to a boil, let cool. Bake your trout (or pike or grayling or whatever), then in some sort of jars with good lids (airtight) start layering the fish with alternate layers of onion and lemon. When the jars are ½ to ¾ full add the pickling recipe. Let them marinate for 24 hours, then serve. Delicious, 'eh?

Notice: Smoked mice for sale . . . lake trout bait for those big, deep Lurking Lunkers . . . satisfaction guaranteed . . . also a handy treat for the family pet. Bag of 50, cold smoked, assorted sizes and colors $29.95. Save on 300 lot, just $110. Contact P.O. Box 4185 Whitehorse Y.T.

STORING EGGS
1. Coat with a thin layer of mineral oil, drain well, place in containers in a cool, dark place.
2. Freezing: Eggs must be removed from shells before freezing. For short periods shelled eggs may be frozen individually in ice cube trays, then packaged and stored. Usually they are separated before freezing. Pack eggs in quantities needed for a single use. WHOLE EGGS: Break eggs into bowl; beat slightly with fork
   1 cup thawed whole egg equal 5 eggs
   3 Tbsp. thawed whole egg equals 1 egg
EGG YOLKS: Beat slightly. Add 1 tsp. sugar or corn syrup to 6 yolks if to be used for making cakes and puddings. Add ½ tsp. salt to 6 yolks for other uses.
   1 Tbsp. thawed egg yolk equals 1 egg yolk
EGG WHITES: Pack without beating
   1½ Tbsp. thawed egg white equals 1 egg white

3. Water-glassing: Dilute sodium silicate with boiling water in a crock. Cool. Immerse eggs in water-glass with pointed ends down. May be kept 8 to 9 months.
muffy

Canning salmon, continued....

After the two hours, remove the cooker from the heat and take off the gauge-weight. Open the cooker carefully, holding the lid on an angle so the steam doesn't come towards you and burn you. With a mitt, take out the jars and put them on the counter to cool. Don't tighten the rings. As the jars cool down, they make a noise when the lids seal.

When they are cool, test for good sealing:

The lids should be sucked down and not loose or humped up. You can see the lid is curved down and also feel it. If you tap the lids slightly with a spoon when cold, you'll hear a clear, ringing sound if all right. If you hear a clunk, that jar didn't work so you should eat that jar of fish right away and not keep it until winter.

Leave the jars to cool all night. In the morning, take the rings off and wash and dry them, so they don't get rusty. If you aren't going to take the jars anyplace you don't have to put the rings on again. Put the jars into their case and store in the cellar.

When you go to open a jar after a few months, check the seal again to see that the lid is still down and makes a ringing noise when tapped. If the seal is bad, throw the fish away. Don't eat it! To open, make a small hole in the centre of the lid with your knife. Then the lid will lift off easily. Throw the lid away.

Some people are tremendously worried about botulism poisoning, so they suggest that you can cook or boil the salmon for ten minutes before tasting or eating.

If you want to "can" moose meat or bear meat in your jars, it takes one hour and thirty minutes of cooking with the gauge-weight set at "10."

If you want to experiment, you can add a little garlic or onion or vinegar or spices to your fish and meat before canning, but remember that our salmon has a very subtle flavour, so don't overdo it.
— *agnes drew* —

GREEN TOMATO RELISH

Mix:
   2 qts. chopped green tomatoes
   2 chopped green peppers
   2 cups chopped onion
   1 pint mild vinegar
   ¼ cup salt
   3 cups sugar
   ½ cup mixed pickling spices [in a cheese cloth bag]

Bring to a boil and cook slowly for 30 minutes or more, stirring occasionally. Remove the spice bag. Makes 4 pints.

pat batchelor

As long as you KEEP your canned goods frozen, they will be okay. It is thawing and freezing repeatedly which harms them.

CANNED SMOKED SALMON

Pack smoked salmon in sterilized jars. To each pint jar add:

   1 small tbsp. vinegar
   ½ tsp. salt
   1 tsp. oil

Process in a pressure cooker for 100 minutes at 10 lbs. pressure.

pat batchelor

TIPS FOR GAME MEAT

For rendering moose fat for lard, add the fat to a pot of boiling water. As the fat is rendered it will float and can be laddled out and poured through a sieve into molds. What is left in the sieve resembles pork rinds and, if fried, is delicious.

Freezing game animals (the meat-eaters, like bear) suspect of carrying trichinosis for twenty days at five degrees fahrenheit for a six-inch piece will kill tricina larvae.

"Shot" meat, where the bullet struck the animal, can be saved by soaking it in cold water with two teaspoons of salt and two of soda. Change the water a few times over the next few days as it gets bloody.

Liver which won't keep too long can be used to make Liverwurst or Liver sausage.

CURING WITH SALT 🧂

Adapted by Agnes from the University of Alaska, Co-operative Extension Service pamphlet F-41, "The Hunter Returns After the Kill." Reprinted with permission.

The basic solution is the same for salting or brining. For each 100 lb. of meat, use 7 lb. of coarse or dairy salt (not iodized), two pounds of sugar (or use honey), and two ounces of saltpeter. The saltpeter is not essential, but preserves color. Sugar helps tenderize and mellows the flavor; the salt does all the curing.

Dry salting is said to be faster and produces a tasty product, with better keeping qualities than brining. However, brining is recommended for regions of extremely dry or cold climate which naturally dehydrates the meat. Throughout either process, the meat should be between 34 degrees and 40 degrees fahrenheit. Higher temperatures may cause spoilage; freezing will interrupt the curing. Trim off any crust and slice the meat into thick slabs.

EQUIPMENT

Crocks and wooden barrels may be used. (Do not use metal containers, lids, or weights in brining or salting.) A clean wooden lid to fit inside the container and a stone or heavy object will be needed to hold the meat under the brine. If salting, it is better to use a container with holes in the bottom for draining excess fluid.

DRY SALTING

Mix the basic ingredients thoroughly. Rub one third of this into the chunks or slabs of meat. Pack the pieces in the containers, and keep in a cool place for three days. On the third day, remove the meat from the crock and rub in half of the remaining salt mixture. Replace the chunks in the reverse order, with bottom pieces now on top (called "overhauling the pack"). After seven more days repeat with the remaining mixture and let stand until cured.

For thick pieces of meat (3 or more inches through), allow 1½ days per pound total time. Minimum time is ten days. Liquid will collect as the salt draws moisture from the meat and should be drained off through the holes in the bottom of the container.

For variety, one recipe suggests a mixture of two cups of pickling spice, two dozen cloves of garlic, two ounces of coriander seed and several dried red peppers be added to the basic hundred pound formula of salt, sugar, and saltpeter.

BRINE

Game meat may be quick-cured in a sweet-pickle solution which takes 28 days. Fit the chilled, smoothly trimmed cuts into a clean wooden barrel or crock. Using the basic formula make a brine with 4½ gallons of water for each 100 pounds of meat.

The water used for making the curing pickle should be pure. Heat the purified water to boiling, add the curing ingredients, and stir until ingredients are dissolved. Skim the surface and let the solution cool to 40 degrees before pouring it over the packed meat. Cover the meat completely, and weight it down. If any of the meat rises out the brine, the entire cure may spoil quickly.

Overhaul the pack about the seventh day, reversing the order. Cover again with the same mixture, unless it has begun to spoil. (See following directions for overhauling). The curing time for the larger, thicker pieces, is 3½ days per pound, and proportionately less for smaller pieces, but with a minimum curing time for all cuts of 28 days.

Overhauling Brine Solutions: Watch the meat in a brine solution closely. If at any time the sweet-pickle corning solution turns sour, ropy, or syrupy, throw it away. Scald the barrel, lid and weights. Scrub the meat in hot water, and rechill it. Repack the meat and cover it with a new chilled solution. Use 5½ gallons of pure water per 100 pounds of meat to make the new solution instead of the 4½ gallons recommended for the first, and complete the curing schedule.

PREPARING [freshening] CURED MEAT

Soak the meat in fresh cool water for several hours, then discard the water before cooking. If it is still too salty, repeat.

STORING CURED MEAT

Remove meat as soon as it is thoroughly cured, then soak in fresh water for two hours. Starting with smaller pieces, remove and scrub with a stiff-bristled brush. Hang in a dry place to thoroughly drip dry.

Roll the pieces in spices if you wish and wrap well in cheesecloth, then tightly with paper. It can be stored up to a year in a dry, cool, dark and well-ventilated spot. If some mould forms, wipe it off with a vinegar-soaked cloth.

Putting Something By

canning, curing, storing eggs next page: jams, jellies, practical cuts, cheese cottage slicer and reconstituting things

NORM'S MARROW SOUP

This is an excellent trail food, prepared in advance at home. We had some on the Carcross-Atlin mail run and only a small potful filled three hungry mushers. I coerced the formula out of Norm Rudolph by feeding him moose steaks. He says that the Indians and the Eskimos always ate bone marrow and they know what's good for them...

Go to the butcher's and ask for cut dog bones. Put all the bones into a big pot, simmer for about three hours, then the marrow will have cooked out.

Remove the bones, add some salted water if desired and cubed spuds, rice, barley, salt and pepper, onions, carrots and parsnips cut in small pieces.

Braise some meat (moose, beef, or whatever) and add it in, too. Let simmer over night, then leave it to cool. Put it into plastic margerine tubs or buy new tubs from the butcher or put it into boilable plastic bags. Freeze.
-b.b.

Never discard any bear fat. Black bear fat is the best fat possible for making pie crusts and donuts. This grease is also an excellent waterproofing compound for your boots.

PRACTICAL CUTS

When preparing a quantity of carrots right out of the garden for canning, pickling or freezing, in lieu of washing and scraping each carrot I simply fill my Hoover spin dry with water and pour in a pail of carrots. Two three-minute cycles leaves them perfectly clean and the tender skins don't need any peeling or scraping. This procedure also knocks off all the roots that may be still on the carrots when you pull them. A wringer washer also does the job quite satisfactorily.

NEW POTATOES OUT OF THE GARDEN

Put the potatoes in a pail and fill with water. Take a broom handle and stir vigorously. Change the water and repeat and rinse clean. A pail of potatoes should take no longer than 10 minutes, and no scraping is necessary.

TO SHELL PEAS

Blanch your pods for one minute in boiling water, then in a wringer washer remove the agitator and put a pail over the centre spindle. Spread a sheet or table cloth over the tub. Hold the sheet there or pin it up with ropes and cloth-pegs (to prevent the peas from flying all over). Now feed the pods through the wringer, pod stem first. The sheet should be arranged so that the peas will go on it and the pods will drop into the tub. Since the peas have already been blanched they will be ready for freezing or canning. A simple fun procedure if you've shelled peas for eight hours like I have.

PICKLE JUICE

Rather than waste your pickle juice after the pickles are gone, simply boil eggs and put them in this juice; keep refrigerated for six to eight weeks, then leave sit for a week to gain a mildly pickled taste. You could also add fresh dill, garlic or pickling spice to this. This method can also be applied to the juice from pickled beets, and gives your eggs a lovely color, but don't add anything else.

The juice from pickled carrots will also do, but then again it's not necessary to add anything else, but, by all means feel free to experiment.

And keeping an eye towards not wasting anything, don't throw away your ends of old soap bars. Simply put them in an old jar and mix or stir occasionally, with warm water. When your jar is full, boil it down and pour into various containers or lids. The color and scent of your new bars are delightful and they certainly beat anything you buy at the store.

Instead of using the old method of putting a plate and pet rock to cover your kraut, use a strong plastic bag full of water over it. This will eliminate the problem of regular skimming by providing an airtight seal over the bowl of kraut.

Good Luck and Good Use,
—Marjorie

Quantity Cabbage Cutting (for Sauerkraut)

OPERATION: PLACE QUARTERED CABBAGE IN HOLDING BOX AND SLIDE BOX BACK AND FORTH OVER KNIFE; AS CABBAGE WORKS ITS WAY DOWN USE BUILT-UP BLOCK TO FEED IT DOWNWARDS.

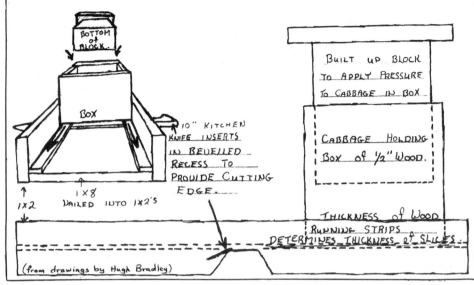

(from drawings by Hugh Bradley)

Jams and Jellies

Anita Tolway makes the jams and jellies that are sold at Curry's at Tagish. When I got to her place, she had just finished sorting leaves out of buckets of huckle-berries (what some people call blueberries). The way to do this is to pour the berries slowly from one bucket to another. The wind catches the leaves and they fly off.

She uses Certo for most of her jellies and finds that the black currant recipe works fine for huckleberry or mossberry jelly...for high bush cranberries use the raspberry jelly recipe.

And from the pulp left inside the jelly bag, she makes a cranberry ketchup that goes well with wild meats or really any meat:

Mash the pulp through a collander to remove seeds. Cook up the de-seeded pulp.

4 cups of pulp
½ cup vinegar
2 cups white sugar
cloves, cinnamon, and nutmeg to taste.

Boil it up and bottle in sterilized ketchup jars.

If you want to make low bush cranberry sauce for the Christmas turkey, wash and measure 4 cups cranberries and add 4 cups of sugar (if you want it a little more jellied and less saucy, use 5 cups of sugar). Put in enough water to almost cover the berries. Cook until it's sauce and put in sterilized jars. Seal with paraffin.

Put some slices of cheddar cheese into your oat meal, the extra fat will keep you warm till lunch.

TREATING CHEESE
A Practical Method for the Bush or Canoe Trip

This method has been used for a number of years using cheddar, Farmer's, and similar types of hard cheeses ranging from very mild to sharp, and will keep the cheese in good shape for weeks and in some cases, where cool storage conditions are possible, for months.

The cheese should be in good condition to begin with and, ideally, free from mold. Any visible mold means the cheese may be far too along for preserving in this way and should be used immediately. Cut the cheese into portions that will be used in a day or two. Wipe the surface clean with a rag wet with cider vinegar which will work wonders in retarding mold formation. Then wrap each portion in its own blanket of cheese cloth (available at some markets or in quantity at a yard goods shop) and dip this covered cheese in a pot of melted parrafin wax. This parrafin wax (available in expensive small packages, or in blocks from stores catering to the hobbyist or home preserver) should not be too hot, well short of smoking. If brought to the melt and held there so it does not get too cool or too hot it will coat the cheese nicely — giving an airtight protected environment.

Dip all the cheese once, then a second time after the first dipping has firmed up. That will usually be enough to protect the cheese for an extended period of time. You can avoid leaving it in the open sunlight and when possible store it free from heat and crushing. After you have used the cheese, the cheese cloth makes an excellent and long burning fire starter.

—Peter Carr,
Carcross Road

MAKING DO WITH WHAT YOU GOT

If you use a recipe book, they'll often call for ingredients that you don't have. This can be especially frustrating if the store is 50 miles away! So here are some substitutes

- 1½ t. corn-starch = 1 T. flour

- 1 cup whole milk = ½ cup canned + ½ cup H₂O
  or 1 cup reconstituted dry + 2 T. butter

- 1 oz. unsweetened chocolate = 3 T. cocoa + 1 T. fat.

- 1 cup honey = 1¼ cup sugar + ¼ cup liquid

in cakes, 1 T vinegar equals for 2 eggs

- 1 t. baking powder = 2 t. creme of tartar + 1 t. soda + ½ t. salt.

oil or meat drippings or lard can be used instead of butter... only use 80% of what is called for.

If you mix powdered skim milk up at a ratio of about 2:1 instead of 3:1 as the directions read, it tastes much better.

Canned Milk

can be used for making sour cream

1 cup canned milk + 1 T. vinegar let stand until it sours & thickens

or for butter, by shaking evaporated milk in a larger jar until it separates.

Rendering.

Remove all tissue from fat... cut up fat & heat slowly in a cast iron pot with a little fat in it. when the fat is liquid, strain through cheese cloth.

... EGGS AGAIN...

POWDERED EGGS
-One egg in a recipe equals 1 Tbsp. egg powder plus 3 Tbsp. water. Either mix and add to recipe; or add egg powder to dry ingredients and water to liquid ingredients.
-Scrambled eggs: 3 to 1 to 1 - (water to egg powder to milk powder)
OR
1 to 1 -(water to egg powder)

THE ADVENTURES OF OSCAR OZONE

As incredible as it might seem, Oscar found himself in a situation for which even he did not instantly have a counter move. Having travelled for four hours by dog team over mountains and glacier to escape the riotous atmosphere of Whitehorse, to Atlin, a small recluse in northern B.C., he came face to face with his all time arch enemy — Rufus Wreckneck — in the form of a bent coathanger. However, he quickly detected this ruse. Instantly he manhandled this intruder, out the door of the cabin whereupon he pounced upon it thrice, and shot it through the heart.

Breathing a sigh of relief, he quickly closed the door, for it was still winter, sat down and lit the pipe. After a pause, he remarked to his companion, a Huskie of course, that it was too bad about what happened to Oscar's brother, Orville Ozone who, after experiencing some powerful rushes, changed himself into a snowflake and blew away.

All of a sudden, the windows shook, the carpet heaved and the walls rippled. Oscar instantly turned into a wastepaperbasket and went under the table. Rufus Wreckneck, after welding himself together, emerged a shapely bobbypin that thrust deep into the gums of a shapely brunette in the corner of the bed.

She woke up without a struggle, letting the blood float into Oscar's abused ear. The sound was incredible, like a sperm screeching and wailing through the caverns of life, onto motherhood, fatherhood and much abuse.

"I have seen the light!" he said in a surprised move.

"How much is a ticket?" the zombie replied.

"It is cheap," the man with the back pocket admitted, as he smiled quietly to himself.

Rome, the eternal city. Sold down the river by a deprived, disgusting bowling ball team from the bottlers of coca cola (who really knew where it was at, in the beginning) and a management team from the Worldwide Church of God.

Aqualungs all over town switched on and honking wildly cruised into Trapper's Cafe, demanding Tootsie Roll Crumbles, the sweetheart of the Discovery gold fields. Two little ones formed a human tire and rolled to and fro around the room, shouting first world war noises and beating time on their gonads with pop bottles to the beat of Mr. and Mrs. Rural America from Alaska. Oscar swallowed the trash in his basket and turned into a Hoover vacuum cleaner but, having no wall sockets available, plugged himself consistently into the cracks in the logs.

Screaming "bust this!" Rufus, masquerading as a shrubbery, subtlely went into seclusion down south drawing pictures of the sand and the sea by the froggy lemon underground, wah dee do dah.

At this point, Mrs. Ozone briskly opened the door to his room and said, "Why aren't you working instead of being a lazy bum?" At this point, he put a gun to his head and blew his brains out.

At this point, Mrs. Ozone briskly opened the door to his room and said, "Why did you blow your brains out?"

"I don't know," he said. "But I sure got a rush."

On the other end of town, events were brewing that, no doubt, would severely effect the outcome of this entire facade. Little known to Captain Paslow (who wouldn't tell his captors a thing), the Ozones were apparently in difficulty, but, in actuality, on their true course of destiny.

True love and mad neighbours in urban settings lay ahead. This didn't mean a thing to Paslow, who was trying to catch fish in a little lake by the seaside. Only Paslow knew something was, indeed, not right. Tearing off his undershorts and stuffing them down the throats of young kissypoos, he leaped off the ledge into the dark night. A right. A left. Another right, and into the Ozone Layer.

He panted; he told himself he shouldn't be in that frame of mind and did a quicky number. "Atlin Fun Days," he thought to himself. "If only it could be here now, like it was, and as it will be."

Moving right along now, he thought he saw Oscar on the edge of the power meter, about to dive onto Rufus, who was posing as a comfy chair. With a scream, "I want it," he leaped onto the soft folds of the chair, past the dirt and into the stuffing, clutching at dust and bellybutton lint from a hundred Atlin parties.

Paslow thought fast and faded into obscurity in a pair of socks, hanging on the side of the chair. Rufus realized readily the ruckus that was about to ensue, and calling out Cherokee Cheerleader songs, he changed his batteries, enclosing Oscar in obscurity.

The clock stopped. For a moment, it seemed as though nothing was going to happen. In the national emergency and bureaucracy deadfoot center, twits ate their shoes and otherwise babbled mindlessly at the crisis. Paslow did not hesitate. Eying a virgin thumbtack in the corner under a couch near the switch that controls the sword rack in the dungeon's fourth floor, the mastermind of Mount Fuji beer and land magnate in central southeastern corner of Ezone, ripped from his socks scene and leapt through six dimensions to the towering bronzed toes of local heroes — which were located somewhere undefinable, but real enough to be believed.

Not believing his eyes, he closed them spun and spun out a cosmic cry of despair. Ozone saw the logic of the scheme. He wasted no time into taking control of the garden out back, concentrating mainly on the potatoes. They watched the commercial together, condemning it in howls of derisive gaiety.

Thinking fast, twenty heartbeats in time, a little piece of damaged merchandise spoke in myriad patterns and asked a question: "Why is a mouse?" parted the air waves to Oscar's mangled mind.

The answer, forthcoming but holding back, was back to back in a commercial concentration centering crudely around the garden. His attention wavering in the heat of the reaction, he wasted no time in going to the dance.

(See Appendum)
appendum (after the ride back):
Raw Purple Destruction, or
Have Another
And Seamus didn't even bat an eye.

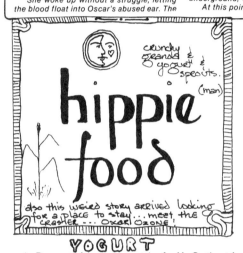

crunchy granola & yogurt & sprouts.
(man)

hippie food

also this weeird story arrived looking for a place to stay...meet the crasher... Oscar Ozone!

YOGURT

1. Buy some plain, pure yogurt (preferably Continental or another brand that has no preservatives in it) at a store to use as a starter. A commercial yogurt culture may be used but they are expensive.

2. Heat homo, 2%, or skim milk at *medium* heat until it forms a thick white foamy layer on top and steam rises from it, (i.e. just barely boiling - 180 F). An advantage to using powdered milk is that you can heat the water first, then add the powder so you don't have to worry about burning the milk. For a thicker, creamier yogurt use extra skim powder (i.e. ⅓ to ½ cup powder to 1 cup of water) or try adding a can of evaporated milk for extra richness.

3. Now remove from heat and let cool until LUKEWARM test milk on inside of wrist till it no longer feels hot. Another test is to stick your little finger in it and leave it there, if it feels hot (but no so hot that you finally have to remove your finger) that is the right temperature. With a thermometer, try for 112 to 120 degrees F.)

4. Place a Tbsp. of yogurt starter in the bottom of a thermos or in the bottom of each glass jar (with sealer lid) that you use. (Run warm water over jars if they are cold.)

5. Slowly pour lukewarm milk into the jars or thermos, stirring gently, mix yogurt starter thoroughly.

6. Store in a warm place - an oven with the pilot light left on for heat (it can be preheated to 200 degrees F beforehand and let cool), - or wrap it in a sleeping bag. If you are using the thermos bottle method, it doesn't need to be put in an oven or wrapped up.

7. Let sit undisturbed for 5 to 10 hours...5 for mild yogurt, 10 for bitter.

8. Refrigerate immediately until set before opening the jars. (With thermos, empty contents out and thoroughly cool them, then you can store it back in the thermos.)

9. Add fruit and nuts or whatever to yogurt but keep about ½ cup plain for use as starter for next time.

-Too much starter added will make your yogurt watery, not creamier

-An old starter will also make yogurt watery. Your starter should be no more than a week old.

-If you use the warming oven of your cookstove to store yogurt in while growing, make sure temperatures don't exceed 110 degrees F.

-If you let the milk cool too much, just reheat the milk and let cool again till lukewarm.

Like sourdough, the more often you make batches, the sweeter the results.

muffy, n.b. and b.b.

GRANOLA

4 cups rolled oats
1½ cups unsweetened coconut
1 cup sunflower seeds
½ cup sesame seeds
½ cup flax seed
1 cup or more of chopped nuts, cashews, walnuts, peanuts (unsalted), almonds etc.
1 cup pumpkin seeds

Mix the above ingredients in a very large bowl (or pot or pail or dish basin or whatever). Heat together: ½ cup oil and ½ cup honey. Remove from heat and add ½ tsp. vanilla. Add to dry mixture.

Bake in a shallow pan in a moderate oven until lightly and crunchily brown, stirring occasionally. While still warm add raisins. Cool before stirring. Chopped dried fruit may be added but I've found they are best added just before serving, otherwise the mixture becomes too moist in storage and is no longer crunchy.

Bran and wheat germ may also be added to dry mixture. Granola is especially delicious served with home-made yogurt and stewed Yukon rhubarb.

-Granola stays crunchier if kept in a cool space.

-The proportions of dry ingredients added don't really matter, you can leave out the wheat germ if you run out, you can add more sunflower seeds and less sesame seeds, you can substitute oat meal for oats.

-Also good in granola is buck wheat, cinnamon and nutmeg. Honey or molasses drizzled on over the mixture in the last stages of baking is good too, but they make the granola sticky and the pans hard to clean. [That's why it's important to add the wheat germ after cooking.]

-I put granola on porridge or with cereal, on fruit, on pancakes with honey, or on peanut-butter and honey [or peanut butter, honey and banana] sandwiches.

---

muffy

"bird"

some things that'll sprout.

mung beans
Radish seeds
soya beans
alfalfa
lentils
wheat

& lots more, too

EXPERIMENT!

SPROUTS

SPROUTS ARE WONDERFUL [and exciting]

If you feel in need of fresh greens and don't live close enough to the grocery store to buy the kind that're imported from California . . . whaddaya do?

Use Wonderful Sprouts — which are three-day instant greens. Just add water and drain twice a day for a couple of days. Use mung beans or alfalfa seeds.

BANNOCK

In its simplest form it is:
- flour
- baking powder
- water
- dash of salt

Use about a teaspoon of baking powder for every cup of flour. Mix in Water until the whole thing hold together. Fry in a pan with quite a bit of lard

If you want to get a little fancier, try Eric's.
- flour (whole wheat and graham)
- sugar (not much)
- 1 egg if it's around
- raisins
- milk powder
- enough cinnamon
- baking powder

Bake slowly in a covered (if possible) cast-iron pan beside fire or over low coals until light brown all over. Make sure you use sufficient lard in your pan.

You can add berries or applesauce to the fancier bannock and maybe a bit of grease right in the bannock and you have fried cake.

Stick Bannock

Make a bowl-like depression in your sack of flour. Add a pinch of salt, 2 teaspoons of baking powder and 1 cup of water. Stir until the dough forms a stiff ball. Roll and stretch out into a rope about 12 inches long. Wind around a stick and bake over a campfire coals, turning the stick as each side bakes.

uncle bill

BUTTERMILK BANNOCK

Buttermilk Powder can be bought by the can in the supermarket. Mary says that it freshens up old eggs and makes the powdered kind taste a little more realistic. (Refer to the can for mixing directions - see the Putting Something By part of the food section for reconstituting eggs.) Here's a recipe using your new-found knowledge about buttermilk powder:

An alternative bannock recipe - a little more expensive but moister:
1 cup whole wheat flour
1 cup white flour
½ teaspoon baking soda
1 teaspoon salt
1 tablespoon sugar
1 cup buttermilk
1 egg
Bake in oil or lots of margarine just like bannock.

w.l.

DUMPLING BANNOCK

Drop spoonfuls of bannock dough into boiling stew about 15 minutes before serving. Weigh the lid down with stones, if necessary, to ensure a tight fit.

mathilde

CAMPFIRE BAKING

(The most uncomplicated method for a happy baking session)

For best results (and a lighter backpack) use a light frying pan with a concave lid - nonstick bottom preferably. Whatever, you need a shallow dish with a tight fitting lid.

Get a good fire going while you are creating cake batter, cinnamon buns, cookies...When you are ready to bake be sure to have shovelfulls of loose, small sized hot coals at hand. With a shovel, or even a large spoon, sprinkle enough hot ashes and coals on the ground to fit evenly under the bottom of your baking pan. Sprinkle coals on the lid of your dish also.

The perfect temperature for baking can be tested by holding your hand over the sprinkled coals - you should be able to hold it there for ten seconds before having to draw it away - if you can hold your hand there for longer the coals are not hot enough.

You will have to change the coals every 7-10 minutes - which should be a delicate operation. Total baking time for each baked good is surprisingly parallel to that of its regular oven time.

a.w.

OTHER USES FOR BREAD DOUGH:

You can make DONUTS by deep-frying the bread dough.

You can make CINNAMON BUNS by taking bread dough, rolling it out to about an inch or less thick and putting sugar, butter, cinnamon and raisins all over the top of the rolled-out dough and then rolling it up...cut slices off and bake by whatever method is available to you.

BUNS - cut off sizable hunks and roll them into balls...put them in a big pan and bake or slow fry or steam.

If you are a real bread freak, check out the Tassajara Bread Book for additional recipes and ways to prepare bread.

BREAD without BAKING

I used to think that a cookstove was the answer, I mean, a person could really get creative with an oven...every time I thought about the store-boughten expanded cardboard that they call bread, it was oh, if only I had a cookstove....

For a while a cookstove was an obsession...I lusted after one, I even thought of stealing one...but in the end, I just adapted.

You can bake bread (if you're not too picky about a crusty crust) on a campfire or a coleman stove or an airtight.

For doing it, you'll need a big pot with a lid - a cast iron dutch oven works just fine...really any big pot with a lid and unburnable handles works...a bread bowl helps...and you'll need a pot or tincans or breadpans that fit into the big pot with the lid.

O.K., heat up some water to a little past body temperature. Put about ½ cup of it in a cup...add a tablespoon of honey or a tablespoon and a little more of sugar in the water, then put in a tablespoon of yeast in the sugared water.

Let it sit for about ten minutes (if it's cold out, sit the cup a little ways from the fire, so it stays around body temperature) while the yeast is sitting, put a cup or a cupanahalf of water (warm to hot) in a bowl, add powdered milk until it looks like milk, put in some sugar if you want, and a couple of tablespoons of oil (this should produce 2 or 3 rather large pools of oil slick shimmering from the surface of the milk).

Interjection - if you use real milk, it should be scalded before using for bread because the bacteria in the milk will prevent the yeast from rising...new yeast is the best to use but if your yeast is old, using a little more will usually be satisfactory.

(If your ten minutes isn't up, put the big pot, described a couple of paragraphs back, on the airtight/stove/fire with a few inches of water in it...put the lid on.)

When the ten minutes is up, stir up the yeast and the sugar and the water, then dump it into the bowl. Dump in some flour (a bit of brown and a bit of white - it's pretty heavy anyway so it's advisable not to use all brown, and all

white would be horrible.) Stir with a spoon or paddle...be gentle, try not to tear the dough.

When you've stirred in enough flour (*enough flour* means that you can put in your hands and they won't come out of the bowl covered with goo) put in some more flour and work it in by folding the dough into itself. Put some flour on a board or a piece of paper on the ground and turn the dough out onto it...with your hands, keep folding and pressing down, then folding, pressing round and round until it feels good - not too squishy and not too dry.

Pour some grease into the smaller pot/pan/can. Fold all the edges of the bread into the centre...turn it over and it should have a baby's bum soft and smooth texture. Put the smooth to the bottom of the pot and move it around so that it gets good and greased. Then take it out and turn it the other way round so that your fingerholds are on the bottom and the smooth side's on top.

For cans, grease the can thoroughly...roll the dough into cylinders that're a couple of inches shorter than the cans...grease the top.

Find an old tunafish tin...cut both ends out and wash it. Put it in boiling water in the big pot, the water and the tuna fish can should be about the same height. Put the pot/pan/can on top of one of the open ends of the tunafish tube...put the lid on...

Wait....go peel a log or cut some wood or read. Keep checking your fire and the water level of the pot and add more if it's getting low...when you eventually get tired of waiting take the tuna tube out and let the bread pan sit right on the bottom of the pot.

The bread is done when the top feels firm....take the lid off so the top can dry out a bit. This is an especially crucial time to watch the water level.

When you're so hungry you can't stand it anymore, take the pan out of the pot, turn the bread out the pan and eat...if you can't afford canned butter (to be really decadent), lard with a sprinkling of salt on it works o.k. (and might even fool your tastebuds if you close your eyes.)

If you're compulsive about things having names, this stuff is called shuffle (from souflee but with its sound heavier and deadened). It's a derivation of b'au, a Chinese steamed rice-bread with meat and sauce in the middle (yum) (cook the meat with sweet and sour sauce) (made with vinegar, soya sauce, honey or sugar or molasses, ketchup or tomato sauce, cornstarch and a bit of lemon in whatever proportion seems sensible to you, then wrap the bread dough around the meat and sauce and steam til done.)

lou

Page 44

CORN JOHNNY CAKES

-1 qt. yellow cornmeal
-1 pt. flour
-½ cup sugar
-1 teaspoon salt
-4 teaspoons baking soda

Mix with water and let stand for ten minutes - do not stir after letting it sit. Drip in a hot pan and turn it over *after* the top has started to set. Dried currants are good additions.

b.

RED RIVER MUFFINS

These are excellent for cold weather — like oatmeal, they stick with you:

In a saucepan combine 1 cup milk, ¼ cup shortening, ¾ cup raw red river. Bring all this to a boil and cook for one minute, make sure you stir it so it doesn't burn to the bottom. Let it cool a bit. Sift together 1 1/3 cups of flour, 4 teaspoons of baking powder, 1 teaspoon of salt, ½ teaspoon of cinnamon and a ¼ teaspoon of nutmeg into a bowl. Stir in ½ cup of raisins and a ½ cup of brown sugar. Blend in cereal mixture with 2 eggs. Stir only until moistened. Fill the greased muffin pans two-thirds full. Bake in a hot oven [400 degrees] for 20 to 25 minutes.

[This recipe was contributed by the Red River box in the kitchen.] Don't worry about the muffins freezing in your pack, because there's enough grease in them to be able to always bite into them.

Molasses Buns

No cabin should be without a crock of molasses for the winter season. It won't spoil, can be frozen and thawed repeatedly, and adds a tang to any recipe. Here's molasses buns instructions the way the Newfoundlanders like them:

Preheat oven to 400 degrees F, then sift together 4½ cups white flour, ¼ teaspoon salt, 3 teaspoons baking soda and ¼ teaspoon allspice.
- Melt together ⅔ cups each of butter and shortening. Stir in 2 tablespoons brown sugar and one cup molasses. Mix together and stir in a cup of raisins and two tablespoons of flour.

Then blend in one cup warm water and add the dry ingredients. Turn dough onto a lightly floured surface and knead gently 8 to 10 times. Roll or pat ½ inch thick. Cut with floured cutter.

Bake on ungreased baking sheet in preheated 400 degree oven for 12 to 15 minutes or until browned. Serve with butter. Makes about forty 2-inch buns.

Newf

APPLE SAUCE MUFFINS

Here's a recipe for when people suddenly arrive and you don't have enough munchies to immediately feed them.

½ cup oil
1 cup sugar
¾ of a teaspoon of salt
½ teaspoon of soda
½ teaspoon of baking powder
1½ cups flour
½ cup applesauce
½ teaspoon nutmeg
½ teaspoon cinnamon
1 teaspoon all-spice

Put it all in your mixing bowl and mix well. Bake in muffin pans or cake pans or over a low heat in frying pan.

mary

Honey is a great favourite with any one I've gone camping with but it is a lot easier to transport if you can buy it early and allow it to solidify in the container. If you must have runny honey, put the honey pot in a pan of warm water on the lowest heat and the honey will gradually liquify.

A sackful of rolled oats will stretch the food dollars and help keep you warm. Porridge in the morning sticks to your ribs, oatmeal muffins in your lunch, oatmeal in the bread, you can make oatmeal soap, feed your dog cooked oats mixed with his other food, and who could forget oatmeal-chocolate cookies? Maybe buy TWO sacks.

COOKIES

Cookies are tasty but time-consuming. Sometimes the wait only increases the pleasure found in the finished project. So I'll share with you the secrets of chocolate chip sweet baby bannocks. If you don't have the patience to wait for them to cook, you can always eat the dough (wonder if raw cookie dough really does give ye worms....or is it just what mom used to say to keep grubby, greedy fingers out of the mixing bowl?)

Put about a ½ cup of lard in a bowl, mash in an equal amount of brown sugar until it's blended and creamy. If you've got two fresh eggs, beat them into the sugarandlard. If not, find a small bowl and reconstitute 2 eggs worth of powdered eggs.....beat them for a while before adding to the sugarandlard.

When all are mixed together and beated to a slight frothiness, put in flour and baking powder...add yer chocolate chips, nuts, raisins or whatever.

Get your frying pan warmed up and put in a good dollop of butter or oil. Divide the dough into good-size cookies and arrange in the frying pan. I don't press them down...they're lovely when they're big and plump and free. Leave them sit on a low heat for a long time. The top of a damped down airtight is perfect, a camp-stove turned down to absolute minumim is o.k., but an open fire is only for people who have some experience managing a fire.

Whichever way is available to you, you'll have to re-position the cookies so ~~that the~~ ones that are cooking faster get a slower heat for a while, and the ones that aren't cooking can take the others' place.

If you don't particularly care for chocolate chips or have none on hand, make peanut butter cookies (glob in some peanut butter with the sugar and lard and eggs), or spice and raisin cookies (cinnamon, nutmeg, and ginger in with the flour), or currant and cornmeal cookies (use a little cornmeal in with the flour) or whatever you think might be nice.

By changing the proportions slightly, excellant slow-fried sweet breads and cakes can be made. You can also steam cakes and they'll have a moist, heavy puddingish sort of texture.

If you follow these trains of ingredients, you may not get a perfect computer designed cake or cookie but hopefully you will have fun experimenting, playing with taste and texture until you arrive at your own method or producing the Ultimate cookie.

lou

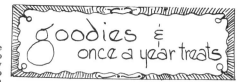

goodies & once a year treats

THREE-OF-A-KIND SHERBERT

3 oranges
3 lemons
3 bananas
3 cups sugar
3 cups water
3 egg whites

Dissolve sugar in hot water add juice of lemons and oranges and the mashed bananas. Freeze until mushy. Add three whites beaten stiffly, fold in gently and continue freezing. Serves sixteen.

pat batchelor

SNOW ICE CREAM

2 cups powdered whole milk
1 teaspoon vanilla
¼ cup honey
¼ cup light cooking oil
1 cup water (approx.)
1 bucket clean fluffy snow

Place powdered milk in large bowl and make a well in centre. Add honey, oil, and vanilla and enough water to make a thick paste without lumps. Continue to add water as you stir, a little at a time, until the mixture has the consistency of thick pancake batter. Fold in the snow a few cups at a time until the ice cream has the consistency and taste you like. Be careful not to add too much snow or the ice cream will be too weak.

muffy

Blowing It (heh heh)

I once had the experience of working with a person who in his own words "knew what the score was" as far as explosives were concerned. Now I myself am no stranger to explosives, though I have no permit, having worked with explosives underground as well as on surface.

At the time we were blasting some stumps off a friend's property, and doing not a bad job of it. Well we came upon this old stump that looked pretty strong, but one thing we didn't know was that the bottom was rotted right out of it, and that which wasn't rotted was eaten out and carried away by certain nameless critters. So we put about 8 sticks under the old thing when we should have put half that, set the fuse and took off for hiding. Well we blew that stump clear out of the ground, right over our heads, and it landed not 20 feet from where we were hiding.

We were well covered, being behind this boulder that was enough to keep the both of us in the clear. I tell you I took one look at that stump, shattered and torn as it was, and it was the ugliest thing I had ever seen. I got up and commenced to yelling and screaming at my partner there, and he did the same to me. So after we finished our screaming we went over to the hole where the stump used to be, and she must have been four foot deep and as much across. We grabbed a couple of shovels and started to fill in the hole when my buddy who hired us to do the blasting comes over and wants to know how come we don't know how to blast properly. Well I told him in short time what he could do with his goddamn stumps, and what he could do with himself.

YIKES!!

So anyways he settled down a bit and told us to go back and blow away a couple more. So that's what we did. And sure enough, we ran across this stump just like the last, so I figured well maybe four sticks this time. Well I tell you that stump didn't move the slightest. We walked over to it, cursed it up and down, then set another charge. Six sticks this time and all we got was a little wiggle out of it. So I figured what the hell let's blow the hell out of it, and hide good. We were about 50 feet away from our last problem stump, so I set 9 sticks under it, lit the fuse and took off. Well that second charge must have loosened her good 'cause with the third charge she took off flying and landed smack dab on top of the other flying stump.

Well that was it for that day. We went straight to the bar and stayed put for two days and, you know, nobody believed us, so we went back there two days later and that son of a bitch had gone and cleared all that land and still nobody believes us.

Mars Bonfire II

PREPARING the LAND

blasting without injury or incident

"Blasters' Handbook" is the bible of the blasting trade, available for $12 plus shipping charges from the Edmonton Office of C.I.L. at 10262-108th Street. It includes sections on blasting stumps and boulders, seismic prospecting, and loads of other uses including "tunnelling" for those of you who weren't in on the fun of the Aishihik hydro project, and "pipeline river crossings" for those of you who want a preview of the next fiasco. With over five hundred pages of concise explanations, diagrams and black-and-white photos, one can hardly help but be impressed by the importance of explosives for practical purposes in this modern world. But how come nobody in the pictures is smiling?

Anyone wishing to do a little blasting should also write to the Explosives Division, Department of Energy, Mines and Resources, Ottawa, K1A 0E4 for their handout booklets which give the latest up date on the Explosives Act and the standards you must follow. Included are detailed diagrams of how explosives are stored and the usual security methods employed. But what I like the best is the advice: "Don't smoke when handling explosives. If you do wish to give up smoking, try a less drastic measure."

STUMP REMOVAL

Just to give an example of the costs and work involved in blasting a few stumps on your land, we quote from the C.I.L. "Blasters' Handbook" on page 357:

One of the quickest and most economical ways of removing stumps is to blast them out. Blasting is most effective in moist firm soil, and not so satisfactory in dry, sandy ground. Green stumps which have a large mass of small tendril roots interwoven with the soil, usually require charges at least twice as large as dead or rotten stumps. Small stumps can normally be best removed by mechanical equipment. Medium sized stumps can usually be blasted out clean at low cost, while exceptionally large stumps, particularly if they are green, normally require a combination of blasting to first loosen and split them, followed by mechanical pulling."

After a brief explanation of where to auger your holes and insert the charges under the stump, the handbook tells you that:

"Under average conditions from one-half to two-thirds of a cartridge should be used for each inch of diameter of the stump, measured at a distance of one foot above the ground . . . Heavy soils such as clay are best for stump blasting because in sandy loam, sand, gravel or loose soils, much of the effect of the explosion is lost. If possible, work should be carried out when the ground is wet, since water tends to increase the effectiveness of the charge, particularly in the lighter types of soil." (pages 358-9)

The cartridge referred to is POLAR stumping powder, 1¼" by 8". So, a green 12" stump in firm, dense soil would need six or seven charges. The cost for dynamite of this sort if purchased in small quantities would be $90 for a case of 145 sticks with fuses.

This means a cost of about $5 per stump.

To carry out the blasting yourself, you will have to obtain a permit from the Mining Inspector (200 Range Road, WHSE). If you've no personal experience yourself you will have to find somebody who does. They will have to submit to an oral exam, the outcome of which is the decision of the mining inspector. Also you will need a permit to carry out the blasting in your particular area.

Both permits are free, and the blasting permit is good for 90 days.

THE ROTO-TILLER

The concensus from the homesteaders and small acreage gardeners that I contacted was that small tillers are useless. They'll jamb on roots, stall in loose gravel and generally self-destruct within a season. The advice, especially for those breaking new ground, is to buy (or get ahold of in some other way) a life-time, powerful tiller such as a "Troy-Bilt."

This machine is billed as a roto-tiller/power composter and will cost you a month's wages, but will allow you to expand that garden for another few bushels of spuds and buckets of peas. Write for the catalogue, and they'll send you lots of info. Discounts for purchases before April 1. Write to:

Garden Way Manufacturing Co.
Dept. 89013
102 St. and Ninth Avenue
TROY, New York, U.S.A. 12180

No Canadian distributor of these products is known. If you can't afford to buy a decent tiller, we suggest you check the rental agencies in Whitehorse and your local store. In each community there is someone who will do your tilling for you for about $15 per hour, or might lend it to you. Just ask around.

"using dogs to generate food, instead of just shooting them to eat."
— anon., Benson Ck, Y.T.

Farming in the Yukon

The first "farming" other than the berry-picking done by Indians was Robert Campbell's venture in 1853 at Fort Selkirk. He had one cow. When the Chilcat Indians burned his trading fort, he snowshoed out of the territory but no one knows what happened to the cow.

By 1875 a thousand prospectors were stomping all over the Upper Liard River Basin and three years later the coastal passes were crossed by about 80 gold-seekers. The trading posts that served them grew gardens and no doubt many of these sourdoughs had cabin vegetable plots, also. Ogilvie Island had noted success.

Then came the gold rush. To feed the open-mouthed masses, thousands of acres of land on the river islands and creek valleys near Dawson were cleared and seeded. Vast quantities of vegetables and forage were raised on farms as far away as Thistle Creek. As the riverboat traffic developed, wood-cutting operations, small towns, mines, telegraph stations, missions, mountie posts and homesteads all sprang up along the rivers. Now the Yukon River, the Stewart, the White, the Pelly — practically every river — had settlers of some sort on the largest islands and major creeks. Most grew at least their own lettuce, rhubarb and root crops. Hay was harvested for the 200 horses pulling the overland stage from railhead at Whitehorse and timothy grass was imported as a supplement.

In 1915 the Dominion Department of Agriculture began to conduct co-operative experiments with interested individuals and two years later established an experimental substation at Swede Creek, one of the gold rush farms. They reported, when closing after eight years of tests, that results confirmed "that a variety of crops can be grown successfully at Latitude 64 degrees North and that yields and quality of the produce compare favourably with those obtained in other parts of Canada a thousand miles to the south." This would not be the last government report to comment favourably on the agricultural potential of the territory.

Throughout the nineteen-twenties, farming was a going concern in many areas: the Dawson area boasted pigs, chickens, cattle for beef and some sheep; one large ranch in the Indian River valley produced 100 to 150 tons of hay annually; Mayo grew "potatoes and root crop almost sufficient to supply the local consumption;" and at Carcross, crops and cattle raised supplied local needs with the Residential School "heavily engaged in farming." By 1931, 41 farms remained.

During the Depression, people — many of them from the prairies — trickled into the Yukon in search of self-sufficiency. Gold mining would always pay wages here even if there were major economic problems in the south. With pennies scarce, home gardening was a way of life. The Yukon's big war-time boom of Canol pipe-laying and Alcan road construction meant local pigs ate better swill from the Army's camps and also connected us with the Peace River area. In 1944, the Dominion Agriculture boys were back, selecting land for a full-fledged experimental farm. They blew it, picking 800 virgin acres at Mile 1019 (Haines Junction).

Not only was the altitude 2,000 feet above sea level, but the summer winds blew cold off the glaciers, and early frosts plagued the area. Still, 23 years of crops (from 1946 to 1968) convinced the workers: "beef cattle found to winter satisfactorily if provided with high-board fences or open-faced sheds for shelter" . . . pigs need protein supplements, too expensive . . . predators worried the shepherds . . . oats and barley grew fine . . . and chickens did well if heated during winter. The farm's early research technique was shaky but in the end it was an inter-government power struggle that closed the operation, not poor results. The Agriculture department and Northern Affairs could not get along, so northern farming research was shifted to Alberta, at Beaverlodge.

Meanwhile, an exploratory soil survey of lands immediately adjacent to the Alcan and parts of the Yukon River to Dawson had estimated there was at least half a million acres of arable land. In 1961, the census counted 222 cattle as residing in the territory.

The same year the 1019 farm closed, D. W. Carr's government report was released. It was a quickie, with little new or profound to say: "farming will probably never be as significant again" as during the gold rush . . . outfitters should control the winter grazing of their pack-horses "remove them as a public hazard from the highways" . . . "should be at least a minimum of appropriate public services provided" . . . "extension and technical advisory services, including advice on veterinary matters, information and guidance in financing and such" . . . "part-time or hobby gardening will continue to have an important place." He suggested trying greenhouses.

Incidentally, Carr, in an accompanying volume, predicted the native will depend less on hunting and fishing as their education and incomes improve. Another shot-in-the-dark missed when he decided trapping "has been declining and will continue to decline in the future." Marten were five dollars then, muskrat were under two and lynx was moving between four and thirty-seven bucks. It didn't matter; no one acted on anything he said anyway.

Then a few of the chiefs started petitioning the federal government for some sort of treaty or land claim settlement. Everyone freaked out when they realized that the Yukon wasn't even legally whiteman's land. The Indians were sidetracked by quick-talking lawyers and well-intentioned liberals and the long process of negotiation began. After a few years, the local land office was told to cut down on agricultural leases-with-option-to-buy. There was a quick scramble as every civil servant and friend of one staked their land and filed. Then it all stopped. No more land. (Unless you had good connections or knew a loop-hole, that is.) (Then the loop-holes were plugged . . .) Land freeze.

Dawson /03

The reason given was "need for a study." So when in 1975, R. W. Peake and Associated reported that the only area with sufficient data was the Takhini-Dezadeash region and that "within this area the first agricultural development should proceed." The department responded by announcing two more studies. Peake had recommended an advisory service, subsidized veterinary service, farm credit, federally-directed applied research and "land be made available to an agricultural development council for agricultural development." Ottawa paid no attention because it had to wait for a land settlement with the Indians to release any crown land.

Farmers and potential farmers lobbied for services and land through the Yukon Agriculture and Livestock Association. The territorial government adopted an "it's not my fault — ask them" approach and tried to be everyone's friend. No one wanted to be their friend.

Meanwhile, agri-experts were helicoptering, driving, boating, and hiking all over the territory. They visited working farmers and lots of useless ones as well. To their great credit, they listened to a few northerners and were shown some good areas. Temporary weather stations, soil samples, polaroid photos, many handful-of-dirt estimations and tons of paper later, two reports were issued.

F. J. Eley and B. F. Findlay authored the first, "Agro-climatic Capability of Southern Portions of the Y.T. and Mackenzie District, N.W.T." and said: "The work reported here must be considered of reconnaissance nature . . . of limited accuracy . . . a first approximation." They suggest no areas can grow fruit trees and that narrow bands along most major rivers can grow cool season vegetables, forage crops, barley and oats. Also the Liard Valley and near Watson Lake are suitable climatically for farming. Other areas are "marginal" economically.

Rostad, Kozak, and Acton with eight others mapped the "soil capability for agriculture" and "grazing capability" over vast acres and prepared "potential for agricultural development" summaries. They identified 63,201 hectares of Class 3 and 4 soil capability (cool season vegies, foraging, barley, oats) and 20 times that much useless land. Similarly they delineated 32,053 hectares for grazing and 221,479 hectares marginal grazing land.

"There is a potential for livestock production or market gardening in certain areas . . ." Also feasible are milk, honey, swine, poultry and eggs, sheep and rapeseed production, all with some limitations . . . They claim that it is lack of over-all heat (low growing degree day heat units) that limits the northern extension of agriculture, more than the short frost-free period. Forages and garden crops would benefit from supplemental irrigation in most years; a rather high incidence of soils very low in potassium, and so on.

Areas have thus been mapped for potential development, and although there are major omissions such as the river islands, the government now has its report and will have to invent new excuses for not releasing land, or have to settle with the Indians. It was not hard for a loop-hole (or battering ram) to be found to allow the proposed pipeline through Indian-claimed land. American consumers, it would seem, are more important than aspiring farmers or Indians.

Much of the historical information in this overview came from the R. W. Peake report, Government of the Y.T., 1975. For any discussion of soils and grazing, as well as general information on farming, we suggest the $18 Rostad-Kozak-Acton, Saskatchewan Institute of Pedology Publications — S174, 1977. The Eley-Findlay agroclimatic capability study mentioned is Project Report No. 33, 1977, Department of Fisheries and the Environment, Meterological Applications and Consultation Division (unpublished manuscript). And forget about the Carr report — everyone already has.

—a. d.

STATION	LAT.	LONG.	HEIGHT (FEET ABOVE M.S.L.)	AVERAGES Based on 1941-70 period of record				EXTREMES Based on full period of record											
				YEARS OF RECORD	FROST-FREE PERIOD (DAYS)	LAST FROST (SPRING)	FIRST FROST (FALL)	YEARS OF RECORD	LAST FROST (SPRING)		FIRST FROST (FALL)		LONGEST			SHORTEST		
									EARLIEST	LATEST	EARLIEST	LATEST	LAST FROST (Spring)	FIRST FROST (Fall)	NO. OF DAYS	LAST FROST (Spring)	FIRST FROST (Fall)	NO. OF DAYS
YUKON TERRITORY																		
Aishihik A	61 39	137 29	3170	24	47	June 22	Aug 9	24	May 30	July 13	July 16	Aug 31	June 17	Aug 31	74	June 29	July 25	25
Carcross	60 12	134 41	2170	12	77	June 14	Aug 31	34	May 11	July 15	July 18	Sept 29	May 11	Sept 29	140	July 15	July 23	7
Carmacks	62 06	136 18	1710	10	67	June 7	Aug 17	10	May 28	June 24	July 16	Sept 16	June 4	Aug 28	84	June 24	July 25	30
Dawson	64 04	139 26	1062	30	92	May 26	Aug 27	73	May 12	July 14	July 19	Sept 17	May 14	Sept 17	125	June 21	July 19	27
Fort Selkirk	62 49	137 22	1435	17	59	June 16	Aug 15	17	May 29	July 13	July 19	Sept 5	June 2	Aug 31	89	July 13	Aug 9	26
Haines Junction	60 45	137 35	1965	26	21	July 7	July 29	26	June 20	July 15	July 16	Aug 18	July 4	Aug 18	44	July 15	July 16	0
Komakuk Beach	69 35	140 11	30	13	26	July 9	July 28	13	June 20	July 15	July 18	Aug 27	July 3	Aug 27	54	July 14	July 18	3
Mayo A	63 37	135 52	1625	30	66	June 9	Aug 16	46	May 16	July 13	July 20	Sept 11	May 25	Sept 9	106	July 13	Aug 2	19
Shingle Point	68 57	137 13	174	14	46	June 26	Aug 12	14	June 8	July 12	July 18	Sept 3	June 3	Sept 3	86	July 10	July 18	7
Snag A	62 22	140 24	1925	23	51	June 18	Aug 9	23	May 29	July 18	July 18	Aug 22	May 29	Aug 20	82	July 10	July 31	20
Teslin A	60 10	132 45	2300	27	60	June 19	Aug 19	27	May 28	July 14	July 16	Sept 12	May 30	Sept 3	95	June 29	July 16	16
Watson Lake A	60 07	128 49	2248	30	95	May 30	Sept 3	30	May 11	June 25	Aug 10	Sept 27	May 11	Sept 15	126	June 25	Aug 10	45
Whitehorse A	60 43	135 04	2289	29	87	June 5	Sept 1	37	May 13	July 4	July 30	Sept 20	May 13	Sept 17	126	July 4	July 30	25

NUMBER OF HOURS OF BRGHT SUNSHINE
1941-1970 averages

	Jan.	Feb.	March	April	May	June	July	Aug.	Sept.	Oct.	Nov.	Dec.
Fort Selkirk	6	75	159	220	263	306	274	232	128	80	16	0
Haines Junction	21	75	161	210	272	271	260	224	144	90	24	2
Whitehorse	42	81	160	230	267	271	250	225	134	96	48	21

June showers bring July flowers.

The men and women of the Atmospheric Environment Department of the Department of Fisheries and the Environment must be thanked deeply for maintaining these records and providing them to us.

If you want a copy of the 30-year averages from 1941-1970, write to Atmospheric. Env., Env. Canada., 35 Dufferin St., Downsview, Ontario.

Send 50 cents and quote the number UDC: 551.582(712), in case it helps. Title of the book is "Temperature and Precipitations" 1941-70. The North — Y.T. and N.W.T.

30-year average is "the current standard . . . as recommended by the World Meteorological Organization" and it "reflects the best possible estimate of the current state" of the climate.

The book is dedicated to "thousands of faithful observers," without whom it could not have been possible.

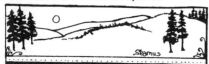

Seamus

Part XV

Everything in town took a swing towards the south in 1977 when they found out they were going to have a pipeline. By 1978 there was a division and the go-getters were downtown while the rest, like Toby, Alex and friends moved out to the country. People said that most of downtown was so southern that if the power failed in winter most people would freeze to death. Maybe, maybe not.

Anyways, there was a fire alarm at McCauley Lodge one afternoon while Alex and I were walking by. The fire chief roared by in his car about 45 seconds later, followed closely by the fire engine, lights and sirens going to beat the band.

Alex was telling me about how modern everything was . . . "And you know Seamus, these people in Riverdale truly expect everything to work like clockwork. It does not but what about some day when something goes wrong . . . it's only a matter of time."

Just then a fireman on a ten-speed bike zipped by, fully outfitted for a fire, chasing the fire engine. It was a funny sight.

"Well, I guess there's always hope, cheesehound."

I believe there is. After all, we don't all live in Riverdale.

FOR MORE ON GROWING....

Cooperative Extension Service, University of Alaska, Fairbanks, Alaska 99701. Northern booklets on gardening and agriculture. Some are written very simply, intended for those who don't read well. Send $.25 for each booklet to cover postage and handling.

Publ. –

P-30	Vegetable Varieties Recommended for Interior Alaska
P-31	Vegetable Varieties Recommended for South-Central Alaska
P-32	Seed Starting and Transplanting
P-33	Fertilizer for the Home Gardener
P-36	What Vegetables Should I Plant for the Most Nutrition and Dollar saving
P-37	Window Boxes
P-38	Tree Fruits and Small Fruits for Alaska
P-39	Vegatables Select for Showing
P-135	Gardens in Alaska
P-137	Controlling Garden Insects
P-139	A Key to Flower Gardening in Alaska
P-230	Beekeeping in Alaska
P-238	A Vegetative Guide for Alaska
P-021	House Plant Culture
P-024	Sidehill Gardening
P-025	Carrots in Alaska
P-026	Raising Plants Under Artificial Light
P-028	Planting, Building-up Rows and Beds
P-1-021	Hydroponics for Beginners
P-1-022	The Compost Heap in Alaska
P-1-024	Potato Storage Management

ON COMPLETENESS

''I never feel complete unless I have a crop in the ground.''

—a quote from (obviously) a farmer

Soil Testing

Roger Pommerville of Agriculture Canada, Public Services Section, tells us: As far as soil testing is concerned, this is a provincial jurisdiction and as the Yukon Territory has no Department of Agriculture, you could try to get it done by the B.C. Department of Agriculture, Parliment Buildings, Victoria, B.C. V8W 2Z7

Factsheets, Ministry of Agriculture and Food, Queen's Park, Toronto. One or two-page infromation sheets, with lots of punched holes so you can file 'em. The research is scholarly, but understandable, covering a wide range of agricultural topics.

Yukon Agriculture and Livestock Association, Box 4703, Whithorse. Meetings currently held the last Sunday of each month at members' homes. Membership $20. a year. Agricultural advice exchanged freely amongst members.

Seed Sources

Thompson and Morgan, 132 James Ave East., Winnipeg, Manitoba R3B 0N8.

If you have a taste for the exotic, send away for their catalogue. You'll probably need a green-house that covers a ten-acre field to fully experiment with their wares, as most of the seeds require a long growing season (which we're sure most gardeners have noticed that we don't have.)

Stokes Seeds Ltd., Box 10, St. Catherines, Ont. L2r 6R6.

Their descriptions of their 600 varieties are reliable and honest. They've got good all-round seeds.

W.H. Perron and Co. Ltd., 515 Labelle Blvd., City of Laval, P.Q. H7V 2T3.

Send $1.00 for catalogue...good selection of both flowers and vegetables. Prices reasonable.

William Dam Seeds., West Flamboro, Ontario. L0R 2K0

Alberta Nurseries and Seeds Ltd., Bowden, Alberta, T0M 0K0

Seed and seedlings for high-altitude, short-seasoned places. Gooseberry, raspberry, and currant plants.

Lowden

s Better Plants and Seeds, Box 10, Ancaster, Ontario L9G 3L3.

Organic stuff. Has a selection of very early tomatoes.

Bishop Farm Seeds, Box 338, Belleville, Ontario. K8N 5A5.

Bulk orders of alfalfa, clover, oats, barley, buckwheat. Will sell in small quantities. Good prices.

Lindenberg Seeds Ltd., 803 Princess Ave., Brandon, Manitoba.

Low prices, and varieties for northern gardeners.

Pike and Co., 10552 - 114 St., Edmonton, Alberta T5H 3J7

200 varieties for the prairies.

The Alaska Yukon Plant and Seed Co., Mail Order Division, North Pole, Alaska. 99705.

They've also got a growing schedule for when to plant north of 60.

HERBS

Otto Richter and Sons, Box 26, Goodwood Ontario L0C 1A0.

Has 300 varieties, including some pretty strange ones. Send $.50 for a catalogue...the common kitchen herbs are pretty expensive compartively.

Neighbourhood Mailbox, 1470 East 22nd Ave., Vancouver, B.C. V5N 2N7.

Lots of spices and herbs for culinary and other uses.

Murchies Tea and Coffee, 560 Cambie Street, Vancouver, B.C., V6B 2N7

Will send you a free price list.

Northern Growing

"Northern Gardening" and "Gardening on Permafrost" are two excellent, well-researched and fairly straight-forward booklets available free from Agriculture Canada, Ottawa K1A 0C7.

Ask for "Northern Gardening 1575" and "Gardening on Permafrost 1408". Tips include: a gently sloping site facing southwest; turn the soil early; the site should have shelter around but with twenty foot clearance; if not trees, use 4 to 6 foot fence; leave a gap in the shelter at the lower part of the garden; don't use too much raw organic matter, compost it first; spread 4 to 6 inches of decomposed organic matter over the garden; dig or plow in the fall, leave the surface rough ; locate compost pile in a warm part of the garden; add nitrogen and hydrated lime to your compost; use fertilizers; sprout spuds indoors; and irrigate during light frosts.

Northern Gardening has a Part 2 on special methods. These are ridging, terracing, mulching, row coverings, cold frames, hotbeds, heating with manure, heating with electricity, shelters and hutches and quonset-type greenhouses. Gardening on Permafrost is based on work by Reverend Father Adam of Inuvik.

"Man is the only animal that is different -trying always to make himself more different. He refuses to see where he fits into nature."

SLUG GARDENING

Near Dawson, I happened into a conversation about gardening with a tall, scruffy-looking wildman. He was dressed in shabby jeans, a thread-bare checkered shirt, worn-down work boots but he sported an almost-new cowboy's stetson. He was talking about fertilizer.

"Dogs," he said and spat past me, a great brown wad of tobacco juice.

I took a step backwards and cross-examined, "Isn't dog shit too strong for a garden? I thought it burnt out the roots."

"Didn't say shit."

"What did you say?"

"Said dogs. Dog. Bury the whole dog," he said while rolling a Drum cigarette. He paused to lick the paper then added, "Wormier the better."

There was a long pause while he fumbled about for a match and, finding one, lit the rollie with cupped hands even though it was hot and windless that July afternoon . . . I wondered whether to prompt him when he took up again on our horticultural discussion.

"Yep. I planted a pot plant right on top of Veraka. Just buried her six inches down so the roots could really get into her. Best pot I ever smoked. Grew big and bushy." He was drawing on the cigarette like it was a joint, holding it with fingertips and savouring the taste a long time before exhaling a thin stream of white smoke.

"Best use I ever got out of that wormy bitch," he said and spat. "Only use too."

—agnes

This chart is reprinted from "Northern Gardening A53-1575/1976" with permission of the Minister himself. May God bless the laddie.

TABLE 2. SOME VARIETIES OF VEGETABLES FOR NORTHERN GARDENS, AND RECOMMENDATIONS FOR SEEDING AND PLANTING

Kind	Variety	Amount of seed or number of plants per 15-m (50-ft) row (g)	(oz)	Distance between rows cm	(in.)	Distance between plants in row cm	(in.)	Depth to cover seed cm	(in.)	Remarks
Cool season crops — seeded directly in the garden										
Beets	Detroit Dark Red, Flat Egyptian, Ruby Queen	14	(½)	50	(20)	3.8	(1.5)	1.3	(½)	
Beans, broad	Broad Windsor, Sutton Giant Windsor	170	(6)	60	(24)	20	(8)	5	(2)	
Carrots	Red Cored Chantenay, Scarlet Nantes Coreless	7	(¼)	50	(20)	3.8	(1.5)	1.3	(½)	
Chard	Lucullus, Rhubarb	14	(½)	60	(24)	18	(7)	1.3	(½)	
Chinese cabbage	Michihli	7	(¼)	50	(20)	20	(8)	0.7	(¼)	
Endive	Deep Heart, Fringed, Green Curled	1 pkt.	—	50	(20)	19	(7.5)	0.7	(¼)	
Kohlrabi	Early White Vienna, Giant of Prague	14	(½)	70	(28)	12	(5)	0.7	(¼)	
Lettuce, head	Great Lakes, Imperial, New York			45	(18)	30	(12)	0.7	(¼)	or use transplants
leaf	Black Simpson, Grand Rapids, Paris Island Cos, Salad Bowl	1 pkt.	—	45	(18)	15	(6)	0.7	(¼)	or use transplants
Onion sets	Ebenezer, Sweet Spanish	680	(24)	45	(18)	7.6	(3)	2.5	(1)	
Parsnips	Guernsey, Harris Model, Hollow Crown, Short Thick	7	(¼)	60	(24)	9	(3.5)	1.3	(½)	must be planted very early
Peas, early	Alaska, Little Marvel	113	(4)	75	(30)	5 •	(2)	5	(2)	
main crop	Director, Laxton's Progress, Lincoln, Selkirk Tall Telephone									
Radishes	Cherry Belle, French Breakfast, Saxa, Scarlet Globe, White Icicle	14	(½)	30	(12)	2.5	(1)	0.7	(¼)	
Rutabagas (Swedes)	Canadian Gem, Laurentian, Victory Neckless	14	(½)	84	(33)	18	(7)	0.7	(¼)	
Spinach	Bloomsdale, New Zealand	14	(½)	50	(20)	12	(5)	1.3	(½)	
Turnips, summer	Early White Milan, Golden Ball, Purple Top Milan	14	(½)	70	(28)	12	(5)	1.3	(½)	
Cool season crops — started inside and transplanted to the garden										
Broccoli	Calabrese, Green Mountain, Itafian Sprouting, Waltham 29	1 pkt.	—	75	(30)	45	(18)	0.7	(¼)	
Brussels sprouts	Jade Cross	1 pkt.	—	75	(30)	45	(18)	0.7	(¼)	
Cabbage, early	Copenhagen Early Market, Early Greenball, Early Wonder, Viking Extra Early	1 pkt.	—	75	(30)	45	(18)	0.7	(¼)	
midseason	Bonanza, Golden Acre									
late	Copenhagen Late Market, Pennstate Ballhead									
Cauliflower	Snowball, Snow Drift, Snow Queen	1 pkt.	—	75	(30)	45	(18)	0.7	(¼)	
Celery	Golden Plume, Utah # 15	1 pkt.	—	71	(28)	15	(6)	0.7	(¼)	
Kale	Scotch Curled	1 pkt.	—	75	(30)	45	(18)	0.7	(¼)	
Onions	Autumn Spice, Sweet Spanish	1 pkt.	—	38	(15)	8	(3)	0.7	(¼)	
Warm season crops that produce satisfactorily in some years from direct seeding or transplanting in the garden, but produce better if transplanted into clear polyethylene mulches in locations protected from the wind										
Beans, bush wax	Pencil Pod Wax, Round Pod Kidney Wax, Top Notch Golden Wax	227	(8)	53	(21)	7.6	(3)	5	(2)	
green	Garden Green, Slender Green									
pole	Blue Lake, Early Wonder Wax	113	(4)	90	(36)	45	(18)	5	(2)	
Corn	Arctic First, Dorinny, Golden Midget, J-6 Cross, Pickaninny	113	(4)	84	(33)	25	(10)	5	(2)	
Cucumbers, pickling	Early Russian	4	(⅛)	106	(42)	60	(24)	1.3	(½)	or use transplants
slicing	Marketer, Mincu, Straight Eight, Surecrop Hybrid									
Marrows	Blackinni, Long Bush White, Zucchini	28	(1)	190	(75)	60	(24)	2.5	(1)	
Potatoes	Norgold Russet, Norland, Warba	7 kg	(15 lb)	84	(33)	28	(11)			
Pumpkins	Jack O'Lantern, Small Sugar	28	(1)	190	(75)	60	(24)	2.5	(1)	
Squash	Buttercup, Early Prolific, Hubbard, Table Queen	28	(1)	190	(75)	60	(24)	2.5	(1)	
Tomatoes	Early Sub-Arctic, Sub-Arctic Maxi, Sub-Arctic Plenty, Swift	25 plants	—	90	(36)	60	(24)	0.7	(¼)	
Warm season crops that only produce satisfactorily if transplanted into unheated or heated greenhouses or shelters										
Cantaloupes	Sampson Hybrid, Sugar Salmon	1 pkt.	—	107	(42)	60	(24)	2.5	(1)	
Eggplants	Burpee Hybrid, Morden Midget	1 pkt.	—	71	(28)	30	(12)	1.3	(½)	
Peppers	Earliest Red (sweet), Long Thick Red (hot)	1 pkt.	—	71	(28)	30	(12)	1.3	(½)	
Watermelons	Market Midget, Sugar Hybrid	1 pkt.	—	112	(44)	60	(24)	2.5	(1)	pollinate by hand
Herbs										
	A large number of herbs including aleriac, anis, basil, caraway, catmint, chicory, coriander, dill, endive, fennel, marjeram, oregano, parsley, peppergrass, rosemary, sage, salsify, savory, thyme	1 pkt.	—	45	(18)	15	(6)	0.6	(¼)	
Perennial vegetables										
Asparagus	Martha Washington	1 pkt.	—	137	(54)	71	(28)	1.8	(¾)	
Chives		50 sets	—	75	(30)	25	(10)	—	—	
Horseradish		25 plants	—	90	(36)	60	(24)	—	—	
Onions		50 sets	—	75	(30)	25	(10)	—	—	
Rhubarb	Canada Red, Macdonald, Ruby	1 pkt.	—	168	(66)	168	(66)	1.8	(¾)	

GREENHOUSE PUMPING STATION

Experiments have been underway to green-house tomatoes using the extra heat from pipeline pumping stations. However, other studies have found plants to be responsive to many different sounds.

We wondered if listening to a pump's whine would make the tomatoes neurotic. Certainly corn would not grow well; it is all ears. So potatoes might do better, with all those eyes and no place for ears.

The ultimate suggestion was peanuts. These could be made into Deaf Smith peanut butter.

casey

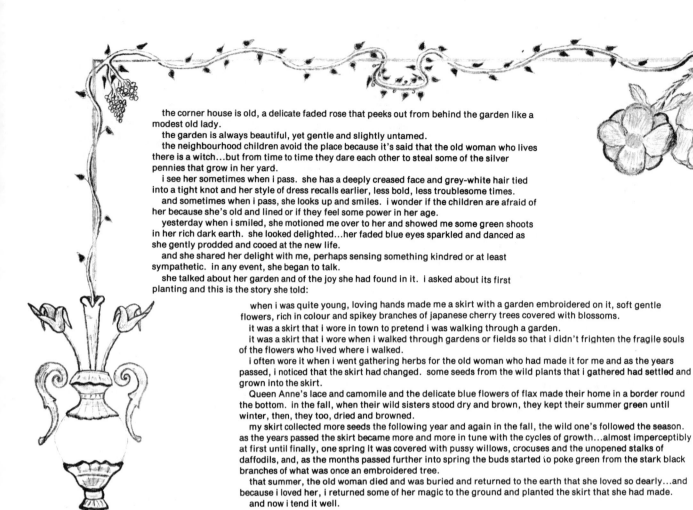

the corner house is old, a delicate faded rose that peeks out from behind the garden like a modest old lady.

the garden is always beautiful, yet gentle and slightly untamed.

the neighbourhood children avoid the place because it's said that the old woman who lives there is a witch...but from time to time they dare each other to steal some of the silver pennies that grow in her yard.

i see her sometimes when i pass. she has a deeply creased face and grey-white hair tied into a tight knot and her style of dress recalls earlier, less bold, less troublesome times.

and sometimes when i pass, she looks up and smiles. i wonder if the children are afraid of her because she's old and lined or if they feel some power in her age.

yesterday when i smiled, she motioned me over to her and showed me some green shoots in her rich dark earth. she looked delighted...her faded blue eyes sparkled and danced as she gently prodded and cooed at the new life.

and she shared her delight with me, perhaps sensing something kindred or at least sympathetic. in any event, she began to talk.

she talked about her garden and of the joy she had found in it. i asked about its first planting and this is the story she told:

when i was quite young, loving hands made me a skirt with a garden embroidered on it, soft gentle flowers, rich in colour and spikey branches of japanese cherry trees covered with blossoms.

it was a skirt that i wore in town to pretend i was walking through a garden.

it was a skirt that i wore when i walked through gardens or fields so that i didn't frighten the fragile souls of the flowers who lived where i walked.

i often wore it when i went gathering herbs for the old woman who had made it for me and as the years passed, i noticed that the skirt had changed. some seeds from the wild plants that i gathered had settled and grown into the skirt.

Queen Anne's lace and camomile and the delicate blue flowers of flax made their home in a border round the bottom. in the fall, when their wild sisters stood dry and brown, they kept their summer green until winter, then, they too, dried and browned.

my skirt collected more seeds the following year and again in the fall, the wild one's followed the season. as the years passed the skirt became more and more in tune with the cycles of growth...almost imperceptibly at first until finally, one spring it was covered with pussy willows, crocuses and the unopened stalks of daffodils, and, as the months passed further into spring the buds started to poke green from the stark black branches of what was once an embroidered tree.

that summer, the old woman died and was buried and returned to the earth that she loved so dearly...and because i loved her, i returned some of her magic to the ground and planted the skirt that she had made.

and now i tend it well.

she looked round her garden and smiled again at the tender little shoots, held like babies by loving earth.

-louise mrozinsky

Part XVI

Toby met a nice fellow named Real at Whitehorse Copper Mine when they both worked there. Real was a really mellow guy, nothing fazed him. He had lived up here all his life and after two years of watching Toby cruise Whitehorse being a "Yukoner," he took him out canoeing down on Squanga Lake.

Toby was thrilled. He was so energetic that he paddled all the time while Real slept and learnt a lot by listening more than talking for once. He was doing fine until he forgot to put the safety on his gun and put a bullet through the hull of Real's father's aluminum boat. Real just kept paddling, turned to me and said "you know, he could be dangerous." He was mellow, to be sure.

Part XVII

Around the fall and spring of 1978 there was a lot of hassle in the government and the commissioner eventually quit because of protest. Toby used to maintain that he didn't care one way or the other, but his true self showed through one day when we were standing outside Mac's News Stand.

The commissioner walked into the store and bought a paper, then came out. For some reason, he always smiled. He smiled all the time it seemed; even when people used to deride him at his job. (I think he just had buck teeth.) Anyway, he came out, stood for a moment and turned to Toby and said: "Well, how's your day going?"

Toby didn't say anything, he just turned away and stared up the street in the other direction. The commissioner never stopped grinning. He just walked away. Toby turned to me and said, "Cheesehound, I can't stand it when people in a lot of trouble talk to me, and don't even know me at all."

I don't know if this has any significance to anything, but it stuck in my mind. Maybe there's some meaning I missed.

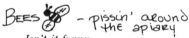

Isn't it funny
How a bear likes honey?
Buzz! Buzz! Buzz!
I wonder why he does?

In 1977, two farmers on the north Alaska Highway got some bees and, after reading **"Winnie-the-Pooh,"** located the hives a prudent distance of half a mile away. Real bears (not of the sensible kind like Pooh, but **real** ones) soon discovered the hives, and the honey.

By the next summer the farmers-cum-beekeepers had gotten wise. They came upon an article in a magazine during their winter reading that revealed a way of dealing with gophers, and they decided to try it for the honey-loving bears. It worked. All they did was pee around the territory surrounding the hives — as dogs do to stake out their areas of influence. Shortly after this process was begun, they spotted bear tracks leading up to the "pee-line." The tracks stopped there, and went off in other directions. The bears had gotten the word. The hives weren't disturbed and that summer the beekeepers got the honey, not the bears.

Same solution for gopher trouble — go piss in their holes. They'll never use them again.

BEES AND HONEY

Sheep at Kirkman Creek

On June 15, 1921 the Dawson Daily News published a letter from Mr. F.X. Laderoute of Kirkman on the Yukon River. He was offering to sell his sheep herd because he was going "outside". The animals were of the Oxford and Merino strains, he wrote, and gave "wool of the finest quality". He stressed that he was completely satisfied that raising sheep was a good investment in the Yukon, a ton of hay sufficient to keep twenty of them all winter. "I kept them in the barn during the nights in coldest weather, but let them out to range each day, even in temperatures as low as 50 or 60 below zero."

– the Yukon archives

EGGS AND CHICKENS
AND EGGS

Chickens are amazing. They have been laying eggs for us for 5,000 years now. Eggs have been dropped from airplanes in tests; in fact a man in Alabama in 1970 dropped a dozen fresh eggs from a helicopter 185 feet high and recovered nine of them intact. They have also been thrown great distances. The current record is 316 feet between thrower and catcher — without breaking the egg. And then people eat them too.

The typical Leghorn chicken in a commercial factory produces about 240 eggs in 12 months. Some records are a Black Orpington that laid 361 eggs in New Zealand in 1930; and a Rhode Island Red hen laid 20 in a single week and seven in one day on Sept. 11, 1971. A century ago the average Leghorn produced 100 eggs a year and by 1960 this figure stood at 207.

Through cross breeding and messing about we have arrived at the month-old tasteless yellow watery eggs from Super-Valu. So many

people think that this is what a normal egg is that they keep on producing them. Here's how they do it, briefly: they bring them into a giant warehouse at the age of five months, when they start to lay and then pen them up, four at a time, in a two cubic foot wire cage. There may be tens of thousands of hens banked up to the rafters in these cages. The eggs roll down onto a conveyor belt which carries them through washers and a mineral oil bath to extend their shelf life.

They live in this environment and lay eggs for 12 months, at which point they become soup or some other form of wonder food. During her life one of these chickens eats 95 lb. of feed, yields 21 dozen eggs, and supplies four pounds of meat at the end of it all as well as feathers and offal for fertilizer and pet food. Rather different from the average farm yard hen you were told about in school, eh?

But you can have six to 12 of your own chickens, which will supply you with some incredible edibles. Let them run around in the sun, peck at a variety of foods, get laid a lot by a funky young rooster, and you should have about an egg every two days from each. That's not much as our gloopy hen in the cage, but good things take their time, and what you get is a beautiful orange yoke, big and thick, with a white that stands up in the pan and doesn't run at all — a real egg.

You can get all kinds of breeds, some are eggless, grown for meat and weigh enormous amounts, some are spun-out little egg layers that speed around brainlessly and lay beautiful eggs, and lots of them. Brown eggs come from certain breeds, the eggs pick up their pigment from the blood of the hen. There is no real dif-

ference between brown and white eggs, but color is pleasing, compared to the chalky white of the warehouse egg.

This is a fairly brief article, information beyond this is available at the bookstore, and personal experience counts for a lot. Common sense prevails when you are dealing with living things in the Yukon. Suppose you order 25 chicks, about two to three weeks old, from Alberta or somewhere and you pick them up at CP Air. Take them home and put them in a big box with some cardboard, straw or cloth in the corners and a light bulb or other type of brooder lamp, hanging above them to keep them warm. Fifty baby chicks require about five feet diameter space, nine feet for 100. The main danger is suffocation from jamming together, and this depends on the bulb as a heat source. Hang it so that the temperature at chick level is about 90 degrees. Too much and they'll stampede to the edge of the box; too little and they'll do the same underneath the bulb. The bulb is raised each week causing a temperature drop of five degrees at a time. If the weather is warm they can go out at three weeks; if it's winter, they'll go to their heated coop at a month.

The coop doesn't have to be the Taj Mahal, but it does have to be secure from other animals that like chickens. Therefore an eight by 10 ft. high fence (wire) buried a foot deep with log bottom and middle pieces should be sturdy enough. Make it 25 ft. square with the coop in the center. The building should be dry, warm, with plenty of food and water, hay for laying and messing up and light to lay in, as they won't lay in the dark. Electricity is handy here — but if you don't have it already you know what to do with lanterns and stoves so we won't go into that. Measure the building about five feet square, five feet high with one or two windows, a sloping roof, and a floor at least a foot from the ground.

Insulation is imperative in the roof and walls. Hay works well on the floor so stuff more in for winter to cut your airspace by about a third to a half. They need about three 3-inch poles, four feet long to sleep on, food and water someplace where it will remain unfrozen, oyster shells or some other grit for their digestion, a lay tray with a ten inch roost for every four hens sectioned with plywood or whatever. You don't have to have sections — they don't seem to care.

For your convenience, the laying bench can be above a bin you store grain and feed in, or garbage cans outside can be used for the food. Make a door big enough for you to get in and out without stepping on or fighting with angry chickens.

Light for 12 hours a day in winter with a bulb suspended above. Heat from a car warmer

down low somewhere will provide plenty of eggs all year except when they molt, once a year for a month. Careful with your heat source: you want it room temperature, 70 to 85 degrees, and away from the hay or you will have crispy critters when it all burns down. This amount of electricity will account for $15 a month maximum on your bill in the Yukon.

Food consists of water, chick starter for the wee ones, hen scratch or straight grains for the hens and hay marsh for the oomph to start them or keep them laying. The average price in Whitehorse for these items is about seven to eight bucks for 50 lb. Vegetables are available by hustling the backroom boys at Super-Valu or Food Fair. They're getting smart though, and it helps to give them some eggs once in a while. Hay is available up here at about $4 a bale. Of course the best way is to have your friend from Saskatchewan to drive back with feed at half the price or lower, and hay at 50 cents a bale! That's where it's at.

You should get three years out of the average chicken. Start them on medicated chick starter, which prevents common maladies that kill lots of chickens. Convert them to growing mash at six weeks and to laying mash at 18 to 20 weeks. Abrupt changes in diet can kill young birds. Augment this all with vegie and meat scraps, bread, fish, sprouts or chinese celery cabbage, which grows quickly, and you will cut the cost of your eggs.

Talk to them, tell them how ugly they are, etc.; be nice to them and they will be nice to you, producing eggs and chicken shit for years, and if you ever get pissed off at one or its time has come, you can off them pretty quick, just grab them off the roost by the feet, carry upside down to the chopping block and zip off their heads. The end.

Mail Order Chicks

Fred's Hatchery
70 Northland Drive
St. Jacobs, Ontario N0B 2N0
(519) 664-2291
Serving small farms and hatcheries, a family business offering 16 varieties to all parts of Canada, including the Yukon, write for catalogue.
CP Air will ship chicks less than three weeks old for about $10. Prices for chicks average about $12 for 25.

Feeds, Hay

BEE'JAC ENTERPRISES
Box 4792
Whitehorse, Y.T.
668-2225
JERRY MITCHELL(Mitchell Trucking)
Mile 905 Alaska Hi-way
(across from Kara Speedway)
Feeds for most livestock — complete line of chicken feeds

SPUDS AND SNOWCHICKS

Stanleigh tells us that the Carcross Community School tried three types of potatoes before settling on "Early Epicure Certified" potatoes, ordered from Kelly Douglas and Company in Whitehorse. Yield was one ton for a third of an acre. Whats that in metric, smarty? And she also says she feeds her chickens snow in the winter when she's lazy, and it doesn't hurt them a bit.

Rabbit Raising

Housing and Equipment
(Yukon and common sense geared)

RAISING RABBITS IN RIVERDALE
get a female rabbit, she's a doe.
get a male rabbit, he's a buck.
put them together and watch 'em f———
add food and water.

Peter and his Playmates

The only recommended hutch is the all-wire one with a floor area 2½ by 3 feet which you can either make or buy. My rabbitry is made up of duplex houses, apartment houses, a girl's dormitory and a hare house for the bachelors. My hutches are of wooden construction with doors made of old chicken wire. The duplex type are set on saw-horses and are about waist height. The dimensions are about ten feet long, three feet deep, and about three feet high. It is divided into two seperate pens which houses a doe and her litter, giving them plenty of room to run, play and grown. The floor of this unit is made out of boards approximately six inches wide with an inch space between each to allow the droppings to go through. These boards are built so they can be turned over. A shelf is built about half way up as a perch which also serves as a great place to put greens for a doe with young. The roof is built on a slope of double boards which is lined with four mill plastic sheetings. It must be rain proof! Rabbits need plenty of shade, light and ventilation. They must be kept clean and their worst enemy is dampness.

Once the littlers are approximately 5 or 6 weeks ole, I keep them in an unused greenhouse which has proved to be a rabbit's paradise. Also I have a wire pen about 8 feet long and 3 feet wide for use as well. The top is made of wood part of which is a hinge door for easy access. Great!

The gestation period for a doe is 29 to 34 days. (Most kindle on the thirty-first day). The nest box should be introduced on the twenty-seventh day after mating. It should be about 8 to 10 inches deep and of sufficient size to avoid overcrowding, but small enough for warmth (like a tangerine or apple box). If using a wire cage-type nest it should be lined with cardboard if the weather is cold, for example, with early May or September litters. This box should be filled with lots of straw, dry grass, or wood shavings but NOT sawdust. Most does will rearrange all this to suit themselves three or four days before kindling. She will pull fur from her underbelly shortly before her litter is born. If enough fur is pulled the litter will survive below zero temperatures, but may perish in above freezing temperatures if there is not enough fur. You can pluck more fur off her and you can also save the fur for future use. Do not mix this fur with fur from other does.

Handling the New Family

The doe should be left as quiet as possible three days before and three days after birth. A doe has only eight teats; should she have more than eight young, they, (they extras), can be given to another new mother. Best to have two does due on the same day. Give the new mother a treat and remove the nest box and count the new born. If it is necessary to transfer some babies to another new mother you can rub vanilla on the foster mother's nose, then mix the adoptees in with her babies. The babies will smell like her own by the time the vanilla wears off. These young must be within a few days of the same age. Don't put older ones in with new babes - too much competition for the nipple.

Until they are out of the nest (about three weeks) only one person should handle them, otherwise the mother may kill them or neglect them. I do handle mine, but only those belonging to very quiet, placid does.

You can determine the sex at three days, but is more accurate at weaning time. By depressing the external gentalia, the mucous membrane can be exposed. In the male, the mucous membrane protudes and forms a circle, whereas with the female, it will extend and form a slit.

Between the ages of 5 to 10 days the young are very poorly co-ordinated and can only "flop-hop" (I call it). Sometimes they flop out of the nest and die. Also on occassion, the doe will jump out while she is nursing and a young will still be sucking on the teat and will be dragged out of the nest - it may die by this rough treatment or by catching cold. After 5 to 7 days it is good advice to remove all excess straw etc. from the nest so they are less likely to flop out. Do not remove any of the fur.

In about ten days the little ones open their eyes. If some seem reluctant to open, you can gently sponge them with cotton balls and warm water a clean one for every eye you bathe. It is not necessary to do this until about the twelth day.

Keep a daily watch on the nest to make sure all the babies are together in one place and remove any that die.

Feed

Rabbits under 12 weeks old should be fed dry grass and dry greens or hay only, as well as pellets, oats etc. - NOT fresh greens and fresh grass - - they are too young to digest it and may die from diarrhae.

Rabbits over 12 weeks old can eat any greens especially grasses. Brome headed grass is lovely. Also garden greens - carrots and beet tops, lettuce, spinach, and kola rabi (their favorite), potato peelings (but not if they have sprouts like an old winter potato).

Rabbit pellets are your most nutrionally sound food as they contain minerals, vitamins, salt, protein etc... In one year my investment has been very small; two 25 kilo bags (55 lbs), $8.00 each, which has gone into the raising of 122 rabbits. I feed this only to my pregnant and nursing does and thier young (until the young are approximately four weeks old). I have these pellets available though a feed dealer and I'd rather support and individual than a store outlet. The service is friendly and your service is their pleasure. He handles all animal feed, rock salt and even oyster shells for chickens. If your interested, go to:
Gerald and Ester Mitchell
Mile 906 Alaska Highway
Mitchell Feeds"

I feed a lot of oats. Fortunately we raise our own which is a great boost to both my budget and the rabbits' diet. Other foods rabbits will eat (none being a complete balance of nutrition) are oatmeal, sunflower seeds, pumpkin seeds, apples, dried corn, dry bread, and cow's milk or dried milk. It is good to give your animals only the amount of food they will clean up in one hour, twice daily, although I prefer to keep food always in front of them. A rabbit requires considerable fibre in his diet thus hay is important. Dried grass which you can put away for winter use is faily good by hay is better. I feed oat bundles and oat straw during the winter.

Keeping Your Rabbits Happy

Rabbits of all ages are happiest when they are kept busy. Willow twigs and small leafy twigs are both food and fun. Small toys are a great sport, like small rubber balls, rubber bone, large marbles, plastic cups and even tin cans. They like to push these around or take them in their teeth and toss them. Their games never cease to amuse or amaze me. And there is no pecking order as there is with chickens.

Breeding

Keep your does and bucks seperate. For the small breeds, your does and bucks should be at least five months of age. The medium breeds should be six months and the giants must be eight months. For a small one, five months or five pounds, whichever comes first.

Your doe, for breeding purposes, must not be too fat and her fur must be excellent, no sheading and plenty of sheen. Although the doe has not great heat cycle, the vulva should be a reddish purple colour - not a pale pink. The deep colour means she is ready to breed.

The same general health conditions apply to the buck. If he is too fat he may be to lazy to service the doe. Check his testicles. If they are completely descended into the scrotum, and the scrotum is full and large, he is a good buck to use. If he has only one testicle, or if one or both are withdrawn into the groin or have a withered look, he may be sterile, or if a litter results, it may be small. This condition is only temporary. One testicle may not yet have descended into the scrotum. If you want reproduction, make certain the reproductive apparatus is in perfect working order - at least as far as you can see.

A maximum of four or five matings per week for a buck occassionally used. Two or three matings per week for a buck in continuous use. The ratio is one buck to ten does.

To breed, take your doe to the buck. Don't blink, or you may miss it. If everything goes right it will be over before you close the hutch door. Never simply leave the pair alone. The buck will mount the doe and fall over backwards or on his side. Now remove the doe. Turn her over and check the vulva to make sure the semen has been deposited there.

The doe's eggs descend for fertilization upon sexual stimulation. This process takes 8 - 10 hours. If the doe should urinate in the meantime, the semen will be washed away. Place her back with the buck for another 8 - 10 hours as another service may be just what is needed.

If the doe is willing the first or the second time and the buck is not try this: Pick the buck up and put him on the doe's back - he will get the idea. If the buck is willing (99% of the time) and the doe is not (occassionally) restrain the doe from mating. Never leave a pair together unattented. They may fight and injure each other.

Is she pregnant? One certain way to know is to weigh your doe at mating. If she gains a pound (on her regular diet) in two weeks (for the medium weight breeds) she is probably pregnant. Two weeks after you have mated the pair, put her back with the buck. If she resists his advances and also growls and whines it is a good bet she is pregnant. If she does not resist the buck, or even if she does, restrain her for a forced mating. Record this date too, because she may not be bred, if she isn't already pregnant, and you will have saved yourself half the gestation period.

An infertile mating or two does humping each other may cause a false pregnancy for seventeen days. Put the doe back in with the buck on the eighteenth day. This female or females cannoth conceive during a false pregnancy.

A good pregnancy test is at three and a half weeks, through the gestation period, throw a handful of straw or dry grass in her hutch and if she starts picking this up in her mouth and carrying it around, I'll bet you anything she is pregnant.

Does and young can stay together for about 2½ to 3 months (depending on the size of your breed) - then you must take the bucks out. Litters the same can stay together if they are all put into the same pen at the same time (no more than a week's difference in age) until they reach 2½ to 3 months. After this time, they get so involved in learning how to hump that they can loose their appetite for food, they can injure themselves, and they can also loose

TRANSPLANTING YUKON TREES

Want to transplant a tree? Here are some tips from the Yukon Lands and Forest Service of the Department of Indian and Northern Affairs.

Choice of the Tree

The best source of transplants is the open area beside roads and powerlines and other rights-of-way; plants from these locations are usually adapted to the types of growing conditions they'll experience in your yard. Though it is possible to transplant small trees successfully in summer by taking special care to keep a large amount of moist soil around the roots, the job is best done during the spring or fall. If you find a plant you want during the summer, mark it in some fashion for transplanting after its growing season has ended.

Soil, Light and Moisture

Most plants will tolerate a fairly wide range of conditions, but they're more likely to prosper in conditions similar to those they grow in naturally. When you take a plant from out-doors, note the soil, moisture and light conditions and try to duplicate them in your yard. Mark which side of the tree faces south. Plants growing in a shady forest will probably grow best in a shady yard, those from an open hillside will need lots of sunshine.

The soil itself is very important. It should be porous enough to allow aeration of the roots, and it should include portions of clay or silt, sand and organic matter (such as peat). If the soil has too much clay or silt it will become waterlogged or it will dry firm and crack; if it has too much sand it will lose water and nutrients rapidly, requiring frequent watering and fertilization.

The Transplanting

Take as much of the root mass as possible and a good supply of earth when you dig up a tree. The roots of a plant growing in dry soil will be unusually long, running deep in the ground, and will require extra care.

Use a cover to hold the soil around the roots while the tree is moved to your home — a burlap bag or plastic garbage bag works well — and be careful not to damage the plant enroute.

Dig the hole for the tree wider and deeper than the root mass. In poorly drained soil, try to improve the soil drainage by adding course material and organic matter to the planting site. Place loose soil under the tree to bring it to the proper ground level and fill in the hole halfway with more soil. Saturate it with water until all the air is forced out, then fill the hole with soil and water again. Take special care to see that the soil level on the tree is the same now as it was when the plant was growing elsewhere, because a difference in soil levels is one of the chief causes of plant mortality.

Care after Transplanting

Trees should be watered frequently — but not drowned — to help their roots reform after transplanting. After an adjustment period of a few weeks, you can reduce the amount of watering to about the same amount the tree would have received in its original site. If in doubt, the general rule would be to keep the soil moist but not wet. Wilted leaves usually indicate too little water.

If the transplanted shrub or tree is a large one, it's wise to prune the crown area shortly after transplanting. Special techniques are required for transplanting large trees, so if you're interested in this, or in transplanting species not native to the Yukon, you should consult publications written on the subjects.

Yukon Trees

In the Yukon Territory, it is necessary to have a permit from the Yukon Lands and Forest Service before transplanting trees from Crown land. Permits are issued under the Territorial Timber Regulations by Yukon Lands and Forest Service officers in Whitehorse (918 Range Road), Haines Junction, Watson Lake, Teslin, Ross River, Mayo, Carmacks, Beaver Creek, Dawson City and Old Crow. If the number of trees involved is small, permits are usually issued free, but if the number is large, or the trees are to be used commercially, a nominal charge is made for each transplant.

---

weight from their extra activities. At this early stage males mount males or females and vice-versa. "Free love" have been in style with rabbits forever.

Breeding stock should be good for two or three summers if you only breed three or four times each summer. In the Yukon, winter breeding is too much bother in my opinion. My rabbits are kept outdoors from the first of May until Thanksgiving or later, depending on the weather. I winter only my breeding stock, four does and two bucks in our root cellar where our winter produce is stored - potatoes, carrots, etc... In really cold weather a barrel heater is used to prevent this produce and the rabbits from freezing. A garage would work as long as it did not get too far below zero. Basements work well too. My hutches have tin trays under the wire mesh floor to catch the droppings. There is no need for odour if one practices common sense and has things properly set up.

Leaving your rabbits out until October assures you of having prime pelts when you butcher them. You will have to remember to give them water four times a day though, as it will freeze.

Common Problems

Cannibalism - Sometimes young does will kill and eat their young. Exact causes are not known but it is attributed to nervousness, lack of water or poor rationing of food. These does should be disposed of. The young should not be examined too soon after kindling as this will excite the doe.

Pneumonia is not uncommon and occurs in the young and the adults in the nest box. Drafty, damp, unsanitary hutches are usually the cause.

Heat can cause death, whereas rabbits can tolerate considerable coldness - even below zero temperatures.

Kill any poor winter keepers or a doe that does not give six or eight little ones on a regular basis, or any that are difficult to breed.

Books

Additional info is outlined in 'The Merck Veterinary Manual' on page 1219. It is published by Merk & Co. Inc. Rahway, New Jersey, U.S.A. My copy was a gift in 1955, so I have no idea of the price now. This is the "bible" for anyone raising animals as it is a reference book of diagnosis and therapy for the veterinarian.

Rabbits young, rabbits old,
Rabbits hot, rabbits cold,
Rabbits tender, rabbits tough,
Thank you sir, I've had enough.

Til the rabbits end........

Cotton-tail Marjorie
Pelly River Ranch
Pelly Crossing

Biftecks sur pied, à l'ombre du mont Archibald... troupeau Hereford au pâturage, à la Ferme experimentale, Mille 1019, route de l'Alaska, T.Y.

Moose Hunting & Skinning

Despite all the macho-hype about the great white hunter, there is little sport in hunting moose. The animal has little chance against a man equipped with a truck or boat, binoculars and a high-powered rifle. That little chance comes from man's laziness. Most people can't be bothered to leave their warm homes and risk being wet, cold, dirty, or tired. That's good for the moose and for those who view the moose hunt as a means of obtaining a tremendous amount of quality meat at a very low cost.

There is no need to do elaborate comparative tests on nutrition. It should be obvious that a moose feeding freely over a large area can get whatever trace elements needed and will be healthier by far than a steer who has never left a factory pen and has eaten cement dust and sawdust and steroids all his life. But for the unbelievers, a moose has 61% less calories, 52% more protein, 91% less fat, the same amount of calcium, 10% more iron, 44% more phosphate, more than 10 times the vitamin A, more Thiamin, 25% more niacin, although only 18% of the riboflavin.

The term 'gamey' is sometimes used to describe wild meat. Moose meat, well cared for, has a distinct pleasant taste that is preferred by many to supermarket beef. Caribou and reindeer taste 'sweeter' and beat beef overwelmingly on every catagory of nutrition. Flavour is less noticeable in females and the young; strongest in mature bulls whether they be beef, moose or caribou.

BE PREPARED

Before you hunt remember that any fool can shoot a moose, but it takes knowledge, hard work and conscientiousness to save as much meat as possible. What people can't eat your dogs will. The first responsibility of a hunter is to have adequate equipment. Each person hunts differently but the following is a sufficient list:

1. RIFLE: it must be sighted in to be at all useful. Calculate your abilities on a rifle range, then halve that for hunting. Buy the correct ammunition. For example, don't use a soft lead bullet in a lever action rifle if you hope for any accuracy. Nylon tipped ones won't get as mangled by the action.

2. KNIVES: if you are taking a "tourist" knife (great white hunter size and made of highest grade steel) bring along a stell to sharpen it and know how to use it. Cutting hair dulls the knife, as will bone work, but it is the fat (which clogs the knife's microscopic teeth) that really dulls a knife. Ask any butcher. Anyone who claims to have "skinned, gutted and quartered two moose without stopping to sharpen up" either doesn't know a sharp one from a dull one, or was butchering lean rutting bulls, and small ones at that.

Many trappers and most natives will take two or three knives, or different size, shape and flexability. A good skinning knife isn't the best boning knife. If you use Swedish or Finnish steel, you can get an edge back on the knife in only a minute or two with a stone, and the cost is only a fifth of the tourist knives.

3. CHEESE CLOTH: not every one agrees here, but most detractors haven't tried game-bags or cheese cloth. Used cheese cloth is available free at most butcher shops, and can be bleached then laundered. Use the cold water cycle as it's old blood you are removing. Or, you can buy cheese cloth by the yard or bolt, and sew up gamebags large enough to hold a quarter of meat. The cloth will help crust the blood and keep some of the dirt, flies, bark chips and spruce needles off it.

4. PEPPER: some people swear by it but I've seen blow flies crawl through the stuff and lay eggs anyways. Pepper is supposed to repel bugs, but I suspect it works best as a coagulating agent to help form a dried crust which prevents blow fly eggs from hatching. Remember that pepper is used to seal leaky radiators, here it also plugs things up. Use generously, a ¼ inch thick over open raw cuts.

5. ROPE AND CORD: my grandad always carries some cord in his pocket "comes in handy" he says. It should be obvious to any camper that rope (30 ft. or more) and cord or twine (strong, so you need a knife to cut it) have a million uses. Many uses emerge on a hunt.

6. AXE OR HATCHET: if you can quarter a moose using only a knife you don't need one. Most people don't have that experience. A hatchet is good for bone-cutting.

7. FLASHLIGHT: in June there is enough light to work all night, unfortunately the season is not open then. In October it is dark by supper time. A radar-light or coleman is fine. Of course many moose have been cleaned by firelight. Not by me.

8. FOOD: cleaning a moose is long and tiring. Bring a thermos of hot tea or soup, some hard tack, cheese, carrots. I pack everything into a large juice can which doubles as a tea billy.

9. BLOCK AND TACKLE: luxuries are handy as long as you are using a motor vehicle to hunt from. Increasing your mechanical advantage with a come-along or other contraption is nice, but not absolutely necessary.

Stash everything in a small duffle or sack so it is handy to take should you have to chase a wounded bull. Of course, that chase shouldn't happen. We've all heard tales of following a trail of blood for 7 miles, then having the ordeal of packing out the meat, so never shoot unless you are confident of a kill, and confident of your ability to save the meat. Rainy, humid weather is blamed for "souring" the meat, so it's better (and more enjoyable) to wait out the inclement weather. Moose lie low during storms, anyways.

The safest shot is aiming at the lungs. A shot there will

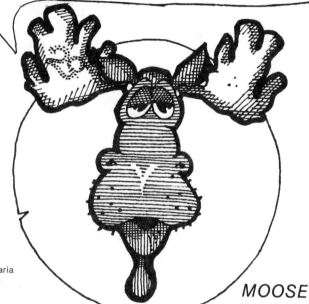

MOOOOSE!

LOST CHOCOLATE MOUSSE

Find and catch one moose. Dip in chocolate (you may have to restrain moose). Usually he runs away as soon as he is let go. Eventually the chocolate washes off from the rain...so it's hard to find the mousse.

MOOSE MILK
by Kathy

one 26-er of light rum
one half 25-er of tia maria
one half gallon of milk
vanilla ice cream
nutmeg and
cinnamon

Mix all booze into large punch bowl. Pour in ice cold milk and add slivers of ice cream over top. Sprinkle spices to taste.

This is a great party drink anytime, but especially at Xmas.
(Ed. Note: Some prefer it with equal parts of booze and milk; that is, one 26-er rum, one 26-er of Tia and two quarts of milk.)

(Also, some prefer overproof rum, and two bottles of Tia and no milk at all. But that's for weirdos, and definitely does not constitute "Moose Milk," unless of course the drink is made by a moose.)

(Not recommended for mooses or persons under 19 years of age.)

MOOSE NUGGERY

Have you ever dreamed of stumbling across a cluster of nuggets? Now your dreams can be answered, partially at least, for these are not nuggets of gold but Moose Nuggets!

People make jewelry from these oval droppings of dried "sawdust." Simply string them together and varnish. Your friends and neighbours will be truly impressed by your Yukon momento.

Remember that nuggets found in the National Parks are protected by a law which is strictly enforced. Nugget collectors must prospect outside park boundaries.

kill him, although you may have to let him stumble around a bit before he dies. Keep a gun aimed at the moose until you are sure he is dead. He might just get up and run away. A second shot right behind the ear will speed up his death.

BLEEDING: a soft bullet tears through the flesh and quite adequately bleeds the animal. But cut away at the jugular if you want, it isn't easy to cut through that thick hide.

GUTTING: try to get the moose into a position where you can comfortably operate. If a leg is in the way, tie it up and back to a tree or bush. If it's floating you can tow the body to a better position. Prompt gutting is essential for colling the meat. Although the moose's circulatory system has stopped, body cells go on living for awhile and produce body heat that would normally be removed by the blood. With no heat removal, the meat will literally cook in its own juices. So cut the guts out and let some cool air in.

The first step is cutting through the belly hide from the chest to the anus. Make your incision through the hide at the breast bone, then use your knife with the sharp edge up, and by pressing the abdominal wall with your other hand, you cut from the inside out. Try not to puncture the gut. (It will smell pretty strong and be unpleasantly messy, but it won't ruin everything if you slip.) If it's a female, cut right through or around the udder, and around the vulva and anus. For a bull, some people advocate tying a string around the penis so that semen and urine do not trickle out. You can tie around the anus also, once you have a knife to cut it to loosen it. It helps to now skin back six inches on each side. Then cut the belly wall carefully and the stomach bag will bulge out. Reach into the cavity near the breastbone and tie off the esophagus (the big tube that brings food from the throat to the stomach). By now the insides will be spilling out, and you have to help by pulling and cutting a little along the backbone, where a little tissue attaches things. To help the organs spill out of the body cavity, you can cut the flank just below the ribcage back to the backbone. For some reason, cutting the left side works better than the right.

Moose are not small animals. Their guts will easily outweigh you, so this isn't a brain surgeon operation. By now you may be frustrated, confused, tired; so relax a moment, take a look around at the mountains, go for a pee, smile at your friend, have a cup of tea, then start all over again.

If the bladder and anus are stuck too securely, you will have to chop through the pelvic bone to free them. This will also spread eagle the back legs. Don't wash out the body cavity with water, scoop the blood out and wipe with grass or moss. The lungs, heart, and wind pipe can also be easily coerced out now that there is lots of room to work inside.

SKINNING: if it is now pitch black out and your buddies are wondering why you're three hours overdue, prop the body cavity open with short sticks, retrieve the heart from the gut pile and go back to camp until the first light in the morning. The natives (who should know) consider the organ meat as the best parts. Sof the first pack trip back is with all the 'goodies' inside the washed out, inside out, stomach bag. The stomach wall is a delicacy like tripe. You can eat the heart right away, just fry some slices.

If it's light, it's best to skin the carcass right away to help the cooling process. This is a long slow job, made much faster with sharp knives. Stop often to touch up your blade, especially when cutting fats. Make cuts along the inside of each leg and extend the belly cut to the head. Roll the hide back as you skin it with long cutting strokes. You probably won't be able to roll the carcass over to finish skinning along the backbone till you've cut it up.

Again, now you can decide to leave the body to cool or quarter it right away. If you are tired but want to keep working, drink lots of water, it acts as a stimulant and won't confuse your metabolism as much as 20 cups of bush coffee or strong tea.

QUARTERING: no one outside the Olympics could carry a butchers hind quarter from a really big bull. Two barely can, so don't cut it that way unless you are right beside your truck. The following method is not that of the

FRYING MOOSE STEAKS

This is the definitive way to fry moose steaks, revealed to us by Norm Rudolph.

-Trim off any skin. Use pepper for seasoning but no salt. (Salt draws the blood to the surface; add salt after cooking.)

-Ham fat is best for grease in the pan.

-Get the pan medium hot first, put in the steaks, and cook at medium heat. Sprinkle a little dark rum on it while cooking.

-If the steak is frozen, watch because the juices will pour out when you start frying it. Be ready and pour off the extra juice to make gravy. (If there is too much liquid in the pan, steaks won't fry properly.)

GUN ADVICE

A few suggestions to new hunters:

In Winter, wipe the gun clean and dry because oil may freeze and jam the action.

Always leave rifles outside and you won't have condensation problems.

Scope should be mounted properly. It will be expensive but worth it if you want to keep it zeroed in.

Watch out for condensation inside cases year-round; let the rifle breathe.

a.d. with b. nixon and n. rudolph

HUNTING RESIDENCY REQUIREMENT

With the impending pipeline invasion, locals are concerned about the impact of so many extra hunters on the moose population. At present, a "resident" has to be here only six months.

From Whitehorse came a suggestion that this requirement be extended to two years. But when the Indian council of elders was asked, they said all permanent residents should be allowed to hunt. "Permanent", they feel, is after about fifteen years, maybe ten.

By this yardstick, the Indians are the majority of Yukon residents in territorial voting as well.

PEMMICAN

The first step is to procure a moose or other large animal. Slice the meat, as thinly as possible into sheets and strips. Build a rack to hang the sheets and strips on and enclose it in a canvas shelter or a smoke house. Make a slow fire of willow or poplar under the meat and keep it going until the meat is completely dried...this takes at least 48 hours.

Put the dried meat in a hide or stout canvas bag and pound it with a mallet or the back of an axe until it's in small chunks...best quality pemmican is completely powdered. Take the best parts of the animal fat and render it. Break the bones up and boil them for the fat in the marrow. Bring the fat to a boil and put it in a container. Add as much of the pounded meat as can be absorbed by the fat. And now you've got pemmican...put it in a hide bag or in some small dishes to set.

EATING PEMMICAN

RUBBABOO...chop off a lump of pemmican and put it in a pot of boiling water. Add whatever you have on hand to make it into soup or stew.

ROUSSEAU...fry the pemmican in its own fat. You might wish to add some vegetables or wild plants.

THIRD METHOD...hack off a lump and eat it raw....good exercise for the jaw as it dries rather hard, but it's a satisfying concentrated food for the traveller with no time to stop. This is a good trail food for cross-country skiing trips. Chewing something will keep your facial muscles moving so they don't freeze.

gramps

GUN CONTROL
Buy Now!

The following are excerpts taken from the pamphlet entitled Gun Control in Canada (working together to save lives), published under the authority of the Solicitor General of Canada.

Starting January 1, 1979, a Firearms Acquisition Certificate will be required by any person wishing to obtain a firearm. The certificates will be issued by the federal government at the local level. Applicants may be required to complete competence training and safety tests in provinces where this provision of the firearms legislation has been implemented.

FIREARMS ACQUISITION CERTIFICATES
Purpose:

Effective January 1, 1979, all persons over 16 years of age wishing to acquire firearms, must obtain a Firearms Acquisition Certificate. This will allow the holder to acquire any number of firearms for his private use. The word "acquire" means to take possession of firearms in any manner, by purchase, exchange, or any other means.

Those persons currently in possession of hunting and sporting rifles will not be required to obtain Firearms Acquisition Certificates for those weapons, but only for new acquisitions. They are not intended to be a license to own, carry, or possess weapons.

The requirement for a Firearms Acquisition Certificate will ensure weapons are not made available to persons with a record of criminal violence, mental disorders associated with violence, or who may pose a threat to other persons.

Certificates are issued at a cost of $10.00 and will be valid anywhere in Canada for a period of five years. Separate certificates are not necessary for additional firearms acquired during the validity of the certificate. Certificates need only to be renewed where additional firearms are acquired after the five year period terminates.

Certificates will be issued free of charge to persons who must use firearms to hunt or trap in order to sustain themselves and their families. No certificate is needed by a person over age 16 who borrows a firearm in order to hunt or trap to sustain himself or his family.

OFFENCES AND PENALTIES

As of January 1, 1979, there are new offences and penalties related to the use of firearms. These are in addition to existing offences and penalties.

Selling, giving, or lending, after January 1, 1979, any firearm to a person not producing a Firearms Acquisition Certificate. (Fine or imprisonment up to 2 years)

Failure to report to police a lost or stolen firearm within a reasonable period of time. (Fine or imprisonment up to 5 years)

Possessing any firearm (without lawful excuse) knowing that the serial number has been altered, defaced or removed, or to alter, deface or remove a serial number on any firearm. (Fine or imprisonment up to 5 years)

GAME ORDINANCE REGULATIONS
Possession of Firearms

A non-resident person, not being the holder of a valid subsisting hunting licence issued under the Game Ordinance or having other lawful occasion, shall keep all firearms securely stowed in the motor vehicle or trailer, boat or aircraft used by him or under his control while in the Yukon Territory and shall not remove the said firearms from such stowage while in the Yukon Territory except upon the direction of a game guardian, peace officer or customs officer.

---

butcher, but your meat won't taste any different.

Remove the breastbone (brisket) by cutting the ribs right through the small white knobs of cartilage on them. The front legs can be cut off at the shoulder blades, using just a knife. Lift the leg and slice deeply at the armpit; there is not bone joint there. Then the neck will make another pack board load. As you detach each hunk of meat slip it into a game bag or two, then prop them up to cool further. The backbone can stay with one side of ribs. Don't forget to rescue the tenderloins in the scramble. Cut beside the backbone with your hatchet.

Hind legs are best cut into leg and rumps for packing, then throw away the feet. If you can save the entire head, do so; if not get the tongue and nose. The hide should then be salted and stretched to dry. If it has to carried a long way, roll it up on a pole and carry it safari style. The bloodshot meat can be saved for dog feed, you could eat it yourself, but it is unpalitable and prone to quick spoilage.

HANGING: if it is too far to carry the meat out in one day, it should be hung on a rack for at least a day or more. Build a hot quick fire of spruce twigs and small branches under your rack. When the fire is high, heap on green alder or poplar leaves for a blast of heavy smoke, and after that keep a smokey smudge of green or rotten wood; this will keep the flies away. If the flies are persistant or the wind unsettled, you may have to build two or three small smudge fires.

The flies are the blue-bottomed shit flies that look like a common house fly, only bigger. They low (blow) eggs that resemble minature rice onto the meat, preferring wet cracks as the eggs won't hatch unless moist. When the eggs hatch they become little worms called 'maggots'. This is completely revolting to city people but mostly because of mis-conception. Maggots are completely edible, in fact are considered a delicacy in some parts of the world not yet visited by television. They won't do any harm except eat up your meat; try to flick the eggs off with the tip of your knife, if some manage to hatch, cut portion of meat away and give it

to your dog. Or your neighbour's dog.

Prevention is the key here; if the blood has not washed off, but allowed to clot, with the cheese cloth and pepper helping, a dry rubbery crust will form after a few days (depending on the humidity and temperature) and inhibit the eggs from getting the moisture they need to hatch.

Never use plastic to store meat in as it will sweat and rot. Put plastic over your compost pile not over fresh meat; use canvas, cheese cloth, or cotton instead.

If there are scraps of meat left unhung, slice into strips a ½ inch thick and drape them over a pole. Turn the strips every four to five hours; your are making dry meat or jerky. Dried strips will keep indefinately if cool and dry, but bloody chunks will be subject to fast spoiling and fly eggs.

BUTCHERING: the organs such as liver, kidney, heart, tongue, and tripe should be processed within days of the kill, as they don't keep long. Either freeze, make into sausages, can in jars or tins, pickle, or invite all your friends over and have a feast!

Ribs can be eaten a few days after the kill as can tenderloins. The thicker the chunk of meat, the longer it should hang.

The neck will become hamburger, sausage or stew meat. If you run into cists while butchering your meat don't worry about it. They are white and about the size of a kernel of corn, and will disappear upon freezing or cooking.

Some people hire a butcher to cut, wrap and freeze their meat. However, hunters who lack refrigeration usually try to make their kill after the weather has turned cold. With a screened meat house, or well ventilated and shadowed cache, meat may hang outdoors all winter. Don't worry about mold on the crust, it improves the flavor. If you don't like it, wipe it off with a vinegar-soaked rag. As meat is needed, a supply is sliced off, or if frozen, cut off with a swede saw, then thawed out and cut into cooking portions. Trim off the crust before cooking. A flat thin piece of meat is called a steak. A big, round chunk is called a roast. Happy hunting and good eating.

THEY'RE ORGANIZED

The Yukon Trappers Association, which is lobbying for action to free more lines, also makes recommendations for changes in laws affecting trappers. The association runs a small office in Whitehorse and works at arranging a better marketing deal than available through the local fur buyers.

GUIDE TO STRETCHING BOARDS

These stretcher patterns show the shape of the skin; however, when making a stretcher, the size of your skins must be considered.

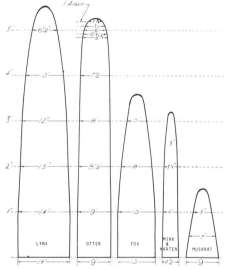

Patterns for Skin Stretchers — *thanks to University of Alaska*

TRAPPING'S FUTURE

Even though the trapper is said to "own" his line, he cannot sell it. He can sell the improvements, buildings, traps, trail clearing and the like — to someone, but there is no guarantee that the Game Branch will assign the line to that same someone when the trapper surrenders it.

Since trapping is a part of the native lands claims negotiations, a line held now by a native is not reassigned to a non-native, presumably so that there will be less expropriations after the settlement. No one has any idea what will be the outcome of the settlement: it could range anywhere from complete native ownership and management of fur resources to the same muddle it is now. A good change is that there will be areas set aside for the exclusive use of natives, with the "white" trappers inside those boundaries given new traplines outside the areas plus some cash settlement.

Presumably the better the line surrendered, based on past production, and the more settled the improvements, the more money the displaced trapper will get.

Trap Numbers

0 — muskrat, squirrel, weasel
1 — muskrat, squirrel, weasel, mink, marten
1½ — mink, marten
2 — fox, lynx
3 — fox, lynx, otter, wolverine   double spring
4 — wolf, lynx, otter, beaver, wolverine
I use mostly 1½ for small animals and 4 for big ones. A 1½ will hold a fox or a lynx but 2 is better.

There are close to 400 traplines in the Yukon. Only about half of those are used but this is changing as the game branch now is starting to take traplines away from those who don't use them. There are two ways of getting a line: you can buy one from someone that has one, but traplines suffer from overinflation these days. The other way is to apply at the game branch for one that is open. To get a line you have to prove three years minimum residency and an applicant with experience has more chances than an inexperienced one. The game branch give open traplines to those people they feel will trap. Try to work as an assistant to someone for a season and then apply for one of your own. The average trapline is about 400 square miles.

Why am I trapping? Because it is in my blood I guess. I wanted to be a trapper when I was a kid; life on the trapline brings me to peace with myself. Right now, the leaves are falling off and there is a skiff of fresh snow on the hills. I am getting my outfit ready for another season on the trapline. It is pretty hectic: run here, run there. I just can't wait to get in for the winter: next week I am flying 70 miles in from the nearest road.

I know that for a while I will miss "civilization." I always do. I miss friendship and it takes a while to adjust to the slower pace one gets into when he is alone. But after a while, things start happening — you start to be part of where you live. The animals get to know that there is a man around, they follow your tracks to see who you are and what you do and you start getting to know them too. And there is the dog team that is a big part, your dogs mean mobility and comfort but also a lot of work. When first snow hits, you lay your trapline and that is when it starts to get in your blood. A few days later you go and check your traps. Every set is a suspense and when there is something in the trap it is like Christmas to a six-year-old. After a while, you get to know the elusive ones — the trap robbers, the smart ones that avoid your sets. Often the game lasts over several years, with you racking your brains to catch them and them having a good feed at your expense. Wolves and wolverines comprise the bigger part of these but all "animals" will teach you a few tricks. That is what trapping is — tricks.

The whole idea is to get the animal to either step on a leg hold trap or stick his head through the snare or trap in case of those "humane" traps. You place the bait behind the trap, not on it so the animal gets caught as he is trying to get to it. The bait is anything smelly that will attract a predator. Rotten beaver meat is my favorite, with a bit of fish oil for added olfactory appeal.

There are about a half dozen basic sets:

cubby set: That is a little stick house built against a big tree or a river bank with a bait inside against the far end, and a trap concealed at the entrance. Good for most animals.

pole set: a pole leaning on a tree with a trap on it and a bait at the end or on the tree. A good set for deep snow.

hanging bait set: a bait hanging from a branch or whatever with one or more traps under it.

the hole set: a bait buried in the snow with a trap over it. Good set for fox, coyote and wolf.

the trail set: a trap hidden in the snow on a trail.

the snare: similar to trail set but with a snare hung across the trail at head level. Good for wolves, foxes, coyotes, rabbit.

As for the tricks, well, hopefully you learn new ones all your life. Each animal will teach you something:

— make a natural looking set
— look for areas where there are lots of tracks
— conceal the trap by putting a piece of white toilet paper over it and sprinkling snow over the whole thing
— brush your footprints around the set
— don't piss or spit tobacco around the set

Those are general tricks but each trapper has his own. You don't set traps thinking that you will get an animal in each one the next day. Trapping takes a lot of patience; you set a trap hoping that you will get something at one time during the winter.

You always hear about astounding prices paid for furs like $600 for one lynx. Don't let that fool you; about five per cent of the furs bring that top price. The average is about half of that. Few trappers make as much money trapping as they would working at a job in town, but most of them wouldn't work in town anyway. Trapping is more a way of life than a job. To me a job is when you sell your time to someone. A trapper is sole master of his time and life.

~ Tanning Hides ~

This flow chart shows the steps that are necessary in preparing a dry or fresh skin for the tanning vat, the tanning process, and the softening. It includes what you do, why you do it, and how you do it or what tools and equipment you use. The author is aware of the many methods of home tanning, but feels it is necessary to mention only a very few. For those of you who have worked with skins or will work with skins, you will undoubtedly read of many different ways to tan, some of which may fill your needs better than others.

DRY SKINS —

(1.) SOFTEN
to each gallon water:
 ¼ cup salt
 1 ounce borax
 2 ounces strong detergent
soak till skin is soft.

(2.) FLESH
scrape off flesh, fat and muscular coat.

(3.) WASH
to each gallon water:
 ¼ cup powdered clothes washing detergent.

(4.) RINSE
cool clean water.
rinse several times to remove all detergent.

A very valuable part of an animal that is very often wasted because no one knows what to do with it is the hide. There is a concise booklet available called "Tanning at Home", that claims people can obtain successful results in their homes by using the methods described. It can be ordered from: Information Office, Cooperative Extension Service, University of Alaska, Fairbanks, Alaska, 99701. (25 cents/copy and 25 cents handling)

This flow chart covers the booklets info.

A #16" kit is available which will do several hides; it contains a gallon of glutaraldahyde, a quart of tanning oils and a booklet. Try: "H and H Enterprises", 501 20th avenue, Anchorage, Alaska 99503.

Reindeer hides can be bought from Canadian Reindeer Limited, Tuktoyaktuk. You can buy reindeer meat at the same time. Great meat. Check with Northward Airlines for delivery details.

FRESH SKINS —

(1.) WASH
cool water.

(2.) FLESH
scrape off flesh, fat and muscular coat.

(3.) WASH
to each gallon of water:
 ¼ cup powdered clothes washing detergent.

(4.) RINSE
cool clean water.
rinse several times to remove all detergent.

**CAUTION: **
ADD ACID TO WATER AND SALT SLOWLY.

DO NOT BREATHE FUMES ACID BURNS.

(5.) TAN
in plastic bucket to each gallon water:
1 pound salt and 4 ounces battery fluid.
(see other formulas in tanning publication)

(6.) NEUTRALIZE
to each gallon water:
1 ounce borax or 1 ounce washing soda.
soak 20 minutes to 2 hours depending on skin thickness.

(7.) RINSE
cool clean water.

(8.) STRETCH
lace to frame or nail to board. Dry 2-6 hours.

(9.) LUBRICATE
apply neatsfoot oil to flesh side in warm room. Wait 10 to 12 hours. Apply tanning oil or leather dressing. Wait until oil has soaked into hide. Dry.

(10.) DRY and SOFTEN
stretch or work in both directions until skin is soft. Sand flesh side if desired.

Weather

There is a saying that "anyone who predicts weather in the Yukon is either a newcomer or a fool." Maybe, maybe not; but there is a weather office in Whitehorse that seems to tell us an awful lot sometimes and anyone who has lived out in the open for long periods of time has come to suspect they can feel what's coming tomorrow. You can call them at 668-2293, Whitehorse.

Actually, weather is a science. It is also a learning process like anything else in the bush.

The following information was gathered by Chilkoot Chuck a few years ago when he became convinced that it was possible to foretell the weather at least 50 per cent of the time or more. We stole it from him.

CLOUDS
Cirrus—feather like high clouds
Stratus—layer clouds
Cumulus—big heaps and puffy cotton clouds

Sometimes prefixes are used, some definitions are in order:
Alto—means "high up"
Nimbo—means "rain cloud"; nimbus is any cloud from which rain falls.

Some generalized rules, not to be confused with strict instances:
Cirrus—storm coming or can mean a change in weather.
Cirro-stratus—if the sun or moon has a circle, a storm may be coming but might miss you.
Alto-stratus—signifies rain, hail, sleet or snow.
Alto-cumulous—it's gonna get colder and will probably be nice tomorrow, though.
Nimbo-stratus—expect heavy precipitation
Cumulo-nimbus—thunderstorms

In general, wind can tell you this:
from the west—clear, cool
from the east—rain
from the north—clear, cold
from the south—warm, sudden showers

MORE NOTES
Here are a few more notes from Chuck:
—Weather basically moves west at 500 miles a day in summer; 700 miles a day in winter.
—Trees rich in fat (birch, poplar) oppose lightning.

Part XVIII
We were on the Yukon River, me and Toby, and we'd been gone a day from Carmacks. During the afternoon we had met some folks who were slightly scared of Five Finger Rapids, and were asking Toby about them. Toby had never been canoeing before, but it didn't show to the folks so he began telling a tale.

"Y'know there's a few choices on how you go: take the left side and keep just to the left of centre. It's okay. Me'n some guys spent an afternoon floating through there in life jackets. But I tell you, one time two guys set out from Carmacks in a brand-new Grumman canoe and new equipment. They got to Five Fingers about three o'clock and somehow managed to flip it over. Well, they went around the bend and there's an Indian camp there, y'see, and these guys were yelling help to beat hell.

"Well the Indians thought it was pretty funny and after a chuckle launched their boats and retrieved the wet ones. The men were so grateful they gave their canoe to those Indians. And they gave their food to the guy who drove them back to Carmacks. These Indians told me this and they also said those two guys had .44 magnum pistols in special pockets of their sleeping bags! Now how do you like that."

The people said that they were definitely impressed and asked when this happened. "Oh last year. You won't see that canoe now, though, because the RCMP came out to check on it and the officer bought the canoe from the Indians for $50, about a quarter of its price in Whitehorse."

He talked like that for a long time. The thing was, you never could tell if he was lying because he believed a lot of what he made up. You can't blame him though; he's entertaining and, if the story's good, it's worth the time it takes to tell it.

—Cumulus clouds are good things until dark underneath; when they get coppery expect rain soon.
—Cirrus clouds are very bad if another layer moves in a different direction underneath.
—If the sky gets overcast fast and rains it will probably not last long. If it all builds slowly, expect long rains.
—High clouds are good but descending clouds bring rain.
—Clouds that run together and lose shape bring rain.
—Leaves showing their undersides signifies a change-wind.
—From a lightning flash to the thunder in your ears is five seconds equals 1 mile in acoustic distance.
—Other signs of stormy weather: red sunrise; a small dew or none at all; muggy, sticky air; rising temperature-falling barometer; bugs out in force; dark clouds to west, dull or dark sunset; clouds at various heights heading in different directions.
Other signs of fair weather: misty, foggy sunrise, heavy dew; falling temperature-rising barometer; campfire smoke rises straight up; spiders spinning webs; ducks and other fowl flying high; high stationary isolated clouds; moderate winds from west or northwest; red sunset.

CONCLUSION
As you can see there is something to say about forecasting weather. My good friend Agnes sums it up rightly when she says, "Lookit, bud, it gets cold as a witch's tit in the winter and either burns or rains all summer." Well, amen to that. It's sufficient.

—*George Marks*

Vegetation
The part of the Yukon which attracts the most wildlife and the greatest human activity is the boreal forest. This is the predominantly evergreen forest of black and white spruce mixed with lodgepole pine and tamarack. In southern areas the spruce often form an impressive canopy which may tower 80 feet overhead. Farther north and at higher elevations the growth is more open with a ground cover of mosses, lichens and small plants. In the northern Porcupine and Peel River basins the tall forest is replaced by woody shrubs such as willow, heath and birch with mosses, sedges and lichens at ground level.

Variations within these forest types are seen in areas which are in some stage of recovery from forest fire kill. Time repairs the blackened graveyard of the conifers with first a show of purple fireweed, then a growth of birch, aspen and poplar with willow and alder. After a burn, 100 years or more is required for the lichen growth of the boreal forest to return.

At alpine elevations over 4,000 feet and in the northern plateaus and lowlands of the Porcupine and Peel drainages, tundra replaces the forest. Tundra is an extensive, treeless area underlain by permafrost. These areas of dwarf shrubs, sedges, cottongrass and lichens are the habitat of many animals such as dall sheep, grizzly bears, wolverine and ptarmigan. However, few people choose to confront this harsh environment for long. This is probably fortunate as the permafrost vegetation is slow growing and easily destroyed.

Within both the forest and tundra areas, muskeg are found. In the southern portion, muskeg occurs in wetlands in scattered depressions. In the north, muskeg results from lack of drainage due to permafrost. Muskeg is recognized by water surrounded by the deep spongy

An Asset Beyond Price
"It may well be, and indeed I am one who is convinced of this, that the untrammelled wilderness itself is the most valuable asset the Yukon has. I believe that before the end of the century, it will be beyond price. As the world grows more crowded, the cities more smoky and populous, as the available open spaces constrict, then the broad horizons of the North are going to take on a new significance. Canada may well be one of the last industrial nations to enjoy the luxury of this untouched open space."

—P. Berton
in Introduction to the YCS publication
Yukon Hydro: A Symposium (1975)

sphagnum mosses which make soft, but damp, walking. Sedges, labrador tea and tamarack grow on the more solid edges of muskeg. Though great for viewing moose, beaver and water fowl, the muskeg is protected by the hordes of bugs which breed there.

The fourth type of vegetation occurs on the rich silt deposits along rivers. Horsetails and aquatic sedges and rushes give way to deciduous shrubs and trees on the higher ground. This broadleafed brush provides food for wildlife and often indicates fertile, farmable land beneath. While the wildlife makes full use of these small areas, man has not yet done so.

—Debbie Jensen

DALL SHEEP IN WINTER

In January, especially when the temperature drops to sixty below, the Dall sheep herd from Sheep Mountain on the edge of the Kluane National Park often are hard pressed to find enough to feed on. When they get really hungry, they come down to the roadside, tip over the litter barrels and eat garbage. One trucker told us that if you are very still, the sheep will come right up to you and eat popcorn out of your hand.

—b. s.

BUGS BUGS bugs bugs buzz buzzzzz bugs BUGS BUGS

This is what we know:

Orange and bright colors repel mosquitoes (we don't know about black flies). If you find yourself with an irresistible urge to dress like a Christmas tree, the more intense the better. Someone down south has even gone to the trouble to list their effectiveness in this order: orange, yellow, green, white . . . The worst colors to wear apparently are the ones most often used up here: blue purple and red purple.

There are repellants. First, to get it over with there is Cutter's, which is fine until you get into real live bug country. The 1977 Silverstreak Expedition after a long trip across the Mackenzie Mountains, arrived in the Liard River Swamps. They are something to behold: 450 feet above sea level and God knows how big.

The first night the tent was covered with bugs so thick that we couldn't see our lines holding it up, and the noise kept us awake all night. The people of the area said that these bugs (the very tiny kamikaze mosquitoes) lasted from May to October and there was no game in the worst part of the area, a rough circle approximately 100 miles in diameter. Well, this is all to try and impress upon everyone that Cutter's didn't work worth a shit here. They liked it! Off in the spray cans seems to do alright until you hit the above-mentioned swamp then the stronger repellants can be given a go. Repex and Nero are two of the stronger ones. Sometimes they will effectively eat right through your clothing.

All these little substances are made of the same chemical. It's called Toluamide, briefly, and is one of the few chemicals known that the critters will pay any attention to at all.

The female mosquito will lay her eggs whether or not she sucks your blood. There are breeds starting to appear around parks and such that are immune to toluamide, through adaptation. Scary, eh? If we forget all the mod-

Who me?

ern crap for a moment we can survive on what the earth has given us. There is always something.

Wild rhubarb juice works, as does citrus juices from oranges and lemons, etc. The early explorers and modern folks have used citronella for an awful long time. Some substances won't relieve the attack but can help with the itching. These are things that draw out the poison and contract the capilliaries. Baking soda works, and ammonia works, as do onions, wet salt and moist tobacco.

That's all we know, except for this repellant, which incidently works quite well. Go to the drugstore for the ingredients.

    3 oz. pine tar
    2 oz. castor oil
    1 oz. pennyroyal oil
    a touch of lavender oil (must be real), and a touch of sulphur can be added for presence.

Soak a bandanna, and hang it on you somewhere, or put some on yourself. Don't wash off for a week and they will never bother you for the rest of your life. Neither will anyone else.

—Eric

It's Their Home

When you're hiking in the country, remember it's not a zoo. The animals are on the loose, and they may not like you in their backyard. Mothers don't like strangers near their children. If you meet a bull moose in rutting season and all he wants to do is make love or fight, get out of his way. Use your head. All bears are potentially dangerous . . . here are a few hints to avoid encountering a bear:

BEARS

Camp off animal or walking trails and near large, sparsely-branched trees you can climb if necessary. If you notice fresh bear signs, choose another area. Cache your food away from your tent, preferably suspended from a tree. Don't store food or eat in your tent. Cook away from your tent. Food smells can penetrate the tent and attract a bear. Bears will eat almost anything. Don't invite a bear with food or garbage. Garbage-trained bears associate food with humans and soon lose their fear of man. Don't leave dirty utensils around the campsite.

Pack all non-combustible garbage to the nearest container. Burying it is useless and dangerous. Bears can easily smell it and dig it up. The attracted bear may then become a danger to the next group of people in that area.

You may still encounter a bear, despite taking precautions. But this does not necessarily mean it will attack. To reduce the hazard:

-if you see a black bear at a distance, make a wide detour;
-if you see a grizzly, leave the area at once;
-keep upwind if possible so the bear will get your scent and know you're there (try singing or making noise, too);
-if you cannot detour or retreat, wait until the bear moves away from your path - always leave him an escape route;

ATTACKS

Most grizzly attacks result from surprising a bear, coming between a sow and her cubs or coming too close to a kill.

NEVER go near a bear cub. You could end up tangling with several hundred pounds of angry mother. Take photographs with a telephoto lens. Bears have a tolerance range which when encroached upon may bring on an attack. Keep your distance at all times.

There is no guaranteed life-saving method of handling as aggressive bear. But some behaviour has proved more successful than others. Running is not a good solution. Most bears can run as fast as a racehorse and quick jerky movements can trigger an attack.

A bear rearing on its hind legs is not always aggressive. If it moves its head from side to side, it may only be trying to get your scent and focus its weak eyes. Remain still and speak in low tones. This may indicate to the animal you mean no harm.

Think about your surroundings before you act. If you meet an aggressive grizzly in a wooded area, speak softly and back slowly toward a tree. At the same time slowly remove your pack and set it on the ground to distract the bear. Climb a good distance up the tree. Adult grizzlies can't climb as a rule, but large ones can easily stretch eight to ten feet up.

Black bears are agile climbers so a tree may not offer escape.

If you have an escape route you may, as a last resort, have to "play dead." Drop to the ground face down, lift your legs up to your chest and clasp your hands over the back of your neck. Wearing your pack will shield your body. Bears have been known to inflict only minor injuries under these circumstances. It takes courage to lie still, but resistance would be useless. Good Luck!

P.S. - When camping, pee between your camp and whatever directions bears may come from, especially if you're there for several days. (See section on bees and bears.)

TREES

The great boreal forest stretches in a continuous belt across northern Canada into the Yukon. White and black spruce, lodgepole pine, poplar, white birch, trembling aspen, alpine fir, tamarack and balsam are the tree species found here. The present forests of the territory have developed from a continuous history of fire and it is only along the rivers that mature forests exist. An exception to this situation may be the Yukon River where at least 300,000 cords of fuel wood were cut for the sternwheelers steaming between Whitehorse and Dawson from 1898-1950.

Approximately 84,534 square miles or 40.8 percent of the territory's total area is estimated to be forested. An estimated 25,870 sq. miles or approximately 28 million acres are productive forests and 58,687 square miles are considered unproductive. This means that about one-third of the 40.8 percent of forested land is useful, or approximately 14 percent of the total area of the Yukon produces trees that can be used for timber. This breaks down even further because it is estimated that only 8,880 sq. miles or about 10 million acres of the productive forests can be reached and harvested. This leaves 17 million acres of land untouched - it is not economically accessible at the present time. This reduces the total area of useful forests to 5 percent of the entire area of the Yukon. No wonder people have trouble finding trees they can use for building a home.

If you do find a good site, here's a tip that might get you those logs free: an individual can cut up to 25 cords of firewood annually without getting a permit. This entitles you to cut trees for building logs and claim them as your firewood - who is to say that they are not to be bucked up in the future?

The Territorial Timber Regulations establish a permit system for cutting and removal of timber for most of the Yukon. For more info, talk to your local Resource Management Officer at Forestry — they can also tell you where the nearest mill for building logs is.

White spruce is the main commercial species in the territory, accounting for 87% of trees harvested ; lodgepole pine accounts for 11% and fir accounts for 2%. The most important commercial area is in the Upper Liard Valley in the southeastern Yukon. It is also the only area that provides hardwood trees for harvesting (70% aspen, 22% poplar and 8% white birch). Because of its location, Watson Lake is the centre of timber production. There are presently 15 - 20 sawmills operating in the Yukon, the majority in the Watson Lake area. A few are scattered around the vicinity of Whitehorse. The biggest operation is in Watson Lake and belongs to Yukon Forest Products Ltd., a subsidary of Cattermoe. It was estimated that there were 35 people employed in the forest harvest industry in 1977.

Timber harvesting has been increasing in recent years and is expected to continue as local demands grow. In 1976-77 there were 47,000 cubic metres (8,322,000 board feet) of lumber produced in the territory along with 24,000 cubic metres (11,000 cords) of fuel wood and 2,300 cubic metres (82,000 of round timber or building logs and posts. The total value of forest products increased from approx. $1 million in 1967 to $12 in 1977. We're cutting more timber almost every year. If we want to continue, reforestation of cut-over land will become more important in the future because trees take over 100 years to grow back here. The Yukon Lands and Forest Service has initiated research designed to test regeneration methods and the suitability of trees and shrubs to the Yukon climate and soil. That's what the Takhini Nursery is all about, and there is another one in Watson Lake.

It appears that our forests are going to be taken care of as long as we don't have too many fires.

j.m.

Look up at the mountain!
...it's a White Rock...
no, it's an Albino Muskox
... it's a Dall Sheep
no.... it's....it's a
Yukon Dall Sheep Igor

BAH!

BIRD SIGHTINGS

Don't bother reporting your latest sighting of a raven, but if you do come across a less common bird in the Yukon, send a note to people who want to know.

All data is forwarded four times a year to the magazine "American Birds," published by the National Audubon Society. Reports should go to:

Helmut Grunberg,
Yukon Conservation Society,
Box 4163,
Whitehorse, Y.T. Y1A 3S9

or Dave Mossop
Yukon Game Branch,
Yukon Territorial Government,
Box 2703,
Whitehorse, Y.T.

The date of the sighting, the number of birds, the location they were seen and the name of the observer should be passed on. If it's a rare beast you come across, send in a detailed description of the sighting and if possible, a photograph.

Any observation at any time of year is wanted. Four seasons are used, and each has their own deadline. Sightings in the winter months of December, January and February should be sent in by March 15. In March, April and May, the spring months, the deadline is June 15.

For June and July (the summer months for birds), August 15 is the deadline. Autumn months are August, September, October and November. Deadline for those is December 15. Happy sightings!

FISH WAR

In 1978 a "fish war" of sorts occurred between Canada and the U.S. because a treaty expired and no agreement was reached on a new one. As a result, all Canadians had to fish commercially only Canadian waters and vice versa for the Americans. Sport fishing by Americans is still allowed in Canada, and the same for Canadians in the U.S., but with one difference.

Canadian sport fishermen cannot use their own boats in U.S. waters. You have to rent one in the U.S. The decision made a lot of Haines people upset because they like us (we're good tourists, I guess), but as of September, 1978, the law still was in effect.

FOREST FIRES

Fires have burned over almost the entire territory within the last 100 years. Old-timers talk about the fire in '58 that came close to reducing Whitehorse to coals and ashes. Large, black clouds of smoke filled the sky, and the city council considered closing the bars so people wouldn't be too inebriated and too difficult to handle in case of an evacuation.

Apparently this fire was started near Lake Labarge by the Armed Forces. I have heard from people who lived here at that time that the Air Force was practicing bomb runs on Richtofen Island when one of the pilots missed and hit the mainland. I checked the Archives to verify this "rumour" but I didn't find any listing of the cause for this fire. All I came across were numberous lawsuits against the Armed Forces by Yukon Forest Services. And that's a fact - you can make your own conclusion.

Every summer, fires start in various locations around the territory. Lightning usually causes them. The dry, hot weather in 1969 created conditions like those in a tinderbox and when lightening struck, fires broke out at Pelly Crossing, Faro, Snafu Lake near Atlin and behind the Texaco Station in Porter Creek. The areas still bear the scars of these fires, and it will take 120-140 years before the trees grow to full maturity and can be considered marketable timber.

The Yukon Forest Service has divided the territory into priority zones for fire control purposes. Under this four point system of evaluation, it is decided which fires are fought, and how much money, manpower and equipment goes into stopping them. Here's the rating order:

1. TOWNS - Any fire within 20 miles of a community gets everything including the kitchen sink thrown at it. Unlimited funding is the rule until the fire is out.

2. ROADS AND RECREATION AREAS - Any fire threatening travel and communication routes and/or tourist--frequented areas is fought. Some financial restrictions limit the action taken.

3. IMPORTANT TIMBER AND GAME AREAS - Any fire in a low priority zone usually is stopped from spreading and will be put out depending on how much money is in the budget, and how many fires are burnig at the same time.

4. UNPROTECTED AREAS - Any fire that occurs is allowed to burn as part of the natural cycle of the land. Usually nothing is done. A fire is left untouched unless used as a training site for fire fighters, or it's getting too big, or it's endangering the caribou herd near Old Crow.

Under these priorities, 88 out of 126 fires were fought in 1977. That's a high percentage, yet under this system only 56,000 sq. miles or approx. 27 percent of the total area of the Yukon is protected. That leaves a lot of land to burn.

A Reciprocal Forest Protection Agreement exists between the feds and the province of B.C. They made a buffer zone along the provincial-territorial boundary where either fire protection agency may take action. A similar arrangement exists between the Yukon and the state of Alaska.

Things may appear to be under control, but don't be careless cause I'm tired of stamping out your fires.

Smokey the Bear

P.S. Campgrounds started when the Yukon Forest Service tried to group together overnight campers as a means of forest fire control.

Taking Care of Our Wildlife

The management of the Yukon's vast wildlife resources is probably the most emotional and difficult political issue facing the Territorial Government. Before you buy your licence and tags and go out to get your moose, here are some things you should know about the other part of game management: the people and the laws.

Wildlife is the only resource totally under Yukon control. All our game laws have evolved over the years since 1901, when Ottawa granted those powers to the Yukon. Our laws are not much different from the other provinces today, because in the last thirty years the government has taken the view that hunting is a form of recreation and a privilege. It used to be that getting one's meat was a necessity, and the law acknowledged the fact. Until 1947, one could buy moose, caribou and other meat at the local meat market, decades after this practice was abolished in other jurisdictions.

Game management is one of the most contentious issues underpinning Yukon Indian land claims discussions. For some reason the Territorial Government opposes giving Indians any larger voice in saying who can hunt in the Yukon, where they can hunt and how many animals they can kill. The prevailing attitude seems to be that only biologists with advanced degrees in their studies can properly determine those things. Of course, game officers everywhere have trouble deciding what they are, biologists or policeman. We should not idly ignore their opinions and advice, but look beyond it, to our own role in this affair.

During the gold rush and after, most of the needs of thousands of people in the Yukon for fresh meat came from game animals. A large herd of caribou used to migrate past Dawson City every year, coming down as far south as Carmacks and Aishihik Lake. Thousands were killed and eaten, as were thousands of moose. In fact, far more moose and caribou were taken during the twenties and thirties than are taken today. What happened to the game? Did anything happen? Yes, but Yukoners didn't have much to do with it.

Before the Second World War and for a couple of years after, fur prices were high and a lot of people made their living by trapping. Most of these people used dog teams, and fed those teams on moose meat. Naturally enough, this accounted for a lot of animals. However, this went on, year after year, for decades. There were always enough moose to go around. Nowadays, we would make better use of the meat,

because processed dog food is both cheap and good, also most trappers would prefer to use Skidoos. But the fact remains, we are not killing as many moose as we used to up here.

Today our perception of the wilderness is gained by the seat of our pants, either in a plane or helicopter, or in a car, or seated on a Skidoo. The country goes by pretty fast; we see precious little. Starting when the Alaska Highway was built, people would drive along and see no moose in the swamps and say "All the moose have been scared away" or "There is a shortage of game in the Yukon." Consequently, they banded together and passed tougher game laws. As time went by, roads improved and vehicles improved so that we see even less of the countryside. Our perception of the wilderness is directly proportional to the speed at which we view it. There's enough moose here for everyone; all we have to do is get off our collective asses to get good meat at relatively low cost.

Yukon Indians know this. In the small communities they retain their knowledge of the old hunting places and the relative numbers of animals there each year. Most of these people know where to go to get a moose. Many of them do so, regardless of the season or the sex of the animal they kill. This is the old tradition that was followed by everyone, Indian or non-Indian until the Alaska Highway came through. Yukon Indians oppose efforts of game officers to find out when, where and how many moose they take, and rightly so: if the biologists knew they'd pass even tougher game laws and jail or fine even more Indians. It has been said if there is to be any violence with respect to the land claims quesiton, it will break out over some incident concerned with game laws.

In 1947 the Yukon Fish and Game Association had grown in two years to be the biggest political lobby in the Yukon. It practically wrote the new game law and were responsible for all the provisions removing most of the special privileges given to Indians since 1901. What they forgot, or chose to ignore, was that Indians provided the Territorial Government with most of its revenue from game, through fur royalties, big game guides — where the Indians' special knowledge of the bush was valued as much as his skill as a guide — and through meat hunter's licences. In fact in 1928, Indians gave the Territorial Government 25% of its local revenues from their efforts in the wildlife industries. The Fish and Game Association was clearly anti-Indian, not because they were prejudiced *per se* but because they had a different idea about how game should be managed. And why not? They were nearly all new arrivals to the Yukon, from Alberta mostly, and they thought they knew it all.

People see moose in different ways, but they all boil down to moose as trophies or moose as meat. Since 1947, the Yukon Government has seen their value as trophies to be more important than their value as meat. This philosophy continues unchanged to this day. Consequently, if you go out to shoot a moose and leave the carcass to rot, the government approves so long as you pay a high enough royalty or trophy fees. If, however, you shoot a moose and try to sell meat that you can't use, or accept a gift of meat taken out of season by an Indian, you are in deep trouble, for there are any number of would-be policemen waiting to nail you.

— Robert McCandless

yesterday, i went for a walk where it smelled like rain. there were
little pockmarks in the dirt where the rain would've made them,
but didn't.

there was a wind blowing that felt like a good day on the river,
just before the clouds break open and force us to huddle under
the sloping, protective arms of a spruce tree.

WILD FLOWERS OF THE NORTH

Adder's Tongue
Anemone, Northern, Plume
Arctic Raspberry
Arnica, or Yellow Daisy
Arncia, Dwarf Mountain
Ash, Mountain
Aster, Pink and Small Blue
Avens, Mountain or Sweet
Bear Berry or Scopolallia
Bear Tongue
Bear Tongue, Smooth
Beefsteak Plant or Lousewart
Bilberry, Thin-leafed or Deer
Bleeding Heart or Eardrops
Bluebell
Blueberry
Bunch Berry or Dogwood
Buttercup, Easter, Marsh,
    or Mountain
Butterwort
Calla, Wild or Water Arum
Casiope
Cinquefoil, Shrubby
Clover, Prairie
Columbine, Purple
Corydalis, Golden
Crane's Bill or Wild Geranium
Cranberry, Alpine
Currant, Black and Red
Daisy Fleabane
Daisy, White
Dandelion
Death Camas
Devil's Bit
Dock
Drummond's Dryas
Dutchman's Breeches
Fireweed, Dwarf
Fireweed or Great Willow Herb
Forget-Me-Not
Gentian, Small Flowering
Geranium, Alpine
Grass, Brome and Cotton
Groundsel or Ragwort
Groundsel, Morning
Hair or Parnassus or
    Grass of Parnassus
Harebell, Alpine
Harebell
Heath, White
Heliotrope
Horsement
Hudson's Bay or Labrador Tea
Iris, Blue
Jacob's Ladder or Sunkweed
Juniper, Blue
Larkspur
Lily, Yellow Pond
Lupin, Arctic or Sun Dial

Maiden/Wax Flower
Marsh Marigold
Meadow Rue
Monkey Flower
Monkshood
Mossy Campion
Northern Bedstraw
Orchid, Franklin or Purple Spotted
Paintbrush, Indian
Pasque Flower or Crocus
Pearly Everlasting or Moonshine
Phlox, Mountain
Plantain, Robin's
Poppy, Arctic
Poppy Moss
Pussy Paws
Rhubarb, Wild
Rose, Wild
Ross Avens
Sage, Wild
Salmonberry
Shooting Star
Strawberry, Wild
Stonecrop or Ice Plant
Sundew
Vetch, Brilliant, Tufted
Violet, Blue, White and Yellow
Wild Chives
Wildflower, Red
Yarrow or Milfoil
Yellow Dryas
Twin Flower

fireweed

The Fireweed is the floral emblem of the Yukon

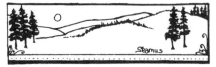

Part XIX

On that Yukon River trip there were some incredible
happenings. At Yukon Crossing, we pulled up to the bank
just about sunset with another fellow from Juneau,
Alaska. He had been telling Toby about life in Alaska and
when he went to Vietnam. (Toby asked him all about
that.)

Anyway, we cleared the bank and saw two guys with
guns preparing to shoot towards the buildings. The shots
rang out just as the Alaskan came up the bank behind us.
He hit the ground right now and motioned to Toby to
come on up. Toby came up the bank, saw the action going
down and got really mad. He whispered to the Alaskan
who disappeared over by the buildings.

"You stupid bastards, you come out here with your
stupid wild west ideas and start shooting the hella outta
everything in sight!"

"Hey buddy, we were just shooting bottles off the log
butts. We're not hurting anybody."

"Then why is my friend lying face down in the grass
over there! You've killed my friend you bastard!"

The two men ran over to the body of the Alaskan and
their faces got really white. One knelt down and just as
his fingers brushed the Alaskan's shoulder, the "dead
man" screamed and jumped up. One tourist fainted and
the other stood there shaking and flushed as Toby and
friend rolled in the grass laughing. They turned to go and
the Alaskan said in the strangest voice.

"Now you two go down to your boat, climb in it and
bugger off out of here. If you hesitate we are going to
totally destroy you by telling the mounties that you did
shoot at us. Is it all very clear?"

The men were already on their way. That night those
two got drunk as skunks and caught a pike in the back
slough. They didn't laugh too hard about that experience.

this is a project we can really sink
our teeth into.

It all began with the construction of a hydrodam on the Mayo
River in 1951. This was the first project completed by the
Northern Canada Power Commission. They've continued
building and developing until the electrical power generating
capacity in the Yukon is 87 megawatts (30 thermal or diesel
generated megawatts plus 57 megawatts generated by hydro
plants). Thermal power comes from a 22 megawatt diesel power
plant in Whitehorse, a 5 megawatt plant in Faro and two other
small diesel plants in Dawson City and Johnson's Crossing. The
hydro-generated power is produced by a 30 megawatt dam at
Aishihik, an additional 6 megawatt dam at Mayo, and at
Whitehorse a 20 megawatt dam on the Yukon River. Now they
want another one.e

We've all heard about the proposals to dam the Yukon River.
Five Finger Rapids used to be the primary site, but now all the
talk and attention focuses on Eagle's Nest Bluff. Maybe public
pressure will stop any attempt to build here, but remember
there are many other rivers and valleys. According to the
report, "The Development of Power", almost every river in the
Yukon has one or more sites that can be developed. Just so you
know too, here's a listing of the top rivers studied for possible
sites for dams.

1. Enough has already been said about the hydro-project on
the Yukon River.

2. THE PELLY RIVER rates as the next best possible bet:
Plans include using Granite Canyon for storage and power,
followed by Bradens Canyon and the Hoole Canyon.

3. FRASER FALLS on the Stewart River with
Independence as a possible secondary project.

4. THE TATSHENSHINI RIVER involving diverting
Dezadeash Lake with the diversion of Kusawa Lake as a possible
secondary stage.

5. At low NWP1 on the TESLIN RIVER.

6. The Upper and Lower Canyon on the FRANCES RIVER.

7. On the BATES RIVER with diversion of Dezadeash
and Kusuwa Lake.

8. Alberdeen Falls on the PEEL RIVER.

9. THE PRIMROSE RIVER scheme involves Primrose and
Rose Lakes and possibly Kusawa Lake too.

The valleys of the major rivers have a relatively flat
U-shaped bottom so large reservoirs are required to generate
enough power to make any dam worthwhile. If plans proceed,
one or more of these rivers would be blocked by dams ranging up
to 400 feet high and flooding some of our richest areas of
vegetation and wildlife. For example, the High Granite Canyon
Reservoir on the Pelly River would wipe out over 200 square
miles of the Pelly and MacMillan valleys. For what?

"You should have seen the one that got away!" Ha! Ha!

Note to the editor of the Yukon Catalogue: I wish to submit this article for immediate publication. It is the work of an investigative freelance journalist, Harry Fritz-Meyer, who entrusted it to me before heading into the bush some months ago. He now is long overdue, and I feel the serious nature of the report overrides any other considerations I may possibly harbour. Please find enclosed the original report, unedited as it was left with me.

Note to Catalogue Readers: Here it is.

It is common knowledge in the Yukon that a consulting firm of engineers has carried out studies on the feasibility of a hydroelectric plant on the Yukon River and adjacent lakes near Carmacks. What has remained hidden, until now, is the possibility for disaster inherent in such a scheme, since a series of lakes that would be affected — known locally as the Chain Lakes — are home to a singularly odd and very dangerous variant of the Great Northern Pike, or Jackfish *(Giganticus stinger)*.

Persons not familiar with the area under study are asked to consult the following topographical maps in the 1:250,000 series — 105L Glenlyon and 105E Labarge. It is not the author's intention to spend time explaining the project as it is understood at this tentative stage, but it does seem likely that portions of the Yukon River near Eagle Bluff, the Chain Lakes, Frenchman Lake and other bodies of water near Carmacks would be flooded as the result of a large dam on the Yukon, and the water would be re-directed through a powerhouse to rejoin the Yukon below Five Finger Rapids.

The Chain Lakes, once an old riverbed of the Yukon but now only joined to their mother by a small creek, Mandanna, would once again become part of the main water course — a disaster the author believes would be comparable in magnitude to the lamentable introduction to North America of the Starling and the dutch Elm Disease. Let it be said that the writer is not a person easily duped and only writes this article after long and painstaking study and dialogues with persons who have seen the danger close up.

Murmurs of the existence of the Giant Jacks came to my ear while carrying on research at Carmacks, the community that would be most affected by such a hydro facility on the Yukon River.

He was reluctant at first, but the man whose startling, face-to-face encounter with these strange freaks of nature started all the rumours and led to my discovery, opened up and told me all about it when he was convinced that to do so would, in the end, save human lives, not to mention several species of fish that utilize the Yukon River system. This man, Peter Heebink, is somewhat of a legend in the Carmacks area for his feats of endurance on the trail as well as his prodigious capacity for green beer and rum. He first penetrated the Chain Lakes region in company of his wife, Ginger, back in the early Seventies. Prospecting and the lure of gold brought them in, but the beauty of the lakes made them drop all that.

Fall found them putting up a small cabin on a tiny island on the biggest of lakes, Mandanna (named like the creek after Miss Mandanna Mack who lived nearby on the Yukon River back in the Twenties). In lengthy conversations I had with the Heebinks, I learned that locals had tried to warn them away from the chain; but those warnings were vague, almost silly. They did notice that the native family who had the region in their trapline territory never ventured far from the Yukon River, but the Heebinks put that down to low fur prices in effect at the time.

Just prior to freeze-up that first year on a cold October morning, when a low mist hung over the lake, Heebink had his first encounter with the strange fish. In his own words, this is what happened. "I was trolling deep with heavy line and lots of weight when something hit the hook so hard it nearly tore the thwart off the canoe. My hands were stupid from the cold and by the time I got the rod untied from the canoe, most of the line had gone singing off into the fog. 'Jesus, that must be one big trout' is what I was thinking as I tightened the drag and hauled back on the rod, sweating all over except my feet, which I had to keep kicking life into. Not one glimpse had I of the fish when suddenly the line went slack and something Green and Huge broke surface a hundred feet away — the Biggest, Maddest and Awfulest looking fish I had ever seen this side of sleep.

"It looked . . . no, it couldn't be, but it did . . . look like a Jackfish, but a God Awful Giant of a Jackfish topping even the biggest sturgeons I could remember seeing as a kid back on the Great Lakes, and not an inch shorter than my 17-foot canoe.

"Before more than three thoughts had crossed my mind — how the hell would I ever get it in the boat?; where's my camera?; or how many dogs would that thing feed? — the situation got right out of hand. Giving up the circling game it had been employing since breaking surface, the damn Jack attacked! Attacked the canoe! Before I could veer out of the way or cut the line, it rammed into the side of the canoe, penetrating that old wood and canvas like a good can opener does to a tin of sardines! There it stuck, half way through. Lord knows how many pounds of furious, snapping, twisting Jackfish! And it the only thing between me and the big swim.

"Beating it over the head with the paddle only seemed to make it madder, but all the thrashing and a little paddling I could get in kept us headed toward the island. Fearful that it would work its way loose and open up the huge hole where it had made its plunge, I took to engaging its attention with various items in the canoe: camera,

hooks, fishing pole; later, my boots and other pieces of clothing. The socks it seemed to savour, fixing its Awful Huge Eyes on me all the while as it ground into nothingness all I threw it.

"Even to this day it makes me sweat all over again to just talk about it, to think of that thing shaking and twisting away at my canoe! Less than a hundred feet separated us from the island when I started bawling at Ginger to get the gun. I never got to use it. With a heave that threw me from the seat, the Jack broke the canoe in two and plunged me (mostly naked by now) into the lake. I guess it never occurred to me, until I looked back, that I would never make it to the island. Right behind me were the biggest set of teeth I don't ever want to see again set between two mad Pike eyes. Screaming (it couldn't have come from me) seemed from somewhere else, but it was all wrapped around with thunder and a high, keening roar. Ginger had fired the 30-30 just at the moment the Pike caught me — and my scream and its death rattle were one!

"When I woke up under the eiderdown, for a second I thought I was convinced it was the most god-awful dream that bad rum had ever given a man. I was saved from a lifetime of repentance, however, by my half-numb limbs throbbing from the immersion in the lake, and Ginger crying by the window. Crying?

"She never stopped wailing when I finally staggered across the room. She just pointed out the window. The overturned and broken canoe I expected, the carcass of that slimy whale of a Jack (awful as it would be) I could have stood. But by God, how many more like it, or even bigger, were tearing around the wreckage or ripping (I can hear the sound in my sleep mostly every night) like sharks at their own dead! Can you imagine it? Circling

were dozens, maybe hundreds, of the Giant Jacks. And deep down in my bones I knew they were here not just to feed. Not, not just to eat. They had come to get Revenge. Revenge! That must mean they travel in packs, like wolves, or thing or something even worse.

"We set about making aircraft signals: HELP! . . . Doctor needed . . . Send The Army . . . Evacuation Requested . . .

"In the next few days we cut up our sheets, clothing and anything else with colour and festooned the island with those aircraft signal things, figuring it was our only hope with that canoe busted. We never did find the signal to indicate 'Surrounded By Giant Pike,' but brother, if they go through with that lousy dam, they had better put that one in the book.

"The book said smoke was a good way of pulling in a plane so we stacked all our firewood round the cabin. That was a bad mistake because the smoke from our burning house obscured everything, and that damn fool water bomber dumped on us! Head to foot. We were both covered in that awful red stuff and no closer to getting rescued. That night was terrible, but more bad luck chased the dawn in. Those Forestry people told a local pilot about our fire, and he flew by to see if he could help, only to have those awful Jacks commence to eat his floats when he taxied in! Two more days passed around that smouldering cabin (we had taken to shooting at them by now) before that pilot got calmed down or returned — with a helicopter this time. We left the island still ringed by those freaks and I tell you true that Ginger and I ain't never going back.

"Like that old old Indian trapper, who I'm sure had a few brushes with them (heard they got his whole dog team one winter when they went through the ice in the narrows. Awful sight that must have been), we soon learned that no one wanted to hear, let alone believe, the story.

"He's no man's fool. If he did make anyone believe, then he would never get rid of his trapline before the country was aswarming with experts and phoney-baloney professors, scaring off the game and shutting down his living for good. Maybe I shouldn't be talking to you now but this idea to flood the Chain Lakes makes my skin crawl, and I just can't sleep worrying about it."

Catalogue Note: The story ended here and was submitted for publication in this form. As was indicated at the beginning, its author has been missing for some months and it has only recently come to light that he had canoed into the Chain Lakes in an effort to get a first-hand experience with the "killer jacks." An air search of the chain turned up a wrecked canoe he was believed to have used and, a short distance away, thrown up on the beach was a severely-mangled typewriter. Nothing more was found.

In view of the serious questions raised by this account, the catalogue is pressing authorities to launch a full-scale investigation into the Chain Lakes pike situation, and is asking the Northern Canada Power Commission and its consulting firms to go slow with anything that could disturb the lakes until more facts are in.

CONSERVATION SOCIETY

Two hundred million dollars isn't much to pay for social and environmental impact of the impending pipeline project, but at least it's something. Unfortunately, the federal government ignored that recommendation (or, rather, dropped it under pressure when negotiating the pipeline agreement with the U.S.). But at least it was made.

But why? Who started all that, anyway? Where in the world would an industry-oriented agency like the National Energy Board get such a crazy idea? They'd never done anything like it before.

They were, of course, preceded by Tom Berger's infamous report on his Mackenzie Valley Pipeline Inquiry. He said "forget that proposal for 10 years" because the social impacts would be too great. So did the NEB just up and decide — out of the blue — to follow the trend and say "Okay. Build it along the Alaska Highway and give the Yukoners $200 million (about $10,000 per person in the territory) to play with so they won't be too mad"?

No, it didn't quite work that way. The NEB wouldn't have even thought of the social costs if it hadn't been for a small group of locals who represent a lot more people than they have on their membership roles.

The group is the Yukon Conservation Society — the only active environmental organization in the territory. They learned a lot of tricks from the anti-pipeliners during the Berger Inquiry and applied them to the all-too-brief NEB study of the Alaska Highway route, and got results.

The YCS has somewhere between 100 and 120 members (in the fall of 1978) but does an amazing amount of work with so few people, and so few funds. Without the group, and without the Indian lobby as well, the Yukon would long ago have been turned into an industrialist's dream.

A lot of what they do is on the public information side of things. For instance, they've held seminars on the Dempster Highway and its effects on the northern Yukon and, lest we forget, the incredible spectacle of the Porcupine Caribou Herd, whose existence is threatened by the highway's presence and use. Representatives of industry were heard then, as well as those of the environment. (A pamphlet on the seminar is available from the YCS.)

Those are just the main things the YCS has been into over the last few years. Not bad, for an organization only 10 years old. It gets into less political things, however, like sponsoring Young Canada Works grants for small-scale environmental clean-up projects and a Kluane Park Awareness Program, which offered an excellent and well-attended slide show at the MacBride Museum in Whitehorse in 1978.

The future of the conservation society promises to be just as busy and demanding as the past. Among their "ongoing concerns and interests" for 1978-79 are:

ON THE PIPELINE
1) construction terms and conditions
2) monitoring government and industry planning
3) pipeline route selection
4) social and economic impact monitoring

ON PARKS AND LAND USE PLANNING
1) management scheme for Kluane Park
2) northern Yukon parks planning
3) public education programs
4) Dempster Highway management proposals
5) land use policy and regulations
6) Wildlife preservation and management

ALTERNATIVE DEVELOPMENT PLANS
1) investigation of small-scale northern technologies. (It's about time someone got into that!)

HYDROELECTRIC DEVELOPMENT
1) Plant "X" (Eagle's Nest Bluff on the Yukon River upstream from Carmacks, conceived by Montreal Engineering, which is thought to be selling its 300-MW dam plans to the Northern Canada Power Commission).
2) Electrification of the pipeline (where we'd flood our valleys, killing wildlife galore, for the sake of the U.S. They'd power the pipeline pumping stations with electricity rather than the natural gas going down south, to save the gas to heat U.S. homes and industry — something like giving the U.S. 300 square miles of the territory to do with as it pleases).
3) Aluminum Smelter proposals. (Although Kaiser Aluminum seems to have lost interest in a proposed site at Whitehorse, the Chamber of Commerce keeps trying to get government to listen to them. Raw bauxite would be shipped to Whitehorse by train, then smelted here with power provided by flooded valleys, dead moose and birds. Now we hear they're looking at Ireland!)

The society's aims are "to ensure the wise use, protection and preservation of scenic, scientific, recreational, educational, wildlife and wilderness values of the Yukon Territory."

Although that doesn't mean they're always breathing fire, they often are. Without them, the Yukon would be lost to madmen profiteers. They deserve everyone's support. Memberships cost $5 per adult, $8 per family and $2 per student per year. They get $3,000 a year from the department of Indian Affairs and Northern Development, virtually all of which goes to miscellaneous expenses like stamps and whatnot, so donate any extra dollars you have to help them out.

They're a good group of volunteers, worth listening to and worth helping. Write them at Box 4163 in Whitehorse (Y1A 3V7), or contact their office in the T. C. Richards Building at 3rd Avenue and Steele Street.

— A.J.M.F.

Birds of the North

Red-winged Blackbird
Boreal Chickadee
Lapland Longspur
Pine Crosbeak
Yellow-rumped Warbler
Red Crossbill
Dipper
Common Golden Eye
Common Merganser
Water Pipit
Black-backed Three Toed Woodpecker
American Wigeon
Belted Kingfisher
Mountain Bluebird
Bohemian Waxwing
Canada Goose
Gray Jack
Canvasback
Clark's Nutcracker
Cliff Swallow
Downy Woodpecker
Common Flicker
Fox Sparrow
Great Horned Owl
Hermit Thrush
Red-necked Grebe
Least Sandpiper
Lincoln's Sparrow
Common Loon
Black-billed Magpie

Mallard, Eleanor
Marsh Hawk
Yellow Warbler
Hairy Woodpecker
Northern Shrike
Violet-green Swallow
Bank Swallow
Northern Waterthrush
Ovenbird
Northern Phalarope
Pintail
Common Raven
Common Redpoll
American Robin
Ruby-Crowned Kinglet
Ruffed Grouse
Rusty Blackbird
Savannah Sparrow
Dark-eyed Junco
Say's Phoebe
Semipalamated Plover
Northern Shoveler
Snow Bunting
Spotted Sandpiper
Traill's Flycatcher
Tree Sparrow
Varied Thrush
Wheatear
Bald Eagle
Willow Ptarmigan

Several other birds, distinct from the foregoing list, have been seen but observations were not sufficiently complete to identify them.

The Extinct Dogfish

Years ago a fish known as a "fisherman's best friend" was abundant in all the Yukon rivers. Anglers agreed the best way to catch them was to throw a worm as far into the stream as possible and shortly after the fish would fetch it back to shore, where they could be clubbed. Indian reports tell of how they used to gather in the narrows and bite at the caribou's heels as they forked stream during migrations. Each spring they could be seen wagging their tails, moving upstream to spawn. It is well documented that the happier fish usually got to the spawning grounds first. The mean ones often developed hunched backs and were called Salmon Fish. Being intelligent, these fish could be trained to roll over by tossing dynamite into the stream. They had the strange instinctive habit of only urinating when they were beside tree trunks. It is believed that through several dry years in the late 1800's all the water bodies in the Yukon dropped and the fish were unable to reach the trees. As a result they all suffered enlarged bladders and eventually one by one exploded to death.

— *Jim Jensen*

Environmental Source Book

Available from: Enquiry Centre
                Information Services Directorate

For free, you get a guide to all kinds of government environment-type departments and agencies in the country. All provincial, territorial and federal government departments appear to be represented, along with their boards, agencies, responsibilities, mandates, et cetera.

A selective bibliography of current writings on environment, including general publications, government publications, publications catalogues, audio-visual catalogues and film loan services is also in this book.

It was designed for the student, teacher, librarian or other researcher. Tells where to go to get more information, and gives helpful advice to the novice on how to get it without too much hassle. (Of course, there's always a hassle with getting confidential government reports. We'll all have to wait for a good freedom of information act for those.)

Anyway, this source book is free for the asking and it's a good start to get you on your way to becoming a protector of the earth and its wildlife. Not a bad hobby at all. And without critics, the government wouldn't do much at all — not things that we like, anyway.

ISBN: 0662-01622-X
Catalogue Number: En 21-23/1978
                Department of the Environment
                OTTAWA, Ontario K1A 0H3

The Northern Southern Protest Poem

Blue sky floating over me
    like an ink
        split out on white heaven
           white mountain
an' me floatin' amongst them
    like some
        wild mixed feather
not knowin' or carin'
        which way I'm goin'
an factories and a northern cross
make a circle of death and of light
        around me.

Down stairs at apartment 1978 (or whatever year it is)
an old diamond driller
        asked me if I knew
        I said I knew but didn't really care.
So go blow — take your wheels
        take your wheels
        spinnin' spinnin' spinnin'
down that road
        leavin' the dust to me.

I turned my collar to the cold
    pulled my cap down low
I heard the Lords of the Forest
    callin' out
        countries for sale
governments really cheap
cities — Lord cities —
    I can give away.

    but these trees of
        summer light
    I'd rather keep.

Blue sky floating over me
    like an ink
        split out on white heaven
           white mountain
an' me floatin' amongst them
    like some
        wild mixed feather
not knowin' or carin'
        which way I'm goin'
an factories and a northern cross
make a circle of death and of light
        around me.

           —Alyx Jones

Canadian Arctic Resource Committee

The Canadian Arctic Resources Committee has done an incredible amount of good work to ensure the north isn't screwed around by government, mindless developers from the south, and the enemy within. CARC was one of the more active participants in the Berger Inquiry and with a lot of knowledge on its side, successfully countered the simplistic arguments offered by the would-be developers.

One way to keep in touch with what they're doing is by subscribing to their newsletter "Northern Perspectives," which is free of charge.

BACK ISSUES OF 'NORTHERN PERSPECTIVES'

A limited supply and the high cost of reprinting compel CARC to charge the following rate:

$.60 plus postage for each issue.

This charge applies to back issues only. Current issues will continue to be forwarded, without charge, to those on our mailing list.

*Volumes that are not out of print may be obtained a xerox copies from CARC at $1.00 each.

      * * * * *

CARC is a non-profit organization, and gratefully accepts donations, which are tax deductible. Donations contribute to the production of the Northern Perspectives newsletter and other CARC research, so it's good if you can contribute a few bucks to pay for what you get free, 'eh?

Chairman of CARC, in case you're wondering, is Dr. Andrew Thompson. He and all his cohorts really give a damn, and if you do too, help 'em out.

CARC has also published several books which may or may not strike your fancy, and they're listed too.

Land Management in the Canadian North — Kenneth P. Beauchamp
—an analysis of land use planning and management in Canada's North with comparative materials from other jurisdictions. The book is a major contribution to the ongoing development of public policy in land use planning, primarily as a reference source.
ISBN 0-919996-00-0 (1976) 105pp. $5.95

Arctic Alternatives — Pimlott, Vincent, McKnight, editors.
—the proceedings of CARC's First National Workshop on People, Resources, and the Environment North of 60°. *Arctic Alternatives* has been widely praised as a comprehensive review of contemporary northern issues.
ISBN 0-969099-5-1 (1972) 391pp. $5.95

Land Regulation in the Canadian North — Peter J. Usher & Grahame Beakhust
—a critical examination of the drafting, implementation, and enforcement of the Territorial Land Use Regulation.
ISBN 0-919996-08-6 (1973) 170pp $4.50

Send order forms and cheques to:
Canadian Arctic Resources Committee
Room 11
46 Elgin Street
OTTAWA, Ontario
K1P 5K6

        —Max Fraser

"A land of gold"

what ever gave you the yearnin',
to drive a thousand miles of dusty road,
what ever gave you the feeling,
to come up here, to the land of gold.

A young mind tends to wander,
a youthful body finds a way to roam,
when you look back at the town you came from,
do you think, you could ever go back home.

There's freedom here way up in the mountains
on the rivers in the valley lyin' low
you feel things up here, that you never felt before
so why in the hell, do you want to go.

There's a little bit of fear, that whispers in your ear,
turn yourself around ——
but who in the hell is fear, to whisper in your ear
it tries to block out all the other sounds.

Two Rivers © 1978

"The only difference between men and boys is the size of their toys."

stan

In Alaska, the settlement was money instead of land, so natives had to buy into the economy of the whites. That was like being dealt into a game of monopoly without knowing the rules, and using their own land as the stakes. So now they play because they have no choice. Some people believe that the white southern Canadians might gain more by not forcing the Yukon Indians to play our sick development-oriented, materialistic games.

—b.b.

On the Trail of '98 — Mining

On my first trip I saw them. I had heard about the tailings piles just outside of Dawson, but never really pictured in my mind the miles and miles of gravel heaped up in piles. This was my first introduction to mining, and I thought the upheaval and destruction of the landscape belonged to the past. Men and women had gotten rich from the gold they wrestled from the ground, and this what they left us.

Today mining is the number one industry in the Yukon. I've heard this on the radio, read it in our newspapers and mining magazines, and seen it on car bumpers, but I never really knew what it meant until a few years ago. I was driving along the North Canol Raod and turned a corner and entered one of the most scenic valleys I had ever seen. The first thing I saw was a mineral exploration camp, then another, and still another. There was no old geezer crawling the back hills with his stubborn old donkey and chipping away at the odd rock with his trusty hammer — no, this was modern day prospecting.

Everywhere I looked helicopters were buzzing around, and tiny moving dots on the mountains turned out to be people seraching for minerals. That same summer I visited Elsa and Cantung, and toured the mine sites and mills at Whitehorse, Clinton Creek, and Faro. I was learning that mining is BIG in the Yukon, and there was more to it than I had thought.

Prospecting is the first step in the story of mining. Claim sheet indexes are available free of charge in each district Mining Recorder's office and at the Supervising Mining Recorder's office in Whitehorse. From the indexes you can order area maps that have mineral distributions plotted on them (last I heard, they cost $1 each). Topographic, aeronautical, geological maps and reports are available from the Regional Geologist, at 200 Range Road, Takhini, Whitehorse, Yukon.

The second step involves staking a claim and recording it. Two-post staking is required for all minerals except coal. There are not nationality or residence requirements for obtaining a claim and there is no provision for a "miner's license". Any person 18 years of age or older may locate, record and hold claims in the Yukon.

Depending on the type of claim you are applying for there are limits on the number of claims that can be staked. For example, an individual can only stake eight claims under the Yukon Quartz Mining Act on any one map sheet (approximately sixteen square miles). Most mining companies get around this requirement by staking claims, flying people from the nearest town to the site, getting the individual to record the eight claims as their own, and then transferring them to the mining company after they are notarized. The "going" rate in Ross River these days has been $50. If the feds had their act together, they would come up with some new legislation so mining companies wouldn't have to play these silly games.

The Yukon is divided into four Mining Districts with respective Mining Recorders at: Box 249, Dawson City; Box 10, Mayo; Box 269, Watson Lake; Room 220, Federal Building, Whitehorse.

The office of the Supervising Mining Recorder for the Yukon is located at 200 Range Road, Takhini, Whitehorse, Y.T. Y1A 3V1.

The third and final step involves acquiring a lease and gaining exclusive rights for mining. In the Yukon, the feds use the following legislation as a guideline to regulate mining:

1. Yukon Placer Mining Act — We live in one of the few places left on this planet where placer mining is allowed. It is the process of mining alluvial deposits by washing them with water. A sluice box is usually used, and gold is what they are after. This act refers to the procedures in locating and staking a claim, and provides a framework in which a miner must work. Placer mining claims are renewable annually upon performance of $200 assessment work per claim.

2. Territorial Dredging Regulations — This act refers to placer rights in the submerged bed and bars of rivers.

3. Yukon Quartz Mining Act — This act refers to hard-rock or "lode" mining. It includes all rock as it lies in the ground containing gold, silver, copper, tungsten, asbestos and any other naturally occurring elements. It excludes coal, gravel, soil, limestone, oil and other related hydrocarbons. Quartz claims are renewable annually upon performance of $100 assessment or payment of $100 in lieu of assessment work per claim. Quartz claims may be leased for a term of 21 years (renewable) after performance of $500 work or payment of $500 in lieu of assessment and after the claim has been surveyed.

4. Territorial Coal Regulations-This piece of legislation involves exploration licenses, leases, and payments for coal mining.

5. Northern Inland Waters Act and Regulations-This act refers to all uses of water. Placer mining accounts for 65 percent of the authorizations issued. Other activities authorized include oil drilling operations, diamond drilling and other hard-rock mining development operations, bridge, wharf and culvert construction, and dredging, dyking and river bank alterations involving dams. The majority of authorizations are issued by the Yukon Territorial Water Board, whose members are appointed by the federal minister of Indian Affairs and Northern Development. Other authorizations are handled by the Controller of Water Rights, DIAND.

Since the days of the gold rush, many valuable minerals have been dug and blasted from the ground. Our history rises and falls with mining and our economy depends on it. Besides the gold that is still being extracted from valleys and streams of the territory, silver, lead, zinc, asbestos, copper, cadmium and tungsten are the minerals being mined in the Yukon today.

Minerals are taken out of the ground by foreign-dominated corporations and shipped off to god-knows-where (mostly Japan) and then we get wages, some taxes and some service economy. Mining is our major source of revenue and it provides the most jobs for people after the government. Because of these considerations, the feds let the mining industry call the shots. They get away with more than they should. There have been some steps taken to reduce the environmental impact of mining, but there is still much more to be done — unless we want to leave behind for our children the same thing we were left with by the people who followed the trail of '98.

P.S. For anyone interested in prospecting and/or mining, here's the name and address of a catalogue you might find useful: Miner's Catalogue, Riggins, Idaho, U.S.A. 83549; (208) 628-3865.

—j. maxwell

A Dawson City Bartender's Soliloquy

Every drunk catskinner
who ever tried to flip a bartender
duble or nothin'
or twist wrists
with the waiter
for the price
of the drinks
thinks he's the first guy
to ever try that.
& every knothole who ever tried
to cage ten bucks off the bartender
on the basis of familiarity
(having passed out on the floor
 every night for the past
 two weeks) thinks
he's the first that day
and the bartender is cheap
and oughta go back
where he came from.
And on those days when
the bartender is hungover
and only wants to sleep
        everybody else wants
        the joint to jump
like that line from Robert Service,
"A bunch of the boys were whooping it up . . ."
while the rest of the time
they play crib and complain about the weather
and the service.
But I'm beginning to feel at home here.
I almost like everyone
in strange kinds of ways
& if I can't have the critics
interpreting my works
as "In depth penetrations
 of the illimitable struggle
 between the counterpoint
 of archaic nobility
 and the whosit."
at least let my patrons declare,
"One thing you gotta say
 for that bartender,
 he knows when to keep his mouth shut."

—Erling Friis-Baastad

a glimpse from the Past...

Mrs. Clarence Berry when asked what advice she could give to a woman about going to the Klondike, replied "Why, to stay away, of course. It's no place for a woman. I mean for a woman alone; one who goes to make a living or a fortune." Such was her comment after travelling with her husband to the Klondike on their honeymoon, spending a winter on the creeks prospecting, and then leaving the country in the spring with a fortune in gold.

Her vivid description of her home and housekeeping bring into focus the daily lives of those women who accompanied their husbands to the gold fields. Arriving on Eldorado Creek in October before their cabin was completed, Mrs. Berry describes their two-room home as having no door, windows, or floor and indicates she had to stand around outside until a hole was cut for her to get in through. The cabin was furnished with a bed and a stove, the stove being a "sheet-iron affair with two holes on top and a drum to bake in."

The cabin didn't have all the modern improvements by any means; no porcelain tubs or hot or cold water. When we wanted a bath we melted ice, heated the water, got the pan we used for washing the gold and did our bathing in that."

There was no lack of visitors. In fact she had nine people to dinner before she even had a table to sit from. Sometimes even strangers would come and eat, often taking any food in sight and then leaving. Nearly every night they had people staying with them because there was such a shortage of accommodation.

After finishing her daily housework, Mrs. Berry would often hunt the dumps for nuggets or pan for gold. One day she is reputed to have picked up fifty dollars worth of coarse gold while she was waiting for her husband to come up the shaft for dinner.

The Yukon Wok looks like a regular Chinese Wok except it's flat on the bottom. Flat-bottomed boats are the thing for river travel in the territory, so the same principle has been applied to campfire cooking. Some people even use these things for gold panning.

You'll find the Yukon Wok great for pancakes, bannock, and similar goodies. The Chinese Wok is better for cooking vegetables and things of that nature. It can be adapted to home-bush use over an airtight or, we imagine, you can just lift a plate off your cookstove and set the Chinese or Yukon Wok on that.

Either come in handy also for washing, feeding the dogs and salads, as long as you clean it before you use it again. Light to carry. Clean it like an iron frying pan.

Understanding the Aurora Borealis

"Was ever such a vision to mortals sent as
Northern Lights in the heavens flaming"
—E. Benediktsson (from "The Northern Lights")

"Some say that the Northern Lights are the
glare of the Arctic ice and snow,
And some that it is electricity
And nobody seems to know..."
—Robert W. Service (from "The Ballad of the
Northern Lights")

There is an old Inuit belief about the Northern Lights, or Aurora Borealis. The great dancing light known as "kenceit" refers to the auroras that flicker and shine and revel in wild delight across the trembling sky during the long winter nights of unbroken darkness. According to Inuit mytholgy, the spectacular displays of lights are the results of torches held in the hands of spirits that guide the souls of those who had just died to a land of happiness and plenty. The sound which is said to accompany this celestial show is the voices of the spirits attempting to communicate with the people of earth. I wonder what they would say to us?

We live in an age of doubt and uncertainty and want facts to explain what we see. The Inuit originally used mythology to explain the presence of the Northern Lights. Now we may not believe their interpretation, yet anyone who has witnessed Nature unveiling her cosmic lights must experience a sense of awe. The forms, the colours, and the motions, all in a state of change, and extending over vast distances of the night sky generate the feeling that here is a natural phenomenon which renders insignificant all man-made creations.

Living in the Yukon, we are in the belt that circles the earth where the northern lights are most often seen. This region of "maximum occurrence" skirts the coasts of Asia, passes over the northern tip of Norway, crosses the Atlantic Ocean to the south of Greenland, and traverses North America by way of northern Quebec, the southern edge of N.W.T., the Yukon and the northern parts of Alaska. Out of four billion people on the planet earth, here we are, a small number or regular spectators to this natural wonder. How do we explain the phenomena? What happens up there in the heavens? What causes the Northern Lights?

Imagine a small campfire burning bright in the night. Smoke rises as usual, and occassionally a small explosion sends sparks flying into the air. Now think of the sun. It's a big ball of gas on fire all the time, burning slowly and steadily and shooting out a constant stream of radiation and tiny particles — just like the sparks from the campfire. Now we've all heard of "sun spots," and seen pictures of these storms on the sun. Each storm means an extra bunch of those little particles are shot into space. Oodles and oodles of these high energy bullets zoom toward us. They soon enter the halo of atmosphere around our planet. They hit the particles and cosmic dust hanging around Earth. Like anyone too speedy or going too fast, they collide — they crash. Flash! There is an explosion and they become like sparks or fireflies. Similar to sparks thrown from a campfire into the air, they want to go everywhere. They want to fly in every direction, but they can't. The earth's magnetic field takes control and determines their movement.

It acts like Zeus. He's sitting in his rocking chair in front of the sun drinking his coffee, watching us fools here on Earth putting on our show. He doesn't know if it's a comedy or a tragedy. He sees the little fireflies born from the explosions in space, and catches them in a jar. Occassionally he decides he'll treat us to a little show of his, so he reaches over and shakes the jar with the fireflies. Lo and behold, we see the northern lights. A gift from the gods! Brightness depends on how vigorous old Zeus shakes his jar. The clue to the color lies within the prism.

Sounds and Forms of the Lights

Have you ever heard the Northern Lights make a sound? Some people swear that they have, and others don't believe them. Residents in or near the auroral zone, like us here in the Yukon, generally think that sounds **do** come from the Northern Lights. The sound most often described is compared to a faint hissing, swishing or crackling sound. People who live in the cities or towns have described it as similar to the rustling of silk. Indians and Eskimos have compared it to sounds like the noise of walking caribou.

These descriptions resemble the sound associated with electricity. For example, a faulty light switch can make a hissing or crackling noise as electrical charges escape into the air instead of following their intended route through the circuit. I've concluded that the Northern Lights can be heard, but some winter evening when you go out and the night sky is alive with light, you decide...

While you are there, you might have fun recognizing and identifying several forms of the Aurora Borealis. The following descriptions are based on appearance only, without any reference to cause, the position of the observer, or the change of time.

1. **A homogenous arc**, when located near the horizon, is seen as a luminous arch across the sky and appears to be a segment of a circle of light. The lower border is usually sharp and well defined, but the luminosity of the upper border fades gradually into the background of the sky. When an arch is overhead, it has the appearance of a thin ribbon of light stretching across the zenith to near the horizon. Often there will be several parallel arcs in the sky at the same time. When this pattern occurs, the arc of greater elevation above the horizon turns back at the eastern end to join the lower arc. This form is the most common pattern, present in practically all displays of the lights.

2. **A pulsating arc** remains stationary, but the entire surface or a portion brightens or fades with a rhythm of a period from several seconds to a minute.

3. **A homogeneous or solid band** is similar to an arc except it is likely to be less uniform, and have a fold or band or pronounced loop along its length.

4. **The rayed arc** is an arc where the length is not uniform or solid, but broken into a series of vertical rays. These rays may be relatively quiet, but more often appear to be in a lateral motion along the arc. This apparent motion is an optical illusion caused by the rapid formation and decay of individual rays.

5. **The rayed band** is similar to a homogeneous band with the addition of vertical rays which break the uniformity. There is usually considerable motion associated with this form, the band itself may move rapidly or the individual rays may appear to be very agitated resulting in intense motion.

6. **A drapery** is an extremely active form characterized by rapidly moving rays and changing colors. When viewed at moderate elevations, this form has the appearance of a band made up of long rays and folds, giving the impression of a hanging curtain. Seen directly overhead, a drapery resembles a wavy band of light with bright spots along it.

7. **A corona** is usually very colourful and changeable and is the most beautiful of all auroral forms. When long rays which are actually parallel to each other extend towards the zenith, they appear to converge at a single point above your head. The apparent union is a matter of perspective and conforms to the impression that parallel lines always seem to come together in the distance. If the rays extend in all directions across the sky, the form has the appearance of a dome. If they occur in only one segment of the sky, the corona has the appearance of a circular fan.

These forms are separate "pieces" or stages in a sequence of an auroral display. Although the aurora commonly progresses

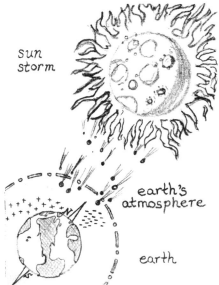

sun
storm

earth's
atmosphere

earth

through the stages just described, there are many variations on the general pattern. The aurora usually begins with the faint homogeneous appearance of an arc low in the northern sky. It may remain stationary for perhaps an hour and then will rise towards the zenith, gaining in brightness and definition. The arc may develop rays, then become a drapery, and finally reach it's climax in an orgasm of colour in the formation of a corona near the zenith. After the corona fades, patches of luminosity endure over a large area of the sky and a flaming auroa may develop. In its concluding stage, the display ends as it began with the formation of a faint arc near the northern horizon.

Size and Direction

It may seem that the northern lights dance only where you are, but observations of the same display over a substantial range of latitude and longitude have indicated the phenomena covers a large area. Height measurements showed that the distance between the upper and lower visual boundaries was many miles. The height and width of auroras have been determined by measuring the apparent change in position of the aurora relative to the background stars seen from two different places.

Depending on the stage or form, the vertical extent of a display ranges on the average from 15 miles in the case of an arc to 85 miles for rays. An arc 3000 miles long and over 100 miles high has been recorded, so the distance seems relative to the circumferences in space. This range may stagger the imagination and raise a few questions in your mind. Good. As we all know, appearances can be deceiving. Remember that the northern lights are occuring far, far away in space and, like the stars, they appear much smaller than they really are.

The presence of auroral displays in such countries as Norway and Australia tells us aurora appears in both hemispheres. Studies have shown that auroras point or indicate a general direction. As you travel towards the poles of the earth, there is a gradual inclination of the auroras towards the magnetic meridian. In the Yukon, the inclination of the auroras towards the magnetic meridian is almost **90 degrees**. This feature is il-

lustrated such that the vertical line represents a portion of the magnetic meridian passing though the point magnetic north and the horizontal line passes through the points east and west.

This doesn't mean that you should be using the northern lights as a compass to navigate through the woods at night. The direction of the arc varies with both latitude and time of year.

Remember that prism? It's the key to colour. First, I'll explain where the light comes from, then clue you in on why we see the various colours of the Northern Lights.

When the sun erupts into a storm of activity, it shoots electrically-charged particles all the way to the earth. These positively and negatively charged ions from the sun enter the upper atmosphere of our planet. In the form of protons and electrons, these high energy "bullets" crash into oxygen and nitrogen particles and cosmic dust already present in our atmosphere. The collisions produce a variety of chemical reactions which result in auroral light being created.

Changes in colour and brightness of the northern lights are due to the relative intensities of the wave lengths in the electro-magnetic spectrum. Added together, they produce what we see. For example, the common green appearance is the product of radiation of that colour. It is normally the most intense component of the spectrum and creates the largest colour effect. Light in colour!

The form or shape and motion given by this light depends on the effects of the earth's magnetic field. Its shapes and vibrating motion has given rise to the name "Merry Dancers" of the night. How do they move like that — jumping up and down and back and forth, and racing across the sky? Why do they move like that?

The moving images can best be understood by referring once again to those little particles from the sun. As those tiny electrically charged protons and electrons approach our planet they encounter the magnetic field. It gets stronger and stronger the closer they come until they begin to spiral around the magnetic field lines which are in a north-south direction. As they come closer and closer to us, the spiral closes to become more of a straight line; and the angle between the directions of the particles' motion and the magnetic field increases.

When the angle reaches 90 degrees, the particles are reflected and retrace their path towards the opposite pole. In effect, the particles are "trapped" like fireflies in a glass jar, bouncing back and forth between the north and south pole in a matter of a few seconds. They travel in a loop-de-loop motion such that the upper portion of their path will be more curved than the lower portion.

Now when these protons and electrons entered the earth's atmosphere, they separated into two fields. Positive charges moved west and the negative went east. Since they are both present, there will be an eastward and westward flow of electrical charges around the world. These opposing flows do not exactly balance. Flow generated by the positively charged particles pre-dominated, and there is a net westerly electrical current. This electricity is visible to us. Living, moving light in colour. We call it the Northern Lights, or the Aurora Borealis.

Well, that's about it. A scientific explanation tends to reduce everything to abstraction, and it seems as though the scientists have solved this mystery of nature. There are many facts and figures about the northern lights, yet there are many more questions still unanswered.

The mystery still exists, and the magic will always be there in this majestic celestial event.

P.S. If you want a more detailed analysis and scientific description, go to the Public Library in Whitehorse and try this book: **Keoeeit - The Story of the Aurora Borealis**. It is written by W. Petrie, and sponsored by the Defense Research Board of Canada.

—j. maxwell

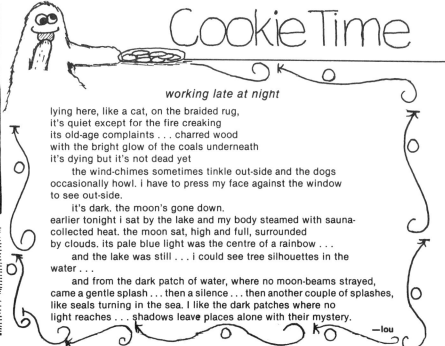

I WONDER WHEN N.C.P.C. IS GOING TO HAVE A SWITCH FOR THEM TOO!

CookieTime

working late at night

lying here, like a cat, on the braided rug,
it's quiet except for the fire creaking
its old-age complaints . . . charred wood
with the bright glow of the coals underneath
it's dying but it's not dead yet

the wind-chimes sometimes tinkle out-side and the dogs occasionally howl. i have to press my face against the window to see out-side.

it's dark. the moon's gone down.
earlier tonight i sat by the lake and my body steamed with sauna-collected heat. the moon sat, high and full, surrounded
by clouds. its pale blue light was the centre of a rainbow . . .

and the lake was still . . . i could see tree silhouettes in the water . . .

and from the dark patch of water, where no moon-beams strayed, came a gentle splash . . . then a silence . . . then another couple of splashes, like seals turning in the sea. I like the dark patches where no light reaches . . . shadows leave places alone with their mystery.

—lou

Song of Harmony

Alone in the woods
  Not lost or forgotten,
The scatched squeaky tones
  of society
Sometimes overcome
And hide the hum

Quiet moments at days end,
  Wood fire crackeling warmth
Cool rapids
  singing softly
I long for you
  And our sweet harmony.

Mary L. Cheney

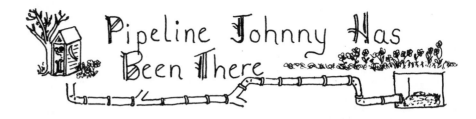

Pipeline Johnny Has Been There

The Yukon has had two boom and bust events which thrusted it into the spotlight of the world. There is a new boom on the horizon - the gas line. The author will attempt to set the stage and then help the reader prepare for this coming event by pointing out some of the "good" and the "bad" that are part of such a project.

The World War Two period of 1942-1944 saw the Yukon become the crossroads for one of the largest construction projects in teh history of the world. It consisted of the Alaska Military Highway, the Canadian Oil (CANOL) road and pipeline (itself larger than the Panama Canal project) and the Whitehorse Refinery (dismantled and shipped piecemeal from Texas). As in the previous boom, caused by the 1898 Gold Rush, thousands of souls poured into the Yukon to participate in this crass program, though it was more organized than the first.

The Yukon is facing its third event of major impact within eighty short (long) years. The proposed Alaska Natural Gas Transportation System will bisect the heart of the Yukon. It is billed as the largest privately financed project in the history of the world. It will even surpass its predecessor the Trans Alaska Pipeline System (TAPS), completed next door in Alaska in 1977.

The author is not attempting to fight or support the proposed gas line. At this time, one should assume that it will become a reality in two or three years. Now is the time to prepare oneself and the Yukon to live and cope with this soon-to-be event and its very real impact.

Knowing of this event's impending impact and *internalizing* it are two very different conditions. Fairbanks and other smaller Alaskan communities knew TAPS was coming, but were ill-prepared to cope with its social and economic affects on the existing communities. Like CANOL, TAPS was such a vast undertaking that whole self-contained cities (camps) sprang up overnight with all the social and other problems of a city, plus many more problems resulting from throwing an army of people together for a short-term crash project.

Few people involved with TAPS ever heard of the CANOL pipeline constructed just 30 years earlier. Consequently, many of the mistakes and inconsiderations made on CANOL were repeated on TAPS. It is interesting to note that the TAPS construction management firm and one of its prime contractors were part of the joint-venture which built CANOL.

A commentator can make the generalistic observation that everything one has heard about TAPS is true, be it good or bad. A related observation is that within almost any aspect of TAPS one wishes to cite, there is both good and bad impacts depending on the viewpoint of the citor. This seems obvious, but it is the intent of this article to point out this phenomenon/condition with respect to the yukon.

To illustrate, TAPS was delayed four years for environmental and other considerations. A lot of positive environmental requirements were incorporated into the finished project. It was also built to withstand the hardest earthquake, highest flood and worst fire known to the region. This was good for the environment and environmentalist, but bad for the consumer who absorbs the costs.

At the same time, some Alaskans who fought TAPS in principle later went to work on it when it became its inevitable reality. The money earned enabled them to develop fully their homestead land with cabin, power, road, well, etc., which they had heretofore been unable to do and could not have done it in the forseeable future. After the pipeline, they went back to doing what they were doing before - but now they had a lifestyle dream fulfilled. This is bad for principle but good for dream fulfillment.

Inflation brought by such a project is probably bad for everybody. This insidious biproject has the most significant impact and is the hardest economic factor to comprehend and cope with. It is also the root of many social problems in the local community.

What one has to internalize (assimilate) is that thousands of "outsiders" will descend upon small, well established and ordered communities with all their human problems. Strangers will appear overnight only to move on before the "local" gets to know them. Often these "pipeliners" only interest in the Yukon will be greed for money. All services will be pushed to the limits, expanded, and pushed again. The "local" will have to compete for everything in his life for two to three years. Afterwards he will have expanded facilities to better serve his needs. There may also be expanded population of left-over construction workers who decide to stay and settle. They may be of different mind and interests than the original community that existed prior to the pipeline.

All in all, mobilization and construction will be an exciting and intense time. There will be more hustle (and hustling) and bustle, entertainment, new people to meet, a sense of urgency and accomplishment(?) There will also be more social disorder - both external/physical and internal/mental: such as increased crowding, alcoholism, gambling, drugs, prostitution, VD, emotional and mental stress.

So what to do about this impending boom situation? Each individual in the Yukon must take stock of themselves with respect to the role they plan to play in this project. Also to *internalize* the effects the project will have on them - both good and bad.

One should have a concrete goal/reason for being involved in the project. It helps to offset the adverse elements. If it is to be a fact of life, then one ought to make the most of the opportunity for themselves and their community.

The community could help by setting up an *independent* (impartial?) information office to co-ordinate with all the participating public and private organizations such as with the territorial and federal pipeline agencies and the contractors. The objective is to get unbiased answers to any and all of its citizen's questions about the pipeline's effect on them. The contractors have such a "single point of contact". with both the territorial and federal agencies; why shouldn't the people?

Mostly it's a case of being aware that in two to three years your Yukon lifestyle is going to be affected positively and negatively. Fortunately, unlike CANOL and TAPS, there is still time to prepare oneself and all aspects of the community for this event so as to lessen the unfortunate social and economic consequences.

Hang in there.

Johnny "just passing through'......

Part XX

Toby knew this crazy guy named Terry who lived in a cabin just outside of Whitehorse and was a drop-out from some form of intellectual life style. Terry was extremely smart when it came to creative thinking, but suffered from the usual plight of intelligence. He was very cynical and often very blunt about life. I liked him a lot because he was honest.

One thing I really had in common with Terry was that he hated cats too. One day a girl who had been staying in his cabin left her Siamese cat there and it shit all over the place. Terry took it and kicked it out of his car about a mile away on his way into town for a week-long stay. Upon returning he found the cat had managed to find its way back, and not only had shit on horizontal surfaces, but had also mastered the art of crapping on walls! So he put it in a box, thinking he would find the girl... All was well until he woke up in the middle of the night and the cat was squatting on his chest, taking a dump on his quilt! He got out of bed, lit the lantern and blew its head off with the 22 and went back to sleep. In the morning he went to throw the corpse down the outhouse but on second thought gave it to Jones, his dog (who told me this story).

Anyways, the reason I found out about this was because I overheard Terry say to Toby, "Well I couldn't put it down the outhouse because I put that little puppy that died of distemper down there, and I liked him!"

THE PAST AND FUTURE LAND

By Martin O'Malley. $8.95. From Peter Martin Associates Ltd., 35 Britain St., Toronto.

For those who want something about the Berger Inquiry rather than Berger's report itself, this is it. The Toronto Globe and Mail reporter takes a typically Torontonian newsman's view of things northern, but since the book is largely quotes of testimony by northern people given to Berger in his community hearings, it's worth the price. It'll blow your mind if you've never been north or never been out of Riverdale. The book is essentially a condensation of the community hearings. Every place Berger visited was included and O'Malley has saved readers a lot of trouble by cutting out the stuff that made the inquiry so tedious, yet so thorough and so important to our country and the public interest.

**Rainer
Genelli
Said
It
All**

August 14, 1975

What really bothers me is this sort of whole imposition of southern values on the north; imposition of people in the north having to face up: "Well, lookit, it's progress. You can't stop it" or something. I wonder how people in Toronto would react if the people of Old Crow went down to Toronto and said: "Well, look, we are going to knock down all of these skyscrapers and highrises and blast a few holes for lakes to make for muskrat trapping, and you people are just going to have to move out and stop driving cars and move into cabins."

Judge Berger: And you told them that was progress.

Rainer: Yes, right, and told them that it was progress. "Well, muskrat skins are $5,000 a piece, and you know, Toronto is a beautiful muskrat breeding ground" or something. Or else maybe an important inquiry for establishing a trapline in the Parliament buildings or something. I don't know. That that is about all that I have to say at this point. If you do come back I might be able to prepare some more things, but I am very concerned about, you know, like fine, a lot of people would be able to adjust, be retrained, you know, get into the pipeline jobs. Whatever. A lot of the people who have come up here to live here — and live here for some reason or whatever else — I am really afraid that we are going to be left behind, and you know, we're left further behind than we are already; and it is a pretty tough go for a lot of people in this town as it is.

Berger: Thank you very much, sir. You made your point very effectively, I think.

ROUTE MAPS TO THE YUKON OILFIELDS
from: Edmonton Chamber of Commerce

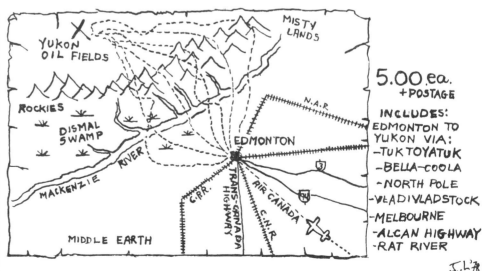

5.00 ea.
+POSTAGE

INCLUDES:
EDMONTON TO
YUKON VIA:
-TUK TOYATUK
-BELLA-COOLA
-NORTH POLE
-VLADIVLADSTOCK
-MELBOURNE
-ALCAN HIGHWAY
-RAT RIVER

"No one going to the Yukon seeking pipeline jobs can afford not to have these detailed and accurate maps of how to reach this most inaccessible region."

—*Bucks Greedy, Pres. of the E. C. of C.*

Dempster Highway Poem

Late in July, we were so broke
I was sure you'd leave me; so I left you
and hitched up the Dempster Highway
aiming for a spot near the Arctic Circle.
When I got to mile 203, I signed on
and went to work.

12 hours a day, 7 days a week
on a chain saw bringing down those
madly tapered northern trees.
Nosy grizzlies, cold rain,
mosquitoes, black flies,
an irritable foreman
and this long haired guy
I worked with squawking,
"Chain saws are bad karma!"
whatever that means other than
I did most of the chain saw work.

At night, too tired to shower
or taste those huge free dinners,
I lay sleepless under the Miss July
foldout tacked to my bunkhouse wall
wondering at the ways of love
that take a man so far away
to please a woman.

—Erling Friis-Baastad
(originally published in a magazine
called "Grain," out of Saskatoon)

HENRY WILKINSON'S PIPELINE INQUIRY

Collected works of Henry Wilkinson
Originally published in the Whitehorse Star

Henry's done it again with his "Everything you need to
know to get an enormously high-paying job on the
pipeline." He even provides book-buyers with a Yukon
passport and a life membership in the Carcross Closet of
Commerce. More importantly, Henry tells us all how to
look and act like a Yukoner so you can be eligible for local
hire. (Anyone who hasn't been resident in the territory
since the summer of 1977 can't be hired in the territory.
Check the union hiring halls in Edmonton and Vancouver
in 1984.)

"These politics and pipelines," he said.
"are levels. Levels of intrigue, corruption,
realities – and as many as the river has
currents."

dick

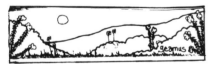

PART XXI

There was a main activity of Toby's that deserves
mention: his bike, a red ten-speed he named "Red Benny."
Woody had a blue one named "Blue Cheer," and Mike,
who liked to go on long trips, had a bike called "White
Powder."

We would go racing around in traffic creating
madness and stopping a lot at places on Main Street to
talk to people, I would get to nose some other dog (who
usually was on a leash, which I thought a rather useless
way to live). One time a car decided to turn in Qwanlin
Mall and drove right through Toby. He flew over the
hood and landed on the pavement in a sitting position,
finger in the air. A buddy working with a sidewalk crew
ran over, all worried. Toby was already up and yelling
obscenities by the time he got there. The car driver was
pretty freaked out, but I guess he should have been.
Toby laid it on thick though because all he got was
scraped hands. Red Benny was unharmed. I got to bark
and growl and be heavy on the cat·in the assailant's car.
That's why I remember it so well.

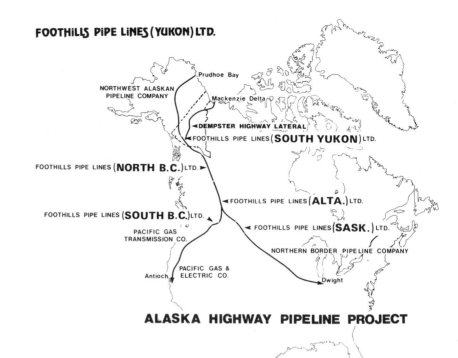

FOOTHILLS PIPE LINES (YUKON) LTD.

ALASKA HIGHWAY PIPELINE PROJECT

ANOTHER DAY IN THE LIFE—

Oh yes, another day, another dollar. Is this what these accursed camps are all about? Why am I here? Dollars and cents, that's what it's all about. More money, I always need more money to keep up this lifestyle. Every morning waking up to somebody else's alarm clock, feeling groggy from the lack of sleep from the night before. The boys down the hall in this goddamn bunkhouse whooping it up again last night like every night, drinking and playing their stereos till all hours of the night and I don't get any sleep. How do they do it?

Get up and off to the kitchen to see how much of that slop they call food I can get down my stomach. I had entertained some ideas about putting on some weight while I'm here, but these cooks put an instant damper on that idea. Eggs that look like painted silly putty, sausages burnt on one side, and God only knows what they did to the other side. I heard once of a fellow who took two pancakes and put them in his moccasins. Said they were quite comfortable, better than felt liners, he said. I believe him. How do these cooks do it? They can take a perfectly simple meal and massacre it. Here am I, working a twelve hour shift, and a damn hard twelve hours it is, and they expect me to keep my body running on this slop? I think I'll become a vegetarian. At least they can't bugger that up too much. Or can they?

Well I suppose I shouldn't complain too much, all things considered, things just aren't that bad. I've got a guaranteed paycheck, something my fore-fathers in mining didn't have. Also they had to carry their year's supplies into this territory on their backs, on their horses' backs, in their canoes, rafts or whatever they could put together. They had the cold of this inhospitable land, irregular supplies, and no hot and cold running water. I wonder how their food was?

Well maybe they had it rough, but so do I. I've got drunk people in my bunkhouse every night, and sometimes I'm one of them. How else can I put up with the boredom and loneliness of this place? How many times must I read the same books, look at the same pin-up pictures, talk the same conversation and listen to the same complaints without going stark-raving mad? I work all day with these guys and when our shift is over they want to talk the rest of the day away with shoptalk. I scream to them, "We've been doing this all day and you want to spend your own time talking about work? Don't you get a little sick of the whole thing?" But I guess not. For some of these men that's all they know — just the job and that's about it.

Some men I've known have drank away a few fortunes and a couple of wives. And you find them doing the same things over and over again. Off to work in some camp for as long as they can take it, then to town to drink, drink, and more of the same. Some men I've met do it the right way. They'll work for as long as necessary to make X amount of dollars to fund some project or another, then they go do it. For those men the camps have their strong points, for others all they are are another way to kick a booze or drug habit, make a few dollars and enough time for another pogey claim. And they go on and on like this for God knows how long. And it scares me when I talk with these old hands and they tell me "Listen, kid, there's no future in this. Get out while you're young. This is all I know and with my education what else can I do?" Yes, it sure scares me.

But camps are not all the blues of loneliness and the stagnation of boredom. You can have an awful lot of fun working your way to whatever goals you've set for yourself. One thing I found out was a good way to hassle and harass the boss. We all know about bosses and how

they, at some times, may be the most bothersome and counter-productive people around. How they can come onto a job that is functioning quite well and in no time whatsoever have everything completely screwed up by their "knowledgeable" changes. Ask any working man how he feels about bothersome bosses. They'll tell you of many instances where the bosses are nothing more than meddlesome pests. But there are good bosses. These men stay in their offices and drink coffee, and talk about their useless employees who have no respect for their positions of authority (ha). In one camp the bosses could not agree on anything, could not get along among themselves, and there was certainly no mutual respect for one another. I could never understand them. But then I don't think they ever really understood themselves either.

I used to take a perverted pleasure in making their already wretched position worse. I would do such things as ask them contradictory questions to confuse them, then before they could answer I would answer the question myself and hussle back to work before they could say anything. One trick I was taught was how to get out of working in the cold, a trick that must be as old as mining itself. You just spill coffee on yourself, then you have to wait till it dries before you go back to the sub-zero cold. And if you've got on two pairs of long-johns plus your work pants that can take quite a while — enough time to drink more coffee and spill another cup on yourself if you feel so inclined. Depending upon the job you are doing

you may get set breaks, or you might just take your breaks whenever they present themselves. This presents itself with more ways of getting in the bosses' hair. If you don't have a set break, then when do you start and finish them? You might just turn the entire day into one long break, and you certainly wouldn't be the first to do so. At one camp the men complain if they don't get so much on-the-job sleep time. They need their sleep, and if they are drinking every night in the bunkhouse, just when do they get their sleep?

Well, when you're finally through the day and it's time to once again brave the dangers of the cook-shack, you might feel that you deserve a meal and that no matter how bad it is you've got to eat something. One thing I learned was to eat as fast as possible, hoping that as little food as possible would touch your by now very sensitive taste buds. Not only is this a good way to get food down your gullet, but it's also a good way to insure that you will live to work another day, and keep those almighty bucks rolling in. If you've managed to hold your food down, you get to go back to the bunkhouse and relax to the same thing you relaxed to the night before. That is, the same records or tapes you've been listening to since your arrival, the same drunks arguing the same arguments, the same pin-ups on the walls, and the same noisy, leaky over-head water pipes. Different camps have varying bunkhouse arrangements, but they all have their basic similarities in single or double rooms, washrooms with toilets that always seem to overflow just as you sit on them, sinks where the hot and cold faucets are reversed, slippery floors that are always wet, and more often than not some drunk sleeping in the doorway in the exact position for you to trip over, break a bone, and miss a few money-earning shifts. Some bunkhouses could be placed on the side of a nice steep hill, so you can get in some good mountain climbing experience, strengthen your legs, and maybe break one on a faster-than-planned descent, especially if you move in the mornings before somebody gets out to shovel the fresh snow. It can be a lot of fun. One bunkhouse I had the displeasure of living in gave me a unique perspective on winter. I had a two-foot ice slick climbing in my window, heading for the floor and if I didn't hack at it occasionally with an axe, it surely would have headed out the door. While busy fighting off this ice slick, I also learned how to move in and out of doors very rapidly. This bunkhouse was so placed that to open an outside door in the dead of winter was to allow the ever-present blizzard to come roaring in and present you with a four foot snow drift. Doing things like this is not what you would call harmonious relations with the other occupants of the bunkhouse. Nobody likes to come out of their room to a four foot snow drift, especially in bare feet.

Now bunkhouses are not all bad. From living in bunkhouses I have met men who had fought in just about every war within human memory. In some cases men who had fought on both sides, at the same time, in the same place. When men like these get together it's something like reminiscing over a just lost chess game. The moves are thought over for both sides, and the wrong decision, the one that cost the game, is discovered. I've also met all kinds of colledge graduate types who have given me a never-ending line of sometimes valuable, sometimes useless information. You'd be surprised at all the arts students working in the camps. Not just summer students, but full time employees, or just full time to the point where most everybody draws the line and says: "That's it! I've had enough. Get me the fuck out of here." So I've had enough with mining camps, survey camps, diamond drilling camps, and I've had enough about writing about them.
—*Jim Montgomery*

THE BACK YARD SMOKEHOUSE

When was the last time you priced smoked salmon, char or goldeye in the local deli or exotic food store? Expensive? You bet it is; anywhere from $4 to $12 a pound, depending on the species, and not nearly as tasty as the smoked fish you could prepare at home.

The best smoke house available, and the cheapest, is the one you make yourself.

With a fair amount of work an excellent smoke-house can be made from plywood, sheet metal, stovepipe and wire mesh. However, there are easier and better alternatives.

Probably the best home-made smoker is an old refrigerator. As these appliances usually have the wire racks needed for laying out the fish, and because they are reasonably air tight and fireproof, they make ideal smokers.

Horst Mueller of Whitehorse modified an old fridge by cutting air vents in the bottom and cutting a three-inch vent hole in the top, through which he has put a short length of round pipe equipped with a damper made from the top of a tin can and a coat hanger.

Horst then punched a hole in the back of the fridge and inserted a thermometer. His heat source is an electric hotplate set in the bottom of the fridge.

A heavy pot is used to hold the smoking wood while a sheet metal "baffle" punched full of holes is placed over the pot and hotplate in order to disperse the smoke. With a minimum of work and very little expense, Horst has made an ideal smoke house.

Other abandoned or broken major appliances can also be used as smokers. Reub Fendrick uses an old freezer while others use washers, dryers and stoves. All it takes is a little ingenuity to turn these junk appliances into efficient smokers.

One word of caution — beware of any fridges or freezers with plastic interiors. If you want to use such an appliance, replace or cover the plastic panels with sheet metal.

Another cheap and efficient smoker can be made from an empty 45-gallon oil drum. With a cold chisel, cut the top from the barrel and also cut a fire box door near the bottom. A baffle should be made to spread the smoke and dissipate some of the heat given off by the smoldering wood.

This baffle can be made by trimming the cutout top of the drum down by 1" all around.

Holes are then punched in the lid and it is positioned about six inches above your pot of wood chips.

It can be held in position either by bricks stacked on the bottom of the barrel or by bolts projecting into the barrel sides.

Next, heavy metal screen should be cut to serve as the fish racks. A 45-gallon drum will efficiently take two shelves. The screen shelves can be held in position by welding or bolting for angle-iron brackets to the sides of the barrel.

The top of the smoker can simply be a heavy piece of plywood with a circular hole about 3" in diameter cut in the center. The draft can be controlled by nailing the end piece of a large juice can near the opening in such a way that the juice can lid can be swung over the draft hole, thus allowing you to reduce or increase the amount of smoke.

Your final job is to punch a hole in the barrel somewhere near the top and insert your thermometer. Once you have your smoker, whatever type it may be, your next job is to prepare your fish for the smoke house.

Very small fish, up to one or two pounds, can be smoked whole while larger fish should be split or filleted. When splitting, simply score next to the backbone and spread apart so that the fish lays flat. When using fillets leave the skin on and don't worry about the rib bones.

Your fish should be washed thoroughly and then soaked in a brine solution made in the following proportions: four cups of salt, two cups of brown sugar, two tablespoons of black pepper and two tablespoons of crushed bay leaves to each gallon of water.

You can experiment with this recipe by replacing the sugar with dark molasses or honey and you may decide to leave out the bay leaves and add instead two tablespoons each of liquid garlic and liquid onion.

Try flavoring your brine for salmon with dill plants. The fish should be soaked in the brine solution for from three to ten hours, depending on how large the fish are, how much brine flavour you like and what salt content you prefer.

You will have to experiment to find your ideal time. When brining, always use a glass, plastic, or earthenware container, NEVER METAL. A plastic garbage can works very well.

After brining, the fish should be lightly rinsed in cold water and then allowed to air dry for up to three hours or until a thin glossy glaze covers the flesh.

The fish are then placed in the smoker, skin side down, and are smoked in a fairly dense smoke at temperatures between 90 degrees F and 180 degrees F for from six to twelve hours. The time and temperature again depend on how you like your smoked fish.

I prefer mine almost dry and as a result would smoke them for the full twelve hours at about 150 degrees F. Probably the best temperature would be between 110 degrees and 140 degrees F for approximately eight hours.

Always set one piece of fish aside during smoking so that you can sample the product in order to determine when the fish is done.

The flavour of your smoked fish depends entirely on the brine solution and the fuel used for smoking. Scrub willow, poplar and birch are some good local woods. Do not use any spruce or pine, as the resins in conifers will taint the fish. Alder, if you can get it, and of course any of the fruit woods, are excellent smoking fuels. Whatever wood you use should be perfectly dry.

The best heat source is an electric hotplate set in the bottom of your smoker. A heavy metal pot can then be filled with wood chips and placed on the hotplate. If the hotplate has a heat regulator, simply adjust the heat to the point where the wood slowly smoulders.

If you don't have a heat regulator just turn on the hotplate until the wood begins to smoulder actively, then turn off the hotplate. If your drafts are set correctly and the wood is dry enough, the chips should smoke for up to three hours.

One or two pieces of charcoal in a hibachi can also be used as a heat source but care must be taken that the chips do not burst into flame.

Just about any Yukon fish can be smoked successfully, with salmon probably the most famous and best tasting. Lake trout in the five to ten pound range are excellent, as are grayling and rainbow. Northern Pike and Lake Whitefish, two of the most underrated game fish, are superlative when smoked.

Your smoked fish will keep for up to three weeks under refrigeration and, of course, you can freeze the product. It has been my experience, though, that no matter how much fish you prepare, it always disappears within two or three days.

So go ahead and try smoking some fish. It's a lot of fun, easy to do, inexpensive and will provide you with some mouth watering delicacies.

—*From The Whitehorse Star*

keeping Busy & making things

TWO CANOE CATAMARAN

For those who like to sail but can't afford it, here's how to make a safe, sturdy catamaran out of two canoes.

The framework is all made from one inch galvinized conduit, the mast is a twenty foot length of 1½ inch schedule forty aluminum. Support cables are made from clothes line cable, and the sail can be home-sewn from ten yards of rip stop nylon available at most drapery stores.

The framework is all bolted together with ¼ inch bolts of various lengths and the framework fastened to the canoe thwarts by 3/8 inch "U" bolts so no drilling of canoe thwarts is necessary. The centre board is cut from a piece of ¾ inch plywood and should be painted with a water solvent paint. Ruddering is done with a canoe paddle from either canoe stern.

Put a turn-buckle on each of the four guide cables running to each end of each canoe. Put a pulley on the mast top and on the end of the boom to enable sail raising and steering.

This craft is extremely stable and can carry four people and all their gear with no difficulty.

Good sailing!

jim jensen

10 YARDS OF RIP STOP NYLON SAIL 18'x8'

CLOTHES LINE CABLE

MAST HELD ON WITH "U" BOLTS THUS ADJUSTABLE

TURN-BUCKLES

TWO 17' ALUMINUM CANOES

SIDE VIEW

PLYWOOD CENTER BOARD

DIAGONAL SUPPORT PIPE

J.J.

20' MAST OF 1½ # SCHEDULE 40 ALUMINUM PIPE

CLOTHES LINE CABLE TO EACH END OF EACH CANOE, WITH TURNBUCKLES

FASTEN FRAMEWORK TO THWARTS WITH "U" BOLTS

"U" BOLTS

18"

40"

¾" PLYWOOD CENTER BOARD

30"

FRONT VIEW

J.J.

Making Your Own Bush Town Hat

This is the pattern for the fedora/panama style hats I have c cheted for various friends the past few years. If I fulfilled all the requests for more, I'd be producing hats the rest of my life so it seems much simpler to pass along the recipe and let you all make your own.

The material I use is synthetic carpet yarn which gives the hat sufficient stiffness and flexibility to be shaped according to your own fancy; or more practically, according to the prevailing sun, rain and wind. These marvelous hats are great sun visors, and they shed rain, can be anchored down in wind with a couple of knotted laces passed through the hat band and can be stuffed in a small corner of your pack, yet keep its shape.   Maintenance is minimal - handwashing and placing it to dry over a small upside down pot or coffee can. The hats seem to acquire more character with age.

MATERIALS: One 3.5 metric crochet hook or possibly a 3 if you have trouble making fairly tight stitches.

5 to 7 ounces of 3-ply carpet or stiff weaving yarn. I order my yarn from a mill in Nova Scotia. It's about $1.35/ lb and you can order a sample card from: John Ross & Sons, Box 841, Truro, Nova Scotia

APPROXIMATE TENSION: In one square inch I get 5 rows of crochet with 4½ stitches to the row.

INSTRUCTIONS: Essentially you are making a circle the circumference of your head for the top, followed by a tube as high as you want the crown and continuing the circle where you left off for the brim. All the terms are standard crochet usage and the basic stitches are explained and illustrated in any craft magazine.

TO MAKE A CIRCLE: Chain 4 stitches and join in a loop with a slip stitch. Into the centre of the loop single crochet 8 stitches. Then single crochet 2 stitches into every previous one until there are 24 stitches in all. Mark your last stitch with a safety pin or a piece of yarn to keep track of rows.

ROW 1: do a row of plain (1 single crochet into each single crochet)

ROW 2: increase every second stitch (i.e. 2 single crochets into 1 stitch every 2nd stitch)

ROW 3: a row of plain

ROW 4: increase every 3rd stitch

ROW 5: a row of plain

ROW 6: increase every 4th stitch

CROWN: When the outer edge of the circle is the same size as the head to be covered (or perhaps slightly smaller as the hat might stretch slightly, and for me this is usually right after increasing every 7th stitch), then continue plain, thus making a tube. Make the tube as high as you want your hat

crown (from 17 - 22 rows after the last increase seems fairly comfortable) and at any point, put in a few rows of any colour you like.

You can use colour to give the effect of a hat band or make the hat a bit gayer by using various colours on the top and brim as well.

BRIM: The brim is made by continuing the circle where you left off. So, if your last increase on top was every 7th stitch, you would mark where you begin your row and increase every 8th stitch, do a row of plain then increase every 9th stitch, etc. Go around and around, trying the hat on now and again until the brim seems the right width then sh off by doing a few slip stitches, pull yarn through and weave in any loose ends on the underside with a wool needle. That's all!

- Helene Xenia Diena D

HOMEMADE BEER

If you've been drinking draft Prinz Brau all summer and wondering what real beer tastes like, and wondering why you passed the breathilizer test after drinking all night, then you're ready to get into the homebrew business. I have been making beer ever since I migrated away from my 79c/6-pack supply. Thankfully, I am not a connoisseur of homebrew, so I have fairly undiscrimin-ating tastes, as long as it is palatable and it works. I have been using the same simple recipe for six years, and friends keep telling me how much better my beer is getting, which is more indicative of their deteriorating tastes than the improved quality of my beer. So, with my apologies to gourmet connoisseurs of homebrew, here is my thoroughly tested beer recipe:

For a ten gallon (ten case) batch buy two tins of hop flavoured malt (the color of your choice), ten pounds of sugar, two packets of beer yeast, and a gross of bottle caps. Heat up a couple gallons of water (Lorne Mountain spring water is best), add the two tins of malt and ten pounds of sugar. You can use between five and ten pounds depending on your mood. Dissolve it all and pour it into a clean twelve gallon plastic garbage pail, making certain it is not your slop bucket. Add enough cold water to make a total of ten gallons (give or take a gallon). When the temperature of this solution (called the wort) is between about fifty and seventy degrees F., sprinkle two packets of yeast on top. A preferred method is to add the yeast to a quart of the wort in a large jar and hasten the consummation of the sugar-yeast relationship (before adding it to the entire batch) with less likelihood of alien yeasts converting your beer to vinegar. Believe me, it takes years of salads to consume ten gallons of beer vinegar.

Now cover the garbage pail with a piece of plastic fastened around the lip with elastic or rubber bands and place in a warm place for about a week. If you're putting it in the loft you'll wish you had filled it there to begin with. Now here's where a hydrometer comes in handy. The bubbling you've been hearing is the yeast metabolizing the white death into alcohol. When under pressure in the bottles the sugar is transformed into carbon dioxide which gives beer its all important bubbles and head. I was sickened to hear of a friend who, before bottling, discovered his beer was flat and poured the entire batch down the sink.

Take periodic readings after five days and bottle when the specific gravity of the beer is between 1.002 and 1.004. If it slips by you and all the sugar becomes alcohol, you will have a reading of 1.000 and will have to add about one teaspoon per bottle (figure it out for the whole batch). Siphon the beer directly into ten cases of beer bottles, with the bugs and cigarette butts removed, and cap with

a bottle capper.

Store in a safe place out of reach of small children and start drinking after three weeks. But, if you don't mind it a little flat and green, commence drinking immediately and save the caps. Pouring the beer properly so as to leave the mung behind from the bottle is an art in itself. And, if you happen to bottle an explosive batch with an overdose of sugar, uncap your bottles in the bathtub, or take it to a party and watch the fun from a distance.

Peter Heinickenbink

Some Fun Things to do in the Winter

See if you can spend an entire day inside without touching the floor of your cabin (staying in bed all day is cheating).

Prepare the Great Yukon Paper Airplane...see if you can make it into a Kamakaze in the airtight or barrel stove.

Use bed springs for an antennae up on the roof for your 12 volt T.V.

Read the dictionary, drag the Reader's Digest in from the outhouse and play "It pays to increase your word power."

Go have a meaningful conversation with the dog.

Stack ashtrays on top of each other and maybe you'll see the funny looking guy from Star Wars.

Go outdoors and try to start the truck so you can go find some people or a bar or something.

The Canadian Government has provided a new pasttime for people who have nothing to do - you can convert your height and weight into metric, convert your house into metric and all your recipes, temperatures as they happen and all kinds of other fun things.

Metric System Equivalents
Equivalents du Système Métrique

Canada metric   Canada métrique

Temperature/Température									
Celsius	-60	-40	-20	-10	0	10	20	37	100	200
Fahrenheit	-51	-40	-4	14	32	50	68	98.6	212	392

Length Measurements Mesures de Longueur		Mass Measurements Mesures de Poids		Liquid Volume Capacités Liquides	
1 in/po	2.54 cm	1 oz	28.35 g	1 fl oz/fl	28.41 ml
1 ft/pi	0.30 m	1 lb	0.45 kg	1 pt/chop	0.57 litre
1 yd	0.91 m	1 cwt	45.36 kg	1 qt/pte	1.14 litre
1 mi	1.61 km	1 ton/tn	0.91 t	1 gal Can	4.55 litres
1 mm	0.04 in/po	1 g	0.04 oz	1 ml	0.04 fl oz'/fl
1 cm	0.39 in/po	1 kg	2.20 lb	1 litre	1.76 pt/chop
1 m	3.28 ft/pi	1 kg	0.02 cwt	1 litre	0.88 qt/pte
1 km	0.62 mi	1 t	1.10 ton/tn	1 litre	0.22 gal Can

chart donated by the cigarette package on the floor.

KNITTING MUKLUK LINERS

PREPARATIONS: You need some 100 % wool. Either spin it yourself or buy it (be sure to check the label—yarn isn't necessarily wool, even if it looks like it). Also get a couple of sets of knitting needles. The packages of 4 needles are best because you can use them for flat as well as tubular knitting.

Find someone to teach you the one basic knit stitch and when you've mastered this (knitting a scarf will leave you an expert), you're ready for mukluk liners. Most craft magazines have clear descriptions and illustrations of this stitch and basic techniques such as casting stitches on and off.

METHOD: Figure out some way of putting continuous stitches on 3 needles. I've found the easiest way to do this is to put all the stitches on one needle then divide them off on the other two needles. Stitches are cast on by making a series of half-hitches. This amount will vary according to the fatness of the yarn and size of the needle - the larger both are, the fewer stitches are required. Ideally, the needles should be about the same thickness as the wool. You may have to experiment a few times until you've found a fit for your leg.

Knit around and around with your basic stitch. A fairly tight knit is a good idea. If using your own spun stuff, leaving the lanolin in makes it more waterproof, but sheep are pretty stinky animals. Knit the tube until it's the length of your leg from the knee down. It's a good idea to have them long enough to turn up over your knees when travelling in deep snow.

When you come to the top of the foot, pick a corner of the triangle formed by the 3 knitting needles. On either side of the corner increase 1 stitch about 2 stitches in from the end of the needle. Every time you knit around and come to these two places, increase another stitch.

When the thing you've created fits over your foot all the way to the end of your toes, (remember this is still a tube with the hole now being the bottom of your foot), knit a couple of rounds without increasing. Cast off your stitches and set aside until your sole is ready.

Flat knitting the sole: This will be done on 2 needles only.

Cast on a few stitches about the width of the back end of your heel. Add a stitch or two over the next couple of rows using your foot as a guide. If the foot goes out on one side, make the increase that side of the centre. Knit away 'til you have something that roughtly covers the bottom of your foot. It's a good idea to keep track of how many stitches are in each row so you end up with another one almost the same. Cast off.

JOINING: Using the same kind of wool, sew the sole to the leg and foot part. If you are going to be using them for slippers in the house, they'll last a lot longer if you sew on leather bottoms.

Mrozinsky

Alice
Custom Dress Making
Box 4402
Whitehorse

ICE SCULPTURES

Sixty below is hard to comprehend if you've never experienced it. When it gets that cold, not much moves. The animals hole up somewhere and any people with brains hole up, too.

But if you live in a cabin, you have to go outside for a pee sometime. It never fails to impress me when I step outside, without a parka or even a sweater, just for a quick leak. All the dogs wag and some whine for attention. They have frost over their neck and face fur and sleep curled up in a hole in the packed snow, face tucked under their tail. I look at them and feel the cold biting into my bare arms and realize that without my cabin, or a fire, or more clothes I would surely freeze to death within twenty minutes — yet they thrive on this cold.

That's usually what I think about as I squat there watching the stars and adding my contribution to the artwork in the snow. It gets to be quite a creation, with the guys building yellow stalagmites and the women carving bas-relief grafittis at sixty below. —*j. b.*

SUB-ZERO PHOTOGRAPHY

Keep your camera warm. Keeping it in your vehicle as much as possible, or inside your jacket or vest when hiking or skiing will ensure smooth functioning in all aspects. This is most important for cameras with battery-operated functions such as light meters; under colder conditions battery function will be greatly hampered, or may cease altogether. A hand-held meter or simple guesswork may be de rigeur.

Sub-zero temperatures have a tendency to make metal to metal moving parts become stiff or even bind. Such things as aperture changes or focusing the camera become increasingly difficult in colder temperatures. Shutters may, if too cold, begin to lag or stick in an open or shut position. These problems are overcome by simply keeping your camera warm.

Care must be taken for your film. Do not be hasty in advancing your film after an exposure. Wind it too quickly or jerkily, and static streaking can occur. Being cold, film can also break. When changing it in the open, take care not to breathe into the camera body — frost will develop, necessitating thawing of the camera. The same goes for lenses. They can also take on a frosty coating and must be warmed to become functional again. When parts do become frosted, be sure they are thoroughly defrosted before taking the camera outside again, as this will only compound the problem.

Bare hands on metal in colder weather can be a painful experience. Where practical, metal parts can be covered in a fibre-reinforced tape. A thin mitten liner can make most camera operations simple tasks. If not too chilly, the finger-tips of the liners can be cut out for greater flexibility.

Rubber lens' hoods should be avoided as they will freeze into impractical shapes which are hard to work around. Metal lens' hoods, on the other hand form a pocket of cold air around the lens, slowing frost formation for a short time if you should venture inside.

All in all, photography in sub-zero conditions need not be unpleasant. It can be most pleasant capturing the subtle hues of our winter light conditions. You need only follow a few simple guidelines to be able to enjoy your hobby. —*Tim Dowd*

Liquid Propane Conversion

Using liquid propane rather than gasoline in your engine can lead to less operating and maintenance costs, longer engine life, and 70 per cent less crap in the air. There are about 250,000 vehicles now running on L.P. on the continent; cab companies, and large trucking fleets have put down an initial investment that is paying off in the long run. Mileage and performance are about the same for L.P. and gasoline, but L.P. is usually about 15 per cent cheaper than gas, and has no lead, carbon, sulphur or gum to screw up your plugs, valves, rings, cylinder walls, oil, or muffler. And again, it's easier on the air we breathe. When considering that L.P. is stored at a low 150 lb. per square inch pressure, and their tanks are built to 250 lb. that makes them about 20 times less likely to break open upon impact than a gasoline tank. Strong argument for conversion, eh?

There are only five basic parts to a conversion kit, and these can be purchased at any L.P. dealer, or in a Jerry kit, from (minus tank) this fellow: Jerry Friedberg, Box 531, Point Arena, Calif. 95468. His kit will cost you about $70. Be sure to tell him whether you have an over or under 150 h.p. engine. Check locally for the prices, then make your own decision, keeping in mind the duty on across border shipping. Your equipment is a converter, which utilizes engine heat to vapourize the liquid, carburetor jets, various hoses and fittings, and the tank itself, which new should cost about $70.

These tanks are good practically forever, so look out for a second-hand one; that should cut the price by about half. Installation is a simple process anybody with the right tools can do, it's just hooking the hoses up to the carbs, and setting your tank down firmly, with brackets bolted in place. Your L.P. people will you how to do it right, or the kit will give you all the instructions necessary to do it yourself.

These people deal in conversion:
Dueck Motors
1305 West Broadway
Vancouver, B.C.
731-7711
You can get a North America wide listing by writing to:
National L.P. Gas Association
79 West Monroe St.
Chicago, Illinois 60603
If you're going to do it, good luck, and remember your contribution to pollution-free motoring. —*mars bonfire 2*

The rising whine of the airplane engines had settled into a throbbing drone and we all felt a gentle pressure backward. Speed built up, the nose left the runway, and we climbed slowly off the ground. I gazed through the window at a wide, green valley, low hills and mountains, and then out the open door at more of the same, my teeth chattering quietly. Wedged between other damp bodies and the wall, I shivered, and though the draft played with my coveralls, it wasn't just cold in there.

The plane droned on and higher, circling the airstrip and the infinitesimal red triangle that was our target. The jumpmaster casually surveyed the valley, the clouds, and then dropped out a paper streamer to test the winds. Circling once more, the instructor directed the pilot to the exit area.

There were three first-timers, two of us on our second jump, and three instructors along for the ride in addition to the jumpmaster, Chris. The differences were quite apparent. The instructors chatted amiably to those ready for their first jump. Their enthusiastic grins contrasted with my partner, who muttered uneasily and fidgeted with his reserve chute. I just shivered and tried to keep my teeth quiet.

As we neared the exit point the first jumper's expression hardened and the grin became a grimace as he clumsily but carefully (oh so carefully!), edged his way to the open, roaring doorway and swung his legs out into the slipstream. The jumpmaster stuck his head

out the door to look ahead and behind, and down, judging the exit point.

He returned and yelled "OK, Ready?"
"Look up, GO!"

The man swung out and dropped from sight, losing even the grimace. The static line went taut and jerked, like a hangman's rope snapping. Then there was a loud banging while it flapped against the side of the plane and Chris pulled it in. The other two first-timers looked at each other, their expressions dimmed only slightly. As the aircraft turned, a small figure became visible suspended beneath a red and white candy striped canopy.

Time crawled while events replayed twice. We continued circling the field and the nearer

my turn got, the more I dreaded its arrival.

The other second timer become more composed as his time came. Again the yell "Ready . . . GO!" His expression of grim determination was drowned in a wave of blank surprise as he fell . . .

At any rate, he's out now, and I'm next: the last novice.

I crawled toward the opening and the roar of the engines. The static line is clipped into place, and with a grin Chris asks "Satisfied?" I nod and he chuckles. I shuffle forward a little more and dangle my legs out into the torrent of air. I gaze down and then quickly back up at the wing. The blur of the propellor is illusory, but comforting. I can't stand to look down. ("Man, that's two THOUSAND feet!") My composure and innocence were exhausted the first time around. This time I know only too well what I'm getting into.

On the first jump my calm appraisal of the countryside, my eager anticipation of the jump, and my practised exit had not obviated the gut reaction. As I threw myself out, my exuberant "Yahoo!" had turned into a strangled "Yeargh . . ." Then my spread eagle had crumpled when I put my head down to see what was below and came to the disquieting realization of my rather awkward position: head down, two thousand feet above the ground, and travelling only forty miles per hour. I made a similar fiasco of my landing, naively coming down normally while travelling *backwards* at five miles per hour. Needless to say, I ended up with a sore tailbone. This dismal review occupied my mind as I dangled my legs in the void and watched the rain clouds whip past the wing.

I look up at Chris and cock an eyebrow in question. Well, what next?
"Okay . . . Ready?"
"Look forward." An eternal pause, then "GO!"

No hesitation — Why bother; after all the anticipation there is nothing else worth thinking. No more mental preparation, no more bad jokes ("Gory, glory, what a hell of a way to die . . ."), and no more prayers.

So I go.

In an attempt at self reassurance I shout at the disappearing plane "Arch Thousand."
"Two Thousand."
"Three Thousand . . ."
Then I think, "Five? Hell, where is that

bloody chute?" Reaching for the reserve, I lose my balance and begin to roll. In reaction I madly claw the air, and regain stability just as a firm tug pulls me upright. I look up to see my nice (and very welcome) parachute billowing full and white against the grey clouds.

With great conviction, I say aloud, "Thank you God. Please forgive me for my foolishness and my doubt."

Before me is spread a vast, open panorama. The Pelly River wanders down the valley toward the afternoon sun. Dark, wet green carpets the valley and low hills. Mountains hem in the north and south, and small lakes gleam like splashes of silver beside the muddy string that marks the Robert Campbell highway. A huge grin spreads across my face as I absorb this incredible scene. Surrounded by such beauty, I can only smile and look around again and again, the rain softly tapping my helmet. I am convinced this is the best way to see the Yukon!

A little belatedly, I remember I still have one item with which to contend, the landing. I yank on the steering toggle to see the target and the instructions I am getting. On course now, I drift over the town and watch the barking dogs. I thank God the wind has slowed and as I approach the field I prepare myself. ("Damn, but that ground is coming up fast!")

OK, ready.
Feet together.
Head up.
Impact!

A sore rear again, but hurting never felt so good before! It surely is nice to be safely back where I belong, but I can hardly wait for next time.

—Glea Piwowar, Faro

Part XXII or "Red Benny's Tales of Intrigue"

I am a bicycle, a ten-speed to be exact. I was born in Japan and bought in Vancouver by a crazy freak who liked to drive fast, get high and amaze me with the speed of his turns. He took good care of me though, and one day Toby bought me and jetted me to Whitehorse.

My first feeling was pins and needles and the constant chafing of gravel along the sids of my tires. Toby bought Michelin tires and filled my inner tubes with "leak-stop," a fiber-resin compound that leaks out new holes and seals them off before the tire is even flat. We would just cruise into a gas station and fill it back up to 55 pounds and we were off again.

We ended up living in downtown Whitehorse which had some rough pavement, but for the most part, was dirt. The cruise downtown was always a favorite. We would zip down 4th Avenue into Main Street and flash through the cars towards the river. Seamus the dog was always by our side, except for long trips. I really liked him, except when he peed on my tires. We got tied together a lot sometimes, depending on whether Seamus would stay around the house. Toby spent more time looking for his dog with me than I care to remember.

Once Toby got stopped by the police when they chased him down 4th Avenue and he cut through Qwanlin Mall to get away. Another car was already waiting and stopped us. The cops were really mad. Apparently we were doing 40 mph and Toby didn't have his hands on me, as usual. And we had cruised like this through the new traffic light on 4th and Main.

Toby never stopped for stop-signs and lights–they were for cars as far as he was concerned. He just kept an even eyeout for everyone, and never got schmucked for years. The only really rough times were when we would cruise out on the Long Lake Road to the sawmills. Sometimes in the really thick dustholes, I would take a hell of a beating. The roots would bend my rims so fast that spokes would pop right out of my axle mounts. The dust would eat right into the gears and brake cables and turn everything into sandpaper.

We walked home twice from about 8 miles out, me him and Seamus, who loved the walk after running all the way out there. Toby'd have to take me into the car wash and steam clean me before I went into the bicycle shop to be rebent into shape.

Isaac Meecham

When I was a kid in Virginia, I
never suspected I'd someday
be living here
              on the delta
where the Klondike River empties
into the Yukon—
drinking beer,
writing letters home
and worrying about the fate
of Isaac Meecham.
I bet I'm the only person in the world
who's worrying about the fate
of Isaac Meecham.
Like my wife said yesterday, "Maybe
you've been chosen to vindicate him."
Raised to consciousness
in the peace-crazed Sixties
I guess I can
if anyone can.
Or should.
Our house was built
during the First World War.
Our attic is filled with ancient copies
of the Dawson Daily News.
A story I read in the first one
I found has kept me thinking.
ISAAC MEECHAM OF
    DAWSON UNDER ARREST
the 1918 headline says.
It seems this Isaac,
who traded between Dawson City
and Alaska points,
spoke out against Mr Wilson
and his war.
The last I heard,
Deputy Marshal John Wood
had left Fairbanks for Nenana
by dog sled to drag
Meecham back to justice.
Mr Meecham apparently thought
the war was fought to capitalistic ends.
He also said the Kaiser should have won it.
I don't think anyone should win
or wage them; perhaps Meecham
was so angry his words moved
faster than his brain. The newspaper,
which was Unionist
and screamed for conscription,
wouldn't want to credit him
with anything more noble than treason
so there's no knowing
for certain. Maybe
he was a good man who hated war
or maybe he loved the Kaiser
or maybe he just loved
to hear himself talk.
At any rate, I suspect
the cell floor was covered
with broken teeth
when they finished
with Isaac Meecham.

—Erling Friis-Baastad

FREE THE YUKON!

Pipeline Engineering:
How to Build a Bomb

Here's the junior molotov kit. First, get your sneakers ready. You've got to be able to run fast — once.

Anyone can do it. Get one empty wine bottle (what the hell, you can use scotch bottles too). Make sure you have 25 cents — no, make that 50 cents for a little gas.

Get that old dish rag that you don't want to keep on using, but don't want to throw out.

You'll also need a couple matches in case one doesn't light. Don't forget your pen, piece of paper, and thumb tack so you can let them know who's responsible

Weapons Department
Yukon Liberation Front
Yahoo!

STAINED GLASS SUPPLIES

Dervo Distributors
650 University Boul.
Berkeley, California
94710

New Renaissance
5151 Broadway
Oakland, California
94611

UNDERWATER DIVING —

There are a surprising number of active divers in the territory. Diving here, we are advised, is not too different from diving anywhere else, although the following considerations should be taken into account:

—Be prepared for a very cold dive.

—Take into account the altitude when calculating decompression rates. For example, Quiet Lake is about 3,000 feet above sea level and there are other lakes at the 4,000 foot level.

—Be extremely careful when decompressing, as there are no facilities here to deal with a serious diving accident and you would have to be flown out to Vancouver. And flying is not going to help anyone who has the bends.

Spear fishing is permitted, but you should check with Fisheries about stocks they are trying to preserve. You need an angling license as well.

COMPRESSED AIR BREATHING STATION
Harry Lowry will fill scuba tanks for about $2.00 at his house at 39 Clyde Wann Road in Porter Creek. Call him at 663-2062 after six o'clock before you come over. Harry has lots of scuba equipment for sale, USDivers, Healthways, and Sportways.
    —d.m.

Ruthie's Plant Dyeing & Home Spinning

With so much of our lives ruled by this technological age, I feel that the more we can depend on ourselves for the goods we need, the better off we are. In a sense, spinning and dyeing with plants has become an extension of a self-sufficient lifestyle for me.

These instructions are very general as it was impossible to cover all aspects of these crafts here. At the end there's a list of books which I've always found helpful. Good Luck.

Dyeing

Plant dyeing has three main steps: 1) preparing and mordanting wool, 2) extracting the dye from its source, and 3) dyeing the wool.

PREPARATION AND MORDANTING

Nature dyes take to any sort of wool - be it homespun, raw fleece or commercially spun wool - as well as cotton, linen, silk and dog hair. They don't take well to any artificial fibres - like nylon or phentax (yuk!). If this is your first dyeing experience, you could try dyeing with some store-bought wool but make sure it's wool and not a synthetic. If you buy a 2 oz. ball of natural shade, you'll know exactly how much yarn you have and will be able to easily split up the ball into smaller amounts.

Whether you're using unspun, homespun or factory spun yarn, the first step in dyeing is to scour the wool of natural oils, dirt, straw and chemicals. Place wool in a pail of water as hot as your hand can bear it with some mild soap like Lux and let it sit overnight. Gently squeeze out water in the morning and rinse. That should do it unless it's "manurey" wool, in which case you can wash it again.

Wool is delicate and should be handled gently. It'll harden and matt if exposed to harsh temperatures and if it's sloshed around in water much.

Next step is to mordant the wool - that is, add a chemical which will help the dye to be absorbed into the wool. Mordanting is done either before dyeing or during the process. To pre-mordant the wool, add a little mordant to water, dissolve and then simmer the wool in the mordant for an hour. Let the wool sit in the mordant bath till you are ready to dye it. If you mordant during the dye process, add the mordant right to the dye bath with the wool.

The accompanying chart explains the most common mordants and when to use them. Traditionally dyers used to put chunks of iron, copper or tin into the dye pot as mordants to vary the dye effects. Root of alum, wood ashes for alkalinity and urine for acidity were also common mordants. Now dyers use mineral salts. Each mordant, while helping to make the dye fast in the wool, also has a slightly different effect on the dye bath. For example, if you have a dye bath of marigolds and divide it into six pots, then add a different mordant to each pot, alum would dye the wool a bright yellow, iron would sadden the dye bath and give you bronze wool, chrome would change the dye to gold, tin would give a bright orange, copper would give an odd shade of green and oxalic acid would intensify the yellow shade originally produced. Without any mordant, the wool would be dyed pale yellowish-gold. So, the type of dye plant you're using dictates the mordant to use. This chart is for a 2 oz. skein of wool.

Mordants are available from drug stores or from: Northwest Handicraft House, 110 West Esplanade, North Vancouver, B.C.

Extracting the Dye

Colour can be eeked out of almost any plant, berry, root or flower as well as from some insects. The trick is to find dyes that provide a strong enough bath (when you've extracted the dye) that it will adhere to the wool and stay fast forever. However, the purpose of mordants is to make the dye fast in the wool.

Having mordanted the wool and prepared a dye bath, the final step is the dyeing itself. When you're sure that you've removed all the dye from the source by simmering it, remove all the dye material by straining through a sieve or piece of cloth. Lay the mordanted wool in the dyebath, or if you're mordanting in the bath, add the mordant, then lay the wool into the bat *damp*. If there's not enough dye bath to cover the wool, add water. Simmer the dye and wool for an hour or until the wool has taken on the desired colour. Remove from heat and let the wool cool in the dye bath.

Later you can squeeze out the dyed wool and hang it to dry. The next day, wash out the wool in warm, sudsy water - gently because the more you wash, the more of the colour will run out.

Dyes

Generally, if you can crush the berry or flower between your fingers and it leaves a stain, it'll provide a dye. Experimentation is surely the key to success in plant dyeing. A basic rule for extracting dye from any source (rosehips, marigolds or whatever) is to crush or break apart the dye plant, leave it to soak for 2 days in enough water to cover it easily, then simmer it for an hour or two in the same water to remove all dye from the plant. Then strain off all the stuff from the liquid and add the wool.

Here are some hints on removing dyes from sources

Use flower heads or petals when they're in their prime. They lose much potency as they die. Dried flowers make lousy dyes. If your dye involves a yellow flower, put in some leaves from the plant as well as flower heads. Usually, flowers give shades of yellow; blues, reds and greens are uncommon.

Berry dyes are challenging. Often a berry dye bath will be a rich, deep purple or red and it won't dye the wool at all. Oxalic acid reacts with the berries to make the dye penetrate the wool better. Add this mordant right to the berries as you're brewing them up. Use berries at their ripest and pick lots and lots. Purple dyes like oregon grape or blueberries give better colour to wool than raspberries or red currants.

Root and bark dyes have to be soaked for at lest 2 days, maybe more to soften up enough that the dye will be released. Dye usually comes from the inner root or bark. Scrape off outer layers to expose the dye source which is usually a yellow colour. The inner bark of a birch tree will give tan, pear and apple bark and some alder barks gives yellow. Oregon grape roots give yellow also. Before leaving roots and barks to soak, break them into little pieces and crush.

Lichens and Mosses: these are my favourite dye sources. Lichen dyeing is always a surprise. Some release great colour after just one hour of simmering. Others must be fermented in a jar with ammonia for a few weeks before they let lose their marvelous colours. With fermentation, plain drab rock lichens can be coaxed into giving amazing purples and pinks. Here are a few lichens and mosses that give good colour by simply brewing them up; both the dark and pale green mosses that hang in clumps like beards on spruce trees give shades of green with alum as a mordant. A bright green, stiff lichen that grows on branches of spruce or pine trees gives brilliant yellow with alum mordant, and bright lime green with copper sulfate. Yellow rock lichen gives good yellow without a mordant, better with alum.

Dye Recipes
onion skins

3 big handfuls of dried outer skins of yellow onions, crushed†
1 tsp. alum (buy from a drugstore)
big enamel or stainless steel cooking pot
1½ qts. water
small skein of wool - 1 oz. of homespun or store bought white and washed well to remove dirt and chemicals

Simmer onion skins in pot with 1½ qts. water for ½ hour. Remove from heat. Strain skins from liquid. Add alum to dye bath and stir to dissolve. Add the wool *damp*, making sure dye liquid covers wool, then return to heat and simmer for an hour. Stir once in a while and lift the wool to check how it's absorbing the dye. When the wool has become a strong yellow-gold colour, (it might not take an hour) remove from heat and let the wool and dyebath sit until completely cool. Later, remove the wool, squeeze to remove water and hang to dry. Rinse the next day with lukewarm water and a little soap, dry and it's ready for use.

† *Swipe the onion skins from a grocery store - everyday they throw out boxes of old onion skins.*

YUKON DYE RECIPES

Lupine (flowers and stems) & copper sulfate mordant = soft green
Mixture of three or four yellow flowers & alum gives soft yellow
Mixture of three or four yellow flowers & tin = brighter yellow
Low bush cranberries & oxalic acid or tin = pale red rose
Blueberries & oxalic acid or tin = bluey/mauve

[*Lichens and mosses are everywhere - Experiment! Try with alum or tin as mordants.*] *I always have made use of the Federal building gardens to supplement my dye pot - lots of marigolds and begonias.*

--- *Addresses* ---

Made-Well Manufacturing Co., Sifton, Manitoba, for 5" x 9" carders ($7.75 a pair - send money order). They also have spinning wheels.

Keith Shackleton, R.R. 4, Campbellford, Ontario, K0L 1L0. Sells unprocessed wool by bag...$ .75 a pound for white, $1.50 for brown or black.

Highland Heather, Grand River, Nova Scotia, B0E 1M0. Already spun wool in either white, or colours, $1.50 - 2.00 for a 4 oz. skein.

Valley Fibres Ltd., 51 William St., Ottawa, Ont., K0A 2N0. Spinning, weaving and macrame supplies...fleeces and flax.

Helio Dyes and Crafts, 2140 W. 4th Ave., Vancouver, B.C. (604) 732-6596. Cold-water dyes - send some money for a catalogue. Try also Behnson Silk Supply on Richards Street in Vancouver. (check the Vancouver phone book at a library for the exact address.)

--- *Book List* ---

1. "Dye Plants and Dyeing", Brooklyn Botanic, 2601 Sisson St., Baltimore, Md.

2. "Your Handspinning" and "Your Yarn Dyeing", by Elsi G. Davenport, both published by Select Books, P.O. Box 626, Pacific Grove, California 93950, U.S.A. These are excellent books for beginners and advanced in cheap softcover. They cover all aspects of both crafts in well.

3. "Anyone Can Build a Spinning Wheel", by W.C. West; "Spinning with a Drop Spindle", Tresh; "An Introduction to Natural Dyeing", by Rob and Christine Tresh; "Home Dyeing with Natural Dyes", by Margaret S. Furry and Bess M. Viemont. These books are published by Tresh Publications in California. They are thin, softcover books full of juicy recipes and advice...between $1.25 and $1.75.

4. "Creative Spinning, Weaving, and Plant Dyeing", by Beryl Anderson. This is a not-too-bad book for knitting with hand-spun yarn and is hardcover with colour pictures.

Mordant	amt.	when to use	effect on dye bath	Beware!
alum	1 tsp.	add to wool in dye bath	use on yellow dyes	too much alum makes wool sticky
iron ferrous sulfate	½ tsp.	add after wool has been in dye bath ½ hour	darkens colours	—
chrome	¼ tsp.	mordant just before dyeing	deepens yellows to orange and gold	light sensitive - is useless if exposed to light
tin (stannous chloride)	⅛ tsp.	add after wool has been in bath ½ hour	brightens all colours, especially yellow	makes wool brittle (use sparingly)
copper (blue vitriol)	1 tsp.	pre-mordant wool	brings out greens	Poison!
oxalic acid	¼ tsp.	add to dye material	use with berries helps extract colour	Poisonous and Corrosive

Spinning

If you have a big ole husky dog or a long-haired canine critter, you might like to learn how to spin the hair off of your beast. Collect the winter coat when your dog sheds it in the spring. Put it in a bag until you have quite a bit.

I'll give instructions for how to make a hand-spindle to spin sheeps wool on and then later, adaptions you can make for doing dog's hair.

A simple spindle for spinning a medium thickness yarn can be made as follows: take a piece of 3/8" dowelling 14" long and a 3" circle of 3/8" plywood. Cut a 3/8" hole in the centre of the plywood disc and slip the dowel into the disk until one end sticks out approx. 2½". Glue it carefully in place. Sharpen the 2½" end, then turn your attention to the other end, and put a notch 2½" from the top. Finish it by sanding the rough edges so the wool won't catch.

Before beginning to spin, take a piece of yarn 18" long and tie it just above the disk. Bring the yarn over the disk, make a halfhitch and bring the yarn up the other side of the disk and make another halfhitch with the yarn in the notch at the top of the spindle. Now, you're ready to spin.

Spinning is basically twisting and pulling fibres of wool or hair till they're in a long continuous yarn with enough twist

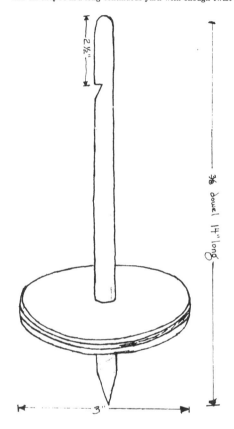

to give the yarn strength - the more twisted it is, the stronger it'll be. Begin with a small handful of well-fluffed and teased raw wool. Hold onto the end of the yarn that's on the spindle and give the spindle a good whirl from the bottom end. Spin till there's twist in the yarn, then hold the spindle between your knees so the twist won't unwind. Carefully lay a few fibres of wool on the twisted yarn so the spin carries the wool into the yarn and as it twists, pull out the new wool you've added so that it doesn't spin itself into a great big glob.

Again spin the spindle (always in the same direction) and let the twist spin the wool, pulling the fibres to make a continuous yarn. Nothing to it! After you've spun enough yarn that the spindle touches the floor, undo the half-hitch in the notch and wind the yarn onto the dowel above the disk. Re-tie the half-hitch.

The surest way to create a smooth yarn is to start with well-teased and carded wool. If you're spinning the wool too thickly and the yarn's all balled up and chunky, with pieces in between that are really tight, try pulling it out a little more as you are spinning. If your spinning is too thin, the yarn'll break and the spindle will crash to the floor. You'll wonder why on earth you're spinning anyway. But take heart!!! Work to develop a rhythm...twist, pull out the wool, smooth it with one hand, twist, pull, smooth, add on, twist, pull, smooth....wind onto the spindle.

 ## Dog Hair

Because dog hair is shorter in length than wool, it's trickier to spin. If you plan to spin mainly dog hair, it's best to build a smaller scale spindle - use ¼" dowelling and

plywood, make the spindle 2" shorter, and decrease the disc size to 2½" in diameter. A set of wool carders (address page 80) is a great help in preparing hair for spinning. If you don't have carders, fluff and tease the hair as best you can by hand. Try to spin the yarn too thick rather than too thin as it's not as oily as wool and slips apart easily. It needs lots of twist. When winding the yarn on or off the spindle, be really careful not to pull or tug it or it may break; washing will help to make it stronger.

With hand-carders you can card lots of different colours of dog hair together and get even mixes; the fibres also form a mat with all the hair going the same way. With dog hair less than 2½" long, I'd say carders are a must but perhaps with perseverance you can spin the shorter hair without first carding it.

Musings of The Lousetown Poet

Hello,

It was quite a while back, in the Gerties' dressing room, that Jenny handed me a little card with bold letters stating: "You're Invited to Contribute to a Catalogue about the Yukon!"

Today I sit naked by the low river in the precious autumn sunshine. The hills are aglow with yellow birches, and cottonwood leaves are crackling in the wind. I've just finished browsing through my journal, and the little white card fell out. I also found two poems I think I like. They were written earlier in the summer when the Yukon River was high and the weather wet and cool. Nudity was touch and go in those days too . . . but then you could look forward to a full summer of naked sunny days.

Now they are more precious than gold . . .

the wind blows the cottonwood snowflakes
they follow the river
the river flows to the sea

the sea becomes one with the ocean
the ocean embraces the earth
the earth orbits the sun

the sun gives me warmth
to dance in the wind

I dance amidst the cottonwoods
they grow beside the river
the river that flows to the sea

the sandbeach has disappeared to the river
to give room for the clouds
to reflect pink up the shore
the rain gave to the river
and the river took the shore

the water is the mirror
for clouds overhead
to be clouds underfoot

on the river
cloudlets melt to one
they look like solid masses
pink and long
reflected on the mirror
pulsating
in the slow and swift
gentle and strong
dark and light
dance of the river

—cathy csepi

Dawson City, Autumn

Once this morning
and once this afternoon,
noisy flocks of geese passed over
going south.
All along the Pacific Fly-a-way
anxious hunters
are unracking their guns.
Here, on the edge of the Arctic,
it's all over for another year.
The dancers and waitresses
from the gambling casino
have all gone back home to their universities.
The black-jack dealers
are off on trips to Europe and Mexico.
The pit-boss is reunited with his wife in Reno.
Joe left with two women
and a fat wallet.
He mentioned Australia.
Those who did more drinking
than working on their claims
get up earlier than usual
and break into a sweat
over the ice on the puddles.
Those whose summer was all work
and no fishing
try to salvage it all
by bagging a moose.
The bars are almost empty.
You can hear winter's feuds
building in the low gossip
of the corners.
This will be my third winter in the Yukon.
I've gone back to walking in the hills alone.
I keep passing the old graveyards
just above town
and thinking of all those sourdoughs
for whom Dawson City
was a one-way trip.

—Erling Friis-Baastad
(originally published in Contemporary Verse II)

SUPPLIERS

CONDON'S YARNS, P.O. Box 129, Charlottetown, P.E.I., C1A 7K3. (902) 894-8712).

They've got all kinds of stuff but the only things that aren't generally available in the Yukon are carded wool (roving) for $2.36 for twelve ounces and scoured fleece (natural white) for $2.66 a pound. You should probably also send 50 cents for a catalogue.

MINAKI TRADING COMPANY LIMITED, Miniki, Ontario, P0X 1J0. (807) 224-3571.

They have sweater patterns and pure wool knitting yarns. Great stuff; super-soft and incredibly strong; doesn't pull apart when you're knitting. Very good directions.

—muffie

BRIGGS AND LITTLE WOOLLEN MILLS LTD., York Mills, Harvey Station, New Brunswick, E0H 1H0.

ICELANDIC WOOL can be gotten through Rammagerdin h.f., P.O. Box 751, Reykjavik, Iceland.

Health Care in the Yukon

Health Centres can be found in Whitehorse, Teslin, Carmacks, Mayo, Pelly Crossing, Haines Junction, Destruction Bay and Ross River. They provide public health programs and limited treatment services.

Nursing Stations at Dawson City and Old Crow provide public health programs, out-patient treatment, and short term in-patient care.

Hospital Facilities in Faro, Whitehorse, Watson Lake and Mayo have 24 hour, out-patient and in-patient services.

Patients requiring more specialized care than is offered in those facilities are transferred or evacuated to larger centres. Whitehorse General Hospital serves as the central active treatment centre in the Yukon. It provides a full range of services — medical, surgical, pediatric, pharmacy, radiology, laboratory, physiotheraphy, psychiatric and out-patient, and offers both acute care and extended care and 24 hour emergency treatment.

A number of physicians operate from three medical clinics in Whitehorse, including general practitioners, surgeons and obstetrics/gynecologists. In addition, Whitehorse is visited periodically by a number of specialists for children, feet, internal medicine, ear, nose and throat, eyes and skin. There are also physicians in Dawson, Faro an d Elsa.

Dental services are available in Whitehorse and Faro.

Ambulance Service is available in Whitehorse, Beaver Creek, Destruction Bay, Teslin, Watson Lake, Carmacks, Faro, Mayo, Dawson City and Haines Junction.

Venereal Disease. The centre in the Yukon for the diagnosis and treatment of venereal disease is located in the Whitehorse General Hospital.

Yukon Health Care Insurance Plan. Territorial law says all Yukon residents are entitled to insured services after three months of continuous residence in the territory. A resident **must** register himself and his dependents in the plan.

If you didn't make enough money to pay taxes last year, you are eligible for Premium Assistance, which means that they'll pay your Health Care Plan fees. You have to apply for this every year.

The territorial government has a pamphlet out called Yukon Health Services, available from the second floor of the territorial building. Phone (403) 667-5233. The booklet or a telephone call will clear up any questions you have.

LEGAL AID

The Yukon's comprehensive Legal Aid program was established to ensure that everyone in the territory is able to receive professional legal advice and assistance if they really need it.

If you have a legal problem resulting from family matters, landlord-tenant matters of any criminal charge, legal aid may be able to help you. The service is available throughout the territory for applicants who qualify, for both civil and criminal cases.

The Legal Aid program recognizes that professional legal assistance is required by individuals with legal problems. If the individual is not financially able to pay for the professional help, the system of justice does not serve that individual as well as it serves someone with sufficient means. Legal Aid exists to make the system of justice fair for every one, no matter what their financial condition.

Legal aid is available to anyone who really needs a lawyer and can't afford one (that is judged by your income). Application forms are available from Outreach Workers, territorial government agents, social workers, welfare workers, probations and corrections staff, native organizations, justices of the peace, RCMP detachments, the magistrate's court registry, native court workers and the legal aid man in the federal post office building at Whitehorse.

Applications are referred to the legal aid committee (consisting of a Yukon Law Society member and two other people).

Sometimes you'll be asked to repay the whole or some of the costs depending on your income, assets and type of case.

The committee will approve legal aid for a civil matter if the action is one which a reasonable person paying for his own lawyer's services would make. Actions which it will not cover include defamation, estates, incorporation of companies or societies or the formation or dissolution of partnerships, real property, transfers, breach of promist to marry, alienation of affections or criminal conversation, arbitrations or conciliations, proceeding relating to any election or proceedings for the recovery of a penalty.
From the Yukon Coalition Project

DAY CARE

Day care services have been in the Yukon for some years, and it is anticipated that sometime in 1979 government standards and a financial assistance program for low-income families will be established. There are five centres providing full day care in Whitehorse, one in Faro and one in Watson Lake. Whitehorse also offers nursery school programs and family day home services. No other Yukon community has a full-time day care centre.

The Yukon Child Care Association – representing interested individuals, groups and day care centres – was established to co-ordinate and upgrade services and to lobby for government standards and financial assistance. The Y.C.C.A. has no fixed address at present and the executive can be contacted through the Victoria Faulkner Women's Centre, 302 Steele Street, Whitehorse, Yukon. Although the Women's Centre does not screen or assess facilities, names and locations of day care centres and other baby sitting services are available through it.

Daycare in the Yukon may be in the same state of unpreparedness as were the Fairbanks centres at the commencement of pipeline construction there. There is no law in the Yukon that establishes acceptable minimum standards for daycare facilities and programs. Daycare does not receive direct on-going funding from the government, and in some cases day-care workers receive only the minimum wage.
—*Lynne Garner, with excerpts from the Optimist Newspaper*

The Consumers' Association of Canada in Whitehorse

302 Steele St., Whitehorse, Yukon Y1A 2C5. 667-4023.

CAC is a voluntary, non-sectarian, non-governmental organization that provides a strong reliable (and local!) voice for consumers. It brings consumers' views to the attention of governments, producers, trade and industry, examines consumer problems and recommends solutions, distributes information of consumer interest, and recommends better consumer laws to the government.

There is no longer a paid co-ordinator in Whitehorse and volunteers — most of whom are always needed — staff the office, respond to messages left on the telephone recorder, and submit articles for the weekly column in the Whitehorse Star. General meetings, open to the public, are held each month from September to June, at the 302 Steele St. office.

Programs offered by the Association include: seminars on such topics as winter clothing, energy saving in the home, Consumer Law and ordinances, buying toys, and game dressing; used sports equipment and toy sales; as well as the publishing of a cookbook called "Wealth in Health" which contains recipies pertaining to northern foods: moose, caribou, fish, cranberries, rosehips, (available from the CAC office for $2.50 a copy).

A Good Insurance Firm

I'll vouch for one insurance outfit that has the right philosophy: saving money for its clients. I insured my wreck for $57 for six months and yesterday I got a cheque for $7.75 back with a note saying that there had been fewer accidents than anticipated, and as a result, The Co-operators was returning a patronage refund.

The name of the company is The Co-operators, with their head office in Regina and a branch office in Whitehorse on Second Avenue across from the library.
—*Agnes*

Grumble Grumble

A true grumbler can have a fine time in the Yukon, there's so much to be dissatisfied with...the local government is run by power-hungry looneys, the cost of food is appalling, the temperatures are riduculous, it's impossible to get land and really the only thing that makes it worthwhile is that you get to join the I'm a Real Yukoner Club which doesn't do much but grumble about all the things that were just mentioned as resource material for grumblers....

There's also the scenery, which is lovely if you're ever allowed a holiday from that boring job in Whitehorse....actually, never mind...just go get drunk at your nearest bar and grumble with all the other people who can't find anything else to do but grumble...it's fun.

That's complete bullshit, just like everything else in this place. It's no fun at all. You guys are crazy. Let's talk about social impact. It may not be fun but at least it's something to do.

anon.

YUKON WOMEN
$2. 190 pages, by JoAnn Bradley, Anthea Bussey, Tracey Read and Audrie Walker. 1975. Illustrated by Claudia Lowry. Printed in Whitehorse. Available at the Victoria Faulkner Women's Centre, 302 Steele St., Whitehorse.

A book about, for and by Yukon women. A Yukon Status of Women council project for International Women's Year. Useful information on legal rights and responsibilities and the availability of health care in the territory. Gives a sense of roles women have played in the history of the Yukon and a glimpse of the lives of some women living here today. Since the book was written in 1975, situations have changed and some of the information is obsolete, such as the need for public transit. All in all, a very interesting and informative look at Yukon women.

—*Diane Seidel*

WELFARE
HUMAN RESOURCES

"We're not just money. That's only a small part – It's mostly services. Like counselling, adoption, group homes..."

The YTG Department of Human Resources was formerly the Social Welfare Branch. Although it is best known for its financial assistance, the human resources workers (as they bill themselves) work in three main areas with the money hand-out as only a part of any programs. In Whitehorse, the workers are split up between family counselling/child protection/individual counselling, and adoption/foster homes/group homes/ therapeutic homes and geriatrics. Outside the "big city," there are small offices in Mayo, Dawson, Faro, and Watson Lake plus two mobile workers providing all services to the North and South Alaska Highway. The South worker also handles Carcross and Tagish; and North worker's jurisdiction starts at Mile 929.

Through the RCMP, emergency service is provided with one worker on-call all night. Basically, this is set up for child protection and crisis situations.

Financial assistance is largely at the discretion of the local human resources worker with guidelines set down by legislation and policy directives. Money (or credit) for shelter, food and clothing can be given out immediately but "special needs" have to be approved by a supervisor. Special needs might include telephone, babysitting and transportation, for example. If you are unable to apply personally at one of the department's offices, an appointment may be made to visit at your home. Phone 667-5674.

New arrivals are told that it is "not the policy of the Department of Human Resources to support job seekers during their job search." To be a resident you must have either a confirmed full-time job or have lived here six months and worked at some time during that period. If you don't satisfy these requirements and are single, you will get only excuses for your troubles. If you are with a family, you can get minimal assistance anyway, perhaps for one week, to pay for lodging while looking for a job. And the government will pay for gas for you to drive your family to the B.C. border. Passing the buck, it is called.

Rates of social assistance are specified in directives. For example: a Dawson single mother with two babies can hope for $208 (food) plus $50 (clothing) plus $36 (incidentals). This is a total of $294 for one month. Shelter assistance amount would depend on the housing available.

What To Expect When You Apply

An appointment will be made for you with a staff member, who will help you complete a detailed application form. It mainly deals with your financial situation. The information you give on this form must be accurate because it's a legal document.

You'll be asked to sign a sworn statutory declaration regarding your financial circumstances. Don't sign this declaration unless you fully understand the questions, or have them explained to you by the worker taking your application. Don't be afraid to ask questions.

Your application will be dealt with at once. Your worker will tell you immediately whether it has been approved or rejected. If it is rejected, you have the right to appeal. Your worker or a supervisor will fully explain to you, on request how the appeal procedure is conducted.. This is not fast – expect a two week delay.

In cases of extreme need, short term social assistance can be given at the interview, such as vouchers for shelter and food. All information about your case is kept strictly confidential.

To Speed Things Up

1. You must bring your social insurance card.
2. If you have a permanent address, be sure to bring a rent receipt from your landlord, or a mortgage payment receipt.
3. Landed immigrant status cards or passports will be required where applicable.
4. If you are employable, it may help to bring a list of prospective employers you have approached for work. It's a good idea to register with Canada Manpower before you apply. Also, bring your last pay slip, if this is available.
5. Bring any correspondence you may have from the Unemployment Insurance Commission indicating your status in regard to benefits.
6. Make note of the following information:
   – when you were last employed, names and addresses of employers
   – when you moved to the territory
   – when you last received social assistance
   – your previous medical plan number.
   – details of your military service.
   – all other sources of income.
   – children's ages and income.
7. The "head" of the family should apply.

Note: If separated, you will be asked to provide current whereabouts, if known, of your spouse (legal or common law).

The department also administers the Territorial Supplementary Allowance for senior citizens and persons permanently excluded from the work force.

The library can also reserve books that are out, and will consider requests to purchase new books. If we can't buy it or if the book is on an extremely specialized subject, we will try to obtain it for you on inter-library loan

On Government and The People

Agnes: The government doesn't like to do anything outside of Whitehorse because they don't understand *at all* what's happening out there. They haven't a clue. Like you can stay out in the bush, on Stewart Island, say, where Rudy Burien is and you can see the government is like a porcupine, sitting on top of Whitehorse, with all those quills coming out of it; they're *flicking* quills all over the place and stuff like that . . . of their influence, but *it doesn't mean anything* to you, as long as one of them doesn't come near you. And if one of them comes near you, you just make damn sure that they know you gotta gun and can shoot the porcupine.

And the porcupine says "Oh, okay" and starts shooting its quills some place else.

A good half of Whitehorse anyways — the workers — are government workers. Now when they get organized, they control the city of Whitehorse, just by their own numbers. When they control the city of Whitehorse and all the MLAs from Whitehorse, they control the Yukon? You've got a few government workers running the whole thing, and that's very dangerous, when you have the government running the govern-

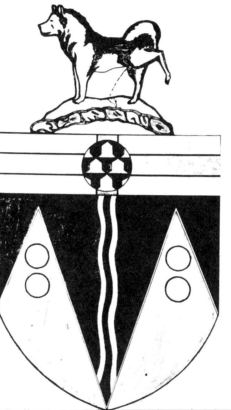

ment. That's what's wrong up here. So what we need is a lot more non-government-oriented things going on, and if we brought up 20,000 freaks, I think that would do it. That's what's happened in a couple of provinces, like Alaska, there's a really, really strong Sierra Club and Conservation Society and stuff like that. And they work hard and they change the legislation. We don't have, like we've got a conservation society, but somehow they don't seem very effective.

Bucky: I've seen the same thing happen. People will come along — a whole, whole group of avid people who are far more politically interested than anybody else has ever been before — but they can't get in (to local groups) because the other people are so deeply entrenched.

—"subversive dialogues"

THE YUKON

Somewhere between cosmic debris and social interaction lies Yukon. Its far far way, and difficult to get to unless you already live there. Not many people on "The Outside" know it exists, let alone know where it is. If they do know about this place, it's because they're among the Vitally Interested who have money invested here, or who have family or friends in the Territory that they like to keep in touch with. People here hardly have an interest in the South. Sure we are affected by decisions made and things done down south, but the general feeling is captured by a popular bumper sticker: "We don't give a damn how they do it on the Outside."

What counts to the 23,000 or so people who live here is their environment (and that doesn't mean the weather). It's the general space they're in: not a lot of traffic, not a lot of people, but a lot of wilderness and space; a lot of opportunity to do anything you want and more freedom than you'll find anywhere else in the Western World. The only limiting factor is one's desire and imagination.

Unfortunately, someone decided to lay $1.5 billion worth of a 4,786 mile, $10 billion natural gas pipeline project on this place, and promised us a second gas line within 10 years of the first one, and probably an oil pipeline in the future, too. They know what happened in Alaska but said lessons have been learned and it won't be quite that bad for us. Promises, promises.

"You can't have a little bit of autonomy any more than you can be a little bit pregnant. Either we run our own affairs or we don't." – Bob Erlam

ARCTIC WINTER GAMES

The Arctic Winter Games were first inspired by a group of teachers who empathized with frustrated northern athletes who always had to struggle in their competition against southern Canadians. With poor training facilities and lack of competition there seemed to be no hope or opportunity for northerners to up their level of skills to southern athletic standards.

So in 1969, proposals for northern games were instigated between the Territories and Alaska to found an opportunity for northern competitors to compete at their own level with people of the same standards and background — the objective here being to give the participants the incentive to improve not

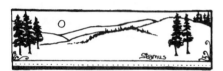

Part XXIII

Whitehorse happens to be blessed with the nicest bicycle shop I have ever seen. There's these two friendly, hard-working guys who seem to always try to do their best for you. I have been in every spring for a straightening of wheels and brakes.

I get taken in early so I can be ready to go when the good weather hits.

There is a side of my life that no one ever ses. I have been spending most of my five years in Yukon hanging from two big spikes in a post in a basement of whichever house Toby is living in. I just hang there in suspended animation and watch Toby do his laundry and put his camping trips together. It's not too bad, though. Lots happens in the winter in a basement. People even sleep there. It's quiet and a nice temperature. The only time I get pushed around is when the furnace breaks down and someone moves me. That's not often.

I have some measure of respect for this treatment because the bikes that stay outside all winter sure look bad by spring. The cold peels the sidewalls right off their tires and washes the oil out of chains and gears, leaving metal and chrome rusted and old. The other way bikes in Whitehorse meet an early death is through theft and violence by the general population of kids on the streets, I've had wheels bent and cables snapped. I've been subjected to having my gears stripped and my seat sniffed. It's a wild world sometimes! I get locked up now.

About every three years my drive train gets replaced and I end up with a new chain, derailer and free wheel. This is quite a job, but things get dangerous when the chain starts to slip. Like the time Toby went to turn super fast to impress this girl and fell on his head. He spent 75 dollars on me after that!

All this trouble and pain soon gave way to the high parts of life in this town, like hopping sidewalks and gliding among people. We used to go silently through the Indian village, where the kids would come out to race us. We'd go tearing along the dirt and through the fields sometimes, The kids always liked Toby because he knew how to ride dirt and grasslands with me.

Toby also knew how to stop me with my pedal lodged in the stone walls beside the doors and then walk cooly into Qwanlin Mall. He knew how to ride me up the sloping ramp to the library door and up to the doors of the Territorial Barn Building, dismount while moving, and lean me gently against the rail. We also went on excursions, like out to Mile 928 on the Alcan, and to Tahkini Hot Springs. On the way back we could do 55 mph down Two Mile Hill and be across town in a few minutes. That was home and my spot under the eaves behind the house.

Life is pretty good for a hot rod bike up here, and I'm lucky to be maintained well. If I don't get stolen, that is, or hit by a truck. We've had some bad scrapes but not in the years since Dave bought a car. Now I just sit around and relate stories to the dog when he is tied up next to me. Sometimes he pees on my tires, but he's good company and never around for more than two or three weeks at a time anyway.

only training facilities in the various hosting communities, but to up the level of athletic skills, and last but not least, to improve relations between the northern regions.

The first games were born in 1970 in Yellowknife, and since then have continued every two years. Competitors join in from the Yukon, Northwest Territories, northern Quebec, Alaska and more recently, Greenland, and are selected by coaches, tournament placement, or by the filtering process of a series of competitions.

Sports included are: alpine skiing, archery, arctic sports, badminton, basketball, boxing, cross country skiing, curling, figure skating, hockey, judo, modified biathalon, shooting, snow shoeing, table tennis, volleyball and wrestling.

New sports are always encouraged, especially those that exclude sophisticated equipment and can cater to the natives' traditional skills such as hunting and snowshoeing (thus the birth of the biathalon event and arctic sports).

FOR SPORTS GRANTS, CHECK:

1. the Yukon Community Recreation Board for local culture, recreation and sport groups in Whitehorse.
2. Y.T.G. guidelines for culture and sport groups operating on a territorial basis, Y.T.G. recreation department.

The postal service in the Yukon is pretty good, as a rule. Problems seem to arise only with the postal system Down South or else with transportation systems in the territory. In Whitehorse, a letter mailed on time one day will be delivered the next in the same town, and to outlying communities as soon as the bus or truck or whatever takes it there. Mail to Outside destinations is dispatched with haste but can get lost at various places along the way, as it is anywhere else in the country and the world.

Uptown Stylishness

Some Women's Centre members were irked by an article which appeared in the April, 1978 issue of Chatelaine. The introduction promised that "this is how the real folks do it." But upon closer examination, one notices that "the real folks" are spending $340 on suits to make them "look aggressive but in a feminine way." The following is the Yukon women's answer to Workstyle '78.

Susan Hellman, F.Y.T., is presently employed as a Curriculum Developer for the Native Alcohol Community Action Project. On the day of our interview, I was impressed by her informality. Clad in jeans, thongs, well-worn denim shirt and grey vest, with a classic black sweater casually draped across her shoulders, she is always in style in the Yukon. Sue maintains that one must always be prepared.

"After all if my truck broke down on the highway a silk suit wouldn't do me much good, would it?" She prefers to spend her money on weekend trips to Dawson and renovations to her cabin rather than on clothes.

"We are cultivating an image," she explains. "This way, Yukon businesswomen are easily recognizable wherever we go."

Women Centre ex-coordinator, Jill Porter, has spent much time putting her wardrobe together. Since the unfortunate disappearance of her laundry last summer, she has had to start from scratch. On the bright side, though, by visiting old friends, going to rummage sales and, more recently, the Salvation Army, she has replenished her supplies. Her wardrobe, like Sue's, is casual with emphasis on comfort and practicality. One added feature is her Chinese dancing slippers (red ones are her favourites).

Janeane McGillvary, steelworker, likes to put on her cotton underpants, and the rest of her clothes on top. She finds this much more attractive than doing it the other way around. After deciding that cheaply made clothes do not wear well, she now buys only good quality garments and wears them for a decade or so. One other favourite piece of apparel for working at the cabin is a broken-in pair of coveralls accessorized by a top-of-the-line Woolworth's scarfette. Janeane would like to see the dilemma of correct dress while labouring in 40 below weather solved by the introduction of genuine blue collars on the ever-popular Stanfield's theme.

Up and coming young law student Emily Drzymala is really dressed for success. With three children and several years of studying ahead of her, "it ain't easy," she says. She's solved the problem, however, by wisely selecting a smart tweed suit from Woolworths, for $19. She now truly fits the image of the "young executive."

—J. P.

Post Office continued....

If you're visiting one of the smaller communities, chances are you won't find the post office open. Hours are short, and depend on when the mail comes in and how soon after that the postmaster (or postmistress) can sort it and get it to the people. Each community gets its mail from Whitehorse at different times of day, different days of the week. The same applies for outgoing mail. So if you're a visitor, you can drop a postcard to family or friends anywhere in the Yukon but don't expect it to get home very fast. If you're after speedy service, you're better off taking it to Whitehorse and mailing it yourself at the main post office on Main St.

Postal Codes

Postal codes apply to every town here with a post office but aren't necessary for local mail purposes since there are no automatic postal machines in the territory. If you're writing from Down South, however, the mail will most likely go through one of those machines so the codes will then come in handy.

They are:

Swift River	Y0A 1A0
Teslin	Y0A 1B0
Watson Lake	Y0A 1C0
Beaver Creek	Y0B 1B0
Carcross	Y0B 1B0
Carmacks	Y0B 1C0
Dawson	Y0B 1G0
Destruction Bay	Y0B 1H0
Elsa	Y0B 1J0
Faro	Y0B 1K0
Haines Junction	Y0B 1L0
Mayo	Y0B 1M0
Pelly Crossing	Y0B 1P0
Ross River	Y0B 1S0
Old Crow	Y0B 1N0
Tagish	Y0B 1T0
Atlin, B.C.	V0N 1A0
Whitehorse	has many

STRONG FAMILIES

Strong families create a strong society. There are fewer who would claim that raising a family in this time and place is easy, however. Very many Yukon families live far from the support of relatives or life-long friends. Job transfers tend to keep families mobile, and make strong relationships with friends or neighbors more difficult to maintain.

For native families, the situation is even more complicated by the white society which controls most jobs, schools, stores and organizations. Naturally it is harder to pass on parental values and develop a sense of mutual love and respect in the face of such factors. All families meet the additional stress of the high cost of living, and many experience the grip of alcoholism.

Yukon Family Services Association is a private agency which seeks to help families deal with these problems and which offers to help many professionals dealing with human needs. Services offered are in three main departments at present: 1) marriage counselling and individual therapy; 2) family life and sex education — outlines, materials and two resource persons who work in the schools or for community groups as requested; 3) Planned Parenthood information and materials regarding birth control, pregnancy, parenthood and child development.

A fourth division of services was requesting funding from the Yukon government. This would be called "Homemaker Service" and would exist to provide emergency help to families. Such help is needed when one or both parents are suddenly unable to care for children or when age or illness means an adult cannot care for himself/herself, yet does not need to leave the home for medical care.

Three full time staff members and two part time persons and an energetic body of volunteers carry out these functions. It often includes program presentations to other professionals like nurses, welfare workers, teachers and ministers. Group programs open to the general public are regularly sponsored, as are special presentations upon request. Individual requests for information or help can be made by phoning Yukon Family Services at 667-2970 or 667-2962, or by mail at #5- 4078 4th Avenue, Whitehorse.

This agency charges minimal fees for its counselling if clients are able to pay. It also must rely on the territorial and federal government for strong financial support, though not government control. By far the largest support comes from its volunteers and board of directors who simply believe that every family made a little stronger builds a society a little healthier.

—Mary Jo Dawe

Skills & Service Exchange Centre

Cost of living got you by the balls? Then get out of the market.

That's where we are — a small but largely begrudging part of the mass consuming market. And I, for one, am fed up with paying $24/hr. labor, plus parts, to some guy to fix my right front headlight. Sure, the headlight needs to be fixed, but can't I get the job done more cheaply? Not by any of the garages in town.

So, I look around for alternatives, ask friends if they knew anyone who works with vehicles, who'd like to make a few bucks. Days go by, headlight's still out and the cops pull me over because of it. They get suspicious, and a few beer, or whatever, turn out to be very, very expensive.

But! Had there been a SKILLS & SERVICES EXCHANGE CENTRE in Whitehorse, I could have gotten the headlight fixed, avoided all that nonsense and saved a few bucks besides.

What, you ask, is a Skills and Services Exchange Centre and how can it save you, and me, a few of our hard earned nuggets?

Basically it's an exchange of services among a group of people, based on the tried and true barter system. People have been practising this system for centuries; what they needed they bartered for, using their own produce, crafts or skills as payment.

It's still in use today, notably in the "third world" countries. And yet it's a practical alternative to our own segmented, specialized, consumer-orientated North American society.

We can all do something: grow food, give massage, make tipis, cook, hunt, sew, repair vehicles. Altogether, the list would be varied and lengthy. However, purchasing these same skills from the usual commercial sources, e.g. day care centres, grocery stores, garages, is expensive.

So why not set up an alternative? Why don't we start doing things by ourselves, for ourselves? Why don't we eliminate the costly middleman and begin dealing directly with each other?

The service exchange centre is not an original idea. A few years ago I read about a similar project in Ontario. I can't recall every detail, but what I do remember is the project was not a loose operation: a plan had been drawn up, there were a few rules everybody had to abide by, all members were listed, along with the individual's available skill or service. It was a small operation, it had been running for some time and it was, at this writing, working out to everyone's advantage.

The exchange centre acted as a clearing house, through which A could purchase say, three hours of B's time. All services are recorded in terms of kind and the number of hours put into the job. When B was finished the job A needed him/her for, A then owed B three hours of his/her time. And A could not get another job done through the exchange centre until he/she paid off that three hours he/she owed B. That way, everyone gets what they want done and payment is guaranteed.

There's no criteria as far as skills and services are concerned. Whatever you can do is of value to someone, probably to more people than you think. Be it darning socks or printing a picture, cutting hair or building a sauna, by pooling our resources, the list could — with imagination and honest self-appraisal — answer just about all our needs.

Sure, there's some honor involved here. This system depends on trust and honesty if it's to work out. But then we know what sleazy operators on all levels have done to this society. And while we haven't totally escaped it up here, there's still room in the Yukon. There's still a chance that we really can leave that type of pollution behind in the smoggy southern cities.

This skills and services exchange centre exists only in my head. I've given the idea and the basic workings. Do you like it? Is it possible? I think it is. There's a fair amount to work out first, like should membership be limited or left open, who'll keep the books, what'll the guidelines be, and so on.

I'd like for us to get together on it, make it a really strong alternative to the way things are now and even worse, the way things will be when the pipeline comes.

Thanks for reading this and remember:
FREE THE YUKON
Kathy Langston
667-2712

─more Post Office─

If you're looking for a specific postal code for Whitehorse, check the postal code book available at post offices across the country.

Postal Rates

The post office has brochures on postal and parcel rates for the country that are free for the public and come in handy if you already have stamps and need to know how much postage to put on. You can also phone your local post office for the rates.

Here's some rates that most people reading the catalogue would use. (Rates effective as of September, 1978, until the next increase.) More detail is available in brochures or by calling the posties.

FIRST CLASS MAIL and post cards
(They haven't gone metric yet)

Weight (up to and including)	Rate to Canada	Rate to U.S.
1 oz.	14 cents	.14
2 oz.	22	.26
3 oz.	—	.38
4 oz.	34	.50
5 oz.	—	.62
6 oz.	50	.74
7 oz.	—	.86
8 oz.	66	.98
9 oz.	—	$1.10
10 oz.	82	$1.12
11 oz.	—	$1.34
12 oz.	98	$1.46
13 oz.	—	$1.58
14 oz.	$1.14	$1.70
15 oz.	—	$1.82
16 oz.	$1.30	$1.94

gees, I forgot my box key... would you get my mail out of there for me? thanks. you're sweet

more Post Office Continued...

SPECIAL DELIVERY will cost you 80 cents per item.

REGISTERED MAIL will cost you $1.25 for value up to $100, and 25 cents for each $100 up to $1,000, as well as the usual first-class mailing rate for the item. Another 30 cents at the time of mailing will get you an acknowledgement that the mail was received; 50 cents after the time of mailing.

CERTIFIED MAIL will get you proof of delivery for 75 cents, plus regular postage.

THIRD CLASS MAIL, like for Christmas cards, baby announcements, and the like to a maximum of one pound will cost you:

for 2 oz.	12 cents
4 oz.	19 cents
6 oz.	26 cents
8 oz.	33 cents
10 oz.	40 cents
12 oz.	47 cents
14 oz.	54 cents
16 oz.	61 cents

NOTE TO AMERICAN VISITORS: The post office says a lot of you send post cards with U.S. stamps on them. Well, they never got anywhere except a bin in the back of the post office building. Canadian stamps are no good in America and likewise for your stamps in our country.

THE WOMEN'S CENTRE
Upstairs, 302 Steele St.
Whitehorse, Y.T. 667-2693

The Victoria Faulkner Women's Centre is operated by volunteers and one paid coordinator as a society that has a purpose of supporting women. It is a special place for friendship, information and the sharing of skills in an atmosphere of women learning from each other. The centre's philosophy advocates the basic rights of women as people, so that women have the freedom to develop as separate, whole persons. The quality of each woman's contribution in society is determined by her good feeling about herself, and her function in a society.

Services: Friendship is the prime concern. The centre offers crisis counselling as required, emotional support, information on housing, employment, child care, legal and medical services. It refers women to resource persons and social agencies as well as receiving referrals from them. The centre also has a fine library.

Programs: In 1978, the centre offered a full slate of programs, including consciousness-raising groups, crisis counselling workshops, dulcimer-building, mukluk-making, yoga, ski tourings and a women's therapy group.

Anytime you're in Whitehorse, please feel free to drop in for coffee and spend some time relaxing, talking or asking questions.
— *The Yukon Coalition Report*

THE OPTIMST

circ. 500 or so. The Yukon Women's newspaper. A collective by the Status of Women Council and some members of the Women's Centre. Starting off as a newsletter published sporadically, it now is a bi-monthly. The purpose is to reach as many Yukon women as possible. Up-to-date news on all feminist issues, such as daycare, abortion, legal aid and profiles of local women. Reports on conferences and the like. Subscriptions $3 per year from the Women's Centre, 302 Steele St., Whitehorse. All contributions such as poems, photos, stories (personal) are welcomed.

Part XXIV

Toby used to go out in the Chilkoot and White Passes in the winter. He liked to go alone and to get away from home for awhile. I always went with him and after I had him trained, it wasn't so bad. But it was touch and go. His fist would touch my head and he'd yell "Go!" At first I was expected to pull a toboggan through deep snow, with all kinds of garbage on it. I didn't really take a liking to this idea. I down right refused to do it right at the Bennett Train station. "Might as well nip this one in the bud," I thought.

In order not to draw a crowd and look stupid, Toby hiked up the tracks until he was around the corner and then he hooked me up. When I wouldn't pull, he commenced yelling and screaming and became a little violent. This hurt, and a few times I thought of leaving him there. But finally it would all stop and he'd settle down.

The time was getting late and he wanted to get away from the train tracks before camping. About half the outfit got dumped in a sack and hung from a branch. Then he pulled the toboggan with me for about five miles. When we were out in the mountains it was wonderful, once Toby got rid of the sled. I packed up, not too heavy, and we trucked around for a week. Just the two of us together was just right with me.

This was all very fine until we had to go back. I got latched onto the toboggan again and we went through the same madness as before--until Toby decided he had to pull it with me. We got back to a spot about a mile from the train station. The rocks began here, and the trail got very steep. To make it all more interesting, the snow was very powdery and drifted deep in front of us.

Toby gave up on me and went ahead to break trail. I just sat there at the bottom and waited for him to come back. He didn't say a word, or give me any attention at all. He acted like I wasn't there. Picking up the harness, he looped it around his shoulders and began to pull. His snowshoes sunk into the snow, and nothing was going very fast, but he was going to do this if it killed him.

I felt bad about this, and began to help him. Leaning hard into the harness, I felt my paws start to sink in the snow, but the trail wasn't bad (he'd packed it three times by now). Then, slowly, another feeling took hold of me, and I started to feel very strange. I still don't know to this day what happened, but everything went red. When I came back to sanity I was standing by the railway, Toby was behind me, halfway up the hill, and I felt sick and shaky. Toby just stared at me, wide-eyed, for a long time. Then, without a word, he gave me a pat on the head, picked up the rope and together we walked into Bennett.

RCMP

The force's history in the Yukon began August 7, 1894 when Inspector Charles Constantine arrived at Fort Cudahy, near the town of Forty-Mile on the Yukon River. Almost a year later he returned with 19 men. Of course he wasn't too popular with the miners (about 260 of them in Forty-Mile), being also a customs officer and land agent. But then he was also justice of the peace, post master, Indian agent and land registrar. A miners' meeting actually defied an order regarding a claim. Constantine dispatched 11 men to Glacier Creek with a warning that to disobey was against Canadian law. The miners relented, and the North-west Mounted Police became the unchallenged representatives of the government in the Yukon Territory.

With the Klondike gold rush, the force became 285 by November, 1898. The rush kept every man on duty all the time in Dawson City, as well as at the summit of the Chilcoot and White passes, where they collected customs on goods entering Canada.

Chilcoot Chuck Says: "Mounties Do not accept bribes"

WINK

HEH HEH HEH

R.C.M.P.

...but you could try tires and other things for their four by fours.

CLINK CLINK

The Canadian government sent the Yukon Field Force, consisting of 200 men, to assist the NWMP to guard prisoners, move gold, and protect banks between 1898-1900. Saloon licences cost $2,500 each, prostitution carried a $50 fine or a month's hard labour. A policeman made $1.25 a day and if caught being naughty was severely punished. One mountie was sentenced to two months in the stockade, then fired for dispensing free tickets to prostitutes to watch the arrival of the Governor General in Dawson.

By 1903 there were 303 officers in the territory, whereas the population had decreased dramatically. There were 793 officers in all of Canada. The reason for this was the boundary dispute with the U.S. at the time and the NWMP were the only representatives of Canada on the spot.

With relaxation after the disputes and rushes the force numbered only 36 men in 1912. Since then the force has steadily increased and today still counts as one of the heaviest number of "police-per-man" areas in the country.

In 1937 the RCMP established an air division and through the war the force became modernized, moved to Whitehorse in 1943 and set up detachments along the Alaska Highway in 1945.

The RCMP remains the sole police force in the Yukon and numbers 97 officers, regular members and special constables. They are all commanded from a fortress-like building on Fourth Ave. by Elliott Street in Whitehorse.

The force in the communities is like this:

TOWN	MANPOWER (August, 1978)	PHONE
Whitehorse	28	667 5555
Watson Lake	7	536-7443
Dawson City	4	993-5444
Mayo	4	996-3222
Teslin	3	3441
Beaver Creek	3	5101
Haines Junction	3	634-2221
(winter)	2	
Faro	3	994-2444
Ross River	3	967-2227
Carmacks	2	5251
Carcross	2	4441
Old Crow	2	2221

Services offered by the RCMP

"Tourist Alert": daily summer broadcast (radio) for people trying to contact others. Phone the RCMP nearest you.

Operation Provident: for business to identify stolen goods. The RCMP issues a number to a business to place on all goods upon application.

River Travellers Registration: tell them where you're going and for how long. If you're not back in time they will come looking for you. May be discontinued due to people who fail to report in after their trips. However, this service still existed as of September, 1978 and the protection is there if you want it.

The RCMP hopes to start a property-identification numbering service for private citizens locally within two years. Until then you can buy an engraving pen yourself and print your social number on the bottom of every valuable item. For further information contact them at the detachment nearest you. May the Force be with you.

—d. p.

TWO DAWSON COMMENTS

From a barmaid: "This is a summer tourist town just like Banff. I know, I've worked in both."

And from a customer of hers: "I've been here seven years, haven't been Outside in five. I've been rich and I've been poor. I don't really work at it or worry about it. It just seems that sometimes you have more money than other times. Doesn't matter to me much. I just spend more and live easier when I've got money. But I'm just as happy without much.

"That's one thing I've noticed about this town over the years: everyone's got money. There's people who are rich and there are lots of poor people. But they are poor 'cuz they want to be. I'm like that sometimes, too 'cuz I don't care if I've got money or not. I have fun either way. Hey, I'll buy you a drink.

Any person wishing to support the NORMAL platform (legalization of pot) can contact them at 2317 M St., North-West, Washington, D.C., 20037. The director is Keith Stroup.

Here's a song about a northern adventure that inspired a story in the Whitehorse Star under the headline "Banjo Jim Facing Draft Charge," with the subheading "Laid in 1967," meaning the charge, not me.

Alaska Busted Blues

I went up to Alaska, driving a panel truck,
Up the icy Alcan, trusting guts and luck.
I'm busted at the border by a guard who said he'd break my knees.
Howard the Duck, buddy you got nothing on me.

They took me to a courtroom, I said, "What you gonna do to me?"
Put you in the jailhouse and throw away the key.
I said, "How you gonna tell all the people what's going down?"
"Get me a lawyer and a newsman, I'll turn this courtroom round."

The lawyers and the newsmen thought the case deserved some play.
They got me on the airwaves, I got to have my say.
Now the people can decide if what I did was right or wrong.
And I can go on writing, playing and singing my songs.

We're gonna keep on dancing, and dreaming of a time,
When we'll all be free to decide what is a crime.
We're gonna keep on fighting, to put a final end to war.
We're not a soldier nation, but we're warriors to the very core.

— *Jim Erkelitian*

Who can vote?

Only Canadian citizens who have reached the ripe old age of 18 have the right to vote in federal by-elections and general elections. Although proof of citizenship need not be produced either at the time of enumeration or at the polls, if challenged for such vital stats, you may be asked to swear that you are a Canadian citizen before voting. So if you have doubts about your status or wish to apply for citizenship, contact: The Court of Canadian Citizenship nearest you. They're listed under "Government of Canada" in the white pages of the phone directory. Don't fret if you can't find the number right off, it's merely camouflaged under Citizenship Inquiries, or Secretary of State or Court of Canadian Citizenship. If you so wish, you can write directly to: Registrar of Canadian Citizenship, Department of the Secretary of State, Ottawa, Ontario, K1A 0M5. If there is not a citizen court in your area, you'll be referred to the nearest one. The granting of Canadian citizenship is supposed to take an average of three months from the date of application. Bureaucracy being what it is, however, it is suggested you don't wait until three months before an election to apply!

An important note to British subjects who do not possess Canadian citizenship: as of June 26, 1975 you were deemed **not** eligible to vote in federal elections ... just one of the nifty little side effects of the new Canada Elections Act which came into force June 26, 1970.

POLITICAL ACTIVITIES OF FEDERAL SERVANTS

Because public servants administer legislation, it is essential that they remain impartial and without prejudice. Active involvement with a political party would decrease, in appearance, if not in actual fact, the impartiality of their decisions. For this reason, the Public Service Employment Act has placed restrictions on the political activity permissible. Under Section 32 of the PSEA:

1. **Public servants may:**
   - attend political meetings
   - contribute financially to a political party
   - contribute financially to a political candidate
   - request leave of absence without pay to run for federal, provincial or territorial political office
   - remain in the public service while running for and holding an elected municipal office

2. **Public servants may not:**
   - work on behalf of a political party
   - work on behalf of a political candidate
   - hold office on provincial, federal, or territorial legislative bodies while employed in the public service

3. **However,** action by the PSC against public servants who participate actively in work on behalf of a political party or candidate can be taken only after an allegation has been made to the commission "by a person who is or has been a candidate for election ......"
   — *National Defence Employee's Newsletter*

FAMILIES NEEDED

"The Department of Human Resources is constantly in search of foster and adoptive homes for children who are not able to be cared for by their families. There is a need for Native families because many of the children coming into care are Indian. Where possible, the worker prefers to place Indian children with Indian families.

"In most situations where children are in temporary care, the worker likes to see them looked after within their own communities because this is most comfortable for the children. Many more Native foster homes are needed both in Whitehorse and the outlying areas. The department also encourages applications from Native families as permanent adoptive homes for children.

"The department can make good use of families interested in children of any age, including infants, although its greatest difficulty is finding homes for older children.

"**Marriage Relationship:** It is not essential that a couple be legally married to foster, but it is important to know they are happy together and are able to settle disagreements in a positive manner. Couples who wish to adopt must be legally married. However, a single person will also be considered as an adoptive parent.

"**Housing:** Again, it is important for prospective foster and adoptive parents to know that there are no rigid housing standards required. It is definitely not essential to have running water, electricity and a separate bed and bedroom for each child. The department would simply like to be sure that there is adequate space in the home for the child and that the home is clean enough so there are no health hazards. The department is more interested in the love and attention a child might receive from a family than the appearance of the house."

whitehorse rec & education programs —

Each spring and fall, the Whitehorse Recreation Department offers a wide range of day and evening courses for the young as well as adults. Some of the classes offered are related to organized sports (i.e. volleyball, badminton, gymnastics) while others deal with more informal activities such as keep fit, and exploration at play. Various arts and crafts courses such as sewing winter clothing and pottery are also available. Evening classes affiliated with the Yukon Vocational and Technical Training Centre are quite extensive and include bookkeeping, mechanics, typing, and welding. The school also offers nonvocational courses a few of which are defensive driving, conversational French, and energy conservation. If you desire further information, the local papers carry full descriptions in advance of course commencement; or you can contact the recreation department (667-6401).

YLCB Liquor Stores

Faro
Dawson City
Mayo
Watson Lake
Haines Junction
Whitehorse (Fourth and Lambert)
Hours: 10:30 a.m. - 6:00 p.m.
Closed Sundays, Mondays and
Statutory Holidays

SQAWK
SQAWK
HIC
SQAWK

FLAP

CBC TV GUIDE, MONDAY TO FRIDAY, 1978
FOR WHITEHORSE
and anyone else that's watching
(Are you there, Old Crow?)

7:00 **Morning Weather Report — Gambling:** A test of your basic beliefs. Try to guess whose weather report you are actually being exposed to. Also today's mystery quiz asks the question: "Where exactly is the Liard Basin?"

7:30 **World News:** Find out why you're too scared to travel Outside anymore. Nothing to do with us.

8:00 **Racing Form:** Live from the Y.T.G. parking lot. Recognize famous people who tied one on last night.

9:00 **Beat the Bylaw:** Our hidden camera is at the Mainsteele parking lot catching the latest tries to befuddle the parking lot ticket machine.

10:00 **Coffee Break:** Live from Martina's Pastry, "The Donut Runner's Review," as gophers from all over town converge to shoot the shit and eat five of the 50 donuts they scored for the office.

11:00 **Mr. Construction:** On the road with Mr. Construction. This week we find out the answer to: "What's wrong with 809?" and "What's in Mr. Construction's thermos?"

12:00 **Post Office:** Today the lunchtime mailers get heckled by the front wicket girls and try not to act embarrassed when told they have nice bums!

Afternoon Programs

1:00 **Dead Air:** Dead Air spends this week in Ross River to find out what goes on in the winter months after Matthew Sills goes south.

2:00 **Community Tours:** Today we ride the water truck around Carcross and laugh a lot. Tomorrow: a tour of Sleepy Hollow with the Whitehorse dog catcher (recommended for mature audiences).

3:00 **Beat the Clock:** Our roving camera tours the highways this week and catches surveyors hiding in their trucks and also we discover in which restaurant the parts runners for all the automotive companies are having coffee.

4:00 **Free Dreams:** A new show dedicated to all those who daydream through the afternoon's work. Today: drifting the Yukon River with the Y.T.G. campground crew.

6:00 **News:** Gives that extra something to Supper Sports — all the sport news that came over the teleprinter that nobody cares about (45 minutes long). Weather: forecast for the next week. Maybe.

7:00 **Northern Realities: Tonight — "Squatting;;** How to deal with front-end loaders. How to live in old riverboats without burning them down. Also, close-up on Whitehorse City Hall plans to extend boundaries to Jake's Corner, Carcross, Braeburn and Champagne.

7:30 **TV Guide Break from CBC North:** In na tik nik nik Mary Tyler Moore a ma ta pik m ga poo bah Scoobie Doo.

8:00 **Yukon Wildlife:** Scene from the Kooper King Tavern. This week "The Beer Strike."

11:40 **Movie:** Tarzan's "Dawson Adventure" or "Gidget Goes Crazy" (a winter in downtown Whitehorse).

T.B.A.: **Friendly Giant:** Cyprus Anvil; **Mr. Dress-up:** Today, how to look like a commissioner; **Muppet Show:** Live from the Terrified Legislature.
— *Sign Off*

YTG Employee Alcoholic Program

The territorial government has a program for helping alcoholic employees. The Employee Assistance Program was started not too long ago for:
   —early identification of drinking as a health problem
   —referral of the employee for proper treatment, so the condition can be controlled before he or she becomes unemployable.

It is not the intention of the program to be concerned with normal social drinking habits, nor to intrude in the private lives of employees, the brochure says. If an employee voluntarily seeks treatment for an alcohol problem or accepts treatment under pressure, his job security will not be jeopardized. Employees under treatment for problem drinking will be eligible for sick leave credits or leave without pay if required.

For further information and assistance, call Alcohol and Drug Services at 667-5627.

—Johnny Sober

POWER for the People?

"I found us a place."
"Already?"
"Yeah, It's a two bedroom house with everything we want."
"Sounds good."
"It is. The only problem is it's heated with electricity."

That recent conversation illustrates an important fact of living in the Yukon: we pay outrageous prices for electricity. Whether you're renting or own your own home, high electrical bills make you think twice about plugging in. Most people that have been around for awhile use as little electricity as possible or try to avoid using it at all costs. It's a convenience that costs so much that even people in Riverdale have turned to alternative energy sources like wood-oil furnaces for heating their homes.

NCPC produces the power and Yukon Electric Co. is the main distributor or supplier of it. The following rates for Whitehorse were in effect September, 1978:

first 40 kwh.	7.43 c/kwh.
next 160	5.71c/kwh.
next 100	4.56c/kwh.
over 300 kwh	3.32c/kwh.

BUT THAT'S NOT ALL. When the total is figured out, multiply by 0.23 cents for every kilowatt-hour, then add that on. That's for a rate increase in May, 1978. The other figures came into effect in January, 1978.

For 1,000 kwhours, a Whitehorse consumer's monthly bill would be (using the January figures) $39.91, and $42.21 with the latest hike. The territorial government has a rebate system that helps equalize electricity costs, especially to those who use less, but the rates themselves promote consumption. As you can see by the figures above, the more power you use, the less you pay. There's a minimum charge of $2.75 for anyone using less than 300 kwh. per month, but if you use just over that, your bill will be $17.36. Fortunately that's where the rebates come in, so the bill to the consumer is a lot less than that.

For more facts and figures, you can check with Chris Pearson at Copytron — he is the chairman of the territory's electrical public utilities board (YEPUB).

The sliding scale of costs encourages us to use energy instead of conserving it. They want more demand than their supply so a case for a hydro-project can be made. Aishihik was supposed to provide all the power we could use, but we all know waht a fiasco it was, and we are still paying the price for it. The Indians in Champagne didn't get any power from Aishihik, and I wonder how much benefit we would get from another hydrodam. Major development like mines would probably get most of it. Even the natives standing on guano cliffs in some banana republic have more sense than stopping their rivers so they can process bauxite and ship it to Japan at prices cheaper than anywhere in the world. Why build dams for the needs of industry that isn't even here and won't commit themselves?

j. m.

This is my land
by mike barnes

Born and bred a Canadian
I was trying for a piece of land
I went up north where there's lots of room
Figured on making my stand
With all of that country wild and free
I was sure that there'd be a place for me
But laws and bi-laws and officers
were guarding every tree.

CHORUS: I say it's insane, just crazy
This can't be happening to me
this is my land and I can't make a stand
Because of some fools bureaucracy.

So I picked me a place out of the way
Figured I'd try my hand
But little did I know of the horror show
When the government let the land
In a line up held inside a room
for four days and nights I'd stand
signing out just to take a pee
and again when I came back 'im.

What can you do
When you're forced to take part in a zoo
Well you don't have much choice
When they're the only ones making the rules.
It seems to me there's a right and a
Wrong way to go about doing things
Why can't I understand the ways that
they do and the ways that they choose.

So I put in my time and was doing just fine
Till the time came along for the sale
We all stood in line
And one at a time
Took our turns at the table
I said "Sir I'd like to have lot #89
I kind of like its looks
And it suits me just fine."
He said "Sorry son, you can't have that one.
I sold it to a friend of mine."

Editor's note: This song was inspired while waiting to buy a lot at Wolfe Creek. For the chords and tune talk to mike.

POWER for half the PEOPLE.

The Yukon Status of Women Council focuses on political action as a means to equal opportunity for women. Since the Yukon's laws, as well as its outlook in many ways, lag behind those in the south, the struggle here is pretty basic. There's little time or practical point in discussing Marxist-feminist theories when labour standards and subsidization are nonexistent. And as an example of ancient history affecting modern lives, the Indian Act and its rank discrimination can't be ignored. Matrimonial law, affirmative action for women, equal opportunities in employment and training, are all areas that desperately need work for improvement. Naturally, this means that the energy, interest and time of Status members are used to their very fullest, with just a bit more needed, asked for and received.

It's been a purely volunteer effort up to now (since the council's beginnings during International Women's Year, 1975). In 1978, however, the Status received a Secretary of State grant to employ a part-time resource person to fulfill the basic, day-to-day activities of the Status, which hopefully will allow members more time and energy to work on research and lobbying projects. In 1977-1978 such projects included making presentations to the Labour Standards Revision committee, participating in the Canadian Unity hearings, and submitting a list of suggested changes to the first draft of the pipeline terms and conditions. The project is, of course, of major interest (but mainly concern) to the council. The horror stories from Fairbanks of inflation, increased crime and accommodation shortages — coupled with the traditional difficulties women encounter trying to get construction-type jobs and lack of social services in the territory — cause a great deal of anxiety. The council naturally wishes to ease the impacts of the project on women, but the size of the task is a little overwhelming. A proposal was being drafted in the fall of '78 to ask for money to hire researchers to look into the problems which have faced women during similar large construction projects, and to find creative methods of prevention.

If you need help, or have a little energy and enthusiasm to offer, contact our resource person, Toni Cowlishaw, at the Women's Centre (667-2693).

—Alison Reid

agnes and chuck, consultants to the world

Agnes and Chuck got together last week and have solved all the world's problems. Unfortunately I was too wasted to get it all down on paper but had a good time. Here are the grand ideas that didn't float away into the ozone.

Agnes figures that since everything that needs getting done in this country is getting done, more or less, and since over ten percent of the work force is out of a job, that means that there really isn't enough work to go around. Her solution is for everyone to work four days a week instead of five and that should make lots of work for everyone. Then all the money going into UIC and Manpower could be paid out in wages. Chuck didn't see how it would make any difference if the civil servants worked only four days or even only two. I guess he doesn't think much of government workers.

Chuck has a crazy cousin from Quebec who explained the Quebecois view of things to him. The way Chuck translated it (there was a lot less arm-waving in English) the rural people and the poor and the young don't see anything particularly obnoxious about English Canadians, at least not enough to break up the country over. What they see the Federal Government as, is a wholey-owned subsidary of American Big Business. Quebec is already owned by the Yanks economically so they aren't too keen on being owned politically as well if they can manage it.

The economic pressure is being exerted now by American-directed industries to scuttle Quebec's independence move. Some Fat Canadian businesses are helping the Yanks, unwittingly or not, by pulling their money out of Quebec. Chuck's cousin thinks that the other maligned areas of Canada and the trodden-under minorities (great revolutionary talk there) should support the move to oust the Yanks from our political scene, including the government. The fight is about a way of life. So Agnes suggested that Canada would be a whole lot better place without Ontario. That's where the troubles lies! Another world problem solved.

DROPPING INTO THE WOMEN'S CENTRE

"A day in the life of a Women's Centre Co-ordinator" seemed, for a brief and reckless moment, like the ideal contribution for me to make to the Catalogue. I eagerly agreed to write it, and — pen in hand — sat down expecting an instant flow of inspiration. The result has been far from instant, and inspiration kind of oozed out in a great garbled mess as I tried to recall some of the finer details of this past year.

It seems incredible now that so much has happened in this little office and still more incredible that we have managed to maintain a certain degree of competence and tolerance through it all. The Centre Co-ordinator's job is full of opportunity. It is an incomparable learning experience in the various aspects of human relations, political involvement, administrative duties, paper-cutting, coffee-making, window-washing, etc. Theoretically, the co-ordinator is required to work only 20 hours a week. She is to work with a team of dedicated volunteers to organize programs and courses, and to staff the centre with well-informed, sympathetic unpaid persons. She should be willing to attend meetings, able to intelligently discuss women's issues while avoiding the use of four-letter words, and, of course, maintain good relations with politicians and other illustrious personalities. From time to time, she will be required to travel to out-of-town conferences, and, in the absence of volunteers, may have to answer the telephone, discuss methods of birth control, pour coffee, change diapers, seek legal advice, sell T-shirts, write press releases, arrange Employment Centre interviews, locate babysitters, vacuum, re-arrange the library and compose nasty letters. In order to be well-informed she should also attend meetings of, and maintain communication with, the Status of Women Council, Indian Women's Association, Business and Professional Women and the Yukon Child Care Association, to mention just a few.

The major difficulty of course, is that although the co-ordinator's salary corresponds to the 20-hour-per-week stipulation, it's a hard job to escape from once the time is up. If the person in question happens to be the type who doesn't like to miss anything, she's really in trouble, and is likely to experience acute energy lapses once in a while. This could possibly explain why a certain past co-ordinator became known for occasionally spending entire days in a local tavern by the water's edge, and escaping to Ontario for weeks on end on the pretense of attending conferences. The experience is really tremendous, though. In the past year we have dealt with an almost unbelievable range of problems encountered by women. Uncomfortable marital and financial situations seem to always be at the top of the list. Rape, discrimination and custody cases have been brought to our attention, as well as the common dilemma of finding adequate housing and child care facilities. We have been contacted innumerable times by women who are simply in town in search of a cup of coffee and a healthy conversation, or a good book. We have sponsored a wide range of programs and courses, both educational and recreational, participated in radio talk shows and written for local newspapers. Above all, we have maintained a sense of humour.

In the face of all disasters (no money, overflowing toilets, disappearing course instructors, criticism from friends, the press and politicians) we somehow not only survived, but did it with style. We hope everyone understands, though, why the files are not always at our fingertips, the floors are often not exactly sparkling clean and we find it necessary to plead from time to time for volunteers. We all realize that volunteer work is not always glorious, nor does it pay the rent, but working with a group of cooperative, non-professional supportive women sure offers its share of rewards. We've all experienced the proverbial burnout, but, with few exceptions, have returned for further abuse. We've got to be doing something right.

—Jill Porter

EVER think CO-OP?

The high cost of living and the desire for more "natural" foods has prompted the creation of food co-operatives in the Yukon and northern B.C. Whitehorse, Faro and Atlin, B.C. now all have active co-ops, and their members are happy with the results, even though they do a lot of work to make things happen.

A food co-op saves its members money because the members do the work that people normally pay wholesalers and retailers to do; and because goods are bought in bulk from wholesalers who deal only with food co-ops, and who have pretty darn good prices.

In Faro, it's the Grubstake Co-op. Talk to people there and you'll find out who they are and what they do. In Atlin, do the same.

The Whitehorse co-op...called the Cheechahco Co-op started in February, 1978 and did two orders that year for about 70 people. It plans three orders per year, and new members can sign up and pay a $10 membership fee just before each order (by doing it that way, the work isn't spread over the entire year).

The selection of goods is wide, and the products are high quality. The food smells fresh and tastes wonderful - delightful, really; particularly the cashews!

People contacting the Cheechahco Co-op at Box 5087 in Whitehorse will be mailed some information. If you're in another northern town and want help to organize your own co-op, ask the Atlin, Faro or Whitehorse people and they'll be glad to help. After all, we're all in this together.

max fraser

Yukon Media

RADIO
CBC YUKON NETWORK
Broadcasts from 6 a.m. to 1 a.m. daily to the Yukon and northern B.C. Good local information programming; much network re-broadcasting and occasionally we'll get a show or two from Inuvik. Listened to widely by rural Yukoners, since it's the only thing they can get!

CKRW
Only commercial network in the Yukon. Broadcasts to Whitehorse and vicinity 24 hours a day, except everything past midnight to 6 a.m. or so is canned music. Claims a larger audience than CBC, which wouldn't be too hard to substantiate. Pop music. Has a local Top 40. *Rock and Roll!*

TELEVISION
CBC NORTHERN SERVICE
Available in most communities. Very little northern programming, but occasionally we'll get a good one. Communities with fewer than 500 people are provided with TV at a fee worked out with the territorial government (which subsidizes most of the cost) since the CBC doesn't have the money to pay for stations in every northern settlement. Their cut-off point for service is 500 people.

WHTV
Provides cable service to Whitehorse. Several U.S. channels and the CTV network as well as CBC. Only CBC is live; rest are delayed broadcasts by one week since they're all videotaped in Vancouver then shipped up here. WHTV has some local programming and local TV news and wants more community groups or individuals to get into the medium. Is attempting to get live U.S. transmissions via satellite which it has already proved viable; but the government isn't agreeing to it yet.

THE WHITEHORSE STAR
Published afternoons, Monday to Friday, Whitehorse. 20

cents per copy. Established 1900; circulation 4,000-5,000. Write 2149 2nd Avenue. Phone 403-667-4481 (news) or 667-4774 (advertising). Independent. CP wire service. Strong local coverage.

THE NORTHERN TIMES
Published mornings, Monday thru Friday, Whitehorse. 15 cents per copy. Established 1978. Circulation, unknown.

THE YUKON NEWS
Published weekly at Whitehorse every Wednesday. Territory-wide circulation about 8,000. Given away free. Local news only.

THE YUKON INDIAN NEWS
Published every two weeks by the Ye Sa To Communications Society. Offices at the Yukon Indian Centre, 22 Nisutlin Drive, Whitehorse. Available by subscription for $5 per year or 15 cents apiece at Mac's newsstand. This paper provides good coverage of Indian issues in the Yukon, the NWT and across the country, as well as in other countries. Mostly local.

ELSEWHERE NORTH
THE ALASKA ADVOCATE
Weekly every Wednesday, state-wide in Alaska. Small, interesting tabloid specializing in things political in our neighbour's land. Box 3035, Anchorage, Alaska, U.S.A. 99510. Fone 907-274-1052/278-3535. Price $25 per year, $0.75 per copy on stands. 50 per year; they don't publish one week in July and one in December.
Good stuff; nice way of learning a bit about Alaska; more real than Alaska Magazine and such. None of "this is the last Frontier" bullshit. Basically political, topical social issues. More or less run as a collective; in spirit, anyway.

THE NEWS OF THE NORTH
Tri-weekly (Mon., Wed. and Friday) published at Yellowknife, N.W.T. Available in Whitehorse at Mac's Fireweed on Main St.

THE YELLOWKNIFER
Published weekly at Yellowknife. Available at Mac's.

THE NATIVE PRESS
Published at Yellowknife. Available by mail.

FASTING
GET YER NOTHING!

Nothing at all.

SOAP

Dorth wanted us to mention fasting. That means eating nothing. Or not eating something. "One of the oldest, cheapest cures for anything that ails you. Cited in every major religion of the world and by Mr. Natural." And Chuck says fasting is good to clear up the *runs.*

PUBLIC LIBRARY

Telephone: 667-5239
2071 Second Avenue,
Whitehorse, Y.T. Box 2703

Hours of Service

Monday-Friday	10:00 a.m. - 9:00 p.m.
Saturday	10:00 a.m. - 6:00 p.m.
Sunday	1:00 p.m. - 9:00 p.m.

Periodicals

The library subscribes to over 300 magazines and retains back issues of those periodicals which are indexed. As many of these publications are on microfilm, a microfilm reader/printer is available for public use. Staff will be glad to assist you in the use of the periodical indexes.

Government Documents

We have federal, territorial and civic publications, including Federal Statutes, Yukon Ordinances and Regulations, the Canada Gazette, statistical reports, and Federal and Territorial legislative debates. Remember to ask for help from the staff since not all of these items are readily available on the shelves.

Children's Books

A collection of picture books and "easy read-ers" is available for pre-schoolers and children in the primary grades.

Other Specialized Material

Telephone Books
Educational Reference Collection
Multi-lingual Books
Records and Cassettes
Encyclopedias
University Calendars
Northern Books
Large Print Books
Atlases and Dictionaries
Almanacs

Photocopying. The library maintains a coin-operated Xerox machine for public use. Copies are 15 cents each.

Children's Story Hour. Most of the year, the library conducts a weekly pre-school story hour for 3 to 5 year olds.

Library Meeting Room. The use of the library meeting room is available to community groups and organizations. It will accommodate about 35 people comfortably. Bookings may be made up to two months in advance.

Art Gallery. Throughout the year the Art Gallery at the library shows the work of both local artists, and rotating displays from outside galleries. Do come in and browse.

MORE BIBLIOTEXT —

Dawson	993-5571
Elsa	995-2442
Faro	994-2456
Haines Junction	634-2215
Mayo	996-2541
Watson Lake	536-7517
Whitehorse	667-5239
Atlin, B.C.	521
Beaver Creek	5171
Burwash	4274
Carcross	4341
Carmacks	5451
Destruction Bay	?
Old Crow	2151
Pelly River	5115
Swift River	6531
Takhini (Whs.)	668-5585
Teslin	3491
Tungsten, NWT	2m 3320

There's a library upstairs at the Yukon Indian Centre in Riverdale chock full of all kinds of books and other reading material. Fiction and non-fiction for kids, and non-fiction for adults, biographies, filmstrips, motion pictures, picture books, newspapers and magazines all dealing with Indian people and Indian issues are there, just waiting to be read, referred to and thought about. The place is quiet and good for just relaxing or doing research in.

—m. f.

the Yukon Archives

Situated on the site of the old Whitehorse morgue the Yukon Archives is now home to the ghosts of the Yukon's past. The books, documents, photographs, maps and diaries held by the Archives record the full extent of the Yukon's colourful and exciting history, from the lifestyles and travels of the native people who roamed the hidden valleys and unnamed mountain ranges long before the first white trappers, through the explorations of Hudson Bay Company factor Robert Campbell, to the gold rush and beyond.

The faces of the thousands who scrambled and cursed their way over the passes and rushed headlong for the gold fields are here. Their words, written by the light of coal oil lamps in frosted cabins, tell of the joys and despair of the northern frontier. The shrill blasts of the riverboat whistle and the watery thump of the huge paddlewheels exist here on film and tape. Mining records and maps recount the fascinating stories of men and women who dug instant fortunes from the gold creeks and who just as quickly lost them. Microfilmed records of the Mounted Police vividly describe the murders and suicides, and the gambling halls and whorehouses of Lousetown. They tell of the men driven insane by the harsh land and relate the epic tales of the "Lost Patrol" and the "Mad Trapper."

In addition to these stories of yesteryear, the Yukon Archives holds topographic maps and river charts, periodicals, and documentation concerning the "silver snake" that is soon to wind its way across the territory.

The Archives is located next to the Whitehorse Public Library on 2nd Avenue and is open from 9 a.m. to 5 p.m. Monday to Friday. Extended week night and weekend visits can also be arranged. Photostatic copies of documents can be made and copies of most of our historical photographs can be ordered at minimal cost. Write for our free descriptive brochure.

So pay a visit to the Yukon Archives. Take a time trip through our past and unearth a wealth of knowledge far richer than many of the fleeting fortunes shovelled from the Yukon's golden streams.

If you can't visit but wish to learn more about the history of the Yukon or about the Archives please write or phone 667-5321.

— Bill Oppen
Sept., 1978

OLD WHITEHORSE
JIM ROBB
- YUKON
1976

RESEARCH IN THE ICEFIELDS
and elsewhere

The Arctic Institute of North Amerca has been conducting an interdisciplinary research program in and around the St. Elias Mountains since 1961. Called the Icefield Ranges Research Project (IRRP), it encompasses a high altitude physiology study which has been going on for eleven years in a high-altitude laboratory at 17,500 feet on Mount Logan; glaciology and geophysical studies on many of the glaciers in the Park; small mammal studies, including mice, ground squirrels and snowshoe hares; caribou studies, geomorphology and the study of rock glaciers in the Grizzly Creek area; botany; limnology; as well as isolated student programs over the years in many other areas. The Institute's small grants fund is set up to assist student researchers in their field work, and this program has been primarily responsible for large numbers of students being able to get into the field in an area which would likely be closed to them otherwise, simply on the basis of expense and logistics.

Publications of the Institute include bound research and technical papers in a variety of fields, conference proceedings, and hardbound volumes on many subjects, including a series of translations from Russian anthropological works. A complete list of publications can be obtained by writing the Arctic Institute headquarters in Calgary (address follows) and the publications can also be ordered from that office.

We have two Helio Courier STOL aircraft on ski-wheels, which are used for transporting personnel and gear to the icefields, including the high camp on Logan. One of the aircraft is currently leased to Yukon Airways out of Whitehorse, and is therefore being used as a charter plane for transporting climbers and photographers into the icefields on a commercial basis. **THE ARCTIC INSTITUTE OF NORTH AMERICA**

**University Library Tower,
2920 - 24th Avenue N.W.
Calgary, Alberta, Canada T2N 1N4**

If you like to study and learn, but you're not into sitting in stuffy classrooms, putting up with boring profs, or staring at those good looking bodies all through the day (the ones that you know won't be putting out all through the night), you can take correspondence courses, and one place that deals with this is the University of Athabaska. It's geared towards those who can't get out to classes, or because of a variety of reasons cannot take up full time attendance at any university. The courses are for credit and can be applied towards a degree, or you could take an entire shit load of courses and get your degree to wall paper your outhouse with. The courses range through the humanities and sciences with tutorial assistance, as well as TV programs and audio tapes to help you along.

The Yukon Vocational & Technical Training Centre

The Yukon Territorial Government has a Vocational School in Whitehorse. It is a controversial place because:

1. It costs money.
2. Some people sleep a lot there.
3. Students get paid to go by the Territory or Canada Manpower and collect U.I.C. as well. If you want to go, remember that you will only get out of it what you put in. Canada Manpower sponsors about 70% of the people there.

The Dormitory has space for 50 people.

The school is open ten months of the year, which is the longest course length.

Courses offered are:
Automotive Mechanics

Nursing Assistant
Welding
Plumbing
Building Construction (Carpentry)
Commercial Bookkeeping
Commercial Clerk Typist
Commercial Secretarial
Community Basic Education
Drafting - Surveying
Electrical
Food Services
Heavy Equip. Mechanics

and Heavy Equip. Operators!

From time to time, as the public demand requires, there is an Air-brake course offered and an Oil Burner Mechanic course every two to three years.

Applications and calendars can be obtained from the Yukon Vocational Tech. Training Centre, Student Adviser, Box 2703, Whitehorse or from Outreach Workers and community schools.

ADULT EDUCATION

The Yukon has a community adult education program based out of the Yukon Vocational and Technical Training Center in Whitehorse. Sponsored by the Yukon Territorial Government, the program has been operating since 1972. It is recognized throughout the Yukon as the Blade/Linc school. The program's objective is to upgrade adults to a Grade ten level of competency in math and English. The Blade (Basic Literacy for Adult Development) program takes a student from illiteracy with no math skills to a Grade five academic level. The Linc (Learning Individualized for Canadians) program covers the Grade six to ten levels. A Life Skills course involves learning communication and creative group problem solving skills. After a person has completed the program they receive a Grade ten diploma.

—*Dorothy Gibbon & Mary Cheney*

These are the people to get in touch with for further information:

University of Athabaska,
14904 - 121st Avenue,
EDMONTON, Alberta

Correspondence Courses are available from British Columbia. The average cost is $15-$20, and complete lists of courses and application forms can be obtained by writing to:

Correspondence Courses
Dept. of Education
Parliament Buildings
Victoria, B C.

The courses are good, made up to be understood easily and are the best way to get that Grade 12 education.

DOMINION HERBAL COLLEGE
7527 Kingsway, Burnaby, B.C. V3N 3C1

A correspondence college dealing in Herbalism, not Naturopathy. The courses come in book form and can be done at your own speed, with all necessary materials included. Sorry, no sample lessons. The course comes in two parts, the first dealing with the anatomical and physiological systems, the second explains the different herbs, roots, etc., their various remedies and preparations and the conditions for their use. There is also available a supplement dealing with diets and formulae.

NORTHERN CANADA INSTITUTE FOR PAPYROMANCY
(affiliated with Papyromancy International)

This small, and sometimes active group is dedicated to the study, development and promotion of the infant science of papyromancy. Papyromancy is the ability to prophesy through contemplating the way people roll reefers. Lots of space for new members. Write to the institute at Box 2703, Whitehorse.
—*b. s.*

FEDERAL GOVERNMENT INFORMATION

Because of some "freedom of information" sections in the recently-proclaimed Human Rights Legislation, the federal government has put together an index of federal information banks. There's one at the Post Office in Whitehorse, and other copies of the same thing might be found elsewhere, too.

Carcross Community Education Centre → Real Education

Carcross Community Education Centre is a community-based alternative high school which provides a total learning experience for its members. Unlike most educational institutions, Carcross is concerned with the development of the whole person — not just the intellectual development of one's mind.

Understanding one's self and others, handling responsibility, acquiring outdoor skills and becoming aware of our relation with the environment are all considered important along with academic and vocational studies.

Much of the Carcross learning experience occurs within the building complex — five houses, two cabins, various outbuildings and the huge three-storey ex-residential school. The main building houses an antique heating and power plant full of working museum pieces, a laundry which floods the basement and eats socks, a bakery with temperamental ovens and a kitchen full of leaky taps. We

also have our luxuries — an expansive library, well-equipped woodshop, three-bay garage, dog team, freighter canoe and sauna. The place has character and, love it or hate it, for us it is home.

While our vocational pursuits offer students educational experiences, they are vital to the community's existence. The physical plant supplies us with heat and offers community members the opportunity to study and train for their fourth-class steam ticket. Work in the garage enables us to keep our vehicles on the road while teaching practical skills. Toys, furniture and cedar-strip canoes are built in our woodshop by students as well as parent members. Home-made bread is baked weekly and a whole array of goodies emerge from the ovens before special bake sales. Community members pool their talents to create a variety of craft items — from caribou antler jewelry to hand knit sweaters. Our logging efforts provide our woodshop with lumber, furnish our cabins and outbuildings with heat and supplement our income through cordwood sales. As student fees don't cover the cost of operating such a complex, we depend upon revenue from these ventures to meet our budget.

Our struggle with self-suffiency prompts us to utilize our resources to the best of our ability. Our garden provides us with produce (and enough potatoes to last through a Yukon winter!). Wild fruits and berries become transformed into jams and jellies for consumption after the snow flies. The amount of protein we eat relies largely on the outcome of our fishing and hunting efforts (in addition to the traditional Carcross soybeans). Activities which may be considered recreation "outside" are essential for our survival.

Where we are

You'll find the Carcross Community nestled in a glacial valley surrounded by mountains in the southern Yukon. Here, in what we feel is the most beautiful place in the north, we have leased 1,600 acres which include Chooutla Lake, waterfront on Nares Lake, a clear-flowing stream and more forest than one could cover in a year of after-dinner walks. We're about 50 miles southeast of Whitehorse and neighbors to the town of Carcross — home of the White Pass Railways's golden spike, the Caribou Hotel, Matthew Watson's General Store and the Tutshi, a very retired steamer.

Who we are

Parent members (or pms, as our staff members are called) form the core of the community. Pms share their skills and themselves to the community for a minimum of two years. Parent members come in a variety of ages, shapes and sizes with a variety of talents and perform a variety of services. Pms are anything from mechanics to social workers, and shoulder all responsibilities involved with running a community — administering, teaching, cooking, cleaning and firing the boilers. Pms live by a Rule of Life, which they themselves write as a group. This is a statement by which they aim to become united, committed to forming a loving community based on the Christian ideals of love and service. The financial incentive for this is negligible — basically room and board plus $50 monthly honorarium. Something much deeper than the superficial needs perpetuated by today's society brings parent members to Carcross and binds them together.

As education at Carcross means education-in-the-broadest-sense-of-the-word, so are our student members students-in-the-broadest-sense-of-the-word. Ranging in age from 16-19, they are as varied as parent members. These young people are individuals who are looking for more than what is offered in usual school

situations; they are searching for alternative academic education, vocational training, a good "people experience" or to be part of something greater than themselves. All come to learn from the experience of living, working and sharing with others.

Workers are special people with special skills who fill special needs. Their commitment to the community is for a relatively short period of time, during which they work closely with the parent body. They too earn the princely sum of $50 per month, and so must be motivated by their desire to see Carcross work. Each of these groups is an integral part of our whole; together they form the Carcross Community.

Beginnings

Conceived in the mind of Bishop John Frame, the Carcross Community began as a dream to turn the Chooutla Residential School into a complex for use as a community-inspired educational experiment. The Chooutla school (which somewhat resembles a hospital ship run aground) closed in 1969 after the building of elementary schools throughout the Territory made it obsolete. Deserted and left to face the Yukon elements for three years, the building acquired many ailments — pipes burst, windows broke, foundations sank and cracked, hundreds of birds nested in the eaves. Costs for professional restoration of the crippled building were overwhelming.

The Bishop's dream was then passed on to a handful of young volunteers who spent a mammoth year of planning, replanning, plumbing, building, financing, digging, cleaning, laughing and painting. At the same time they struggled to form a community which would provide young people with an ex-

perience which would be educational in the broadest sense of the word. In September of 1973 the community opened its doors to the first students.

Since that time, many people have passed through the community's doors. Each year has been shaped by the members present. Although community goals and ideals have remained unchanged, methods of achieving them may vary; no two years have been the same. Carcross has remained flexible enough so to allow each community to find better ways of realizing their goals. This has involved Carcross with an expansive Community of 90 as well as a closer community of 35; a full high school curriculum (offering every course under the sun) and a reduced program emphasizing upgrading. The 1978-79 school year will be one of intense evaluation and rebuilding; parent members, workers and a minimal number of students will work together so to provide a Carcross Community in 1979 which will best meet the needs of today's youth.

The Carcross Community is searching for people who would like to offer themselves, their spirit and their willingness to help our community grow and flourish. If you would like to join our community and share with us, or request further information, please write: Carcross Community Education Centre, P.O. Box 26, Carcross, Yukon Territory, Y0B 1B0.

THE GUMBY PAPERS

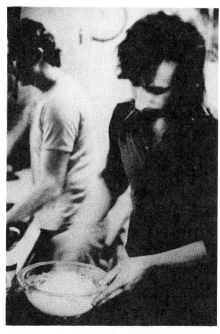

Below are some transcrips of on-the-scene reporting from an Arctic Circle camp.The camp no longer exists.The job is finished and so all those wasted days and nights are a forgotten dream.

A man called D.P.Gumby was a bullcook in this camp and managed to capture the moods of his work-day just before he quit.There was much more than these four episodes, but these are all we can print for now.We are still looking for Mr. Gumby to get his permission to use these articles.

Rumour has it he was locked up shortly after his release from camp.

Please let us know if you know of his whereabouts.

RAVEN'S REVENGE REVUE
(Part 3....the job)

Our hero, D.P. Gumby is sweeping the floor where the men take their coffee break.However;the time is 3pm and the men on night shift are filing in after sleeping 4-5 hrs. They are still in a comatose state and so for that matter is DPG.

DPG:ohhhhh rum tum tiddle doo
    rumm t gummdiddle poo....
MAN:Hard at'er eh?
DPG:that's what they say(continuing
    to sweep)
Man:yep
Another man:yep
"man:looks like she's still snowing
    out
Man:yep
DPG:move your feet
Man:yep
"man:yep
"man:yep
MAN:plane come in today?
DPG:nope
MAN:any mail for me?

DPG:nope
MAN:Leroy still out?
DPG:yep
man:yep
man:yep
THEN....another man comes in. Our
    hero now has a mop.
Man:Hard at'er eh?
DPG:That's what they say
Man:Looks like she's still snowing
    out
"man:yep
"man:yep
"man:yep
DPG:Move your feet
Man:Plane come in today?
MAN:nope
"man:nope
"man:nope
Man:any mail for me?
DPG:nope
Man:Leroy still out?
DPG:yep
Man:yep
MASSIVE MABLE comes out of the
    kitchen, on her way to her
    room,talking as she walks.
MM:Good morning how are you all
    it's still snowing outside
    the plane didn't come in
    today so I don't have any
    picture back do you like the
    cookies Leroy is still out
    and he may be back tomorrow
    but maybe not untill next....
Man:yep
MAN:yep
"man:yep

RRRRRAVENS' REVENGE REVUE
(Part 4.....The plane is in)

The scene opens today on our hero, D.P.Gumby(DPG),outside the office area with four people who are about to embark on the plane to Whitehorse(wonder-city of the western dream).Also present are Donald the demented first aid man

and the office page-boy,Scooter. It is around noon and our hero is hungry and still partially asleep...
SCOOTER:515253545556575859.......
    606162636465676869.
DON:Alright is everyone here do
    you have your bags why didn't
    you tell us you quit I know
    he's pissed but I'm trying to
    ignore him...and you...well
    carry him then.
Man1:I've been here 68 days and.... ,
Man2:I've been here 102 days and....
Man3:goddamotherfuggershitterneg-
    grspialloverpiss..............
DPG:You got fired eh?What room
    were all you guys in?
Man1:I've been here 68 days and....
Man2:I've been here 102 days and....
DON:I think I hear the plane....
Man3:pizzinmerightoffuggemallany-
    wayniggercuntpiss........
RRRRRRRROOOOOOOOAAAAAAAARRRRRRRR-
ZZZZZZZZMMMMMMMM
Out they go into the truck,man1
and man2 carry man4 who has been
comatose since he arrived and only
is going out because his buddies
take him everywhere with them in
the hopes that someday he will tell
them who he is. Man#*@$%¢* is
wondering whether to crack our hero
in the head or kick the door to the
office but forgets everything when
the truck starts up. Watching them
go are Scooter and our hero.
Scooter:402403404405406407408409-
    410411412413414415416417418$i*3
DPG:How many guys are coming in do
    you know their names is there
    another one today?
Scooter:421422423424425426427428......
    three....no I don't....no.....
    429430
The truck comes in and out gets
Donald,three men who are clearly
having a mystical experience(one -
is obviously right out of the
Capital Hotel bar and is walking
on the spot against the wall.
Donald:Go get your rooms this guy
    will show you them and come
    back and sign in except you
...continued on page 96

DON'T COME HERE LOOKING FOR WORK!

There are no jobs in the Yukon. It is a closed shop to most people who come here. It is basically taking care of its own. This is a natural game set up with rules and limits, which, once learned, can be used to profit the individual who is willing to try his luck. Luck is not perhaps a good term, because getting a job up here is less a game of luck and chance than most people realize.

Any "game" has its key to understanding and manipulation — and this one does too. If you think you can come up here and tap in on a pipeline or a road construction project without knowing anyone, then think again. Remember there are many people who live here who work on construction projects and a decent percentage of them are looking for work at any given time. The "boom & bust" tale is not being told here — just increases and decreases of various degrees. The pipeline may possibly be built starting 1981 but three of the four major mines in the Yukon may be out of production by then too. The north is like that.

Road construction takes unskilled labourers (of which there is a surplus here like everywhere else) and machine operators (of which there is a whole squad waiting for the big jobs to open). Pipeline companies are training most of their own personnel and once again it's "who you know." The only jobs listed in the Whitehorse Star at the time of writing (summer) are for clerks in department stores and chambermaids. Not your average boom town now is it? Even agencies like manpower and union halls give preference to those who come back year after year — those who live up here, work and play, get rich in summer, broke in winter. These folks get preference — always, without fail.

Are you still reading? If so, hello and welcome to the honest part of this article and the first rule of "job-hunting" in the Yukon. Don't believe anything of what anyone tells you. First, the best way to find out what's going down is to go sit out in front of the Post Office or go have a beer in some tavern that has a spark of youth left in it. The grapevine is the very best source of information on any subject and can be followed up quite quickly. Move fast; everything else does. Second, go to Canada Manpower if you're into red tape and mediocrity and spend some time there. If they tell you to come back for an appointment in a week just raise a little shit, like go see the MP for the Yukon and explain it to him. It's surprising how fast the wheels of government move when they're greased a little. The most common problems at Canada Manpower are the refusal to release information and the almost dictatorial powers of some counsellors within the organization. Remember that *they are there to serve you*, not to comment on your hair or clothing, or to tell you what an asshole you are. It's changing, but slowly.

The government jobs are all handled by Manpower. You are not allowed to go and see the people beforehand to try and impress them, so don't let on you did. If you didn't visit your objective you're wasting your time going to interviews where the person was picked out last week. Don't be afraid to look good — remember that they always try for the best person for the job so act like that person. Lie a lot and be cool. If you're good it's okay to bullshit verbally; just don't sign anything until you're sure you can get away with it.

You may think this is all very shocking but this is 1978 and a degree in computer maths will not get you an 80 hour week with a highway contractor playing in the dirt because you're over-qualified; and a grade ten education won't get you a job sweeping floors in a building because they want grade 12 now. To get the job you want, you've got to be who they want. So act accordingly, and have some fun too. Face it, that's what your future employer probably did. The union halls hire for those who are members. For those who aren't it's another hustle and a tough one, too. The only way to do it is by sheer pressure of presence. Smile three times a week and tell them how much you want the job. They'll get sick of you in a hurry and give you something to do or just tell you to beat it. Don't be afraid to confront people up here. Some of them will treat you like a slug, but a lot won't. There is nothing a person can cut you down for except the interruption if you've got the spunk to put on a good act and make your visit pleasant. Leave 'em smiling. It's probably a bitch of a morning in the office.

That's about all we're going to tell you. The first part of this article still holds true — "there are no jobs unless you know somebody," but there is an additional phrase up here that goes: "You may get a job because you're somebody someone wants to know." Someone asked, "What are you going to say about Unemployment Insurance?" Well, first of all it's not enough money to live nicely up here because of the high prices.

Second, it's not going to further your peace of mind unless you've already got a good nest egg from working. Thirdly, lots of people get told to go back south where there are more jobs than here. Fourthly, some people cheat and get away with it; a lot try and don't. Fifth, if you end up here on UIC or Welfare, don't ask for too much. You won't get it. Too many people up here work too hard to have any sympathy for almost anybody.

To return to the start of this piece: "The Yukon is a closed shop to most people who come here. It is basically taking care of its own."

— *e. p.*

WOMEN AND WORK
(Outside the Home)

Yukon workers are covered either by the federal **Canada Labour Code** or the territorial **Labour Standards Ordinance**. Territorial public servants come under the Public Service Ordinance and the Public Service Staff Relations Ordinance. The *Labour Standards Ordinance* has provisions in regard to equal pay for the same work performed under similar working conditions except where such payment is made pursuant to "(a) a seniority system; (b) a merit system; (c) a system that measures earnings by quality or quantity of production, or (d) a differential based on any factor other than sex." This means that unless one of the listed factors pertains to a job women must receive the same wage as a man for the same work performed under similar working conditions.

Complaints in this area should be addressed to the territorial government Labour Standards officer.

The **Fair Practices Ordinance** regulates hiring practices in the area of discriminatory practices, etc. When choosing an employee, an employer cannot discriminate on the basis of race, religion, religious creed, colour, ancestry, national origin, sex or marital status. Complaints under this section can be handled by the labour standards officer. The **Fair Practices Ordinance** also prohibits discrimination in any term and condition of employment and in advertising in respect to employment as well as in accommodation on a number of grounds including sex and marital status.

For complaints in which the federal government is the employer, write to: A. R. K. Anderson, Director General, Anti-Discrimination Branch, Public Service Commission of Canada, Ottawa, Ontario, K1A 0M7.

For complaints involving employers such as banks, telephone companies, etc., that fall under federal jurisdiction, write to: Fair Employment Practices Branch, Canada Department of Labour, 340 Laurier Avenue West, Ottawa, Ontario, K1A 0J2. Copies of any complaints should also be sent to: Sylvia Gelber, Director, Women's Bureau, Canada Department of Labour, 340 Laurier Avenue West, Ottawa, Ontario, K1A 0J4.

One booklet which might be useful is put out by the Labour Canada Women's Bureau, called "The Law Relating to Working Women" and contains information about legislation on working women throughout Canada.

Wanna Be A Miner?

There's your friend. There he is after spending eight months at Elsa, working in the mine. How's he doing?

"I dunno, man. Just got back this morning."

"Far out. Good to see you. How was it?"

"I dunno. I'm pretty bushed. Sure glad I got outa there, though. It's about fucking time. Now I can get back to real life again."

Later, when he's got his shit together a bit better and when he's in better spirits, you hear him tell you:

"That's a strange place. I'm like a lot of the other guys. You just go there to work and that's all you do, man. I mean you work, smoke dope, work, smoke dope, maybe someone's got some cocaine, then you eat and listen to some music and maybe read a book and then you sleep and it's back to work. Eight fucking months. A lot of really shitty work. But at least it broke the boredom.

"Everyone in there is goin crazy unless they already are. Some people really like it there, though. It's really weird. I don't know how those guys do it. They're just there. It's all they've done. They've had the same job and even the same fucking room for 15 or 20 years. They might have worked their way up the ladder a ways but shit, man, how can anyone live there for that long at that fucking mine? It's all they've done. It's all they know. I'll bet some guys have a quarter of a million dollars in the bank. No bullshit! They never spend any of the money they make. They just stay in the bunkhouse when they're not working and watch TV or maybe they beat off once in a while. But what I was gonna say is there's this one guy there who **really** doesn't know what to do with his dough. Or maybe he just wants to be nice to everyone. He goes to the store every week, like clockwork, and comes back with a bag of groceries, or maybe two. He puts them in the garbage or somewhere else and just leaves them there. I don't believe this guy's for real. He just leaves all this stuff in the garbage. He buys it then throws it all away. Then everybody else goes through it and takes what they want. It's neat. There's everything from peanut butter to Drano, if you're into that. All kinds of shit. It's really unreal, man. That place sure does weird things to people. Or maybe the people are just weird anyway.

The Last Night At Fire Camp No. 22

For the past three days,
we've been climbing
up and down through the burn
on the side of our mountain
toting pulaskies and shovels
and "piss-cans" full of water
until there was nothing left
of the fire, not even
a few smokes.
There'll be little to do
for the next 24 hours
but keep an eye open
for the chopper
that will take us home.
We look out over the delta
where the White River
dumps its volcanic ash
into the Yukon.
The sun sets about midnight.
The sky is purple and gold,
royal colors,
and we feel like kings,
laborers lounging around,
swapping jokes,
digesting steaks,
drinking coffee
taking it all in:
probably the first
and last men ever to sit
on the top of this
particular mountain.

— Erling Friis-Baastad
(originally published in Contemporary Verse II)

you've been here before you were fired not you him not you,him.

SCOOTER and DONALD disappear leaving DPG to do his proverbial job.

DPG:Alright come with me and I will endeavor to conjure you some rooms.

Man1:I don't want a room out there. (walks off in a different diection).

Man2:Goddammotherfuggemallcocksuckermotherfuenshittalloverpiss.

DPG:Here....(opens door,dodges

blow to the groin and quickly splits.)

(back at the office)

Donald:Here is the mail did you give them their rooms who is that walking against that wall there was also a New Cook here she is.

DPG:Are you the new cook can you walk can you follow me to your room?

New Cook:What?

DPG:oh no.....

New Cook:What?

(Part 5......The plane goes out)

Our hero, D.P.Gumby is standing outside the offices with Donald the Demented the first aid man and other assorted people.

DON:Alright is everyone here do you have your bags why didn't you tell us you quit........
RRRRRROOOOOOAAAAAARRRRRRZZZZZZMMMMMM.....There is the plane now I know he's pissed but I'm trying to ignore him....and you....well you'll have to carry him then....let's go.

DPG:The hell with that if he's going to be such a vegetable then he can bloody well stay.

DON:We don't want him.

DPG:You don't want anyone that you've got here.

DON:sssshhhhhh not so loud we are laying off 6 labourers today.

DPG:That's great.You'll get your contract done in record time that way.

(Enter Biggy McWheel)

BMc:Then I told the little weasel

of a labourer that I was the camp superintendant and blah-blahblahblahblah.............

DON:Come on now let's go get in the truck do you have everything...........

DPG:Hey Biggy whats that on your leg?

BMc:(turns to vegetable)Why you ... #@*&%#"@?...............

DPG:He likes you.

There is a commotion and heavy (very heavy)footsteps at this point and in walks Massive Mable. You can hear the plywood flooring complaining under the weight.

MM:Hello hello hello here we go on the plane I'm going......

DPG:Oh fuck, here we go.......

MM:.....to see Leroy and be with my daughter for thanksgiving and see the baby and come back next week or the week after that or the week after that I hope the kitchen can do without me what is the time is the plane in maybe I should check my mail I usually get lots of mail even though it is almost always papers and lottery stubs and did you know I won.......

THE FLOORBOARDS:#$@*&*$%#@@&*%$#%$#"

DON:Let's go......

DPG:Yeah shutup and get in the truck and don't talk to me ever again.

MM:urp.......

Everyone gets in the truck and goes up to the airstrip.

MAN:welltheweatherlooksbabble-jabberwooftweet.....

DON:yep

MAN2:yep

Man3:yep

MAN2:hey was there any mail for me who will get my room did you drink all that scotch you had why are you staring at me like that?

DPG:What?

Man2:Yeah alright.I guess I have been here a long time.

MAN3:I've been here 102 days and....
And now......

RRRRRRRRRRRRAVENS' REVENGE REVUE
(Part 869.....Cleaning a room...)

D.P.Gumby is at work,merrily whistling a catchy tune and smiling warmly to all the people who drift past the door on their way to the can.The pictures in this little room reflect upon beautiful ladies in quaint country scenes,and,like all other rooms the occupants have their jolly little habits that make life in camp such a staggering ecstacy.The particular hobby of this lovely little room is to get so bent and twisted out of shape that they can go without paying attention to the time-warp.His friendly partner joins DPG for this small cleaning job.

DPG:(opens door and steps back)oh-mygod....its Drunken Foreign Mech's room.

PARD:Wow.....

DPG:Do you want to use my knife to scrape that off or go for a chemical approach?

PARD:Here;you do the beds and find out where this trail of food leads to.

DPG:The closet don't open it!

PARD:Don't worry we can't go into peoples stuff so we'll leave it.

DPG:But what about the smell?

PARD:We'll tape it shut,airseal it.

DPG:Yeah, maybe the job will end this month.

PARD:Well let's get at the bed...

DPG:Give me a hand here the sheets are stuck together.

PARD:Oh-oh it's the old cement sheet effect.

DPG:Don't get too close it's starting to smoke......

PARD:Here;dump this old coffee on it and let's abandon ship.

DPG:My foots stuck and I can't... there it's OK let's go.

PARD:I'll open a window and seal the heat off;frozen stuff doesn't smell.

DPG:Hurry;it's dripping into the hall and then people will know about him.

PARD:(slam)There it's done,let's go have a coffee.

DPG:OK I'll go change and meet you in the kitchen.Maybe we can forget that one until next week.

(later...)

MAC:Don't you ever work your jobs so easy and everything.......

DPG:I think I'll quit....

MAC:.....all you do is sweep the floor and throw blankets.....

(at this precise moment, Drunken Foreign Mech. comes by and sort of speaks.)

DFM:Gribblegrobblemuzzletweet-wooftoodle.

MAC:yep

MAN:yep

ROOM:yep

DPG:Make it out for today I'm leaving tomorrow.

MAC:Oh yeah?

DPG:yep.....it's time to go walkin' with the dogs in the woods.

MAN:That mechanic's pretty good on the job isn't he.......

Someone:What?

D.P.gumby:woof woof.

Nakina

Nakini is a northern Indian Village on
the CPR railroad line. The train stops
for mail. I saw this village on one of
my trips Out-side — it is Overy quiet,
sleepy & built of white & Red board.
This is a poem about it.

Nakina

No more snow to fly
Still she keeps you sleeping
Nakina I see you
though, Nakini I don't hear you
blanket white she hides
22 white clap sheds she smiles
Broad eyes she cries
Red angel's trail
Hunters of the high wind
     full of wild Rice.

Nakina   white snow
white sheds
Red trim she bleeds
    and evergreen
grey snow
grey sheds
Red trim she bleeds
    and evergreen
a yellow ochre dream
    she kneels.

Nakina in the willows
watch out for the wolves
  and the fishers very keen
and alcohol keeps them
     mean

        alyx/ones.

calculating the length & amount of a POGEY claim

Now called just "U.I.," instead of "U.I.C.," pogey is a way of life for a lot of northerners. Legislation has changed a bit but the difference is not much in areas of high unemployment, like the Yukon. Since the regional rate of unemployment is always above nine per cent here, the "VER" or Veriable Entrance Requirement means you need ten weeks of insurable employment during the 52 weeks before you apply, or since you last filed for pogey.

To figure out how long you can collect, you need to know your number of weeks worked. To do this, get all your job separation slips and look in the spot on the form saying "number of weeks of insurable employment." The UI people calculate the length of benefits by adding three numbers. The first number, call it A, is the number of weeks on your separation slips, up to a maximum of 25. The next number (call it B), is zero unless you have worked 27 weeks (just over six months) or more. If you have worked more, subtract 25 from your number of weeks worked, then divide by two. The result is B. (For example, 31 weeks worked means 31 minus 25, for six; divided by two equals three. So B would be three in this case, and A was the maximum at 25.)

To calculate C, the third number which the UI people call the "regional extended phase," you will have to make a phone call to the Whitehorse UI office when you have been paid for A plus B weeks. Ask only "what is the current Regional Unemployment Rate (or "RUR")?" It will be something over 10, and even could be as high as 20, depending on the latest statistical folklore from Statistics Canada, or StatCan. Take the regional unemployment rate, subtract four, then multiply by four. This is "C," although it can only be as high as 32. So if the regional unemployment rate is 12 or more, C is 32.

Now you can get your total number of weeks possible by adding A plus B plus C. However, if this total is more than 50 you still only get paid for the maximum 50 weeks.

A few examples:

1) Assume your number of weeks worked is 10. Then A will be 10 and B is 0. After 10 weeks, you phone their office and find out the RUR is, say, 10.5. That gives you a "C" of 26 more weeks for a total of 36 on your UI claim.

2) Assume you worked 31 weeks. That means "A" will be the maximum 25, and B is 31, minus 25 equals 6, divided by two gives you a B of three. When you phone after 28 weeks, you'll find out the unemployment rate is something more probably like 18 per cent, so you'll get a "C" of the maximum, 32. A plus B plus C equals more than the maximum of 50 weeks for your claim so you'll get the maximum allowed, of 50.

3) Assume your weeks worked is 18, and the RUR is more than 12. Then A is 18, B is 0 and C is 32. You are eligible for the maximum, 50 weeks of pogey.

Remember, of course, that the total number of weeks of benefits includes the penalty period assessed if you quit your job, time for holiday pay, et cetera.

How Much

Check those separation slips and calculate your average weekly insurable earnings over the last 20 weeks worked. If you worked less than twenty, calculate the average of only those weeks worked. To find an average, add up the total insurable earnings from the separation slips of those weeks you want, and divide by 20 or the number of weeks work. This number, divided by three and multiplied by two, is your rate of benefit. The maximum is $160 per week before deductions and the minimum is $32.

Example: Your slips say total insurable earnings are $2,700 for the 18 weeks you worked. Divide out, this gives a weekly average of $150. So your rate would be $150 divided by three (50) and multiplied by two, for $100. You'll get $100 a week for almost a year if you aren't able to find more work.

Future Changes

Pierre, our noble leader, might have something up his sleeve to try before the next election. The current talk is about a change that will require 40 weeks worked during the past two years. This won't affect seasonal workers who are able to work on 20 weeks, collect until the next year, and work 20 weeks again. But it will hit hard at someone who was on a 10-weeks-worked claim and was collecting for 42 weeks. That "poor guy" would have to go out and work for 30 weeks. The trauma of seven months work might completely undo the minds of some of our pogey regulars.

        —a d

D.P.G's socio-economic inquiry into Camp Life

Camp is: A place that does not really exist. It has no history and no future. It has no plans and no memories.

Camp is: A meal (good or bad), a bed (they're all the same), and a paystub in your drawer every two weeks.

Camp is: A place where you keep your mouth shut because you learn you have nothing to talk about except camp. (Ed. note: See "Gumby Papers.")

Camp is: A place where you are attuned to the slightest rumour, whisper of closures, firings, hirings and other camps.

Camp is: Where you see the same people again from another camp you were in.

Camp is: A good (hopefully) book to read and a maturing attitude toward girlie pin-ups as a matter of Mental Survival.

Camp is: Mental Survival, if you're there for

Part XXV

One time on the river, (I've forgotten which one), Toby and I ran into couples from the south, also canoeing. They were pretty straight–kneeling in their canoes with life-jackets on, etc. Toby was nude and couldn't have given a shit. They passed us by but we canoed a long day and ended up at their camp.

It seems that on this particular trip, Toby had packed a lot of good fresh food and because we had only been gone a few days, there was lots left. He walked up the bank, said a few words, and they offered him the use of their fire to cook his supper. Apparently they had just eaten. Toby outdid himself. He cooked a huge steak, squash with butter and sugar, a lettuce, tomato and avocado salad, and to top it off, produced a bottle of Mommesin Red. Boy did he pig out.

All this time the southerners were drooling. Toby kept offering them some and they would decline, until finally one of them asked "Do you always eat like this way out here?" And my man answered, "Hell yes, on this river there's no portages or any bad rapids - so it's just a lark; anyways it beats the hell out of freeze dried beef stroganoff."

There was a general silence around the campfire. One of the girls cleared her throat and said, "That's what we just ate for supper." Toby almost shit his pants laughing. As a matter of fact he kept laughing all the way down to his canoe, and brought back another bottle of wine and a box of food.

"Oh we're not hungry, besides it would take so long to make and it's getting dark."

"Nonsense, you're in the Yukon. It won't get dark tonight; you're free as a bird and you're acting like caged animals. Hell, I've got something here that all four of you can make in about three minutes."

"What's that?"

"Shrimp cocktail on lettuce with white wine – superb".

"Oh my god!"

"Well, do you want to eat or not?"

"You're damn right I do," said the girl, and started poking around in the box.

"It's all there, and while you're at it - could you make one for me?"

We had fun, but what an ass he was. I never got any shrimp cocktail – just freeze-dried dog food.

the duration.

Camp is: Dreams based on your wildest fantasies — alone in your room.

Camp is: A meat grinder for your soul: it swallows you, grinds you up and delivers you to someone's plate as their workhorse.

Camp is: A beginning of a lifestyle you hope to move into — i.e., school, money for another start in the country.

Camp is: An ending when your lover gives up on lonely nights.

Camp is: Resistance to those who are determined not to be affected by it.

Camp is: A womb for those who can no longer exist without it, socially or monetarily.

Camp is: Where you give up your freedom of choice for a solid helping of chance.

Camp is: Escape by booze, escape from booze.

Camp is: Escape by drugs, escape from drugs.

Camp is: ATCO trailer rooms with a bed or two in each, a table, one or two cupboards, plywood walls, linoleum floors, plastic ceilings.

Camp is: Non-existant to your friends. They forget about you. After all, where *have* you gone compared to life in town?

Camp is: Continuous. There will always be another one.

Camp is: Education. You can grow up, grow old and spend your last days in one.

Camp is: A place we swear never to go back to.

The first thing about camp that is important is to realize fully **why** you are there. For the most part, it's money. Debts, Dreams and Duty rule the wallet of us all who end up in camp. You must not lose this thought, this reason.

"Ha!" you say. "It's not likely that'll happen to me." Well, okay. But men die of old age in camps. There have been hundreds of thousands of dollars to their names and men also die of strange things at ages of 18 to 21 who stayed too long, be it four months or two years.

The second thing is that talk is cheap. There is nothing to talk about, so unless you can say something intelligent (not "Bill's a dink") you might as well shut up first and listen to how stupid everyone else sounds.

The third thing is that all you have to look forward to every day is work, meals that can make or break you and a bed made by a man who makes them up to look at, not to sleep in.

The fourth thing is your own — what are you going to hold onto while in camp? A dream? A memory of home? A skin book?

And so with these four main points we come to some basic facts of Mental Survival.

1. Camp is made up of very simple minds and characters.

2. You want to try and maintain sanity and still communicate with someone.

3. You want to try and maintain sanity, and *act* like you're communicating with someone.

4. You are a very real part of what you see,

About your best chance for employment is at one of the mines. They have a very high annual turnover, something around 100 to 110%. This means that approximately 1,000 persons come and go every year, according to Manpower. You could contact the mine or mines of your choice from Whitehorse and tell them that you're here and you want a job and this is what you can do. Chances are they'll say something like "call next week, and we'll see".

You could also go directly to the mine office and camp there. This seems to work better than sitting in the beer parlour, although people have tried it and lucked out. If they know you are right there, and intend to stay 'till hired, your chances are much better. Also, if you happen to be a status Indian, they pretty well have to hire you because the mines have promised to hire more native employees and they can't attract many. Even if you've never worked in a mine before, you could get a job as a labourer, and work your way to a higher paying job. Mining is all learned on the job. You may or may not like mining - that's your choice; but if you come looking for the super-jobs, mining may be your only choice.

— mars bonfire two →

and what you see isn't always very good for your ego, your pride or your Upward Mobility in society at large.

It seems to point to two ways of dealing with it all — you can be a member of whatever crowd holds court in camp, or be a recluse. Either one works really well, depending on what you want to put into it.

If you work for DPW you will find yourself out of a job if you are reclusive. They all like to be neurotic together. If you work for a contractor the opposite holds true — nobody bothers a man who keeps to himself and doesn't bother anyone else.

Still, the unknown will always be present. There was a bullcook who woke up two hours late one morning scared he'd be fired and found that the four people he worked with were already fired for being awake and saying naughty things to the boss. In camp they can do anything to you — that's what they're paying you for. Unions notwithstanding, they get away with anything if they do it fast enough. Unions can be bought, too, just like you.

What you need when you go into camp is as much of an environment of your own that you can take with you. This consists of things such as:

1. **A Stereo.** Not a big one or you'll have 'em all drinking in your room and using it as a slop-bucket-ashtray. Preferably very small speakers that don't disturb anyone else, a **good** cassette deck and a small but good pair of headsets. Suggest AKAI cassette deck GXC-39D and Sansui SS35 monitor headphones. Tape your favourite music from friends when down homeward; you get a better tape than store-bought and it's close to one third the price of buying those tapes pre-recorded.

2. **Some Pictures.** Three or four of nice things that make you smile but won't leave you longing for home, etc. Remember that you may hate those pictures and those tapes by the time you leave. If you looked at the Venus de Milo at 6 a.m. on your way up and out to the Arctic Circle in December you'd probably call her a dog by nightfall.

3. **A Small Piece of Rug** four feet square or so to give your feet some reason to feel in your room after work and first thing in the morning.

4. **Writing Materials.** Your mind is most creative in an environment that stretches your emotions. This contrasts with the fact that camps are some of the most non-creative places you will ever experience. But some nice leatherwork, drawings and poetry of the soul have been turned out in a bunkhouse room.

5. **Books.** (Left till last because of their importance.) They are the lights in the darkness, retreats into fantasy, the movies of the mind. A good book, a fair sized one at that, will get you through three to four weeks of sleep-work-eat-read-sleep just fine. So in reality, three heavy books will get you six paycheques, lonely as hell and on your way out. But at least you were entertained by something other than a sticky copy of Hustler and your hand. (Not that masturbation isn't a going concern in camp life, but (1) your own fantasies you conjure from the last girl you communicated with are always better than Larry Flynts', Hugh Hefners', etc. There is no quicker way to get bushed than that; (2) Masturbation is a Personal Awareness and you have lots of time to do it right, unless the rooms are two-man, which is rare up north nowadays.)

Seeing as books are the main source of pleasure (if you're not a reader, then maybe booze is the answer!) all we can do now is go into a list of good ones found true by lending them around camps and always not seeing them for three weeks (short time for 1,000 ± pages) and having been passed on with a smile.

—D.P.G.

SOURCE BOOKS

PUBLIC WORKS. $10
By Walter Szykitka. 1,024 pages, photos, illustrations. Links Books, Music Sales Corp., 33 West 60th Street, New York, New York, U.S.A. 10023. Distributed by Quick Fox, same address as Links.

A huge 8½ by 11 inch volume that looks like it's got a helluva lot of information in it. "If I ever wonder how to do something, I look in that," said one reader. Author Sykitka said he started out to put together the ultimate "how to" book. "The idea," he says in the volume's introduction, "was that, if you found yourself lost in the wilderness and had no other possession than that book, you would nevertheless be adequately prepared to survive." He wanted to produce only one volume, however, not an encyclopedia, and limited himself to just over 1,000 pages. "Public Works is the result. And although I am well aware of its shortcomings, I am also satisfied that it contains so much fundamental and useful information that I don't hesitate to say that everybody ought to have a copy." There's nearly two million words in it. A great source book.

WOOD HEAT
by John Vivian, Rodale Press, Emmaus, Pennsylvania, 1976, 313 pages illustrated with line drawings, about $6.

"There are several products on the market that purport to remove creosote from your flue. They go by such names as Fluesweeper. First of all, they are nothing but rock salt that you can buy by the hundred pound sack for loose change. And they work by vaporizing the salt which combines with the creosote to make it catch fire. . . . If you are going to install an airtight stove, do your planning as if a flue fire is inevitable, then do your best to avoid having one by cleaning the flue. . . . And, during the day, have an open fire when you can — door full open."

Very complete. Includes sections on wood heat chemistry, reclaiming heat from the stovepipe (with a bibliography credit to Yukoner Mike Wassil), building a fireplace, stove-top cooking and lots more. And after you've read it, you can use it for kindling, too.

B.C. MUSEUM PUBLICATIONS

An excellent and inexpensive handbook series has been published by the British Columbia Provincial Museum. The thirty-five titles range from "The Amphibians of B.C." through grasses, fishes, barnacles, ferns, edible plants, mosses, dragonflies and many others. Most cost one dollar, with the most expensive being the colour edition of "Common Mushrooms of B.C." at $5. Although the material is directed at our immediate southern neighbours, much of the information applies to the southern Yukon.

Also available are five "occasional papers," six "museum method manuals," five "anthropology memoires" and a handful of other papers and an annual journal, "Syesis."

For a complete price list write to: "Publications," B.C. Provincial Museum, 601 Belleville Street, Victoria, B.C., V8V 1X4.

The only disappointment that we have noted are the poor bindings on these books, especially as they can expect rugged use.

Tips for New Camp Cooks

Keep dinner simple. Meat with two veggies. Rice only once a week. Never repeat a meal in a week. Ask before making spaghetti — some people won't eat "foreign food."

Order lots of luncheon meats, spam, that sort of thing. The nastier the better; drillers especially love junk food.

Use shake and bake, package foods, cake mixes to make things easier. Put instant pudding mix into the cake mix to make it less fluffy.

Always make a dessert. Men love pies, canned fruit, and especially chocolate flavours.

Breakfast: get up one hour early and make LOTS of coffee and make pancake batter in advance. Don't make scrambled eggs in advance.

Lunch: order cheese and cold meats. They can make their own lunches. Lots of variety, but keep a few surprises, like hard-boiled eggs. If some stay in camp, don't make a big lunch, just soup and sandwiches.

Take a few projects and some books to read because you'll have free time during the day. If there is some plywood around, build a small sauna by a creek.

— Joyce

WISH AND WANT BOOK
From the Cumberland General Store, Route 3, Box 479, Crossville, Tennessee, U.S.A. 38555.

The Cumberland Store's catalogue is full of delights. There are Connestoga Wagons, oxen harnesses, ice cream churns or, as they explain it, "a comprehensive selection of down-to-earth tools for living the good life." This catalogue costs $3, but is well worth it for nostalgia buffs and back-to-the-land types who can't afford their tools anywhere else.

We have been warned that the store is flooded with mail orders and can't handle the volume, so turn-around is slow. They are very honest, though, and will eventually get around to your wishes and wants.

The company that publishes Alaska Magazine (Alaska Northwest Publishing, Box 4-EEE, Anchorange, Alaska 99509) has a wide variety of books — fact, fiction and how-to, including the best book I have yet seen dealing with the construction, design and maintenance of wood cookstoves, camp-stoves and airtight or downdraft type heaters by Ole Wick. Full of drawings with a heavy emphasis on building your own, this book is great. (Check in the Alaska Magazine for correct price and the order form.) They've got lots of other good publications as well.

— Peter Carr

"THE PEOPLE OUTSIDE," 1971. By Jim Lotz, et al. Studies on squatters and so on. A thorough research on the situation up to 1971:

"There is abundant evidence that squatters are not considered a problem in the Yukon unless they become too visible, or they are located on land that is needed for other purposes. . . . The squatters served the city, providing a labour force that could not be housed at low cost elsewhere, and the city served the squatters. The relationship was mutually rewarding, and fairly stable over the years. . . . One thing is certain — that if the squatters of Whitehorse were all removed, the cost of running the territory would increase, because everyone would have to be 'properly housed,' while at the same time many stores and services would lose a captive market." from page 2

Interesting chapters on the legal side of the matter and squatter relocation. Available at the Whitehorse Library 309.712. A must for political activists.

— a. d.

MAGAZINES AND PERIODICALS

HARROWSMITH
bi-monthly from Camden House Publishing in Camden East, Ontario, K0K 1J0. $7 per year; $12 for two.

The best, and getting better all the time. A true Canadian production that has discovered and catered to people who want to do things for themselves, instead of paying big fuel bills and buying things at stores they could raise themselves. Good for anyone into wood heat, farming and gardening, log building, solar, raising chickens and other livestock, wind, water, buying land. At our publication time, they were planning a "Best Of" edition to meet demand for their sold-out back issues. They've got a good selection of books to sell, an excellent sourcebook for new readers.

NATURAL LIFE Magazine
Box 640, Jarvis, Ontario.

"Access to self-reliant living" is the magazine's subtitle, and it lives up to that. A Canadian production, it's probably less well known than Harrowsmith and since it has less than half of the former's circulation. Not a "glossy" format, but printed on recyclable newsprint, even the cover. Lots of letters from readers are printed, and sometimes those are just as informative as the articles. Lots of sources listed in each edition. Seems a good product. Highly recommended.

THE MOTHER EARTH NEWS
bi-monthly from "today's turned-on people of all ages. The Creative Ones. The Doers. The folks who make it all happen. Heavy emphasis is placed on alternative energy and lifestyles, ecology, working with nature, and doing more with less." Box 70, Hendersonville, North Carolina, U.S.A. 28736. Fone 704-693-0211. $14 by subscription in Canada, $12 in The States, for one year (six issues). $2.50 per, on newsstands.

Has lots of stuff — ideas, products — about what it claims — getting by with less (they say getting more, actually). Good rag, puts a semi-warning about the products it advertises on its page five who-we-are box. "More than a magazine . . . a way of life" is its slogan.

I wrote this after Airma told me about a friend of hers who split the Yukon because all the men here just love their old trucks.

Mechanic's Love Song

Your hair is like the flowing grease
That flows down from the trans
Your eyes are like two bearings rolling
Round the bearing pan.
Your voice it is so heavenly sweet
It gives me such a thrill
Like the idle of a finely tuned
Three-twenty-seven mill.

The first time that I saw you
Walking with a little swing
My mind recalled my pick-up truck
With brand new shocks and springs
The first time that I kissed your lips
And held you tightly, dear

It was just like feeling that surge of power
As you shift her into passing gear.

I'm the best mechanic in these parts
With the best little pick-up, too
And you're my little crescent wench
You know I love you true
I love you as the trany loves
The oil all around her gears
Like my chev you were born in fifty-four
And that was a vintage year.

I'll hug you like the planetary gear
Snuggles up against the shims
I'll kiss you like a four-barrel carb
Jets at 600 r.p.m.'s
I need you like the battery
Needs the generator
Like the solvent loves to dissolve the grime
From off the carburetor.

— "Banjo Jim" Erkelitian

METRIC MILEAGE

The mileposts along the Yukon's highways are mostly gone now, which presents a big hassle for a lot of us who drive them and like to know where we are, how far we've gone and how far we've yet to go in our journeys on gravel, dirt and calcium. The kilometre posts (K-posts, pronounced Kayposts in Europe, by English-speaking people anyway) are hard things to get used to unless you've got a little system down for calculating a conversion. The problem was presented to one of the catalogue producers, who put his brain to it. Something simple for figuring "metric mileage" follows:

Instead of figuring five eighths of a mile equals one kilometre and one mile equals eight fifths of a kilometre and trying to do weird multiplication and division in your head, figure that:

80 kilometres is 50 miles
40 kilometres is 25 miles
20 kilometres is 12.5 miles
10 kilometres is 6.25 miles
one kilometre is .625 (or roughly five eighths) miles

The problem comes when you get K-posts on the Alaska Highway that read "1390" or somesuch.

Keep in mind that the conversion isn't really precise in the "80 is 50" system. Actually, one kilometre is .621 miles, but it's close enough.

Another system, perhaps simpler, depending on the way the mathematical part of your brain functions, is to just multiply by point six.

Twenty Km. times .6 is 12.0, or twelve miles. Close enough. The 12.5 miles in the 80 to 50 system is more accurate (the **real** 20 Km. mileage is 12.420), and probably a lot better if you're running on empty.

Other distances to be kept in mind with the "80 to 50" conversion system:
160 km. is 100 miles
320 km. is 200 miles
480 km. is 300 miles
640 km. is 400 miles

Hitch With Canoe!

For less than it costs to take the bus ($35) you can take your canoe, pack and yourself back from Dawson City to Whitehorse if you hitchhike with a sign that states you are willing to share gas. You will get faster results than those hitchhiking without a canoe! —w. l.

Gas at Tok

If you're driving to Dawson via Alaska, fill up at Tok. When you work out dollar and gallon exchanges, you are paying Whitehorse prices for gas there. In comparison Koidern charges $1.50 and Dawson $1.30. —w. l.

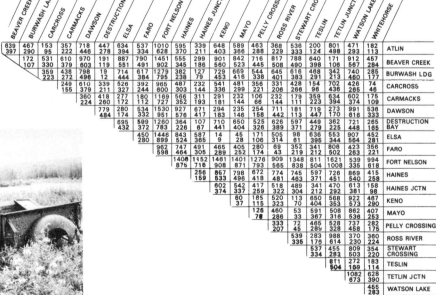

ROAD DISTANCES via ALL - YUKON ROUTES (325 - Kilometres, 163 - Miles)

BEAVER CREEK	BURWASH LANDING	CARCROSS	CARMACKS	DAWSON	DESTRUCTION BAY	ELSA	FARO	FORT NELSON	HAINES	HAINES JUNCTION	KENO	MAYO	PELLY CROSSING	ROSS RIVER	STEWART CROSSING	TESLIN	TETLIN JUNCTION	WATSON LAKE	WHITEHORSE	
639/397	467/290	153/95	357/222	718/446	447/278	634/394	537/334	1010/628	595/370	339/211	648/403	589/366	463/288	368/229	536/333	200/124	801/498	471/293	182/113	ATLIN
	172/107	531/330	610/379		191/119	887/551	790/491	1451/902	555/345	299/186	901/560	842/523	716/445	817/508	788/490	640/398	171/106	912/567	457/284	BEAVER CREEK
		359/223	438/272	798/498	19/12	714/444	617/384	1279/795	382/238	127/79	729/453	669/416	544/338	645/401	616/383	468/291	342/213	740/460	285/177	BURWASH LDG
			249/155	610/379	339/211	526/327	392/244	965/600	487/303	232/144	541/336	481/299	356/221	331/206	428/266	154/96	702/436	426/265	74/46	CARCROSS
				360/224	418/260	277/172	180/112	1169/727	566/352	311/193	291/181	232/144	106/66	232/144	179/111	359/223	634/394	602/374	175/109	CARMACKS
					779/484	280/172	534/332	1530/951	927/576	671/417	294/183	235/146	254/158	711/442	181/113	719/447	273/170	991/616	538/333	DAWSON
						695/432	599/372	1260/783	364/226	107/67	710/441	650/404	525/326	626/389	597/371	449/279	362/225	721/448	265/165	DESTRUCTION BAY
							450/280	1446/899	843/524	587/365	14/9	45/28	171/106	505/314	98/61	636/395	553/344	907/564	452/281	ELSA
								962/598	747/464	491/305	465/289	405/252	280/174	69/43	352/219	341/212	808/502	423/263	356/221	FARO
									1408/876	1152/716	1461/908	1401/871	1276/793	909/565	1348/838	811/504	1621/1008	539/335	994/618	FORT NELSON
										256/159	857/533	798/496	672/418	774/481	745/463	597/371	726/451	869/540	415/258	HAINES
											602/374	542/337	417/259	518/322	489/304	341/212	470/292	613/381	158/98	HAINES JCTN
												60/37	185/115	520/323	113/70	650/404	568/353	922/573	467/290	KENO
													126/78	460/286	53/33	591/367	508/316	862/536	407/253	MAYO
														333/207	72/45	465/289	528/328	737/458	282/175	PELLY CROSSING
															539/335	283/176	988/614	370/230	360/224	ROSS RIVER
																537/334	455/283	809/503	354/220	STEWART CROSSING
																	811/504	272/169	183/114	TESLIN
																		1082/673	628/390	TETLIN JCTN
																			455/283	WATSON LAKE
																				WHITEHORSE

TRANSPORTATION COSTS

(Sample rates only as of January 1, 1978)

BUS:
Coachways — 667-2223
Whitehorse — Watson Lake $15.35
Whitehorse — Vancouver $90.30
Whitehorse — Edmonton $73.20
Norline — 667-2223
Whitehorse — Dawson City $35.00
Whitehorse — Faro $25.00
Whitehorse — Mayo $32.00
AIR:
CP Air — 667-7881
Whitehorse — Vancouver $125.00 plus $8.00 tax
Whitehorse — Edmonton $125.00 plus $8.00 tax
Whitehorse — Watson Lake $40.00 plus $3.20 tax
Watson Lake — Edmonton $102.00 plus $8.00 tax
Watson Lake — Vancouver $110.00 plus $8.00 tax
Northward — 668-2101
Whitehorse — Dawson City $75.00 plus $5.90 tax
Transair — 668-5121
Whitehorse — Yellowknife $138.00 plus $8.00 tax
Wien Air Alaska — 668-2311
Whitehorse — Fairbanks $78.85
Whitehorse — Juneau $38.90
Whitehorse — Anchorage $103.00
Trans North Turbo Air — 668-2177
Whitehorse — Faro $55.00
RAIL:
White Pass & Yukon Route — 667-7611
Whitehorse — Skagway $70.00 round trip
AUTOMOBILE RENTALS:
Hertz — 667-2505
Avis — 668-2136
Tilden — 668-2521 (Whitehorse)
　　　　994-2710 (Faro)
　　　　993-5437 (Dawson)
Whitehorse Motors — 667-7866
Sample prices:
Small car — $19 day, 19 cents mile, $95 week
Big car — $24 day, 24 cents mile, $120 week
¾ Ton — $22 day, 22 cents mile, $132 week

Watson Lake — Daily scheduled jet service to and from Edmonton and Vancouver via CP Air; charter air service; scheduled bus service north and south; taxi; car rental.
Whitehorse — Daily scheduled air service to Edmonton, Vancouver. Scheduled air service also to Anchorage, Fairbanks, Yellowknife, Winnipeg, Juneau, Inuvik, Watson Lake, Faro, Dawson City, Ross River and Old Crow; charter air service; scheduled bus service north and south; taxis; car rentals; railway.
Haines Junction — Chartered air service (helicopter); scheduled bus service north and south, and to Haines, Alaska.
Destruction Bay, Burwash, Beaver Creek — Scheduled bus service north and south.
Carmacks — Scheduled bus service north and south; chartered air service.
Pelly Crossing — Scheduled bus service north and south.
Mayo — Elsa — Keno — Scheduled bus service south; chartered air service; taxi; scheduled air service (Mayo).
Dawson City — Scheduled air service; scheduled bus service south; taxi; car rental; chartered air service.
Faro — Scheduled air service; scheduled bus service; taxi; car rental.
Ross River — Scheduled air service; chartered air service; scheduled bus service.
Old Crow — Scheduled air service only — twice weekly.

FREIGHT RATES
effective September 15, 1978

CP Air — Whitehorse to Vancouver . . . $14 minimum charge; $.41 lb. from 41 to 100 lb.; Priority Handling — minimum charge — $18.20.
Whitehorse to Edmonton . . . $16 minimum charge; $.34 lb. from 41-100 lb.; Priority Handling — minimum charge — $21.
Transair — Whitehorse-Yellowknife . . . minimum charge $16.50; $.41 lb. to 100 lb.; $.39 lb. 100 lb. and over.
Whitehorse-Toronto . . . minimum charge $24; $.57 lb. to 100 lb.; $.53 lb. 100 lb. and over.
Northward Air — Whitehorse-Dawson City . . . minimum charge $14; $.34 lb. to 100 lb.; $.32 lb. over 100 lb.; $.29 lb. over 500 lb.; $.21 lb. over 1,000 lb.
Whitehorse-Inuvik . . . minimum charge $14; $.39 lb. to 100 lb.; $.34 over 100 lb.; $.31 lb. over 500 lb.; $.24 over 1,000 lb.
Coachway Bus Lines — The bus lines do not handle anything over 100 lb. Rates go down every 10 lb.
Whitehorse-Edmonton . . . minimum charge $7.25; maximum charge $22.75 for 100 lb.
Whitehorse-Vancouver . . . minimum charge $8.45; maximum charge $27.60 for 100 lb.
Norline Bus Lines — Whitehorse-Dawson City . . . $9.30 per 100 lb.
White Pass & Yukon Route — The following rates are for general merchandise up to 500 lb.
Whitehorse to Vancouver . . . 100 lb. — $14 . . . 200 lb. — $24 . . 300 lb. — $34 . . . 400 lb. — $44 . . . 500 lb. — $54.
Whitehorse-Edmonton . . . 100 lb. — $18.65 . . . 200 lb. — $29.65 . . . 300 lb. — $40.65 . . . 400 lb. — $51.65 . . . 500 lb. — $62.65.

Driving our roads

A million words could be written about driving unpaved highways in the Yukon. Several thousand were, but later found to be too many; they were scratched. Here's just a few that say the same things.

1) lots of people, especially tourists, get in accidents here because they don't know how to drive gravel highways, or because they're too tired or otherwise unable to comprehend the full reality of the situation and deal properly with it.

2) the roads get very slick when it rains. Those are times to drive carefully.

3) never stop suddenly. It freaks out other drivers, and conditions might be so bad (dust, sun, both; rain, dark, both; taillights covered by mud) that someone following closely behind won't be able to see you stop.

4) constantly keep a watch out behind you to see if anyone wants to pass and if you're in their way. Let them by: reduce your speed by 10 or 15 m.p.h. and pull slowly over more to the right-hand side of the road. Don't be afraid to use the shoulders.

5) compute your travelling time at an average 50 m.p.h. if you're going to do 60 and 70-80 in the long, straight stretches. Always give yourself lots of time, especially if you're tired. If you're unfamiliar with gas availability and restaurant frequency, see tourist brochures.

6) if you've got your headlights on, traffic coming at you can know you're there a lot sooner than all-of-a-sudden. Likewise, they can see you sooner. It's safer that way, for all of us. Headlights need plastic cups, available at many places, to protect them from flying rocks. You're guaranteed to lose your lights if you don't have them.

7) your windshield will get cracked unless you mount a big screen at the front of your vehicle. Accept the fact and forget the screen for windows.

8) protect your radiator from holes, etc., by placing a screen in front of it.

9) radiator holes can be plugged with lots of pepper. Just pour it in.

on the move

10) your gas tank can suffer similar fate unless coated with rubber matting or somesuch. Plugging a gas tank is harder (pepper is not recommended for that!), but you can use small screws, soap, a bit of cloth and Seal-All (good product) in any combination to plug it up. Check 10 miles down the road to see you've done a good enough job.

11) by checking your air pressure before you go and along the way you can reduce the chances of flats. Take the weight your vehicle is carrying into consideration and refer to your "auto care" guide the manufacturer lays on you. Carry two spares anyway, plus a good jack; "jack-alls" are recommended.

12) if a tire does go flat, don't slam on the brakes. Take your foot off the gas, hang onto the wheel, put your foot on the clutch if you've got a standard and do your best. Use the brakes only when you're going pretty slow. Don't drive past 40 m.p.h. along much of the Dempster because a lot of it's surfaced with slate (very sharp: one catalogue groupie had three flats in 10 miles 'cause he drove too fast there).

13) expect snow any time of the year in the Yukon, especially up the Dempster.

14) water for cleaning your windshield is available all along the highway — ponds, creeks, etc. all have it, while at gas stations it's usually a hassle to get. Be self-sufficient. It's also a good idea to carry a hand-wiper with you. When you can see that your windshield will soon be covered with mud from another vehicle either passing or going the other way, turn on your water-thing *before* the mud hits. Visibility is restored more quickly that way.

15) speeding tickets are rarely handed out for doing more than the limit on unpaved Yukon highways.

16) when you're doing a good clip and you want to pass a truck, chances are he's seen you and will flash his backup lights at you when it's clear to pass him.

17) there is little traffic on the Yukon's highways. If you're leading a long line, though, let the other pass. Then you can all enjoy the open road.

18) Have a beer and relax. Drinking in vehicles is allowed in the Yukon, as long as the driver is not impaired and 19 years old or more. Beer cuts the dust better than anything else. Fruit juices are good too, and smell better if you've hit a pothole as you took a sip.

bicycling in the yukon

Anyone can have a good experience cyling in the Yukon, and it's an excellent way to see some beautiful country. All the major roads — Alaska highway, Klondike, Mayo Road, South and North Canol and Robert Campbell highway — are cyclable. Off each road lies routes to good fishing lakes, rivers, or creeks, and excellent hiking mountains. It's limited only by the strength of your legs.

What You Need

A sturdy bike is necessary, whether it's an old clunker or a new ten-speed. There are only about 100 miles of pavement in the Yukon so you can expect the bumps and jolts to wear your bike and tires. A wide, heavy treaded tire is best. Always carry a tire patch kit and the necessary tools to do the job. You can buy a 10-speed repair kit in Whitehorse for about $7. This includes a tire patch kit, oil, applicator, variety of wrenches and tire removers. For longer trips carry a spare tube and pump, also if you can carry a spare tire, do so. Extra light oil is essential, as the dust and dirt of the roads gets into your gears and drive chain. Make sure your front hubs, crank bearing, head bearing, and coast brakes have a good application of multi-purpose grease.

By far the easiest way to carry your gear is with saddlebags located over the rear wheels. Once you have your holding rack in place (about $8.50) you can save some additional cost by sewing your own pair of canvas saddlebags.

These should be lined with plastic or water-proofed, and old tent flaps work well.

For yourself, a raincoat and your fenders should keep you dry enough to stay on the road, if you feel so inclined. Transport trucks have a tendency to throw rocks from their tires, so beware of them as they pass you. Also Winnebagos can be unwelcome as far as their ability to throw rocks, so beware!

You can cycle in the Yukon from about late April to late October. September is especially nice, as the air is fresh, the sky is clear and the colors of the poplar, aspen and birch are the richest. On a good day you can average between 30 to 50 miles a day, or just take the day off and go fishing or hiking or whatever suits your fancy at the time. One thing to watch for though, is that the department of highways spray the roads with calcium chloride and water to help keep the dust down and harden the surface. This can be especially slippery when wet, so again beware. If the road seems impossible to travel on then by all means don't. Some locals even cycle in the winter, but just in the towns. If you plan to, just dress warm and don't carry any bottles with you.

The best bike shop in the Yukon is the Bicycle Repair centre behind the Hudson's Bay on Fourth Avenue. The shop is run by John Hill and his son Rick. They are amazingly knowledgeable and friendly, with all the things necessary to keep your bike in top shape.

You'll also find their prices reasonable. They told me that last summer ('78) they sold twice as many wheels than the year before, and that most were because of theft. So lock your bike down well, through the wheels to something that will not move — such as a steel fence. Also mark the frame and wheels with an engraving pencil, so you can easily identify stolen parts.

If your bike is stolen, report it to the R.C.M.P. They also have a bike pound where yours might be, if lost. Hopefully.

Bicycling can be an excellent way to exercise, as well as a magnificent way to see all the beauty this territory has to offer. I've cycled around Missouri, California, Italy, and Newfoundland. One fellow I know bikes back and forth from California to Alaska, via the Yukon, in search of his favorite season, or maybe just a job.

Whatever the reason, it's a good time. Enjoy it.

— Zeke Scopik

One more morning by the river
with the ice mist closing
   between hand and mouth
daring not to walk over—
      the ice is still too thin
and lowly drunks
      full of farts
by the railway station
and railway grease
the brakeman's lantern
      in the fog
(you know him "hey Tex")
moving ever so slow
   you read yourself
      into novels
of drunken railway heroes
   and Kerouacs
mixing with the natives
who've been there all along
sleeping in a box-car-
      side-track-switchman's shack
and switching t-shirts to keep warm
for the winter sun
      is just
   two more mornings away
an' you hope a buddy comes
an' spots you a dime
to make it over to the Regina Inn
      at nine
the crystal mist of no winds north
   the cooler hours of time

and you just couldn't make it
      south this year
   you're too old for that.
            Alyx Jones

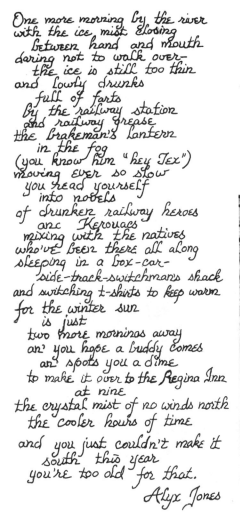

...W.P. & Y.R....Wait Patiently & You'll Ride

Trains are something special, and they're fun to ride, unless perhaps you're a regular commuter on one, because they were the standard mode of transport for people for a long time, which gives train ride that special "olden" feeling.

You get more than that special feeling when you ride the White Pass and the Yukon Route between Whitehorse and Skagway. It's a train but that is no regular passenger car you're riding in. If it isn't an original 1900 model, it's an awfully close replica. No fancy meal or bar or observation cars of modern-day trains — just a comfy seat in a small, narrow car with 40 or so other people (if it's full, which usually is the case in summer time, and a pot-bellied

heater at one end.

The ride takes about eight hours for the full trip over the (you guessed it) White Pass — one of three passes the white man saw fit to use in opening up the Yukon from the Pacific Coast. (The others are the Chilkoot, of Chilkoot Trail and Chilkoot Chuck fame; and the Chilkat Pass, named after the Coastal Indian band, now a route for the Haines Highway.)

You stop at Bennett Station for a lunch of stew, beans and pie (paid for by your ticket), and carry on to that neat little town Carcross along the shore of Bennett Lake after a long, beautiful climb from the coast. Some awfully pretty scenery there. Crossing the 2,900-foot barrier between the coast and the inland part of the continent never fails to impress people and get them wondering about the grandeur that was created. You don't tire of it, even after several trips.

CHOO-CHOOS LIKE MONEY, TOO

Cost for the ride in summer is $70 return from Skagway to Whitehorse (or vice versa) or $35 one way either way, but a better way to do it from this end is to drive to Carcross and save yourself $16 on the fare and three slow hours (two anyway) on the train, which chugs slowly between Whitehorse and Carcross. Fares are lower in non-summer months.

Carcross to Skagway costs $54 return ($27 one way)

Whitehorse to Bennett and back costs $39.90, while

Carcross to Bennett and back is $34 return.

Other rates can be obtained by calling White Pass at 667-7611 in Whitehorse, or writing to White Pass at Box 2147, Seattle, U.S.A. 98111.

All ticket costs are in U.S. funds, so expect to pay more while the Canadian dollar is below par with the U.S. one. White Pass says they're in U.S. funds because their ticket office and all their tariffs are set at Seattle — another holdover from the Gold Rush days, we presume.

Winter Driving

In a land known for its ice and snow, winter driving is an expensive and often risky business. Here are a few ideas that might help you start your vehicle, stay on the roads and survive the winter.

1) To drive a vehicle, you have to start it. If you buy heavy duty jumper cables (the cheap kinds break) you'll save money 'cause everyone needs a boost sometime. If your gas line is frozen, you can dump gas down the carburetor and start it. This is not good for your engine but occasionally it's necessary. Carry the usual tools for minor adjustments and repairs — pliers, crescent wrenches, screw drivers, hammer and a little can of ether comes in handy if you want that extra get up and go.

2) If it's 30 below F (in Celcius, that's minus 24.5), you're straining your vehicle if you try to get it going. If it's 40 below (both scales read the same here), you're hurting it. If it's 50 below (minus 55.5 celcius), it's going to cost you to go anywhere.

3) Be patient and let your vehicle idle until it's good and warm. In the long run this will save time, because your vehicle won't stall out, and your battery won't die from you trying to start it while waiting for a tow truck, or a boost or push from a fellow motorist passing by.

4) Driving conditions are different in winter. Common sense makes it smart to go slower than in summer. It's easier on your vehicle and it's easier on you to take your time. Sand bags on the back of your vehicle are good for traction and handy in case you get stuck. Studded tires cost more money than the ordinary ones, but they're probably worth it.

Don't drive too close — leave lots of space between you and the next vehicle. Back off the gas just before a corner and gently accelerate when in it. Allow extra time to cross an intersection or turn onto another road. Accelerate and decelerate gently, and try to drive as though you have no brakes because once you use them you lose much control of the direction of your vehicle. Occasionally, ruts grab your tires and want to take

charge so hang on to the steering wheel at all times. If you have any trouble at all, you have got to steer out of it.

5) Stopping in winter can be a problem, even if the road looks bare and dry. It might not be. Packed snow roads at cold temperatures are almost like pavement, but there are a couple of things you ought to know. Glare ice is one thing, and black ice is another.

Glare ice generally occurs when temperatures are above zero (F — about -20° C). Asphalt roads have black ice and it's more dangerous because there's no chance for traction — none. If you find yourself in a skid, try to steer your way out of it — don't use your brakes unless you are desperate. When you do, pump them. Hopefully you'll stop. If you have to decide between oncoming traffic and going off the road, hit the ditch. Your chances are better there than those at Gerties, and the stakes are bigger too.

6) Once you're in a ditch, have fun getting out! If you are prepared, you'll have a shovel, tow chain and maybe a come-along to use as a winch, just in case someone in a four-by-four doesn't come by.

Be ready for the worst, especially if you're going on a long journey. It's always prudent to wear your parka and carry a few extra things like blankets, sleeping bags, candles and matches, pocket warmers and some food. That short list ought to be enough to get anyone through a storm or other unfortunate circumstances until help arrives. Whatever you do, don't leave the vehicle unless you've got a dogteam in the back. Let them find you. If you do take off, leave a note of your plans, when you left, etc. It might help them find the body faster.

7) In case of an accident and injury, contact the RCMP as soon as possible.

8) If planning a long journey on the highways listen to up-to-date reports on what highways are open to traffic and the conditions of the roads. Let someone know you're heading off in to the ice and snow.   j.m.

hitching a ride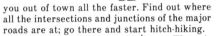

. . . my thumb and me have been around the world and back again so many times that I've stopped counting. We've all hitch-hiked sometime. It can be a cheap and carefree way to travel, an art-form really, or it can be terrible (but usually only when you make it that way). Anyway, here are a few tips I've picked up from thumbing rides in the Yukon.

Love,
sissy hunkshaw

1. If you are near a town or city, get to outskirts as soon as possible. There you won't be bothered by the number of non-stopping vehicles passing. They're not going anywhere anyway so don't worry about it. Walk, stick your thumb out when cars come. Locals are more likely to pick you up if they see you are doing something for yourself, and it'll only get

you out of town all the faster. Find out where all the intersections and junctions of the major roads are at; go there and start hitch-hiking.

2. Have lots of time and patience. There is **not** a lot of traffic here, but there are lots of things to explore in the ditches, and some close contact with sights that in a car would go by too quickly to really appreciate. If you're hitching in the summer, you may find a long line of people in front of you in junction towns like Carmacks, Stewart and, of course, Whitehorse.

3. Distances between most places are long and the facilities scarce along most highways, and non-existent on others. Check your maps for info. Most lodge owners do not like hitchhikers. You've always got to leave your pack outside, too. Try to carry enough stuff to live for a while, a tent, a sleeping bag, some food, and an axe (during my morbid fear of being attacked by a grizzly bear on the road, in the dark, I sometimes think fondly of the axe that thumbed up the Alcan with me: completely lousy axe but it cut tent-poles and kept the men a little wary of pouncing on me. Not that they would, anyway, but sometimes a woman hitch-hiking alone has to think about these things).

4. If you are around a town or city and need a place to stay, we happen to have a growing hostel association. (Check the hostel section of the catalogue or phone the hostel association in Whitehorse.) Use it. Last summer someone was killed by a car when they were sleeping beside the highway.

5. If you are hitch-hiking at night, find out where the truckers stop and try to get there. Approach truckers **after** they are finished their meal and/or coffee and are about to leave. Ask politely and if you are one of the rare ones they like, you might be lucky and get a good long ride.

6. Rides are given more by locals than tourists. The camper people, it seems, trust only other camper people. Before jumping in the vehicle and losing the warm bed in Whitehorse, ask the driver where he is going so you

don't end up getting left out in the boonies 100 miles from nowhere, unless, of course you don't mind being there.

7. If you don't have to, don't hitch-hike in winter. Just because it's 50 below doesn't mean that people will stop and give you a ride, although chances are better than summer.

8. When you do hitch-hike in winter, be prepared. The days are short and it's cold. Dress warmly and keep your head covered — you'd be surprised at how much body heat can be lost from there. A pocket warmer is a good idea, and don't be afraid to start a fire by the road. Try to stay close to buildings for their shelter in case of a storm or no ride.

9. Keep moving when it's really cold. Stamp your feet, clap your hands and start walking around in circles or up and down the road. Leave plenty of room for a vehicle to stop and pick you up. Don't expect cars to stop if you're walking a long hill. Motorists can't use their brakes as much in the wintertime, and they usually need all the speed they can get to climb the hill.

Curves are another bad place for cars to stop. Move off the road and give them plenty of room. If you happen to get a ride in the back of a pick-up and it looks like it's the best you can get, take it. A sleeping bag can protect you fairly well and there's less wind-chill if you huddle right down on the floor. Fellow fresh air companions like dogs are good to snuggle with. Try to get yourself into the centre of their pile for warmth, if they don't pile on you and lick you silly first.

10. If you really want to keep moving down the road, there is one bus that plies the Alcan Highway and another one that travels back and forth between Dawson and Whitehorse. That's it.

An Open Letter To The Motoring Public

We thought that some of you might be wondering about those strangely immobile figures, right arm outstretched, mitted thumb aloft, that sometimes hover by the highway. We have the answer. These people are known as hitch-hikers. They are standing there showing you the direction to or from town, as the case may be. The proper procedure upon encountering one is to smile and drive on by.

Under no circumstances should you pick these people up. They are freezing. The colder it is, the better they like it. With fortitude, you may be instrumental in helping one of these people to achieve his her dearest aim: frozen feet.

Of course the temptation to pick up a hitch-hiker is tremendous — you'd be doing something few others do. You'd have some company for the ride. You could even fantasize that you're the rescue helicopter which would pick this fellow up where he similarly stranded in the bush.

Actually, when I have a running vehicle, I am sometimes unable to resist the temptation of picking up a hitch-hiker. Although I know it's not the done thing, sometimes they're fun and they help warm up the car. Kidding aside, give us a ride. . . . We're fascinating.

————————with love from two highway statues ——

MOTORCYCLES —
TRAVELLING THE ALCAN

It can be done. A few dozen drive the highway each year, so you won't be establishing any world records.

The following maintenance advice comes from a factory-trained Husqvarna mechanic who has driven up here for years . . .

Use good (expensive) brand-name tires and carry extra tubes.

Oil chain two or three times a day because of dust.

Check airfilter and clean every night or 300 miles if road is dusty. Just blow out with air hose at gas station.

Check spoke tightness each day.

Carry spare plugs and points.

Inspect entire bike every night for loose bolts and nuts.

Eye protection is a good idea. And, of course, a good helmet and good raingear. Sit out the rain if possible.

Remember that parts are available for only a few brands in Whitehorse.

—a. d. with ¾

VISITORS

Here's a few things travellers visiting the Yukon should Know:

1) The Yukon is a territory of Canada, not a part of the United States. The Klondike Gold Rush took place here, not in Alaska, which is next door to us in the U.S.

2) Fire permits are required if you plan to use open fires. They're free from RCMP, Forestry, Territorial Agents or Game Branch personnel. Check fire danger listing when you can, and be careful. Most of the Yukon has been burned once already and we don't need any more man-made fires.

3) Yukoners love their wilderness and its wildlife so don't go poaching game or you'll be dealt with by "Yukon justice", if not the courts.

4) If you want to hunt and aren't a resident you have to go to an outfitter. Write or talk to the game branch at YTG for more information.

5) You can fish a lot for almost nothing. Licences cost !10 per season or !3.50 for five days for non-residents. Please obey catch limits.

Most banks are open from 10 a.m. to 3 p.m. Monday through Friday, but not every town has one. Regular hours are kept in larger places like Watson Lake, Faro, Dawson City and Whitehorse. The Credit Union in Whitehorse has longer hours and the Bank of Montreal at the Qwanlin Mall is open Saturday mornings. Most banks have affiliations with U.S. banks but if that's where you're coming from, check your home branch about getting money sent to you in the Yukon. Credit cards from the U.S. are usually valid here, including BankAmericard, Mastercharge, American Express and affiliated gasoline cards. Most gas stations here are Chevron/Standard. Gas costs a lot more here -- $1.10 or so in Whitehorse for regular to $1.40 in Faro, but the gallons are larger by one fifty than the U.S. ones.

A few visitors have pointed out to us that Yukoners seem to be obsessed wit guestbooks. True enough, there is one at every information centre, tourist attraction, historic site, museum, and even in some private homes. With that in mind, we are happy to note that "Soapy Smith" and "Cassidy, Butch" both signed in at Fort Selkirk in 1978. Apparently they are doing a preliminary survey of the potential for their line of work when the pipeline passes through.

YUKON HOSTELS

The Yukon Hostelling Association (part of the Canadian Hostelling Association) is an ever-growing presence and service in the territory that is welcomed by both locals and visitors alike. Until recently it operated only one hostel in Whitehorse. That was started by another group when too many young people were coming into town with backpacks and no place to stay. Then the hostel association was formed. In 1979 it will offer four "city" hostels and a bevy of rural hostels along rivers. (Plans for the latter weren't firmed up by our press time so phone or write the people below or check in at any of the other hostels for details if you're planning on visiting us.)

The "city" hostels will be:

WATSON LAKE HOSTEL
Mile 635 (kilometre 1021) on the Alaska Highway, on the border of British Columbia. **Open:** June 1st to September 15th. **Capacity:** 30 beds, breakfast and dinner available. **Reservations:** Write to Box 602 Watson Lake, Yukon or phone the YHA office 403-667-4471.

WHITEHORSE HOSTEL
Mile 916 (kilometre 1447) of the Alaska Highway, on the Yukon River and at the terminal of the White Pass & Yukon Route Railway. **Open:** June 1st. **Capacity:** 60 beds, breakfast and dinner available. **Reservations:** Write to Box 4762, Whitehorse, Yukon or phone the YHA office 403-667-4471.

CARMACKS CASTLE
Mile 102 (kilometre 163) on the Klondike Highway in the Carmacks Community Centre, on the Yukon River. **Open:** June 1st to September 15th. **Capacity:** 30 beds, meals available. **Reservations:** Write to Box 4762, Whitehorse, Yukon or phone 403-863-5191 or 403-667-4471.

DAWSON TENT HOSTEL
Mile 327 (kilometre 526) on the Klondike Highway, on the Yukon River in the heart of the Gold Rush Country, at the junction of the Klondike and Yukon rivers. **Open:** June 1st to September 15th. **Capacity:** 45 beds, breakfast and dinner available. **Reservations:** Write to Box 510, Dawson City, Yukon or phone 403-993-5351 or 403-667-4471.

The YHA also plans canoe trips, chilkoot pass hikes and a series of lectures for 1979. and there will probably be more; so, again, check the YHA for what other things they've got happening (also for cancellations or changes in case some things don't work out as planned).

Yukon Public Relations Award
Honorable mention goes to our pal Smelly Goggle, who, in a fit, drove south in his old bent up Toyota pickup to visit the bright lights of Vancouver. Apparently he maintained a total nonchalance while driving down Theatre Row as his two huge dogs humped each other in the head in the back of the truck.

CAMPGROUNDS

The Territorial Government's campground service maintains forty-eight campgrounds and thirty "other areas," supplying firewood, picnic tables, privvies, firepits, a few kitchens with stoves, wells and dumping stations. The locations of all the sites can be found in the YTG Tourism map folder, "Travel Yukon" which is available free from their Whitehorse office or any of the information centres along the highways. None of the government's campgrounds have electrical hook-ups or showers or any of the fancies of life, but there are a few commercial campgrounds around Whitehorse and in Dawson and along the Alaska Highway that can provide for the less hearty. There is a fee charged to use the government campgrounds for non-Yukoners, a measly $10 per vehicle per season or $2.50 each night.

The Campground Service has gone a bit overboard with signs and railings everywhere, but if you had put up with the idiot stunts of some tourists, you might be forgiven if you wanted to treat everyone like fools.

The new firepits in 1978 were an attempt to make an enclosed cooking facility as well as allowing for a bonfire afterwards. The firepits are poured concrete pentagons with folding grills. Unfortunately they seem to self-destruct, probably because they aren't made of heat-resistant cement, but that problem will help provide employment over those months when it is dark and cold and the last tourist is safely home in bed in Florida.

Those planning on using the firewood provided should bring along an axe to split it, as it often comes in six inch diameter chunks which aren't nearly as easy to light as presto logs. Also bear in mind that after a weekend, there usually won't be any wood left until the attendant makes his next visit. In a pinch you could probably cook quite a few meals with all the burnable garbage left in the barrels and scattered around.

Our vote for the worst place to put a campground has to go to the site under the bridge at Carmacks. How anyone can sleep with all the semis roaring overhead is beyond comprehension, unless perhaps the real reason for the torture is to drum up business for the hotel and bars.

A. D.

Yes sir, campers.... if you burn all your paper & plastic garbage, the litter barrels won't fill up so fast or attract marauding bears

G.S.

a note for tourists on the Thirty Mile – Yukon River

For years now I've wondered what the white stringy matter is that can be found seen floating in the water of the Thirty Mile River section of the Yukon River, just below Lebarge. Some thought it was fish guts and others figured it must be toilet paper from Whitehorse's sewage. The answer, thanks to Doug Kittle of the Environment Protection Service and W.G. Whitley of Northern Affairs' Pollution Control, is now revealed. The white fibrous material has been tentatively identified as "a species of filamentous nonmotile green algae similar to dichotomosiphon". A better identification would require a properly preserved sample and a specialist in algae. This algae when dead was bleached in the sunlight to give it the 'paper colour.'

Sternwheelers, Steamboats, Paddlewheelers

Yukon history was written by its steamboats. The Yukon River once had the largest fleet of riverboats north of the Mississippi River. In fact, river navigation as a science reached its flowering right here, long after Mississippi traffic had declined to a pale memory.

Steam power is the original "alternate technology." How else can one describe power that moved thousands of tons of ship, barges and freight on fast, dangerous rivers powered by cordwood, with slow-moving engines that never wore out? There were steamboats on the Yukon River every summer from 1869 to 1955 — nearly 100 years, yet the basic ship did not change in its design or operation. In fact, the design of a stern-wheeled riverboat goes back to about 1830, on the Ohio River.

The river steamboat has to move cargoes "uphill" in fast, shallow rivers at an economical speed. It has to be cheap to build and operate, and it has to be safe. A flat hull solves the first problem and powerful engines allow it to move upstream, against the current; however, the problems are only starting. The hull has to be able to bend in the middle without breaking in half. This problem is solved by adding "hog poles" towering above the upper decks like the girders of a bridge; they keep the hull from working or twisting out of shape.

The boats have to be cheap to build because they were frequently lost through running into boulders or snags or other mishaps, and their replacement costs had to be low. Yukon boats were built from West Coast fir. Three of them — the Whitehorse, the Dawson and the Selkirk — were built in 1901 in Whitehorse in merely 43 days by a work force, imported from Seattle, of about 250 men. The total cost of the three boats was only $30,000.

The boats were cheap to operate. For decades the British Yukon Navigation Company (BYN) used to buy cordwood along the river at five to seven dollars per cord. Going downstream, a boat might use as little as a cord an hour; upstream, though, it might use ten. The operating cost for most boats averaging both upstream and downstream was about $1.50 a mile: not bad when you figure it moved sometimes three hundred tons of freight and up to 100 passengers.

The big problem was safety for the ship and its passengers. Everything depended on the crews. The pilot had to know the river; every bend, bar and rock, day or night, at every stage of the river. In the beginning the boats used to carry massive spars, slung with block and tackle. If the boat ran aground, the crews would sling these spars down over the bows and use them to lever the ship back into deeper water. After twenty years of learning the river, the pilots got to be so good that they took the spars off the boats: they didn't need them any more.

The following table gives times taken by steamers without barges to make the run to Dawson during good stage of water in Yukon River.

From Whitehorse	36 to 40 hours
Lower Laberge	33 hrs.
Hootalinqua	30
Big Salmon	27
Carmacks	20
Yukon Crossing	17
Selkirk	12
Coffee Creek	9
Stewart	5
Ogilvie	3

—(from Dawson Daily News, June 18, 1931)

In the old days, steamship boilers blew up with terrifying regularity. In the 1850's the U.S. government passed a steamship safety law which required boilers to have gauges and safety valves, and to be tested annually. They saw that boat operators would invariably compromise safety for speed and power and therefore, profits. Naturally enough, the law was denounced as an infringement on free enterprise. Canada has always had tough safety laws and Yukon boats have a near-perfect record.

Before the gold rush, the Americans dominated Yukon River traffic with boats operating out of St. Michael on the Bering Sea. Immediately after the Klondike discovery every shipyard along the coast started turning out riverboats. Most were towed thousands of miles north to the Yukon's mouth, loaded with cargoes for Dawson City. The White Pass and Yukon group of companies cracked this monopoly by building a railway to Whitehorse and a shipyard for its own boats. Soon it established its own monopoly on the river and made it cheaper to get freight 460 miles downriver to Dawson, instead of hauling it 1,600 miles upstream from the sea.

After the gold rush tapered off, the boats continued to carry heavy mining equipment and pipe to Dawson along with that community's dwindling need for supplies. Throughout the twenties and thirties BYN operated anywhere from six to ten ships in a busy, 16-week season. While the company's first boats were patterned on the proven designs of the Columbia and Missouri riverboats, it soon evolved its own designs which were vast improvements on the early boats. The Klondike in Whitehorse is the best example of the work of the BYN engineers. There is no other boat like it in the world. Even the big tugs presently working the Mackenzie River using 1,600 horsepower and four propellers would be hard-pressed to equal the Klondike's performance as a work boat.

After a brief flurry of activity helping to build the Alaska Highway, Yukon riverboats went into a slow decline. The last boat was hauled out in 1955, except for the Keno's poignant last voyage in 1960. The end of river traffic meant the end of a way of life for hundreds of people. **— Rob McCandless**

THE OLD STERNWHEELER!
The remnants of the past exhibited on every corner
Tutshi towers over the tallest buildings
Abandoned of beings but not of souls,
She still creaks and whines when the winds are high,
Ice covers her decks in winter
Fireweed invades her dark bows in summer,
How strong her yearning must be!
The freedom of open water only a few feet away,
Like an old lady watching children play,
In the very spot where now motor boats roar by
Sure she's wise to them
But there's no envy only a silent sigh,
Their time will come, but unlike hers,
Where she carved the way
They followed . . .
Where she tumbled and rolled
They dared not venture . . .
What she did,
They can't imagine . . . Tutshi

—Mady

FERRIES

Here's some information the Alaskan state government put out in 1978 about its "marine highway." For the latest information, write them at:

State of Alaska
Department of Transportation
and Public Facilities
Div. of Marine Highway Systems
Pouch R
Juneau, Alaska 99811

Southeast Alaska Departure Schedule
Summer 1978 (May 1-Sept. 30)

FROM	TO	DAYS
Prince Rupert	Skagway	Mon-Wed-Fri-Sat
Seattle, WA	Skagway	Tue and Fri
Skagway	Prince Rupert	Sun-Wed-Thu-Sat
Skagway	Seattle	Mon and Sat

These trips also serve the communities of Ketchikan, Wrangell, Petersburg, Sitka, Juneau and Haines.

Cabin space is not available May 1 through September 15. Travelling as a deck passenger is generally no problem and some vehicle space is still available during this period. We would encourage you to stop over at ports enroute. There is no extra charge for this as long as the stopover points are noted prior to ticketing. In this way, cabin space is usually not necessary.

The fall and winter schedule (October 1, through April 30, 1979) will be available for booking approximately July 15, 1978.

If you wish to make a reservation be sure to include:

1. Your name and address
2. Number in your party and ages of children.
3. Overall length, width, and height of your vehicle (connected length if pulling a trailer).
4. Telephone number
5. Two alternate travel dates in case we are unable to confirm your first choices.
6. Indicate stopover ports.
7. Indicate if you will travel without stateroom accommodations.

CUSTOMS

Goods Canadians can bring back that are duty and tax free:
- after forty-eight hours absence, personal goods up to $10, and those up to $50 once a calendar year.
- after 7 days absence, personal goods up to $150 once a calendar year.
- gifts under $15 Canadian (except alcohol and tobacco), *original* art works of art (not copies) over $20.
- coins and stamp collections, hearing aids, original paintings over $20 signed by the artist, sculptures over $75.
- persons over 16 yrs.; 200 cigarettes, 50 cigars and 2 lbs. of tobacco.
- those of legal drinking age in the province or territory they're entering; 40 oz. (1.1 litres) of wine or liquor OR 288 oz. (8.2 litres) of beer or ale.
Some Duty-free goods liable for 12% sales tax:
- camera accessories and some musical instruments.
Some goods subject to duty and tax:
- radios, TVs, stereos, records, tapes, calculators, cameras, and ski, golf, and tennis equipment.
Note: There are restrictions on several items such as firearms, used motor vehicles, imported CB radios, livestock, animals and their products, meat products, plants, fresh fruits and vegies, so check with your local customs office.

the mini-bus story

The Yukon Women's Mini-Bus Society (YWMBS) sprang from a Transit Committee of the Yukon Status of Women Council, a group which has a strong commitment to upgrading the quality of life in the Yukon, and in particular, in Whitehorse.

The YWMBS developed a system designed for and geared to that segment of the population who would not or could not make the trip by any other means. It was felt that a public transit system could fill the gap between the taxis and private cars by providing an intermediate transportation alternative. Increased accessability and mobility could eliminate feelings of isolation and non-involvement.

We encountered many problems in the planning stages. An obvious and very major problem was that no member of the Society had ever been involved in any form of transit operation. Consequently we had to learn as we researched. Our research eventually led us to develop a proposal which was far removed from our original concept of running three used vans at a zero deficit! Our proposal was first presented, to anyone who would read it, in October of 1974.

The learning process necessitated constant revisions and updating of drafts as one idea after another was explored then rejected or accepted. Because of our inexperience we lacked certain tools which would have speeded the planning process. We actually drove and redrove routes with stop watches in hand to develop schedules. Our strength was that we knew our city intimately thus easing the process of locating routes.

The second stumbling block was government bureaucracy. We were negotiating with three levels of government: civic, territorial and federal. Communication between governments as well as between governments and ourselves was at best, sporadic. We were all novices in the political arena and had to learn how to deal most effectively with government red tape.

We encountered problems because of the nature of the Society. We were a group of women not on familiar terms with either the business or the political community. We therefore lacked credibility. It took many months before our proposals were viewed seriously.

Finally, in July 1975, the Ministry of Transport announced that the Federal Govern-

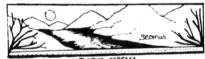

PART XXVI

One evening Toby and Woody were sitting on the porch, talking about nice things while Whitehorse slowly went to sleep. Toby was talking soft, and describing great things. We were ready for the word, as Toby began to speak. "You know how you often think of what a perfect day would be, 'eh Wood? I just thought of one this afternoon when we were lying around in the yard.

"I thought of waking up on a little island in the middle of a small river. The sun was just before ten of eleven and the sky was a few thin wispy clouds against a perfect blue. I was with a lady who loved me as much as I loved her, and the cheesehound was off chasing rabbits most of the time. We had blueberry pancakes with maple syrup and butter, and the coffee went down smooth as silk.

"The day was spent cruising in the canoe taking turns lying on top of it, nude against the sun. I sat with my paddle and stroked little patterns in the water while the sun danced on the canoe and through the woods. Animals stood and watched us go by, and we were so mellow and high that they never moved.

"After, we stopped on a sandbar with some ancient logs on it and had lunch. I watched her swim in the river and dry off in the afternoon warmth. When our bodies were warm and dry we made love in the hot sand, all alone and free. And the afternoon went by, cruising on the river, forever moving, forever changing, eternally young and sparkling in the sun.

"There was fresh trout for supper and lots of scotch to drink while the three of us watched the sunset over the river in the distance, where perhaps we would be tomorrow. I said goodnight to the world, kicked at the dying ashes in the fires; and crawling into bed, arms surrounded me and I drifted to sleep, content...."

No more did we speak, as the sun slipped behind the horizon. We didn't have to; for it would happen someday.

Being a Mini-Bus driver in Whitehorse is no easy task. You know the old saying: "through rain, snow, sleet and ice fog." Ice fog. Yes folks, that's when the visibility is zero in downtown Whitehorse. The cars are kept running, and only the brave are on the road — and the dedicated, underpaid Mini-Bus drivers. Anyone who works for Mini-Bus has to feel a little dedication. The short history (herstory!) of the system is enough to make anyone appreciate the work put into it. If I was asked to write "A Day In The Life" of a mini-bus driver, and sum it up in a few short sentences, I would say how most of the time, it actually is a "fun job" thing — like having to stop the bus every couple of miles to clean the mud off the lights during spring breakup, or having the passengers wipe the frozen snow from the windshield wipers, or driving in 40 Below with no heat! These are some of the things that make it so unique and exciting.

Of course there is the personal contact with the passengers since there are no bus stops (except downtown), a good holler stops the bus right in front of your house. Next time you're in Whitehorse, flag us down.

We're the bright green ones on the road.

Oh, and you know what? I've been driving bus for two years and wouldn't trade it in (not even for the pipeline).

—*Diane Seidel*

ment was prepared to contribute $80,000 for the purchase of mini-buses for a trial transportation system. Ironically, the Mini-Bus Society was not directly informed of the decision but heard the announcement on a local radio station.

We began operation in February, 1976 running three buses with one additional as a spare. It soon became apparent that we were badly understaffed. In the first three months of operation the management was carried by one person working 60/70 hours per week. After three months the concept of job-sharing was introduced. The manager's job was shared by two women each working 30/35 hours per week on half salary. Society members again provided back up support — they washed buses, answered phones and prepared advertising campaigns.

The System now owns five mini-buses and operates four of them over 750 miles of fixed routes each day. The buses are flagged down anywhere on their route except in the downtown areas where there are bus zones. We have always exceeded our targets for passengers carried, while remaining under budget. We are presently carrying between 750 and 900 passengers per day.

Our beginnings and have been part of a four-year struggle to demonstrate that the people of a community can, if determined, achieve seemingly impossible goals. It has been an interesting study to watch how the attitude of the government, of politicians and of the business communities has changed towards us over the four years. It seems to have gone from indifference to incredulity to a reluctant admiration.

For me, personally, it has been a tremendous experience. As general manager, I have had the support of a strong Society whose members were willing to devote much time and energy to make this system a success. I have had to learn to deal with government, with business, with the media and, most importantly, with the general public. There have been days when I wonder why I ever got into this business. Temperatures of -40°C, long hours of darkness, broken down buses, icy roads and demanding passengers all make the days pass quickly. We have enlisted passengers to push buses out of snow banks, drivers have kept to schedule by driving cars or trucks to notify passengers that the bus was unavailable, society members have washed buses and I've changed tires.

I look back on the days when people told me we'd never survive, that northerners would never use a bus service. We were told that women couldn't drive buses in cold weather and that they wouldn't be able to handle the passengers. A driver once overheard a conversation between two men, one of whom was obviously a visitor. The visitor remarked that he understood that Whitehorse had a new bus system and that it was run by women. The second man answered, yup, there was a bus system and that women seemed to drive buses and manage the system. He fell silent for a few seconds and then added, "But I'm sure that the husbands of these women are doing the real running of this system; women couldn't do it alone!"

The system works and it grows. We carried 9,000 passengers in August, 1976. In August, 1978 we broke all our records by carrying over 20,000 people. The system will continue to expand as Whitehorse grows and every effort will be made to keep the system innovative and flexible, responsive to the needs of the residents. It's been frustrating, maddening, terrifying, exhilerating and rewarding!

—*Joanne Linzey*

WHO WERE THOSE GUYS, ANYWAYS?

Hyder, Alaska and Stewart, B.C. are hailed as being "in the land of scenic splendour" by the brochure the Stewart "Chamber of Commerce" puts out. It's doubtful there's still a chamber anymore because there's little commerce left since the Granduc mine shut down in '78. Stewart is dying, economically, so Hyder loses out too, being the free-wheeling little Alaska town about two miles of pavement around the corner that quenched the miners' thirsts. Despite the loss of economy, the splendour is still there, as it is all along the West Coast. But more than anything else, the places are known for the drinking in Hyder.

The bars themselves are hard to describe, since the scene was tainted during observation by some really good LSD and an acquaintance dressed with a purple cape and who reminded one of some sort of Wizard Lord, or devil, depending on the thought pattern at the moment. But even if you're stoned on acid you can recall there were three bars that operated in eight-

hour shifts to keep the town and its visitors wet, or completely corned, depending on the mood.

There's shotguns behind the bars so don't cause too much trouble.

It takes a while to get there from here: you've got to drive the Stewart-Cassiar highway from near Watson Lake. But you can approach it from the south, too, between New Hazelton and Terrace.

Tourism might be the only thing Stewart can count on to keep itself going, but whether it wants tourists is unknown. Cassiar Asbestos mine products are being routed through there now so port activity might be helping them along soon, too.

Whatever the fate of Stewart, it's a neat little place if you want to check it out. For more information, write the Stewart and District Chamber of Commerce, Stewart, B.C., and see if anyone's still there.

—*Art*

Car Maintenance for the Winter

1. Get the car ready before winter! First frost — get it done or it can cost lots.

2. Check anti-freeze level for 60 below F. A garage will check it for free or buy the gauge for $5.

3. Fan belt in good shape. Buy a spare.

4. NEW air filter if paper. Clean if oil-bath-type filter, new oil.

5. New plugs and points. Do yourself.

6. Check condition of spark plug wires, distributor cap and rotor; in good shape or replace.

7. Set timing. Borrow timing light from a friend if possible to be more accurate.

8. Clean, light-weight oil in motor, either 5-30 multi-grade oil or straight 10-weight.

9. Drain windshield washers.

10. Battery in good condition, check specific gravity with gauge. Clean posts and terminals with battery brush or wirebrush and jack-knife.

11. Tires in good shape. Snowtires at least on back (but can get away without in real cold). Tube tires if possible — or you will end up putting tubes into your tubeless. Two spares.

12. If your electricity is free, get battery blanket.

13. If heater isn't working well, try flushing out the heater core with air or rad cleaner.

14. Some sort of block heater or circulating engine (in-line) heater.

15. Oil pan heater! Can do serious damage without one (may be lucky, but may blow it completely). Electric or propane.

16. Block off rad with cardboard or tarp. Experiment, block off more if colder. If really cold, belly tarp is a must, keeps running gear warm.

17. Don't buy gas-line anti-freeze. Buy methyl hydrate in any drug store or hardware store. Put some in all the time, a cupful for first three fillups, then when cold. Especially important in heated garage. Keep gas tank full. (Buy a locking gas cap?)

18. Special for 4 by 4 vehicles, put lightweight oil in differentials, lightweight (winter) grease at grease points.

19. Good to get two sets of keys so we can lock and leave running for five minute errands.

20. Keep winter clothes, a flashlight and jumper cables in trunk.

— ¾ with a. d.

Skidoo Warning

Are you getting excited about pulling out that new Christmas sled to take junior for a drag behind your macho skidoo? Well beware — a baby in Quebec had his eyeballs frozen solid on a similar venture and is now totally blind. Dad was so besides himself he went so far as to destroy his beloved skidoo by drowning it in gasoline and blowing it up.

Also a warning to motorcyclists! Richard Pantes, an avid motorcyclist, while on his way to Teslin in October, froze his eyes so severely he couldn't focus. Fortunately they have since thawed out and are functioning normally.

CAR STARTING IN COLD WITHOUT ELECTRICITY

For starting your car or truck in the really cold if there isn't any electricity to heat it up, you'll need a "tiger-torch" (propane torch) and a length of stovepipe with a 90 degree bend at end to direct the heat underneath the oil pan. Also you'll need a bottle of O.P. Rum to keep you warm while you watch it to make sure you don't start your car on fire. Especially in Old Crow, this would be embarrassing.

— ½ with o. d.

Other suggestions

—drain oil and heat it up and put back in (if this is necessary, make sure there's someone around to brush the snow off your back . . . it's miserable twisting the bolts anyway, without coming back out from a warm up and the next time you got back under getting frozen to the ground.

—warm up the battery to re-charge it. It is faster to put it in a pan of warm water to warm up. Or just bring the battery inside every night and leave it near the stove.

—the solenoid takes a shit-kicking in winter. If the car won't start, check that.

—your whole vehicle takes a shit-kicking in the winter . . . if you really need to be somewhere else, maybe you should consider a snow-mobile, or a dog-team, or just skis. Or get a garage built.

—preventive medicine — get up once in the night to start your truck/car . . . that way it keeps itself warmed up, especially if you put a blanket or tarp over the hood.

— lou, etc.

---

rub-a-dub-dub, where's the grub?

When you're eating dust from that Winnebago that won't let you pass, and you're picking dirty, black boogers from your nose (we call them "Alcan Oysters"), you are not likely to be thinking of food. Good. There are not many worthwhile places to stop to eat. Decent food at a reasonable price is a rarity. Most restaurants and lodges around the Yukon want to give you as little as possible, and charge outrageous prices. Usually it's plastic junk food, too. Remember — they figure they will never see you again. They want your money, and don't really care about you 'cause you're just one in a hundred thousand passing through their door. Expect the worst, and maybe you'll be pleasantly surprised. Maybe!

I've driven all the roads in the Yukon. Yes, every one of them. I've spent many an hour behind the wheel savouring the thoughts of a good meal, and I've planned many a day's activities and travelling so I could eat at a particular restaurant or lodge. Here's a list of decent eating spots and gastronomic delights. They are a trip in themselves.

1. Along the Alaska Highway:

First place to stop is at Teslin Mile 804 Motel and visit their cafe. Home-cooked meals, great hamburgers, and thick, tasty soups are found here. For desert, try the pie.

Just past Mt. Mudpack and a little ways down the highway is Johnson's Crossing Lodge. It's the only place I've ever eaten pumpkin pie and ice cream for breakfast. This is numero uno as far as I'm concerned. It's my favourite! Treat yourself to home cooking at its best, and meet some fine folks. They're real! Unfortunately, they're closing their doors this November 1st (1978). They've been there for 20 to 30 years and now they are reducing the services they provide. They want some time to themselves. Too many tourists and too many hunters from Whitehorse on weekend excursions up the South Canol Road means too many demands. They want some peace, so I understand. I can relate to that, and hopefully you will, too. Whatever they offer, you can be sure it will be good because they care.

I stay away from Jake's Corner, like a lot of other people do too.

Now, we all need to stimulate our palates. Once or twice a year, it's nice to treat your taste buds to gourmet foods. In Whitehorse, we all patronize the GG (Golden Garter). It's the place to go to. Apparently the Monte Carlo rates highly, too. Annabelles provides a refreshing alternative of good quality cuisine and it's a nice place to sit. They have no liquor licence so you can bring along a favourite wine to have with your meal. In all these places, you get what you pay for — they are reasonable prices.

Driving down the road towards Alaska, you can't go wrong having a meal at Mother's Cozy Corner at Haines Junction. Burwash Lodge is neat, and worth the brief drive off the highway (only open in the summer). Are you prone to attacks of the munchies? Pine Valley Lodge is a nice place to stop for tea and cookies. Ida's is the hot spot in Beaver Creek.

2. Along the Klondike Highway:

How do you handle a hungry man? Take him to Braeburn Lodge. It is a must, the favourite place of almost everyone travelling this road. Truckers eat here, and hippies too. They're famous for the biggest sandwiches and hamburgers in the Yukon. They are the biggest portions I've ever seen anywhere. The cinnamon buns are so good that Valdy wrote a song about them, and someone from CBC named the airstrip there the "Cinnamon Bun Strip."

At Stewart Crossing you can get a solid meal most of the time.

When you're trucking around Mayo, there's only one place to go. Ravens ate the food out of the back of the truck while we were eating at the little trailer restaurant. I think they got as good a deal as we did but it's the only place there.

Moose Creek Lodge, 20 miles west towards Dawson, is rather a unique place. Friendly people serve generous portions of pie and (mmmmm) gingerbread. Rumour has it that they also make a take-out pizza. Stop and find out for yourself. P.S. It's the only service station that I know where they pump gas by hand.

You get more for your dollars at the Klondike River Lodge at the Dempster Corner. The food is fair and the prices reasonable compared to the thievery that goes on in Dawson.

3. Along the Carcross-Skagway Road, the Caribou Hotel in Carcross is the place to grab a bite to eat. Plants and famous parrots provide pleasant distractions to the tourists.

4. Along the South and North Canol Roads, Ross River appears to be the place to eat at. It isn't. Who wants those tiny bubbles in your tummy? No need to pay for indigestion.

5. Along the Haines Road come growlie time, turn in at the Dezadeash Lodge. It is another favourite of mine. The combination of home-cooking and hospitable people make it memorable. Do yourself a favour and stop here.

6. Along the Robert Campbell Highway:

There is not much in Watson Lake. If you do eat here, go to the restaurant at the Belvedere Hotel. It's not bad; it's not too great, either. I'd stop at the Shamrock-Tomahawk Lodge at the junction of this road and Nahanni Range Road. It's worth trying if for no other reason than there is no other places worth mentioning until Carmacks. The Trucker's Roost in Carmacks at the junction of the two highways is, according to most people, superb.

7. There are no lodges or restaurants on the **Nahanni Range Road.**

8. Along the Dempster Highway, there is one place to eat near Eagle River. It's part of a restaurant-bar-motel-service station-office-complex that is subsidized by our government. I'm boycotting it because it's a cancerous growth that doesn't belong there. I'd appreciate it if you would do the same. Let 'em stew in their own juices.

When travelling the roads of the Yukon, the best bet is to take your own food. It is definitely cheaper and probably more nutritious. You can have a movable feast by packing enough grub to last you on your journey.

P.S. Remember to pick up your garbage and take it with you. Don't litter the country.

— *Starvin Marvin*

FLYING
the Yukon Territory

Flying in the Yukon is an exciting and rewarding way to get around. The long distances and the limited road system make this high-speed personal transport system a great convenience for those who do any amount of travel here. Government control has given flying a very high safety record and has improved aircraft reliability to the point where mechanical failures are next to non-existent. Flight training has brought pilot standards up to where a trip to Faro for a private pilot now is a safe delightful hour's jaunt through the Big Salmon River country rather than a five hour battle with the trucks on the Campbell Highway.

ON YUKON MOUNTAIN FLYING

Our mountains are like mountains anywhere: high, hard and lots of them. The following hints are condensation of a brochure published by the Ministry of Transport (MOT) for the Penticton Seminar on Mountain Flying.

Weather — Get as much information as you can before the flight and be prepared to do an unscheduled landing or a return to a safe place to land. Never push visibility beyond your ability to do a 180 degree turn.

Wind — Be cautious of wind direction and its effect upon up and down drafts. Be looking for places where mountain formations will cause wind shears and associated turbulence. Ridges should be approached in such a way as will allow you to get away if downdraft conditions are found.

Ice — Bad stuff for a light plane. Make sure it is all off the wings before takeoff. If it starts collecting in flight, change altitude and arrange to land at the nearest possible site.

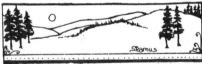

PART XXVII

Back in the early 70's, the winter still came down hard in Whitehorse. Toby said it wasn't so bad if you had your act together. You needed a lover, a dog and a cozy place to live; and also you had to be prepared for the silence of the north when it came upon everyone.

We knew a fellow out on the Long Lake Road who went by the name of Bob. He came into Whitehorse about once a week at first, just to shop and see a few folks. Around Christmas and New Years though, he began to get lonely and used to stay in the bar on a Friday or Saturday night.

We used to walk together out to his cabin. He would tell me stories and treat me good. It was a nice place, but small and there wasn't much distraction from the snow outside or the dark log walls inside.

Rendezvous was okay. Everyone got wrecked and had a wonderful time, and then it was March. Bob went home one day and put his rifle to his head and pulled the trigger. I found him the next day, sitting against the wall, on his bed, frozen solid.

A lot of people knew him and took it a little hard in places, but he was only one of about five that winter. For some reason March is the worst month. It seems to creep up on those who haven't got it together and let themselves get depressed.

Toby reckoned that he didn't need all the aforementioned comforts - but he said he wouldn't stand the winters up here alone for more than three years.

He is basically right. The price for your freedom is the ability to rule your life and put it in the order in which you want it lived. The Yukon's winter is still the greatest test of a man's ability to maintain his mind.

White Out — This is where the eye can pick out nothing that is useful to judge a horizon. Can come on very suddenly and cause vertigo and at least considerable confusion.

Temperature — Don't get caught by a hot high day that puts your density altitude way up and the aircraft's performance way down.

Experience is the real teacher of northern mountain flying. A seasoned pilot will have his own list of things to watch for and he begins to rely on that almost sixth sense. One of the characteristics of these mountains is that as one goes north, the tree line comes down and when those barren slopes are covered with a layer of fluffy snow and just a little light snow is falling from that gray evening sky, there is very little to look at.

The Yukon has more than its share of mountains. Between the Tintina Trench in which Ross River, Watson Lake and Mayo are located, and the Mackenzie River, there is nothing but 400 miles of massive, majestic and very unforgiving mountains. The major problem is finding out what sort of weather conditions exist out there. You could fly right through a weather system that the aviation weather facilities don't even know exists. Therefore a pilot must learn to assess the weather he is flying in and make decisions based on his experience and his ability to deal with the conditions in that area. For the average private flyer the commercial guys are usually more than happy to help out with local information if approached intelligently. Often they will help with finding a place to crash out for a snowbound night, and occasionally by finding a good party.

ON GAS

The north is littered with the good old 45 gallon barrel. These have been the cause of not a few sputtering engines and adrenaline rushes. They collect water. They can, if conditions are right, collect a lot of water. A barrel with a fuel company seal on the bung and a date less than a year old and which has been stored lying on its side if in the open, can (if filtered properly) be used with perfect safety. If it hasn't got a seal, then the label that says 100/130 aviation fuel probably means that it has stove oil inside. If it is standing up, it will be filled with water. The combination does not burn well in a rented Cessna. Old gas will go stale as the additives settle out. This will take some years but to use gas less than one year old is a really safe limit.

When using a barrel pump try to arrange the inlet so it is about four inches above the bottom of the barrel. This will help with the water as it tends to settle to the bottom. Besides, you need something left to run the skidoo on. For filters, the time tested chammy (chamois) is unbeatable. There are several in-line filters designed for installation on pumps but if stuck don't pour unfiltered gas into an aircraft. I have seen brand new barrels with paint flecks in them.

ON COLD WEATHER FLYING

Aircraft in the north require some attention before winter sets in. A winterization kit is produced by most aircraft manufacturers for their various aircraft. It will be designed to redistribute the cooling airflow in the engine compartment. Home-made kits and taping of holes should be checked out with an engineer as the engine cooling system is fairly carefully designed. Other work, such as oil changes, are described in the operating manual for the aircraft.

Engine warm-up in cold weather should be accomplished carefully. The warm-up should be fairly slow as a six-quart lump of oil takes time to thaw. When heating with a Herman Nelson, or a master heater or, if necessary, a tiger torch, the aircraft should not be left as this operation can result in a fire if a gas leak exists. An engine blanket is necessary for operations in the cold and there are some good fireproof ones available. With a tight fitting engine blanket, an in-car heater will keep the engine warm all night in very cold temperatures.

ON GEAR

The Air Navigation Orders have a list of emergency equipment to be carried in sparsely settled areas which includes the entire Yukon. Most operators have devised a kit that is a product of aircraft size, the government list, their ingenuity and often bitter experience in some loon-shit filled swamp. If you have occasion to make one up, ask around. I prefer an organic approach. That is lots of dried beans and fruit for food. Hard candies are fairly high in calories. A new paint can makes a good waterproof container for the food and other small items and makes a good cooking utensil as well.

If you are about to head out as a passenger in a light aircraft there are some things it is nice to have in your pockets if you have to go camping somewhere you didn't expect to. Grab a couple of books of matches as you leave the bar. The Swiss Army Knife can be a real asset, as could be a bottle of bugdope. If it's cold out, it is a good idea to wear your parka as it will be fairly difficult to put it on while descending for a landing in a willow patch. If there are lots of loads such as a camp move, make sure your personal gear such as sleeping bag and clothes fly the same load that you do.

Information Required on a Flight Plan

1. aircraft type and registration
2. transponder
3. air speed in knots
4. point of departure
5. route
6. destination
7. proposed time off
8. time enroute
9. locater beacon
10. communications equipment
11. navigation equipment
12. number on board
13. name of pilot, licence
14. nature of dangerous cargo
15. additional info as may be requested or useful. Colours, survival gear, etc.

— JOHN HILL

cross country skiing

As a frustrated downhill skier living in the Yukon, one of the first things I did was trade my downhill skies for cross country skies - a trade that is becoming increasingly difficult. My equipment was obselete anyway, and I had become disillusioned with long lift lines and the materialistic fashion conscious ski cult.

I anticipated missing the speed and exhileration of soaring down majestic mountains, but instead have become hoplessly addicted to the solitude and variety that cross country skiing offers, without having to give up that speed and exhileration. As a true addict, I feel compelled to afflict others through some exciting information about skiing in the Yukon.

This has to be one of the best areas for cross country skiing for many reasons. Firstly, the cold dry winter climate is ideal for snow conditions from December to March. Waxing couldn't be simpler, as black or special green was is suited for any temperatures between -20 to 20F, which is the typical range during these months. Green and blue will serve as a kicker at the warmer end of this temperature range and above. Save the klisters for April or avoid them completely and start summer early. The snow depth by December is normally deep enough to cover the low vegetation and the dead fall that may be littering your trails and will gradually increase in depth until March, with rarely much melting occuring during these months. So the transitional snow conditions common to the southern climates rarely exist - not that there is no enjoyment in the art of waxing and skiing wet snow, but it does simplify the waxing process for the beginner and the after-work-skier.

The cold is rarely uncomfortable since skiing is a very active sport and sweating is more common than freezing. Inevitably, you continue to strip down as you continue your ski as your blood gets circulating. Wearing layers is advisable over say just a down jacket, in order to eliminate the sweating problem. Below -20F there is no wax on the market that will deliver a good enough glide to make skiing enjoyable so it is a good time to pack trails or open new ones with snowshoes.

Creating your own neighbourhood ski trails is half the fun of skiing. The Yukon's terrain in the most habitable areas is ideal for cross country skiing. There are the wide open valleys with rolling hills, open ridges and the

Cool evening. i can smell winter coming, though the leaves haven't changed, and the back of my mind calculates cord wood and winter supplies.
wondering where i packed my long johns, where i stored my muks. wondering where i'll find a toque as toasty as the one i lost last spring.
it's First Northern Light Night for an american hitch-hiker going back to california. he calls us out to see the soft glows of pale green in the sky.
i look forward to winter, when the lights swirl and sing and the colours change, walking through the snow late at night and whistling the light a little closer.

numerous chains of lakes, especially in the southern Yukon. Off the Carcross Road for instance, we developed 30 or 40 miles of ski trails. Develop is hardly an appropriate word since much of the area has remnants of old logging roads and existing trails. A good portion of the trails follow bare or sparsely growing poplar ridges, leaving only a few miles that needed any clearing. I cannot emphasize enough the enjoyment and creative satisfaction one gets from planning and packing a new trail. It is usually best to pack with snowshoes, as initially it won't be skiable and it is easier to cut limbs and pick up debris without ski poles in the way. In areas without ridges and old trails, it is best to become very familiar with the terrain before doing any clearing and cutting. Most important is making sure that beginner runs are not too steep, the downhill sections do not have sharp turns to them, and they allow adequate room for making turns. For more difficult trails, one intentialy seeks steeper meandering downhill runs. It is preferable that all trails are circuits and that they can be skiied in both directions. Half way through the first winter, our neighbourhood had created such a maze of ski trails of such varying degrees of difficulty that we found it necessary to spend an entire evening mapping and naming all the trails, so we did not have to give a lenghty description when referring to a particular trail. We made several copies to distribute ot newcomers. This also eliminated the possibilities of skiers taking a trail too difficult or long for them.

There is also trail making on a larger scale, which allows for overnight or weekend long circuits. It is preferable to select trails with as much variety as possible. The trip will be much more interesting if it includes old roads, lakes, ridges, hills and some bushwacking. Some examples of tested ski trips are: from Carcross to Atlin via Nore's Lake, Striker's Pass, Taku Arm, Jone's Lake (trail to Atlin Lake). For those with more enthusiam for bushwacking, there is the Annie Lake - Alligator Lake - Coal Lake - Cowley Lake circuit. Both trips are about 60 miles and take about four days to ski. I find February to March the best time for long ski trips because there is more snow and the weather is milder for winter camping.

by Peter Heebink

Aviation History in the Yukon

Pilots who would like a better perspective on their heroics, or passengers who don't appreciate Northward's punctuality, are invited to read two excellent articles by Jeanne Harbottle on the early days of flying in the Yukon. The articles were published in the ALASKA JOURNAL in the Autumn issues of 1973 and 1974. The first is entitled "Clyde Wann, Father of Yukon Aviation" and the other is called "White Pass Aviation and Its Rivals." Both issues are available at the Archives

The Myth of the Yukon

The Yukon is the cussedest land I know.
A frozen mass of perpetual ice and snow.
Located somewhere just beyond the North Pole
where it's far too cold for any mortal soul.

At ninety below the ground beneath you warps
and you fear you might wake up a frozen corpse.
Everything frozen, and if that ain't so bleak
imagine peeing ice cubes when you take a leak.

Folks don't have time in winter for sport and fun.
They're too busy chopping firewood by the ton.
In the dark winter when the wind always blows.
they're shovelling tunnels through forty feet of snow.

If the cold don't get ya, there's the wolves and bears
or falling off mountains, and other nightmares.
But if it's rivers and canoeing that you crave
the Whitehorse Rapids can carry you to your grave.

In the summer you'll find muskeg and deadfall,
mosquitoes and blackflies as thick as a wall.
It's said they can carry you away, at their peak.
Summer is hell, but it only lasts a week.

Of course the preceding is a distorted lie.
But only those that live there know exactly why
we let the world believe it, without a doubt
to keep it to ourselves and keep outsiders out.

by Peter Pike

staff photo
"The Rock and Roll Moose Meat Collective"

Front Row: Agnes Montgomery-Drew, Bruce Batchelor, Louise Mrozinsky, Jim Maxwell, Nora Batchelor, Max Fraser, Allison Wood
Centre Row: Radar "Ricochet" Shy-Guy, George Marks, Eric Petersen, Stanleigh Cole, Mars Bonfire II, Jim Montgomery, Donna Ward, Tony Mrozinsky
Back Row: Dangerous Dan McGrew, Swede Saw Sam, Beaverly Taylor, Albert T. Johnson, Jean Légaré, Tim Dowd, Casey Cheesehound, G.I. Joe

Rock + Roll Moose Meat

The Loot Whole Moose Catalogue is dedicated to:

mom & dad
and
the old Beatles

writers: (in no particular order)

Mars Bonfire II, Agnes Montgomery-Drew, Max Fraser, Eric Petersen, Bruce Batchelor, Jim Montgomery, Jim Maxwell, Louise Mrozinsky, Kay Chappell, Helen Dobrowowski, Joy Proulx, Beaverly Taylor, Peter Heebink, Jan Weagle, Peter Carr, Jim Jensen, Debbie Jensen, Mady Theil, Dorothy Gibbon, Jon Ruldolph, Jean Légaré, Erling Fris-Baastard, Dave Clark, John Hill, Zeke Scopick, Bill Oppen, Alison Reid, Tim Dowd, Glen Piwowar, Walter Lanz, Al Foster, Jill Porter, Rick & Avril, Frank Turner, Jim Erkelitian, Marjorie Bradley, Robert McCandless, Jim Vautour, Manfred Janssen, Mike Barnes, Diane Johnson, Alyz Jones, Ruth McDougall, Cathy Csepi, Kathy Langston, Diane Seidel, Lynne Garner, Mary Cheney, Joanne Linzey, Alison Wood, Mary-Jo Dawe, Chilcoot Chuck, George Marks, D.P. Gumby, Harry Fritz-Meyer, Albert T. Johnson, Muffy MacDonald, Pat Batchelor, Dan Carruthers, Lee Carruthers, Tom Roscoe

graphics and artwork:

Front Cover watercolour by Stanleigh Cole/back cover by Tony Mrozinski / headings, titles, borders by Nora Batchelor, Tony, Louise Mrozinski, Stanleigh, Heather MacKenzie/Lost Moose & Seamus borders, Whelan-Karin tent, and Natural Edible illustrations by Stanleigh/Table of Contents by Nora /Page 5 by Diane K. Taylor / Dog Packs, Cabins, stove diagrams, water system, Y.T. Crest, blowing it, Pike by Tony / Chilcoot Chuck cartoons, Dall Sheep dog, YLF, RCMP, Crowbar, Mooose, all by Graham Swanson / Wolverine Mushing Zen, 180 and 1 uses Alternative Housing, Bradford idiot by John Lodder (who asked us to plug his forthcoming Yukon Komix)/Stackwall by Dave Clark / Solar by Stanleigh & Nora / A.M. Radio and Catamarans by Jim Jensen / Fish Camp, WhiteHorse vistas by Jim Robb (artist in the territory for twenty years, last of Yukon Beatniks) / Bean Sprouts by Lou/Dancing Moose by Stanleigh & Tony / Tanning hides by Jim Vautour / Northern Lights by Sunil Bhandari / RRMM logo by Terry Emslie from the Scott Lyle Collection

photography:

Page 1 - Rhubarb - Martha Louise Black - Yukon Archives (Y.A.) / Pg. 6 - Seamus - Y.A. via D.P. Gumby / Pg. 6 - Traf - Eric Petersen / Pg. 6 - Log Cabins & Skyscraper in old Whitehorse - Ralph Nordling / Pg. 7 - Mountains - Ralph / Pg. 8 - Big Salmon Cabin - Max Fraser / Pg. 9 - 1942 Alaska Highway Camp - R.A. Cartter - Y.A. / Pg. 9 - Spring - Ralph / Pg. 10 - Old Couple - Jim Robb / Pg. 11 - Map - Dept. of Energy, Mines & Resources / Pg. 12 - Paddling - Joy Brown / Pg. 14 - Needle Rock - M. Menzies - Y.A. / Pg. 15 - Ice - M. Menzies - Y.A. / Pg. 17 - Atlin Lake after Storm - Peter Carr / Pg. 19 - Aerial View of Glacier - Bonnie Burns / Pg. 19 - Angus - Joy / Pg. 20 - Dog with Pack - Umberto / Pg. 22 - Porkie Quills - Jane from Dawson / Pg. 23 - Sleigh - Janet Prenty / Pg. 23 - Toboggan - M. Menzies - Y.A. / Pg. 24 - Old Couple - M.L. Black - Y.A. / Scratch and Sniff / Pg. 26 - Stackwall - Dave Clark / Pg. 26 - Children Playing - M. Menzies - Y.A. / Pg. 27 - Tipi - Dorothy Gibbon / Pg. 27 - Dome - Ralph / Pg. 28 - Lester the Woodcutter - Eric P. / Pg. 29 - Carcross in Winter - Umbie / Pg. 30 - Big Salmon Village - Max Fraser / Pg. 32 - Toilet - Raunchy Haunch / Scratch and Sniff / Pg. 34 - Children in Tub - M. Menzies - Y.A. / Pg. 35 - Greg & Casey - Miss Brazil / Pg. 35 - Table & Lantern - Alyx Jones / Pg. 39 - Eating Out - P. & B.H. / Pg. 44 - Log House Interior - Joy / Pg. 45 - Cookstove in Carmacks - Chris Flynn / Pg. 46 - Dogs Plowing-

(photography con't) - M. Menzies - Y.A. / Pg. 47 - Fields of Klondike City - H.C. Barley - Y.A. / Pg. 48 - Garden - Agriculture Canada / Pg. 49 - Cat & Carrots - Donna Ward / Pg. 50 - Sheep - M. Menzies - Y.A. / Pg. 51 - Chickens - Agriculture Canada / Pg. 51 - Bird - Bruce Martel / Pg. 52 - Cabbages at Haines Jct. - Agric. Canada / Pg. 53 - Tree - Donna / Pg. 53 - Cattle - Agric. Canada / Pg. 56 - Otter - Umbie / Pg. 56 - Bull - Y.T.G. Tourism & Info / Pg. 57 - Karen & Joy / Pg. 58 - Lake & Mountains - Ralph / Pg. 59 - Quigley Creek Campfire - Gregory Skuce / Pg. 60 - Ravens - Mady Theil / Pg. 60 - Loons - Bruce Martel / Pg. 61 - Foxes - Y.T.G. / Pg. 61 & 80 - point rack - M. Menzies - Y.A. / Pg. 62 - Eagles Nest Bluff - Joy / Pg. 62 - Porcupine - Bill Qwill / Pg. 64 - Lapie River - Ralph / Pg. 65 - Peak - Y.T.G. / Pg. 66 - Placer Mining - Dave Mac-Lellan / Pg. 67 - Open Pit Mining in Faro - Y.T.G. / Pg. 67 - Gold - Dave MacLellan / Pg. 70 - Wall Tent - Donna / Pg. 70 - Looking - Joy / Pg. 71 - Stu - Eric P. / Pg. 71 - Scenery - Umbie / Pg. 72 - Tent Bush Camp - Y.T.G. / Pg. 73 - Frosty Gears - Kathy Sprague / Pg. 74 - Jumping for Joy - Umbie / Pg. 74 - Mushroom - B. Martel / Pg. 75 - Jim & Deb - Max / Pg. 76 - Flowers - Mady / Pg. 76 - Klondike Kate - Univ. of Alaska Collection - Y.A. / Pg. 77 - August Snowfall - Agnes Drew / Pg. 78 - Parachuting - Joy / Pg. 79 - Stu & Mudpack - Eric P. / Pg. 79 - Divers - D. Mac-Lellan / Pg. 80 - Ruth & Casey - Bruce Batchelor / Pg. 81 - Mistah - Ralph / Pg. 81 - At Farrago - Umbie / Pg. 82 - Ellen - Joy / Pg. 83 - Terrified Gov't Building - Ralph / Scratch and Sniff / Pg. 84 - Flying Bird - B. Martel / Pg. 84 - Jim & Kay - Eric P. / Pg. 85 - Children - Joy / Pg. 85 - Puppeteers - Joy / Pg. 87 - Hotel Stephen Fire (1977) - D. MacLellan / Pg. 89 - City Hall - Ralph / Pg. 91 - Tom - Y.T.G. / Pg. 91 - Where's Rudy? - Y.T.G. / Pg. 91 - Lost in Ozone - Dawson Jane / Pg. 92 - Carcross Community People - Paul Rapatti / Pg. 93 - Stanleigh's Tent - Umberto / Pg. 93 - School Spuds - P. Rapatti / Pg. 93 - Wood Camp at -50° F. - Umbie / Pg. 94 - Wall Tent - Joy / Pg. 94 - Ralph & Mike - Colleen Nordling / Pg. 95 - Hugh - Bill Atkinson / Pg. 95 - Mining - D. MacLellan / Pg. 96 - Tramway - Vancouver Public Library - Y.A. / Pg. 97 - Joy & Melanie - Casey Cheesehound / Pg. 98 - Friend - Joy / Pg. 99 - Buggy - Ralph / Pg. 100 - John, where to now? - Greg Skuce / Pg. 100 - Canol Truck - Stu Withers / Pg. 101 - Haines Road - D.P. Gumby / Pg. 101 - Team & Car - M.L. Black - Y.A. / Pg. 102 - Rainer - Pauline Worth (Betty Grinwis Collection) / Pg. 102 - Truck in Forest - Jane from Dawson / Pg. 103 - Iskut's lead dog - Bruce B. / Pg. 104 - Grant - Ralph / Pg. 105 - Sternwheeler - Alan Moutter / Pg. 107 - Carol - D. MacLellan / Pg. 108 - Old Abraham - Y.A. / Pg. 108 - Amphibious Leoning Keystone Commuter - C. Haines - Y.A. / Pg. 108 - meets the Modern Age - Van Bibber Collection - Y.A. / Pg. 109 - Rotsa Plenty - Bruce B. / Pg. 109 - Carcross Bridge - Umbie / Pg. 110 - Staff Photo - Courtesy of Ratso / Scratch and Sniff / Pg. 111 - Donini Bottle - Eric Tolton

other people who helped in some way:

Libby Barlow, Dennis Menard, Mike (BMW) Cavanaugh, Steve, Caroline, Joanne, Ed Leishman, Barb Preston, Wayne Touriss, Aja, Barry Barlow, Jan Slipetz, Mike & Diane ... and all the others who we might have forgotton.

special thanks to:

- Donna Ward for assisting with developing
- Ken Faught of Tundra Silkscreens for re-doing some photos; Howard & Gary & their staff at Arctic Star Printing; Byron Keebaugh and Meridian Printing of Lloydminster
- Jill & Carl & Bauer's Auto Beauty Shop in Winnipeg; and John, Eric & Pat Batchelor for financial faith
- The People at the Carcross Community who provided us with a place to get together and helped us feel at home: Jason Olher, Wes Johnson, Robin Trudel, Tom Rounthwaite, Eric Tolton, Mike MacMillan, Donna Pendziwal - MacMillan, Umberto Willner, Heather MacKenzie, Charles Corbet (Charlie Chaplin), Cecily Leyden, Kath Amundsen, June Payne, Stanleigh Cole, Sunil Bhandon, Cath Constable, Janet Rushant, Geoff Rushant, Gisèle Normand
- The People at the Bakery, Betty, Rainer, Joann & baby Sarah
- The Fireplace in the Brown House
- The sauna
- The mountains around Carcross - for reminding us of what's real.
- The dogs for waking us up.
- To Valery Valiant for not breaking down (yet)
- The good herb for providing the essence of our motivation & mystification meetings
- The loose horse that hung around our front yard eating Casey's dog food
- and to all the people who said they'd do something for the catalogue and didn't, but who tried anyway.